Family Wealth Management

Family Wealth Management

SEVEN IMPERATIVES FOR SUCCESSFUL INVESTING IN THE NEW WORLD ORDER

Mark Haynes Daniell
Tom McCullough

WILEY

Cover art: Shutterstock
Cover design: Wiley

Published by John Wiley & Sons Singapore Pte. Ltd.
1 Fusionopolis Walk, #07-01, Solaris South Tower, Singapore 138628

Other Wiley Editorial Offices
John Wiley & Sons, 111 River Street, Hoboken, NJ 07030, USA
John Wiley & Sons, The Atrium, Southern Gate, Chichester, West Sussex, P019 8SQ, United Kingdom
John Wiley & Sons (Canada) Ltd., 5353 Dundas Street West, Suite 400, Toronto, Ontario, M9B 6HB, Canada
John Wiley & Sons Australia Ltd., 42 McDougall Street, Milton, Queensland 4064, Australia
Wiley-VCH, Boschstrasse 12, D-69469 Weinheim, Germany

ISBN 978-0-470-82429-0 (Cloth)
ISBN 978-0-470-82907-3 (ePDF)
ISBN 978-0-470-82908-0 (ePub)

Typeset in 11/13 pt. ITC New Baskerville by MPS Limited, Chennai, India.
Printed in Singapore by C.O.S. Printer Pte Ltd.

10 9 8 7 6 5 4 3 2 1

Mark dedicates this book to a wonderful young lady,
Julia Bornemann,
with all best wishes on her own career
and plans for a life truly wealthy in all things that count.

Tom dedicates this book to the loves of his life,
Karen, Kate, and Ben.

Contents

Foreword **xi**

Preface **xvii**

Acknowledgments **xxix**

INTRODUCTION AND OVERVIEW: A CRITICAL TIME FOR FAMILY INVESTORS **1**

Chapter 1 Setting Out a New Approach to Family Wealth Management 3

Chapter 2 Arriving at a Point of Inflection in the History of Family Wealth 23

Chapter 3 Addressing the Differences between Private and Institutional Investing 45

Chapter 4 Reinforcing the Importance of a Disciplined Investment Process 57

THE SEVEN IMPERATIVES **71**

IMPERATIVE 1 ESTABLISH FAMILY VISION, VALUES, AND GOALS **73**

Chapter 5 Documenting Family Philosophy, Vision, and Values 75

Chapter 6 Determining the Purpose of Wealth and Setting High-Level Financial Goals 89

Chapter 7 Structuring Assets and Aligning Investments to Serve Multiple Purposes 105

Chapter 8 Integrating the Family Business into Wealth Management Strategy 119

IMPERATIVE 2 SET A PRACTICAL FRAMEWORK FOR FAMILY INVESTMENT 133

Chapter 9 Rethinking Modern Portfolio Theory, Considering Goals-Based Wealth Management 135

Chapter 10 Reviewing Different Approaches to Asset Allocation 149

Chapter 11 Comprehensive Risk Management 165

IMPERATIVE 3 SET A LONG-TERM FAMILY WEALTH STRATEGY AND DEFINE THE ASSET ALLOCATION MODEL 185

Chapter 12 The Elements of Long-Term Strategy 187

Chapter 13 Investing for the Future: Mega-Themes and Principled Investment Management 199

Chapter 14 Long-Term Strategy Document (Example) 217

IMPERATIVE 4 DRAFT THE ANNUAL INVESTMENT POLICY STATEMENT AND REFINE INVESTMENT TACTICS 235

Chapter 15 Drafting the Annual Investment Policy Statement and Refining Investment Tactics 237

Chapter 16 Rethinking the Role of Traditional Asset Classes 249

Chapter 17 Assessing Alternative Assets and the Search for Recurring Alpha 267

Chapter 18 Selecting Individual Investments and Investment Managers 285

Chapter 19 Investment Policy Statement (Example) 299

IMPERATIVE 5 MONITOR PERFORMANCE AND RESPOND TO THE NEED FOR CHANGE 309

Chapter 20 Monitoring Performance against Internal Goals and External Benchmarks 311

Chapter 21 "White Water Investing" and the Management of Wealth in Turbulent Times 321

IMPERATIVE 6 SELECT AND MANAGE AN ECOSYSTEM OF TRUSTED FINANCIAL ADVISORS 327

Chapter 22 Designing the Ecosystem and Selecting Advisors 329

Chapter 23 The Role of the Family Office 341

IMPERATIVE 7 ENGAGE AND EDUCATE THE FAMILY 359

Chapter 24 Determining the Right Wealth Distribution Strategy 361

Chapter 25 Preparing the Family for Successful Management and Transfer of Wealth 375

CONCLUSION **393**

Chapter 26 Pulling It All Together: The Successful Management and Transfer of Wealth Across Generations 395

Bibliography **403**

List of Essay Writers **407**

List of Figures and Tables **409**

About the Authors **411**

About the Raffles Family Wealth Trust **415**

About Northwood Family Office **419**

Index **423**

Foreword

In 1999, Warren Buffett spoke wisely, as ever, about "investment complexity," and his words are well worth remembering for all family investors. He said:

> Investors should remember that their scorecard is not computed using Olympic diving methods. Degree-of-difficulty doesn't count. If you are right about a business whose value is largely dependent on a single key factor that is both easy to understand and enduring, the payoff is the same as if you had correctly analyzed an investment alternative characterized by many constantly shifting and complex variables. The truly big investment idea can usually be explained in a short paragraph.

In the financial services industry, "simplicity" is the enemy, as complexity is more psychologically intoxicating, and makes it easier to sell fee-laden financial products to investors—and helps to keep us glued to the various channels of the ubiquitous financial media. Sadly, there is far too much that is focused on in the media and celebrated in the popular domain that distracts investors and matters little.

As an investor who has focused on working with legacy families for many years, I have often reflected on the investment landscape over the past 30 years (more or less a complete generation) and ponder what that past portends for the future investment environment. I believe now that what is needed more than ever is a strong framework of simplicity for investors, a coherent approach bolstered by a few key tenets that matter to long-term financial success.

A Different Environment

Investors, families, and institutions alike are living in increasingly complex and bewildering times. Today's investment environment seems a world away from that of just one generation ago, in the early 1980s. New issues such as globalization and the rise of emerging market power, macroeconomic forces, the Global Financial Crisis (GFC) of 2008, systemic risks, sovereign debt defaults in major countries, unprecedented monetary policies, climate change, high-frequency trading, investment fraud, and other aspects of our financial life now play important roles in family wealth management.

Additionally, driven by the global information technology revolution, sparked by the proliferation of the Internet, accelerated by powerful mobile devices, and enabled by the availability and speed of wireless data, we are living in an "always-on, data-everywhere" society. Media companies have done absolutely brilliant jobs convincing investors that they must stay constantly tethered to their communication devices, for fear of missing the latest breaking news that may impact their investments, however irrelevant, inconsequential, and short term the issues are that they are communicating.

The combination of the shock and impact of the GFC of 2008, the very real substantive challenges facing investors, and the high-velocity and high-volume barrage of information has frozen many investors into a holding pattern of sorts—unsure of the right investment strategy to follow to protect and compound wealth. One clear sign of fear, confusion, and uncertainty is the capital flow over the past five years into bonds and out of stocks, despite interest rates lower than those during World War II in America and a strong rally in many stock markets.

A Brief History of Investing

It's worth a brief look back to see how we got to this situation. Following a long period where most investors held a straightforward portfolio of bonds and public stocks, in the early 1980s a new era was born. This era can be exemplified by the genesis and rise of firms like the Blackstone Group, a firm founded with initial seed capital of $400,000, which has grown into one of the largest private equity firms in the world over the past 30 years, and now has over $150 billion under management.

This early era of alternative investing, characterized by active engagement with opportunities in private equity, venture capital, real estate, liquid alternative assets (such as hedge and credit strategies), and even extending into new forms of investing in natural resources, was a halcyon era of profiting from uncrowded investment opportunities. The relatively attractive returns of these new sectors, when compared to traditional asset classes, were enhanced by a strong private versus public arbitrage, which led to outsized returns for investors in these new, privately traded asset classes for most of the 1980–2000 time frame.

Average return profiles for private equity, as the industry really got buzzing in 1990, were nearly 22 percent annually over the ensuing decade ending in 2000. These returns complemented terrific returns in public stocks and bonds. Diversified portfolios offered high returns and moderate volatility; an increasing number of families began to follow the so-called diversified endowment portfolio model.

After the brief—and reasonably isolated—Internet bust in 2000, the period 2000–2008 was essentially characterized by high and consistent returns across many asset classes. Everything seemed to be working in harmony until the pent-up crisis of 2008 took hold in a deeply flawed system and brought the prices of nearly all financial assets down sharply and created a very real risk of a collapse of the global financial system.

Coming out of the 2000–2001 correction, the U.S. Federal Reserve followed a standard protocol of lowering short-term interest rates in an effort to boost economic growth. This let loose a global search for income and yield among investors, empowering the enormous boom in credit-related instruments and derivatives that ultimately came unglued in the GFC. Debt became abundantly available, which led to exceptionally strong capital flows into leveraged investments such as private equity and real estate.

Rebalancing, Risk, and Return

However, as more capital flowed into previously uncrowded alternative asset markets, prices and risk went steadily up and, correspondingly, returns went down. Deal quality deteriorated and many deals went bankrupt when credit dried up rapidly in late 2008. Investors who bought into the classic endowment model, which promised equity-like returns with less "risk" (measured by volatility) by allocating wealth across a wide range of alternative asset classes, were shocked to find that nearly all of their investments dropped sharply in value, regardless of asset class.

Diversification to the underlying risk factors wasn't as strong as expected. Only cash and bonds provided ballast to the downside, and they usually held low weights in most endowment-type portfolios. Most alternative asset classes require moderate economic, interest rate, and inflationary conditions to perform well. They have very high correlations to equity markets so, as many families found out, to their surprise, their portfolios were less diversified to key factor risks than they thought and also highly illiquid, opaque, complex, and expensive.

Meanwhile, a simple 60–40 weighted portfolio model to global stocks and bonds has out-performed the vast majority of diversified portfolios since the onset of the financial crisis. Accordingly, in this increasingly complex and confusing environment, one of the most popular investment strategies—that of the endowment model as undertaken by family investors and smaller institutions with less access to high-performing managers and a less robust stream of endowment contributions than the big Ivy League players—is being questioned by families and institutions alike.

A Better Way Forward

Many families are thus looking for a better way forward in the future than they have found in the recent past. It is in this context that Mark Daniell and Tom McCullough have written a topical and insightful book. I believe that this book is an excellent contribution to the thinking about the topic of family wealth management, and is an important work for all those in search of an investment strategy well-adapted and refined for the new world order.

With their usual superb grasp of financial history and investment fundamentals, the authors integrate critical family-related strategic issues into their thoughts as well. This provides a fresh and challenging perspective for many who have never thought through the role the family really plays in family wealth management.

For most families, the overarching objective of their family investment office is to preserve and compound capital over the long haul. Families, unlike most institutions, are blessed with the ability to be very long term in their investing philosophy; equally important as an edge is a family's ability to be flexible in how they chose to invest.

However, setting up and maintaining the right investment philosophy, financial strategy, governance and constitutional model, decision-making processes, and practical approach to investing to take advantage of these valuable inherent opportunities is a very difficult challenge for any legacy family.

In my experience, those families that have had the greatest success over time achieve and act on an understanding of the insights brought to life in this intelligent and thoughtful work by the authors.

I believe that this book will become an important reference guide and actively used "playbook" for families and investment managers around the world as we all navigate through the clearly challenging investment waters ahead.

Stephen J. George, CFA
Founder and Managing Partner
Panorama Point Partners, Ltd.

Preface

This book is the product of a truly international effort, bringing together two coauthors on opposite sides of the world to address a global topic of great interest to both of us.

Although friends for many years, this book benefited from the difference of perspective and experience we were able to bring to our joint effort. Over the period in which we were drafting this book, our views coalesced around the set of principles and shared observations underlying their genesis and application.

We hope that the views expressed herein achieve their stated purpose of helping you to protect, enhance, and benefit from your own family wealth as best you can.

There is no easy option for any family wealth manager—and in fact there never has been—but with the benefit of the examples and insights contained in these pages, we hope that we can make that journey less onerous, more informed, and, in the end, as successful as you can possibly be in achieving your deepest aspirations for both family and family wealth, and for yourself as well.

Statement of Purpose: The Challenge—and Value—of Preserving Family Wealth

It is our hope that the ideas and examples contained in these pages will help family leaders and their advisors to protect the family's hard-earned wealth and compound it successfully over time.

The purpose of this book is to help families to make and implement sound investment decisions, consistent with that unique family's philosophy of wealth, long-term vision, and common values. In so doing, they will create superior, sustainable returns for the benefit of both living and future members of the family and those they choose to serve with their wealth.

To achieve this goal, it will be essential to continue a number of successful past practices, but also to do some things differently in areas where old models, approaches, and instincts have proven wanting in a challenging new world order.

Riches to Rags Is Not the Only Option

The well-worn phrase "from rags to riches to rags in three generations" exists in virtually every country around the world in one form or another. This phenomenon, while frustratingly common, is not the only path available for a family with substantial wealth.

In these pages will be found ideas and examples of an approach that can reduce the risks of catastrophic loss of wealth, and also some ideas about the ways successfully wealthy families have built and preserved their fortunes over time and across generations, and in so doing found alternatives to the erosion of family wealth and stature suffered by so many others.

A Higher Synthesis of Family and Finance

Throughout this work we will raise the issues of family and financial fortune as two parts of a whole that are inextricably intertwined. They are so interrelated that both need to be addressed and considered in full and proper measure throughout the diagnosis, design, and implementation phases of a wealth strategy. Family wealth management is as much about family and its individual members as it is about finance and individual investments.

The pursuit of the long-term goal of family wealth preservation requires family leaders to master the management of both family and finance and to avoid the traps and pitfalls experienced by others. This is a balancing act that requires the simultaneous mastery of both change and continuity in the constantly evolving world of family wealth management.

The Unique Nature of Family Wealth

There is something unique about the nature of family financial wealth as compared to other kinds of family assets, business successes, or trading positions.

Family wealth does not exist as a kind of transactional substance in a global zero-sum game. If one family loses a defined sum of money through excessive spending, family dispute, poor planning, or a bad investment decision, there is rarely an offsetting gain of equal or superior proportion for another family. It is just a pure and simple loss.

The Fire Metaphor

Money can, at its essence, be thought of as a kind of energy. The best analogy for the kind of energy represented by family financial wealth may be that akin to a warm and illuminating fire. If tended properly and protected from adverse interventions or influences, those flames can burn for many years. However, if scattered without purpose, left unattended, or exposed to harsh conditions, the flames can burn lower, or even be extinguished altogether.

If the flames are left to die out, there is almost always no counterbalancing increase in energy or offsetting benefit arising elsewhere. The fire simply dies out entirely on its own, vanishing from sight, perhaps never to be rekindled.

The reduction or extinction of wealth is thus a loss of an illuminating energy that could have benefited the family and its individual members, and also contributed to the greater good of the communities in which that family lives, works, and invests.

Lasting Impact of Loss of Wealth

Research also shows that the loss of family wealth can even have a negative effect on families for generations as a lingering sense of regret, festering anger at the loss of what once was and is no more, and a burning desire to resurrect what was lost can consume the lives of individuals long after the wealth itself is gone.

However, the preservation and enhancement of family wealth can have a long and positive effect on the family as a whole and its individual members. Given the right amount of attention, tending, and activity, the flames of family wealth can burn long and bright to the benefit of the family and all those who come into contact with its members and enterprises.

Addressing the full needs of a family wealth management program can be an engaging exercise across branches, generations, and any other divides in a family of wealth. It can both improve financial management and strengthen the bonds and sense of common purpose within the family as well.

The Family Is Always at the Heart of Family Wealth Management

The financial challenges, which can be daunting, may, however, be less difficult than the many human issues arising with regard to the culture, individuals, relationships, generations, transitions, and challenges within the family itself.

To be successful, a family wealth plan needs to address both family and wealth in equal measure. The difficulty inherent in the human side of family issues was perhaps best captured by a family and family business leader who stated with no little exasperation, "I don't know why they call these people issues the 'soft' issues; they should really should be called the 'even harder' issues. . . ."

Although difficult and diffuse, these soft issues may be the most important factors in determining whether a family retains and enhances its fortune, or loses financial wealth in an entirely avoidable set of conflicts, mistakes, and family errors. While catastrophic loss of family financial capital may seem like a remote possibility today for you and your family, a quick review of the list of the once wealthy—and the many reasons they lost their money—may provide a sobering view of what can, and often does, happen.

The records of history are humbling indeed.

No Universal Solution

Our views are not meant to provide a one-size-fits-all approach to every family's financial needs. Rather, they should be seen to provide useful input to help families follow their own visions, adhere to their own values, and determine their own investment philosophies and practices.

While there is no single playbook that will guarantee consistent, long-term investment success, we do believe there are some basic common elements critical to successful investing. We have outlined them in these chapters.

Adaptation to Change Is the Key to Survival

It may be worth remembering that Darwin did not say, "Only the strong survive." Instead, his true words were, "It is not the strongest of the species that survives, nor the most intelligent, but the one most responsive to change."

The great changes in the economic and financial world we face, from macroeconomic risks to rising fiscal pressures and government policies to microeconomic opportunities, will have consequences that stretch across an entire generation of family investors.

How we respond to those changes, and the investment challenges they bring, may well make the difference between sustaining family wealth and stature, or falling prey to the all-too-frequent decline from riches to rags potentially accelerated in a modern interconnected world.

Constant in Purpose, Resilient in Adversity

It must be understood that success in family investing is not merely about stepping through a mechanical process on an annual basis, or allocating assets on an informed and forward-thinking basis.

Families who have experienced success over an extended period know they need to invest time, effort, and thought on a continual basis in the pursuit of their financial and family goals. However, even for the insightful and dedicated family, things often do not go according to plan.

Unforeseen events from within or outside the family can have a devastating effect on family and fortune, and these crises will often prove to be the greatest tests of a family and its leaders. Wars, disasters, deaths, nationalizations, crises, crashes, corruption, and conflict, to name but a few causes of loss of financial wealth and family stature, provide challenges through which the most exemplary family leaders navigate with steadfast attention to, protection of, and, where necessary, regeneration of family wealth.

An Integrated and Holistic Approach

In all cases, the elements of an approach to successful investing will need to be considered individually and separately, and also as part of an integrated whole where one element can affect many more, and where the results may be substantially driven by the interconnection of factors as much as by any one single factor or event.

It may well be that defining, measuring, reporting, and managing the integrated whole is one of the highest priorities of all in the job of a family wealth manager dedicated to the preservation and enhancement of family wealth.

Investing Differently

The new approach to investing advocated here is all about families investing in a different way to preserve their own fortunes and to assure their own family's future.

Just as family wealth management is as much about family as financial wealth, investment needs to follow insight, form needs to follow substance, and the right amount of resource made available for investment in the few things that truly matter. Families now need to invest their limited time, effort, and money very selectively in a plan that will best ensure their own long-term future. That future can unfold in the best possible manner only if families invest their financial wealth wisely, and also invest time and effort (and money) to address the nonfinancial risks and opportunities that can have a fundamental effect—catastrophic or positive—on their family wealth.

The nature of investment in the new world order thus needs to be different from the past in two very important ways. First, it must be well and quickly adapted to reflect historical lessons learned and the realities of the new economic order—a "new normal" that carries with it both new opportunities and the challenge of investing successfully in a colder economic climate. Second, the best approach to family wealth management also needs to reflect the necessity of addressing both family and finance together, the two eternal sources of family wealth preservation or loss.

The Elements of Investment and Finance

To begin with the economic and financial challenges of family wealth disciplines, the areas for active investment include an understanding of the broader context and the global investment opportunities (and risks) available, the development of a family purpose-led approach to asset allocation, the selection of appropriate investments, and the development of an ecosystem custom-tailored to meet the family's long-term objectives and worthy of its trust. These areas for investment are addressed in these pages and captured in the integrated framework in Chapter 1, and elaborated on in each section of this book.

We are now in a world in which we need to work harder and invest more to get less. We need to analyze more deeply, take more risk, allocate more capital, exchange more views, and engage more actively in managing the costs and quality of our advice to get less in return. We need, as a result, more skills, more relevant information, and an integrated worldview and model of investment that can get us through this difficult period, and also those inevitable crises that will emerge in the future.

Nothing is forever, but a balanced and enduring approach may pay far greater dividends in the long run for those investing families willing and able to adapt to changes in the environment, to both think and act differently in different times.

On Family Matters

Investment is also required on the family side, which was the area most often neglected by families in the past. Specific sums of money need to be set aside and targeted programs developed to understand and share family history, culture, values, and vision; to construct effective systems of family leadership and governance; and to create and implement programs in the education of each generation according to its needs, and in the continuing education of adult family members.

Investment is also possible to address individual development and family succession plans that are so crucial in keeping the ship steady in turbulent times and across generations.

If all we invest is money, then our chances of retaining our family fortunes and stature are dramatically reduced. Without investment in both family and finance on a coordinated basis, there may be no return when we need it most.

Achieving Consistently Superior Results

The combination of these two elements of family and fortune into a single investment framework for the family, we trust, will not simply be an academic exercise, as our intention is far more practical.

It is our hope and aspiration that you will find in these pages some relevant new ideas and useful approaches you can apply directly to support the achievement of your own family's long-term goals, investment objectives, and wealth management plans—proven ideas and approaches that can inform and guide real decisions and action in the capital markets and within the family itself.

In so doing, we hope to have contributed to the preservation, enhancement, and growth of your own family's wealth, ensuring both continuing family prosperity and all the individual benefits and enduring opportunities that true family wealth can bring over time.

Overview of Contents

Although the subject matter of family wealth management needs to be addressed on an integrated and comprehensive basis, we have divided our observations and examples into seven discrete components. These individual elements of strategic thinking can also make up a step-by-step approach to the development and implementation of an effective investment strategy for your own wealthy family. By unbundling the task, we hope that it becomes more manageable, especially for the new citizens in the land of substantial liquid wealth.

The investing world is a far more complex and difficult world than in the past. Changes in capital markets, volatility, interest rates, valuations, capital availability (or not), gross domestic product (GDP) growth, and bailouts or deficit funding of banks, cities, states, counties, companies, countries, and currencies have all contributed to a particularly challenging current environment for family wealth management—with a future that looks no less tricky for some years to come.

In its overall approach, the subject matter presented here addresses many of the issues relevant for family investors and their advisors in the new world order. The chapters contain information and insights related to the history of family wealth, the current and future economic environment, investment lessons from the past, observations on the future, a new approach to portfolio theory, asset allocation and portfolio construction, guidance on active management, coinvestment, sustainable and principled investment, aggregate portfolio and risk management, and some of the unique psychological aspects that distinguish family wealth management from institutional investing.

The imperatives, set out in the contents and described in summary below, create order and a useful taxonomy or checklist for the thoughtful investor looking for a forward pathway that is better adapted to the markets of the present and the future than that provided by old models that may have been found wanting through recent periods of crisis and recovery. These imperatives, and their combination, provide the backbone of a goals-based and family-centered approach to wealth management.

- *Introduction and Overview: A Critical Time for Family Investors.* In this first section, we address the current challenging environment in which families are making investment decisions.

In addition, we describe some of the principal differences between private and institutional investing—and some of the hard lessons learned by family investors over time. These initial chapters set out the benefits of a disciplined approach and the broad context for families to begin to develop their own integrated approach to the management of both family and family wealth.

- *Imperative 1: Establish Family Vision, Values, and Goals.* Before beginning to set out the strategies, tactics, and oversight of specific financial and real investments, it is essential for family investors to determine the philosophy and purposes of family investment and to align the family's investment process with its overall long-term vision and guiding values. In this section, we address the setting of high-level family wealth goals, along with the opportunities to structure assets to achieve multiple purposes and, if appropriate, to integrate the many aspects of a family business into the family's approach to wealth management.
- *Imperative 2: Set a Practical Framework for Family Investment.* There are many ways to approach family wealth management, with the best approach driven by a family's unique history, capabilities, and interests. Portfolio theory, goals-based wealth management, and the most useful models and approaches to asset allocation and risk management all need to be thought through and adapted as necessary before setting out a disciplined (and documented) program of family wealth management.
- *Imperative 3: Set Long-Term Family Wealth Strategy and Define the Asset Allocation Model.* One of the great advantages families have over institutional investors is the ability to be more creative, to take on different types of risk, and to take a longer time frame for investment strategy. Under this imperative, the elements of long-term strategy are raised for consideration. The content of a long-term strategy document is presented, along with an example for your review.
- *Imperative 4: Refine Investment Tactics and Draft the Annual Investment Policy Statement.* Successful investment is as much about the timing of investment as it is about strategic asset selection. Here, the search for alpha and the evolving role of different asset classes in a family portfolio are discussed. In addition, an example of an annual IPS is provided to see

how the disparate assets may all be pulled together into a single operating portfolio.

- *Imperative 5: Monitor Performance and Respond to the Need for Change.* Over recent years we have seen dramatic change in the investment environment and the performance of different assets, both financial and real. Adapting to different environments is essential. Keeping a close view and control over portfolio performance, cost, and risk is essential to investing successfully in an environment that may require adaptation to survive and prosper.
- *Imperative 6: Select and Manage an Ecosystem of Trusted Financial Advisors.* Every family will need a set of advisors to manage its wealth, from brokers to bankers to custodians, to name but a few. The definition of the best possible system, along with the selection and management of the best available participants in the family's network of advisors and influencers, can make an enormous difference in the final outcome of a long-term family wealth plan. The role of a family office and its alternatives are discussed here as a key part of a family's support system.
- *Imperative 7: Engage and Educate the Family.* The final imperative addresses some of the "soft" issues necessary for a family to increase the odds of keeping family wealth intact. Family culture, distribution policies, and educational programs can all make an enormous difference in both performance enhancement and risk reduction. The savviest of families address these family issues in tandem with the technical aspects of family wealth planning and execution. Perhaps most important, family wealth management provides a practical context, a clear step-by-step approach, and an overall approach that allows family investors and their advisors to integrate these broad insights into a coherent and custom-tailored plan of action.
- *Conclusion.* While it is important to build from the bottom up, it is also essential to take a top-down perspective to ensure that all aspects of the plan work together as intended, and that the overall strategy is well adapted for the internal family dynamic and external environment in which it is to be deployed. This final section addresses the importance of

pulling together all aspects of family wealth management into a complete, coherent, and fully aligned set of activities.

In the end, it is our hope and aspiration that the content of this book should enable the reader to develop a successful approach to family wealth management in the new world order, well-suited for his or her own unique family and applicable over an extended time frame and across many economic cycles, both positive and challenging.

Throughout this book, you will also find short essays on topics of relevance from subject matter experts from around the globe. Their contributions all served to add breadth and depth to the discussion and to "shine a different light" on the important issues families face in the management of our financial and personal affairs.

Acknowledgments

In the creation of any book of this breadth, it would be impossible to cite and thank all those who have had an influence in its creation and on its content.

Coming after so many years of study, experience as both advisors and investors, and through collegial discussions about the topics we have addressed here, there are countless experts, sages, professors, friends, colleagues, clients, speakers, teachers, and authors of other works whose ideas and experiences have contributed substantially to the results of our own endeavor. We would like to thank them all for their dedication, caring, knowledge, and inspiration that have helped us on our journey.

We express our sincere thanks to the colleagues and friends who contributed their intellectual capital and practical wisdom to this volume: Jean Brunel, Basil Demeroutis, Jane Flanagan, James Garland, Stephen George, Stephen Horan, James Grubman, Dennis Jaffe, Ed Lazar, Heinrich Liechtenstein, Thierry Malleret, Erwann Michel-Kerjan, Rick Pitcairn, and Mykolas Rambus.

We also extend our thanks to the many contributing authors who so kindly provided the short supporting essays embedded in this book, small demonstrations of wisdom and practical experience that have both illuminated and informed in so many areas of relevance and interest to our readers.

In addition, Mark would like to thank Stephen J. George of Panorama Point Partners, Ltd., who was instrumental in getting this book under way; Mandy Young from the Raffles Family Wealth Trust, who played her usual stellar supportive and organizational role through much of the development of this book; Jennifer Jacobs and Sarah Chalmers for their excellent editing skills; Asad Jumabhoy for his thoughtful comments on an early draft of the manuscript; and Sara Hamilton of the Family Office Network and Mark's coauthor of *Family Legacy and Leadership*, for providing insight, encouragement, and selfless friendship along the way. He would also like to thank the friends who have provided support and guidance, most notably George Svanidze in Tbilisi; Rupert Phelps of BNY-Mellon in London; Thierry Malleret in Geneva; Nicolas Oltramare and Andreas Baer in Zurich; Julio Cazorla in Barcelona; Tom Hutton in the United States; Tileman Fischer in Munich; Suridah Jalaluddin in Kuala Lumpur; Irman and Liestyana Gusman in Jakarta; and Jaya, Narain, Sunny, Will Adamopoulos, Juliana Ng, Alex Krefft, Claudio Mariani, Jimmy Hsu, Iu-Jin Ong, Roxanne Davies, Chew Mee Kirtland, Chris Wilson, and countless others in Singapore.

Mark would also like to acknowledge and thank his coauthor, Tom McCullough, for his exceptional dedication and countless contributions to this, his first, book. May it not be his last.

Tom would like to acknowledge and express his gratitude to his business colleagues and partners at Northwood Family Office, Scott Hayman and Eric Weir, with whom the approach to private wealth management outlined in this book has been developed, discussed, and put into action over many years, and to the families who have entrusted their lives and wealth to Northwood's care. Thanks, too, to Mia Cassidy for her tireless assistance and positive spirit, and to Sharon Mendelaoui for all her diligent work on the graphics in this book.

Tom would also like to thank his many colleagues in the private wealth industry, too numerous to mention, who have contributed to and honed his thinking about these very important issues of family, wealth, and the thoughtful management of both. It has allowed him to develop an approach to family wealth management that puts the family and their goals back at the center of the wealth management process, where they have always belonged.

Tom would also like to express his appreciation to his colleagues at the Rotman School of Management for the vision and foresight they have shown in introducing a professional, integrated private wealth management program in the MBA program at the University of Toronto, and to the students who have contributed to the program. Tom would also like to express special thanks to coauthor Mark Daniell, who, as an experienced author and gracious gentleman, brought perspective, collegiality, and good humor to a challenging but stimulating task.

Finally, Tom wants to express his gratitude to his wife, Karen; his children, Kate and Ben; and his family and friends for their support and encouragement—and for giving him the freedom to pursue his passions, including writing this book.

INTRODUCTION AND OVERVIEW: A CRITICAL TIME FOR FAMILY INVESTORS

CHAPTER 1

Setting Out a New Approach to Family Wealth Management

"*It is different this time.*"

These have been described as the five most dangerous words in investing. Many investors over the centuries have suffered greatly by ignoring the lessons of the past and the immutable principles of investing.

Unfortunately, in some ways it actually *is* different this time in the world of family wealth management.

Families are beginning to understand that there are enough changes of sufficient magnitude in the economic landscape today, and in the full set of pressures of all kinds facing modern families, to require them to think and act differently in the pursuit of long-term family wealth goals.

Especially in times of turbulence, adversity, and change, prior approaches to investing need to be reviewed and, where needed, changed and adapted for application in a new world order.

Under the new rules of the game, the failure to make needed change and invest differently may well be the greatest risk of all.

Continuity and Change

Although much has changed and much will need to be changed, not all of the lessons of the past should be discarded. There is a good deal to carry forward from the proven principles and approaches developed and tested over time; the lessons of history are not to be forgotten, but the rules of the future also call out for consideration.

Successful investment in this new world order will require preserving the best of the past while simultaneously managing important change to prepare for a difficult and uncertain future. It is all about adopting the "best practice" of the past and also putting in place the "next practice" of the future.

Investing differently in the new world order is thus about both continuity and change, about the concurrent consideration of past and future, and, as always, about helping a family to articulate and achieve its broader family aspirations and its specific financial goals.

The family itself is always at the heart of family wealth management.

As in the economic sphere, changes in the modern family have also pushed the nonfinancial aspects of the family past a different kind of tipping point and into a new world where marriages cannot be counted on to last, where children are increasingly separate from their parents, and where global families have less time together and, perhaps, less in common with their siblings and cousins than in past, less mobile generations. Education and engagement of the family across these increasingly disparate generations and other family divides may be among the wisest investments a family can make in risk management, succession planning, and long-term family wealth preservation.

For well-structured families, governance and leadership roles can also be important elements in the mix. The best-led families with experience stretching back over multiple successful generations of wealth preservation and enhancement will have a fully integrated approach to family governance, asset structuring, family roles, and the successful management of family wealth.

These nonfinancial issues are an essential part of family wealth management and need to be integrated into a holistic approach to the family and its wealth as a shared, multigenerational enterprise.

A Unique Time for Family and Finance

What makes this period of time uniquely challenging is the set of trends and events that have pushed family issues and family investing past a point of inflection and into a new world where not all historic assumptions can be relied on going forward, and not all lessons applied successfully in the past may continue to work as well as they once did.

It may be necessary to review basic assumptions about portfolio theory, asset allocation, risk, expected returns and distributions, and to think afresh about what realistic goals can be achieved and reset distribution expectations and other actions to realign family wealth management with both long-term family visions and the realities of the new world order.

The principles and practice of old allocation models, for example, may be necessary, but no longer sufficient, input for a less hospitable investment climate. Long-held views on such issues as correlation, volatility, liquidity, currency exposure, and real after-fees-and-carry performance in alternative asset classes may need to be reconsidered. Overall portfolio objectives, dynamics, risk, and costs will need to be measured and managed along with individual investment performance.

Most successful investors understand that Modern Portfolio Theory's (MPT's) definition of risk as volatility is only one piece of an overarching investment strategy. The role of risk, especially systemic, tail, correlation, counterparty, currency, and value risk, has come under renewed scrutiny as a result of the global financial crisis (GFC) and its aftermath.

Managing well in turbulent times is an essential skill for family investors pursuing a goal of multigenerational wealth preservation. In such environments, investors need to take a different approach to their portfolio strategies and tactics than in more stable and prosperous times. Being able to switch from one mode to the other when needed can make all the difference.

Even the basic role of core asset classes, such as cash and fixed income, may require reconsideration and "repurposing" in an overall portfolio when markets become more adverse and the economic climate turns dark and cold. Many practitioners of endowment models found that they did not hold enough cash and fixed income when the GFC hit, while unfortunately most "diversifying" asset classes, structured notes of various kinds, and other products suffered large decreases in value and provided less liquidity than expected.

However, cash and fixed income proved to be a source of value preservation amid declining markets around the world, and also provided a reliable source of value and liquidity for capital calls, as collateral, and as liquidity for liability management as well.

In this new world order, the balance between change and continuity may have shifted for families, pushing them across a threshold where they may want to stop, reconsider, recalibrate, and realign their activities at a very fundamental level before moving forward again.

A Comprehensive and Balanced Approach

There are many elements to this new model. It is first and foremost focused on unique family needs and goals. It is more agnostic toward market fluctuations and more aligned with investor cash flow needs. It takes into account multiscenario planning; it focuses on influencing factors investors can control and predict, setting aside those they cannot; it eschews high fees and product-oriented sales; and it understands that beta can be had very cheaply and alpha has value but is not readily available across all asset classes. It tilts toward direct investment, where possible, to benefit both family and finance, and its principled approach takes into account factors beyond just the financial. This new approach increasingly combines the intelligence and financial capital of multiple families acting in concert to pursue attractive coinvestment opportunities.

Such an approach is well-suited to maintaining performance in a more volatile climate characterized by unpredictable swings in market values, major systemic challenges, low growth, higher risk, and fewer opportunities for alpha or substantial income generation in a world awash with cash.

Resetting Expectations

Families must adjust their expectations for capital growth and income—and hence review distribution assumptions and policies—to reflect the reality of the markets in which they operate. But they also must hold fast to their long-term financial goals and overarching family aspirations, not losing sight of the long-term vision regardless of the chattering voices that tell them otherwise or tempt them toward a pursuit of the investment flavor of the day.

It is this tenuous balance between steadfastness and adaptability that each family must find to secure and defend its own prosperous future.

Investing Differently

The Seven Imperatives of Successful Investing in the New World Order

The essence of the approach developed and practiced by successful families and their leaders can be captured in seven interrelated imperatives that, when implemented with discipline and care, can make a world of difference to a family and the long-term preservation of its wealth:

Imperative 1: Establish Family Vision, Values, and Goals
Imperative 2: Set a Practical Framework for Family Investment
Imperative 3: Set a Long-Term Family Wealth Strategy and Define the Asset Allocation Model
Imperative 4: Draft the Annual Investment Policy Statement and Refine Investment Tactics
Imperative 5: Monitor Performance and Respond to the Need for Change
Imperative 6: Select and Manage an Ecosystem of Trusted Advisors
Imperative 7: Engage and Educate the Family

Family-Centric

The approach defined here restores the primacy of the family in the family wealth process. The process should be family goals-based from start to finish, addressing both "hard" and "soft" elements of the family, its members, group culture, and its wealth management strategies along the way.

As a first step in the process, it will be important to understand what a family is trying to accomplish, what are the most important values (as reflected in real belief and action, not just as drafted in a values statement), and how individual family members wish to participate in the process of managing their family wealth. If there is a current patriarch, strong family leader, or single point of contact for investment strategy, then the personality, ambitions, capabilities, and limitations of that one person will also be critical to understand and engage in the process.

From the outset, the family's philosophy of wealth—whether assets are held for the unrestricted use of the current owners or held as stewards for future generations—needs to be clarified up front and that philosophy needs to be respected throughout the process.

While driven by family objectives and principles, this approach also takes into account the need to learn the lessons of the past on how to avoid the many pitfalls of individual investors as revealed in the work of experts in behavioral finance and investor psychology.

Structured and Managed for Multiple Purposes

Because substantial family wealth both serves more than one purpose within the family and is normally intended to last for far more than one generation, the structuring and oversight of family wealth should clearly reflect these different purposes and support the realization of a family's long-term financial objectives.

Families may choose to allocate their assets into separate groupings or legal entities to ensure that specific objectives are met. They can also engage in planning and structuring, which often includes trust and corporate structures, multijurisdictional approaches, tax management, and family law planning. Careful design can help ensure that family wealth is successfully protected and preserved across many generations.

The role of tax planning will, in many jurisdictions, increase in importance. Many governments, saddled with large annual deficits and debt burdens (and fueled by populist "soak-the-rich" sentiment) will look to the wealth and income of privileged families to raise revenue, bridge deficits, and, eventually, reduce the mountains of debt built up from the end of the Second World War onward.

Although tax is a major consideration in structuring assets, it is not the only one. While many families use structures to manage income, capital gain, wealth, and inheritance tax, some families also use these same vehicles for other, more qualitative purposes such as protecting assets, segregating assets for a particular (e.g., philanthropic) purpose, institutionalizing family values, and controlling distributions of income and capital.

Often, structuring and investment policy go hand in hand. A trust for a young member of the family may have a long-term capital appreciation bias, while funds for an older member may be more income sensitive as health care, spending, and philanthropic needs rise.

Based on a Different Model and Practical Framework of Investment

For many families, disappointing financial performance and their failure to achieve objectives over an extended time frame are signs that a different approach is needed.

The results for many families coming out of the GFC have precipitated a rethinking of MPT and its associated passive approach to asset allocation, investment, and expected asset class correlation in adverse markets. At the same time, there is also a reevaluation of the relevance to family portfolios of a purely Swensen-style investment model that became a catechism for many families, endowments, and smaller institutional investors over the past pre-GFC decade.

A new approach to family wealth management is required—one that is founded on identifying and funding client goals, scenario modeling as a key part of asset allocation, and an integrated and active approach that considers all components of the family's holdings and structures.

> **Warren Buffett: On Modern Portfolio Theory (an Imperfect Model)**
>
> "Investors should be skeptical of history-based models. Constructed by a nerdy-sounding priesthood using esoteric terms such as beta, gamma, sigma, and the like, these models tend to look impressive. Too often, though, investors forget to examine the assumptions behind the models. Beware of geeks bearing formulas."
>
> *Source:* Berkshire Hathaway, Letter to Shareholders, February 27, 2009.

Considering a Goals-Based Approach to Wealth Management

One of the lessons learned from the crisis is that a more practical and human approach to investment may be more suitable for an investing family than a pure portfolio theory–based approach. This family-centric orientation is commonly called *goals-based wealth management* (GBWM), and it assumes that the true definition of risk is the potential inability of a family to achieve its goals, not only the volatility of its current investments. This approach is driven by a family's specific goals (usually multiple in nature); the mathematics of investment, risk and distribution; and the principles derived from historical lessons learned.

In the GBWM model, investors set out to achieve multiple objectives in one coherent approach.

Investors who have a clear perspective on why they are investing, what the money is for, when they need it, and the level of priority of each intended use will be better served no matter what asset allocation approach they ultimately choose to employ to allocate their funds to specific asset classes and individual investments.

An Integrated, Disciplined, and Documented Approach

Although the list of individual elements of a family wealth management plan is long, and the strategies and tactics are not simple, each plays an important part on its own and as part of the total picture.

A well-conceived integrated family wealth framework approach ensures that decisions are not made in isolation, but rather on an integrated, holistic basis. Figure 1.1 illustrates the multiple

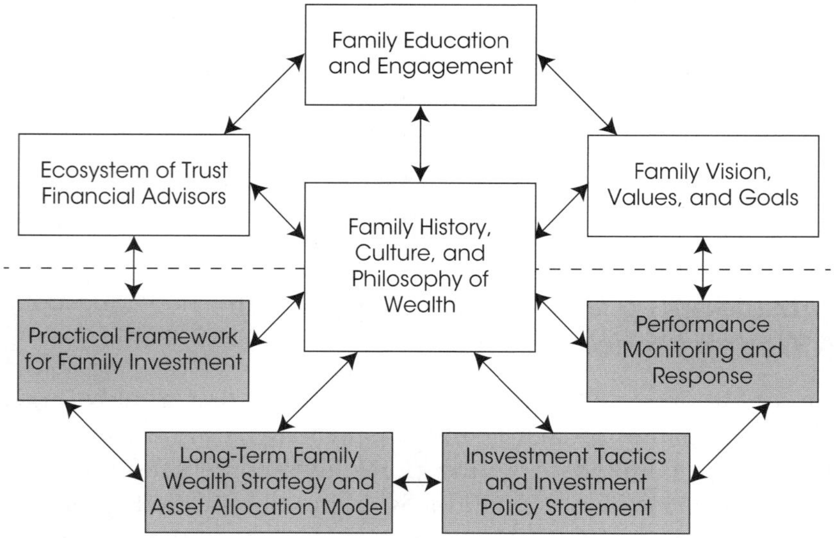

Figure 1.1 Integrated Family Framework

components that need to be included in an integrated family framework. The framework has to be robust enough to hold firm through various challenges, yet flexible enough to adapt as the world changes.

One of the salient characteristics of a best practice approach to family wealth management is wealth plans that capture and describe all of these integrated components in clear, simple, and practical written documents. Of these wealth plans, there are two that stand out in importance:

- *Long-term strategy (LTS) document and strategic asset allocation model:* The LTS provides guidance on the family's philosophy and purposes of wealth, family vision and financial goals, and its guiding investment policies and principles long term. By its nature it is comprehensive in content (addressing all seven imperatives) and is multiyear, and possibly even multigenerational in point of view and expected application.

  The soft issues need to figure prominently in the LTS, including any issues related to family governance, culture, family education and engagement, succession, and leadership.
- *Investment policy statement (IPS):* The annual IPS is as granular as the longer-term LTS is strategic, with both entirely aligned and reflecting the same family vision, values, and investment objectives.

  The IPS will contain a forward view of at least one full year of the relevant macroeconomic environment and capital markets, set investment tactics, and reprise the role of each asset and asset class in the context of that market and overall portfolio, and will define the coming year's specific targets for return and distribution. That approach will be driven by a defined asset allocation model, risk parameters, and preestablished tactical ranges for each class.

Managed by the Horizons, Not the Headlines

Precisely because the churn of events and flow of information seem to be accelerating with each passing year, it is necessary to impose a more thoughtful order on a chaotic and endlessly interconnected series of world and capital market events. In the past decade, there have been instances where some of the major stock market exchanges have been closed for a few days and the frenetic pace of trading, financial press, and prognostications fell silent. It is instructive to imagine how an investment environment would differ from ours where the stock markets opened for trading only two days per month, allowing investors to exchange shares at the market rate, but then were closed for the balance of the month.

It is quite likely in this scenario that investors would spend more time thinking about the fundamental value of their stock holdings than the minute-by-minute prices of their holdings.

There has always been more volatility in the perceived "price" of assets than the drivers of "value" creation themselves. Good investors consistently reject the belief that successful investment requires a focus on the day-to-day price-focused market system and pay attention to long-term fundamentals rather than the Wall Street and popular media short-term hype and gloss.

Families, unlike institutional investors whose performance is scrutinized on a quarterly basis, have the ability to be long term in their investment horizons. Yet, possibly due to emotions and the self-interest of the family's financial ecosystem, families far too often fail to use this inherent long-term thinking and investing edge to their own advantage.

Headlines and sound bites have to be over the top to compete for consumers' attention and are often nothing but a distraction for the thoughtful investor.

"This [media barrage] has," as one large family office chief investment officer (CIO) summed it up, "absolutely nothing to do with investing."

Fully Global in Seeking Opportunity

Not all the news in this new normal and the emerging world order is bad.

As the world of risk evolves, the world of opportunity increases as well. Volatility creates opportunities. Unprecedented growth of middle classes in emerging markets creates opportunities. Markets and currencies that lurch downward may provide unique buying opportunities. One person's environmental concern is another person's long-term attractive investment opportunity. For instance, the negatives for investors associated with environmental degradation can be offset by investments in clean technology.

Historically, families tended to focus their investments within their own home country and currency (back in the days when countries had their own currencies). This now needs to change as the best opportunities for capital growth and income generation can arise anywhere, while diversification principles and family priorities can lead to participation in an expanding world of asset classes and geographic areas for investment.

Sustainable and Principled Investing

Defining and implementing a principled approach to investing, in line with the family's vision and values, is one of the most important elements of the new paradigm. Going beyond philanthropic contribution and a negative screen on individual investment—for example, not investing in tobacco, alcohol, gaming, or firearms—and undertaking a principled approach will have an impact on each stage of the family wealth management process.

There is a whole new vocabulary cropping up in the area that includes such terms as *impact investing, venture philanthropy, social capitalism, philanthrocapitalism,* and other similar labels for an emerging fusion of "doing well" and "doing good." In these models, financial return targets are not lowered to accommodate social returns, but investors simply integrate wide-angle social issues into their financial and operating planning in order to drive a balanced approach that is aligned with both family values and financial aspirations.

Integrating the Family Business into Family Wealth Plans

A family business is often the largest source of family wealth. The family business and its ownership, governance, management, and leadership may also play an important role in a family's internal culture, social stature, and economic prosperity.

Many family leaders and family office CIOs make the mistake of leaving the family business out of their thinking about family wealth management, when a more thorough approach and a fuller understanding of a family's balance sheet would benefit from a view of the portfolio that looks at the collective asset base both with and without the operating business.

The incorporation of a family business into the asset allocation model can have a fundamental impact on decisions made in the family's overall wealth strategy, including issues of capital and income contributions, cash and debt drawdowns, risk, cash flow, leverage, currency, sale timing, family role definition, and other considerations common to all assets in the portfolio.

Defining and Managing Risk

Risk management is one of the central goals of a family wealth strategy. Managing risk is difficult at the best of times, but there is now evidence that the nature of risk is evolving. It also seems that the probability of negative outcomes will increase and the scale of potential impact will increase. Unfortunately, the set of risk management tools most used in the past have not done the job as expected, or as needed, in the recent financial crisis.

Even the definition of risk may need to be revisited to supplement the single variable of volatility with a more nuanced and tailored view. Family investors are searching for a new way to think about risk and ways to protect themselves and their capital going forward. There are many different definitions of risk: volatility, permanent impairment of capital, underperformance, absolute loss, loss of purchasing power, and failure to protect capital.

For some families, the best definition of risk may simply be "not being able to meet your goals" once established on a reasonable basis.

Supported by a Fully Aligned, Effective, and Efficient Ecosystem

The family financial "ecosystem" is the combination of family, internal family resources and external suppliers, and the web of advisors and influencers who make up the interconnected system that shapes and defines a family's wealth management strategy.

One of the greatest disappointments with the external advisory component of the ecosystem relied on by many wealthy families was the extensive profiteering by their private bankers, along with other advisors and asset managers, which became abundantly clear during the GFC. Rising markets from 2003 to 2008, in particular, made it relatively easy to mask a disturbing level of financial "productization," leverage, and high-fee models adopted by financial institutions and advisors.

Much, if not all, of investors' available alpha was eaten up by high aggregate fees, augmented by generous carry arrangements, high water marks, commitment and placement fees, commissions and profits embedded in structured notes, and other in-house vehicles. And they were often opaque from the family's perspective and undisclosed by advisors. These arrangements remained intact despite painfully poor results in the portfolios under management as values plummeted.

In the run-up to the GFC and in its unfolding, the weaknesses in many family ecosystems were exposed, triggering a rethinking about the role, benefit, and cost of external resources and internal family office staff as well.

If Berkshire Hathaway Were a Hedge Fund

The overlay of expensive investment fund fees can not only reduce the return on risk capital, but it can also fundamentally alter the economics of a fund investment. Berkshire Hathaway illustrates the point. Warren Buffett has had spectacular investment performance over almost half a century, averaging over 20 percent per annum, which would have turned $1,000 since inception into $4.3 million by 2009.

> However, if instead of running Berkshire Hathaway as a company in which he co-invests with you, Buffett had set it up as a hedge fund and charged 2% . . . as an annual fee, plus 20% of any gains, of that $4.3 million, $4.0 million would belong to him as manager and only $300,000 would belong to you, the investor.

This assumes the hedge fund manager had the same performance as Buffett. Those who did worse would have returned even less (!) to investors.

Source: Terry Smith, "Straight Talking," www.terrysmithblog.com.

Monitoring Performance and Cost against Internal Goals and External Benchmarks

The performance and progress against the multiyear LTS and the annual IPS need to be monitored to ensure that high-level decisions and policies are turned into effective action on the ground, and that the family's overarching vision does not get lost in the daily battles for capital preservation, growth, and income generation.

Performance should be measured against preselected benchmarks on an after fees and tax basis. These benchmarks can serve as the basis for compensation in an aligned family resource and third party ecosystem. Results should be measured net of all advisor costs, commissions, and carry. The results must also be measured against the family's own internal objectives, which may, in some cases, conflict with external benchmark measurements.

Once the plans for the journey are set, navigating along the way can be substantially aided by the creation and application of a "strategic dashboard," which captures all of the relevant performance monitoring measures and proposed corrective actions in one regular report. This dashboard measures financial performance against plans and benchmarks, looks at costs versus budget and benchmark, and also tracks nonfinancial metrics that support the achievement of the family's long-term ambitions and plans.

This monitoring reflects the old notion that "what gets measured gets done," and keeps the full array of issues summarized in one single report, which will help family leaders and their advisors to effectively manage the progress and take corrective action.

Family Engagement and Education

One of the salient differences between private and institutional investing is the need for a program of engagement that includes education of individual family members, beginning at an early age. By ensuring that family members are motivated, informed, and involved at the right age, and armed when and where needed with the right knowledge and wisdom, families will have a far better chance of successful wealth management in the current generation, and of a successful transfer of their wealth, intact and well-prepared, across many future generations.

Paying attention to this essential set of enabling activities—part of a program to address the "soft" issues within the family and the hard skills required to make good investment decisions in the market—can be of great value in achieving a family's longer-term family vision and its associated financial objectives.

An Integrated and Holistic Approach

A thoughtful wealth management strategy ensures that decisions are not made in isolation, but rather on an integrated, holistic basis; it can help families to pursue their overall vision with a sense of certainty that all of the elements necessary to combine to create that vision are being addressed on a coherent and forward-looking basis.

Consistent with Family Approach to Governance and Leadership

The establishment and operation of a system of family governance and leadership is a hallmark of a successful legacy family. Well-organized families will often have some combination of a broad family forum involving all family members, annual family meetings, a family council, and a foundation board, in addition to the traditional business and investment boards.

Similarly, a family constitution, compact, or mission statement can clarify family vision, values, and principles of operation that need to be aligned with wealth strategy, and may help to orient and guide its long-term direction.

Business Family Parallel

Business families will understand the concept of integrated management. They are used to running their companies in an integrated way with all of the senior managers in each area of corporate responsibility (e.g., manufacturing, sales, accounting, marketing) sitting around the table on a regular basis determining the strategic direction of the company and operating it on an integrated basis. The role of the CEO is to bring the various disciplines together to meet the needs of their customers.

In the same way, the management of wealth should be approached on an integrated basis. The required areas of expertise (e.g., investment, tax, legal, estate) will be different from a business, and the required leadership will be different from that of a traditional CEO. Figure 1.2 illustrates the principle of integrated management in business and financial families.

A well-organized family will be able to pull together its governance structures, individual roles and responsibilities, aspects of its culture and leadership model, and its investment process into a seamless whole.

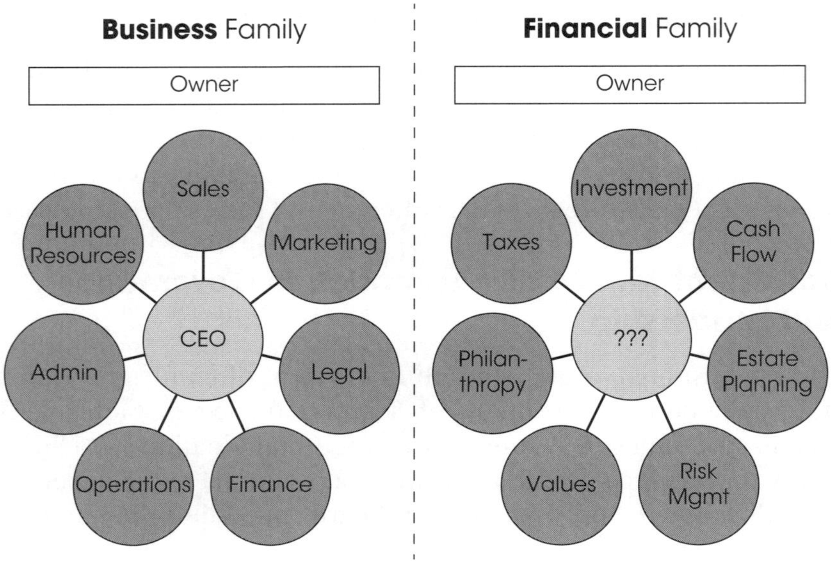

Figure 1.2 Structure of Business and Financial Families
Source: Jean Brunel, Brunel Associates, Presentation at Private Wealth Management Summit, La Quinta, CA, June 2008.

Unchanging Purpose in a Changing World

One of the common characteristics of a point of inflection like the one we are now facing is a wider-than-normal range of potential outcomes and an exceptionally strong link between current decisions and long-term consequences. It is thus especially important now for family leaders and advisors to make the best possible decisions and navigate toward the best possible outcomes in that wide range of available options.

Although much of this book is about long-term evolution in the investing environment and the resulting requirement to adapt a family's approach to wealth management, the fundamental purpose of the exercise does not change.

Successful family wealth management is now, as it always has been, all about creating a common pathway forward to help families realize their visions, respect their values, and achieve their investment goals in a disciplined, sustainable, and efficient manner.

Similarly, within the family itself, many core family and financial objectives will remain constant through all economic and investment cycles, such as the desire for family unity, harmony, and individual happiness, as well as the need for family income, capital preservation, growth, and control within the investment portfolio.

A positive outcome will be far more likely to come to fruition if all relevant ideas are considered, a disciplined family-centric process is followed, and both continuity and change are embraced in the right proportion.

This approach will provide the best opportunity for a family to move forward toward the ultimate goal of continued prosperity, harmony, and the fulfillment of its full family potential over time, and even across many generations.

A Tale of Two Families

Two of the greatest family fortunes in history were created in the nineteenth century. One family thrives and prospers to this day. The other collapsed. Why? It's all a matter of addressing both family and finance at the same time—a pure financial focus is a much higher risk and has a much lower probability of success than a more balanced approach.

Cornelius Vanderbilt (1794–1877)

Cornelius Vanderbilt created one of the greatest fortunes in world history, valued at his death (in 2007 dollars) at $167 billion. He left 95 percent of his estate to one son, and divided the rest among his other children and his wife, leaving a tiny portion to charity. Four of his children contested the will, one of whom ultimately killed himself over the escalating feud about the financial inheritance. Economist John Kenneth Galbraith said that the Vanderbilts showed "both the talent for acquiring money and the dispensing of it in unmatched volume," adding that "they dispensed their wealth for frequent and unparalleled self-gratification and very often did it with downright stupidity."

Confirmation of that view came only 48 years after Cornelius's death: One of his direct descendants died penniless. And, within 70 years of his passing, the last of the 10 great Vanderbilt Fifth Avenue mansions in New York City was torn down. So great was the destruction of the Vanderbilt family and its wealth that for decades through the mid-1900s, the press referred to it as "The Fall of the House of Vanderbilt." The family became known more for its palatial estates, lavish parties, and romantic scandals than for its business interests. William K. Vanderbilt, grandson of Cornelius, said of his inheritance: "It has left me with nothing to hope for, with nothing definite to seek or strive for. Inherited wealth is a real handicap to happiness. It is as certain death to ambition as cocaine is to morality."

Cornelius employed a legion of attorneys and accountants. In fact, his planning was based completely on the "two-legged stool" of estate and financial planning that dominates the planning arena to this day. He did not consciously prepare his children to receive their inheritances, create a pattern of communication among the family, or organize them for ongoing success. Simply stated, he did not prepare his heirs for their inheritance before dropping one of the world's great fortunes into their laps. The result: When the Vanderbilt family held a reunion in 1973, there were no millionaires left among them.

Sir Nathan Mayer Rothschild, 1st Baron Rothschild (1840–1915)

The rise to prominence of Europe's Rothschild family is far more than a tale of banking or politics. It is also an example of how any family can intentionally prepare and organize their children to be independent, successful individuals as well as members of a unified family, no matter their financial status. By the time Sir Nathan Rothschild came to lead the family's enterprises at the turn of the twentieth century, the name Rothschild was synonymous with banking and finance. So great was their power that on several occasions the House of Rothschild, as it came to be known, actually bailed Germany and England out of economic catastrophes that threatened their very existence.

The Rothschild family philosophy on passing inheritances from one generation to the next is very different than Vanderbilt's. They actively mentor the children. For example, they establish "family banks" to lend money to those children who wish to start businesses or pursue other careers, and they monitor and advise the ventures in which the children participate. At the annual family gatherings (which have been held for over 200 years), the values that have sustained the family for generations are affirmed even as their vision for the future is sharpened and clarified. (And if a family member fails to attend the annual family gathering, they are locked out of the family bank!) As part of that vision, the family supports a program of philanthropy in the arts, medicine, science, and education.

Vanderbilt did financial planning, which grows and protects the money, and estate planning, which prepares the money for the heirs. The Rothschilds added a third "leg" to that model: They use heritage planning, which prepares the heirs to receive their inheritance. Building upon that more stable platform has helped to keep them unified, strong, and prosperous for generations, no matter what is happening in the world. By putting individual achievement and family unity ahead of the money, this three-legged planning model takes money out of the "requirements for success" equation altogether. The result: *Any* family can complete heritage planning for their unique circumstances.

Source: Rodney C. Zeeb, JD, CEO, and Ryan D. Zeeb, President, The Heritage Institute.

CHAPTER 2

Arriving at a Point of Inflection in the History of Family Wealth

They, looking back, all the eastern side beheld Of Paradise,
so late their happy seat . . .

John Milton, *Paradise Lost*

These prophetic words of John Milton, capturing the sad sense of loss upon the departure of Adam and Eve from the Garden of Eden, are well-suited to describe the feelings many families have about the difficult investment climate we are now facing, far removed from the rosier economic climate that characterized many prior years.

Although some of the choices we face still seem consistent with this now-past era, and some of our current investing activities are nothing out of the ordinary, other aspects of family wealth management are undergoing a deep and irreversible evolution that will last for the remainder of our investing lifetimes—and beyond.

Perhaps no families feel it more acutely than those who live in countries who are suffering most in the current global investment environment, and those more positively situated on the cusp of a growth-driven transition from a developing nation to a more sophisticated community of wealthy families and investment opportunities.

In some critical areas for all families, things have indeed changed forever. In these areas for family investors there is, as for Adam and Eve, no going back.

A Point of Inflection

The dictionary definition of a *point of inflection* is "a point of fundamental change, a transition from one state to another." This is the perfect way to describe the depth of change we are seeing as we transition from the old environment to the new, edging beyond the "tipping point" past which fundamental approaches need to be reconsidered; new ideas need to be developed, tested, and implemented; and practices no longer relevant need to be left behind.

Past this point of inflection, we need to adapt to change and do some things differently from the way we did them before.

This is not the product of an isolated event, nor even of events and decisions taken within one short period of time; it is the result of a number of seemingly independent factors, trends, and patterns, coming together to change the balance and direction of events for a sustained period.

On the economic front, some economists are predicting a protracted multiyear period of difficulty in Organisation for Economic Cooperation and Development (OECD) markets while deep-seated issues work themselves out; others speak of a lost generation operating in an adverse environment of even longer duration. Still others see a speedier return to a more positive economic environment, but none sees the clock being turned back in a manner that will make old approaches fully suited to the new future facing the global community of family investors.

A Century of Dramatic Changes in Family Fortunes

The five decades from the end of the Second World War to the beginning of the third millennium have been a golden era for the creation of substantial family wealth around the world. Even taking into account the problems of 2008 and beyond, the list of the uber-wealthy grows longer every year. Booming economies in China, India, and other emerging markets, along with ever accelerating developments in the technology and media worlds, continue to generate ever longer lists of new millionaires and billionaires to join the old, who have proven themselves successful in maintaining their wealth over time.

A similar creation of great fortunes could be observed during and after the Industrial Revolution of the second half of the nineteenth century. During this period, vast fortunes were built on the back of industrialization and international expansion, particularly in America. Many great historic fortunes were forged, just as they are today, through taking advantage of the evolutionary—and even revolutionary—change in technology, resource prices, the rise of the emerging markets (in those days including the United States), and continued globalization of trade and investment opportunities.

At the same time, within our own generation, great fortunes have been lost due to cataclysmic events, market collapse, poor strategic decision making, inadequate planning, lack of risk management, and family discord and disputes, which have all wrought havoc on the unwary and the unprepared.

This past century will be long remembered for its destruction, as well as its creation, of family fortunes.

Ghosts of a Gilded Era

Forbes magazine, long associated with the definitive "Rich List," posts a fascinating list of America's wealthiest families from 1918.

Perhaps most interesting is that not a single one of the families cited in 1918 could be found on the Top 20 Rich List nearly 100 years (three or four generations) later (see Figure 2.1). In fact, not one of these great families even made it to the Top 100 Rich List of 2012.

This is particularly striking as the family fortunes of the Rockefellers, Vanderbilts, and others of the Gilded Age on the 1918 list would amount to over $100 billion in today's dollars—each.

Also interesting is that nearly all members of the 1918 list were WASPS (White Anglo-Saxon Protestants), nearly all were male, and their fortunes, in the main, were made and stayed in America.

Not only have these leading families faded over time, but they have also been replaced by a far more international and diverse group of modern-day billionaires.

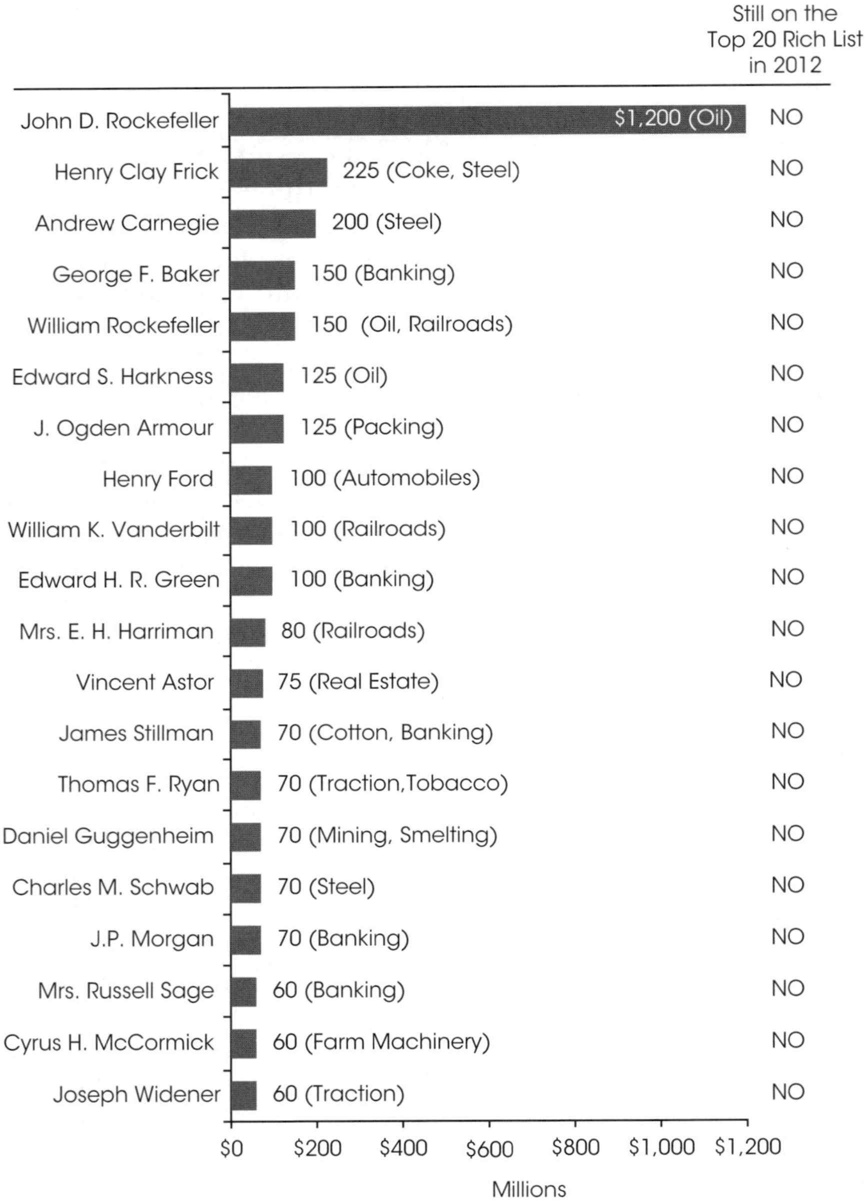

Figure 2.1 Forbes Top 20 U.S. Rich List 1918
Fortunes are in 1918 dollars.
Source: Forbes, www.forbes.com/2002/09/27/0927richest_15.html.

Losing Family Wealth and Stature

In looking at these families and others who have fallen prey to the curse of riches to rags in three generations, a small number of recurring stories and patterns are found time and time again.

The traditional oft-repeated patterns and sources of family wealth destruction include:

- *Time and the inevitable impact of large numbers.* Families tend to expand exponentially in number, while real wealth often grows only arithmetically. That means that the family wealth per person naturally diminishes over time. In the absence of a family system that concentrates wealth in a shared legacy portfolio or dynasty trust, or passes on wealth in a concentrated manner, such as in the traditional system of primogeniture (where the eldest child receives the bulk of a family's estate), many families find their wealth dissipated through no great error in investment or excess in distribution.
- *History.* As previously pointed out, economic crises or political revolutions have substantially reduced or eliminated many great family fortunes. Whether it is an aristocracy eradicated by political revolution, a religious or ethnic group whose assets are confiscated by a hostile government, or even an entire nation's wealth subsumed by the state (as in Russia in 1917 or China in 1949), the loss of family wealth to the forces of history can be tragic. In the past 50 years, we have been living through a time of exceptionally peaceful relations between nations, which has allowed a relatively conflict-free pursuit of economic goals. A longer view of history would suggest that it is only a matter of time before the forces of discord "cry havoc and let slip the dogs of war" and the environment takes a turn for the worse.

  The potential for conflict is increasing as geopolitics enters a more strained period in Asia, the Middle East, and parts of Africa. Everything from access to energy, water, and mineral resources to the simmering "war of civilizations" between radical Islam and the Western powers will create a real test of family leadership in a crisis context.
- *Taxation.* One long-established European aristocratic family recounted an illustrious history of wealth preservation from

its fourteenth-century roots across more than 30 generations in an unbroken line. The continuing wealth was, in part, generated by hiring and renting out soldiers to nations and chieftains eager to wage war across Europe's bloody centuries. Despite a history of successful navigation through political and economic crises from the Napoleonic wars onward, the family is now simply "clinging to the dregs of a once great fortune" due to two generations of high-tax regimes in Europe and England similar to those shown for the United States in Figure 2.2.

- *Family relationships, disputes, and marital discord.* In every jurisdiction, unfortunately, there are examples of family fortunes destroyed by disputes, legal battles, and expensive divorces. Countless family businesses have also been brought low through conflict, poor leadership, and the toxic mixture of bad family dynamics and their intrusion into a shared family business.
- *Bad family values and practices.* Poor governance structures and practices, excessive spending, inattention to investment and business disciplines, drinking, gambling, and other human vices have brought down many family fortunes. Just as good values can be the bedrock for the creation of an enduring family

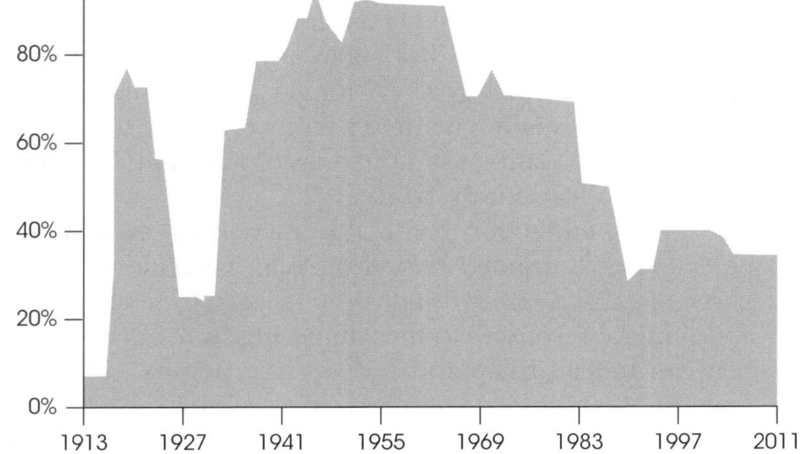

Figure 2.2 Historical Highest U.S. Marginal Income Tax Rates

legacy, a lack of cohering values and a lack of discipline can contribute to the ultimate decline and demise of a family's wealth and stature.

- *Poor investment decisions.* Poor decisions are an obvious source of economic loss, and have brought down many families. While there is no vaccination against bad decision making and bad decision makers, the approach outlined in this book is intended to improve the quality of the management of wealth and mitigate such catastrophic losses where possible.
- *Predators in the family ecosystem.* The wrong advisors, with poor skills, bad motivations, or both, are another notable source of great loss of family wealth.

Vast and Rapid Accumulation of Wealth

While great wealth accumulated by a privileged few has been the hallmark of civilizations for thousands of years, this recent era has been notable in its rapid creation of family fortunes from many different areas of endeavor.

With the advent of the technology age, the opening of global markets, deregulation, the end of empires, the rise of former colonial countries, the end of Communism, the era of easy credit and property booms, the rapid growth in alternative asset funds, an exceptional leap upward in CEO and senior executive compensation, and the rise in oil and gas prices, among other factors, more billionaires (now totaling more than 2,000[*]) and millionaires (more than 11 million[†]) were created than ever could have been expected at the beginning of this long bull run in family fortunes.

However, the ability of even the most celebrated of wealthy families to retain their financial status and resulting social stature has been severely tested by the flows of history, disruptions in the markets, and changes in the family.

Over the past century we have also seen a dramatic change in the stability of the family as a unit; a repetitive history of wars, depressions, and panics; and a history of substantial dissipation of family wealth.

Getting rich is rare, but staying wealthy over time is rarer indeed.

---

[*]Wealth-X, "World Ultra Wealth Report 2012–13," 19.

[†]CapGemini, "World Wealth Report 2012," 17.

Profile and Trends of the World's Wealthy

by Mykolas Rambus

Contrary to popular belief, the majority of ultra-affluent individuals are self-made, having built their own fortunes and inheriting little to no wealth at all. Three out of four individuals with substantial means are self-made. The remainder (one in four) receive their wealth from inheritance.

But, most curiously, half of the inheritors go on to build far more substantial fortunes than that with which they started. While in the past this may have been a small trend, it is likely to increase substantially as the primary holders of America's and Europe's wealth, the so-called Baby Boomers, embark upon the largest wealth transfer ever recorded, from parent to child over the next 20 years.

A family's geocultural context has been an important, if not deciding, factor in the circumstances that lead to great financial wealth. The United States has for some time possessed the world's most vibrant, diverse, and dynamic economy, providing an ecosystem in which great entrepreneurs flourish. This is why today the United States still has more ultra-affluent individuals than anywhere else in the world, for now. Including the United Kingdom's growth, the United States and progressive Europe are at the end of a 100-year wealth creation cycle, whereas Asia is just beginning.

By 2025, Asia, as opposed to the United States, will have the highest concentration of ultra-high-net-worth (UHNW) individuals of anywhere in the world, driven off the back of business builders who are able to tap into both global and local markets efficiently.

On balance, and steadily growing over the next 100 years, inherited wealth will be a larger proportion of the global ultra-affluent landscape, and by historical observation, nearly half will engage in business activities that may boost their families' accounts.

Both Latin America and the Middle East, where inherited wealth makes up more than 50 percent of all family fortunes, provide effective examples and in some cases road maps of how to incorporate effective planning, education, and advice to acquire, develop, and benefit from new business activities.

The shift is clear and has already begun. New wealth is being created en masse in growth economies, especially Asia—North, South, and Southeast. Families are migrating from west to east, from tax focused to tax advantaged. And perhaps most important, children are being educated in an ever increasingly global village of ideas, techniques, and relationships, developing entrepreneurial talents, should they wish to use them.

The world's ultra-affluent today possess $25 trillion in aggregate net worth, and are likely to continue to drive the global economy via the necessary expansion of their family's holdings.

Mykolas Rambus serves as the chief executive officer of Wealth-X, a global authority on UHNW individuals and worldwide standard for professionals working with the ultra-affluent. Wealth-X is headquartered in Singapore.

Three Generations of Crisis and Challenge

A brief chronicle of events over just one century shows why many of these fortunes may have suffered from events beyond the family's control.

While the global financial crisis (GFC) and its subsequent bursting of asset bubbles may have had a negative effect on many fortunes, this is just one of many notable examples of devastating economic downturns over recent centuries:

- 1901: First New York Stock Exchange (NYSE) stock market crash of more than 50 percent—in the middle of a recession.
- 1907: Panic and subsequent bailout of the financial system by J. P. Morgan and a group of wealthy individuals.
- 1914: World War I (1914–1918) and the end of Ottoman, Austro-Hungarian, and German empires.
- 1917: Bolshevik Revolution destroys private wealth in Russia.
- 1929: Stock market crash and depression (1929–1940).
- 1939: World War II (1939–1945).
- 1949: Communist revolutions at the end of World War II destroy private wealth and capitalism in China and elsewhere around the world.
- 1973: Oil crisis followed by stock market crash, inflation, high unemployment, high taxes, and banking crisis.
- 1970s: Confiscatory tax regimes in the United Kingdom, income tax at 83 percent, capital gains at 98 percent.
- 1981: Socialist election victory in France and nationalization of banks and other companies.

- 1982: Global recession and Latin American debt crisis.
- 1989: Japan's Nikkei Index begins collapse from a high of 42,000 to an eventual low of under 10,000.
- 1992: Black Wednesday and European exchange rate mechanism (ERM) currency crisis.
- 1997: Asian economic crisis and subsequent emerging markets collapse.
- 2000: Tech Wreck begins and broader stock market collapse with major indices just recovering to pre-2000 peak levels a decade later.
- 2007: The GFC begins to unfold.
- 2012: France, already claiming 44 percent of gross domestic product (GDP) in taxes, announces an increase in personal income tax to 75 percent tax rate on high earners.

The first lesson that can be taken away from this brief but dramatic history is that any family leader or advisor to a wealthy family's portfolio of investments should expect that there will be a major external economic, political, or military crisis every 10 years or so, with a lesser event every 3 to 5 years.

Internal family crises are an added "bonus," which can crop up at any time to threaten a family's wealth and well-being.

Past the Point of No Return

In some areas, the "new normal" may well be, for some time yet to come, a world of risk with less-than-adequate return. Investing wisely, searching for yield and protecting capital—all longstanding objectives of many family investors—are no longer so easy to achieve.

The new investing world has been described as having passed the point of no return. Both identifying and managing this change, and retaining the valuable foundational elements of continuity, are what this book is all about.

One rueful asset manager joked that the "point of no return" also signaled the start of an era where there was no yield, or no "return," on capital. His clients and other investors were facing a world of continuous risk with little, or even no, real return on the wealth placed at risk in global capital markets.

Where We (Thought We) Were

Just over 10 years ago, the investing world was spiraling upward on a seemingly unending flow of good news, unrelenting global growth, and the production of a continuous set of attractive investment opportunities in all asset classes. The property market, stocks, bonds, private equity, technology-driven venture capital, emerging markets, and commodities were all in the ascendant. Even poorly understood collateralized debt obligations (CDOs), collateralized mortgage obligations (CMOs), derivatives, and structured notes seemed to be playing a useful role in the portfolios of unschooled and, as yet, unwary family investors.

Volatility, real interest rates, inflation, and geopolitical risk, in the wake of the collapse of the Soviet empire, receded into the investment background as fortunes were made across virtually every market and financial, geographic, and asset class.

The macroeconomic picture was similarly rosy. Most of the major economies were growing steadily, albeit at very different rates, employment was rising, the dollar was strong, and the euro had recovered from its early postlaunch swoon.

Not surprisingly, stock markets relished this good news. From 1987 to 1995, the Dow Jones Industrial Average rose each year by about 10 percent (on average). From 1995 to 2000, it tacked on growth at a solid 15 percent a year.

Never in history have we seen such a positive pair of back-to-back decades as the 1980s and 1990s. Unfortunately, this good fortune is neither typical nor likely to recur anytime soon, given past distribution of returns.

In fact, as hard as it is today to remember the emotional and analytical climate of those halcyon days, the major concern expressed was whether the economy was "too hot" and might need a gentle tapping on the brake to moderate the positive momentum of the markets. The main challenge was to find a way to manage the context to a point where things were "just right" for an extended period of time, in what was being called the "Goldilocks Economy."

Unfortunately, this period came to an abrupt and painful ending for many family investors.

The extremes in the performance of equity markets, and the potential for down decades like the one we have just completed, force long-term investors to think through the implications for their own family investment models and approaches (see Table 2.1).

Table 2.1 Dow Jones Industrial Average—Returns by Decade

Decade	Increase/Decrease
2000s	-8%
1990s	+318%
1980s	+228%
1970s	+5%
1960s	+18%
1950s	+239%
1940s	+34%
1930s	-40%
1920s	+132%
1910s	+8%
1900s	+51%

All Good Things Must Come to an End

Within the first decade of the new millennium the entire world had turned upside down. Twice.

The collapse of the Internet bubble just after the turn of the century imploded the Nasdaq index. The NYSE dropped 50 percent from its peak in 2000–2001 and, 10 years later, just made it back to where it was in December 1999, marking a dead decade for equity capital returns, as shown in Figure 2.3.

Included in this go-nowhere decade was extreme volatility, including two massive market downdrafts in which some equity investors saw their portfolios drop by 35 percent (2000–2003) and 55 percent (2008–2009).

For the emerging markets, just 10 years before the onset of the GFC, the Asian economic crisis was unleashed. It began on July 2, 1997, with the decoupling of the Thai baht from the U.S. dollar, and saw some Asian stock markets like Indonesia's fall by as much as 85 percent in U.S. dollar terms. The crisis then grew and spread rapidly to other non-OECD markets in eastern Europe and Latin America.

These more fragile economies have now worked through three major global crises, and their local implications, in one short decade.

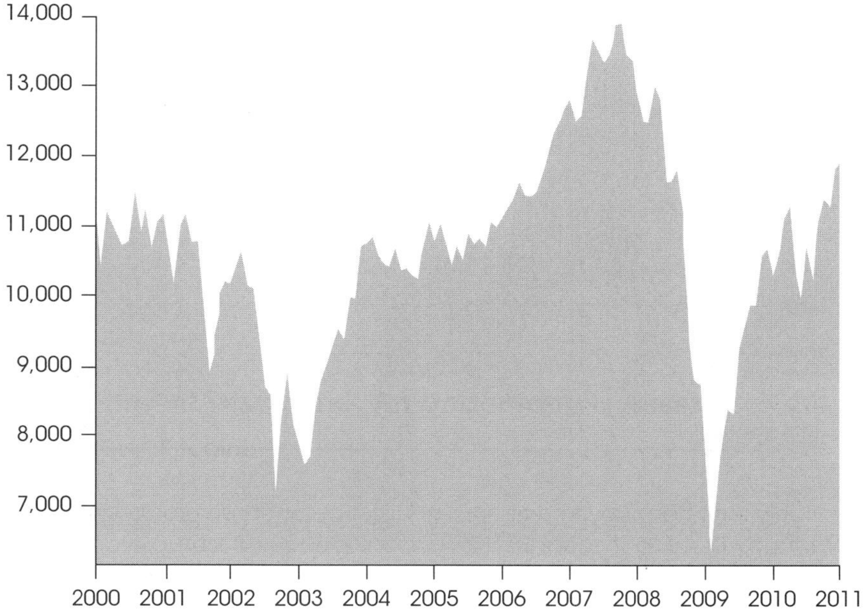

Figure 2.3 A Dead Decade: Dow Jones Industrial Average, 2000–2010

The Great American Wealth Implosion

As the equity market's relentless rise ended, so also did bubbles in property, mortgage-backed securities, bank stocks, and other financial assets. Each of those unsustainable market valuation peaks either imploded or deflated rapidly, tipping the world's economies into a set of difficulties from which they have taken many years to stabilize and begin a halting recovery.

The impact on many families was abrupt and deep. The average American household saw its net worth drop by 40 percent at the bottom of the market, wiping out more than a decade of value accretion from property, shares, and savings (see Figure 2.4). Not only did the portfolio of assets decline in value, but the opportunities to generate income or a recovery in capital value were also challenging.

The property market in the United States alone dropped up to 30 to 40 percent (depending on the region) from its peak in 2006 and 2007, and even more in some hard-hit cities. By mid-2011, more than 11 million households had plunged into a position of

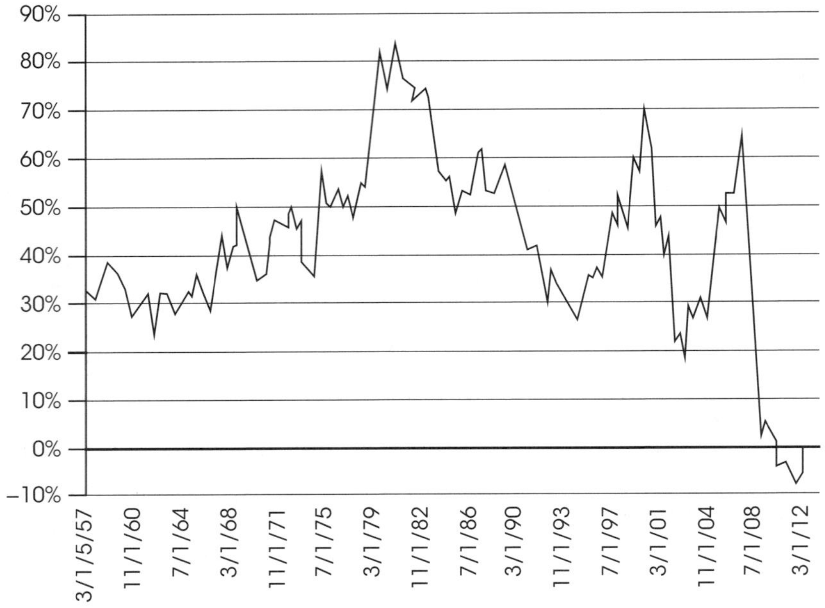

Figure 2.4 U.S. Household Net Worth, Percentage Change from Five Years Earlier

Source: Gluskin Sheff, The Big Picture Conference, October 2012; Bloomberg, Business Insider.

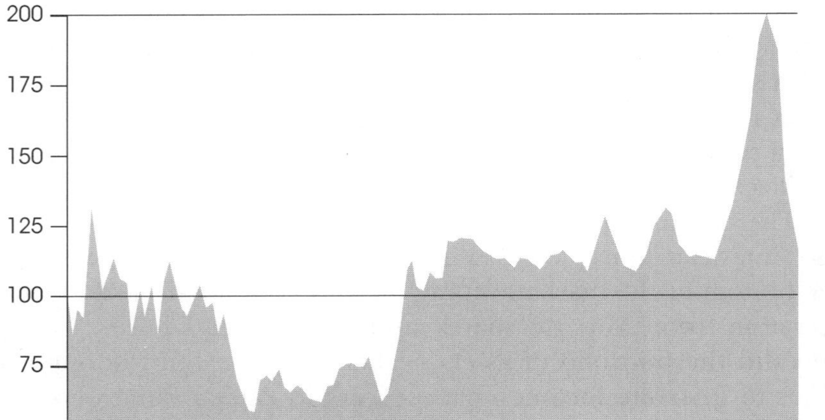

Figure 2.5 A History of U.S. Home Values, 1890–2011

Source: Case-Shiller, benchmark (1890 = 100), annual data prior to 1953, quarterly thereafter (through 1Q12).

negative equity, where the amount due on a mortgage exceeded the value of the property. In the worst hit areas, the so-called "sand states" and large "new build cities" in Florida, California, and Nevada, families investing or living at the epicenter of the damage saw values decline by up to 70 percent from their precrisis peaks to postcrisis lows as shown in Figure 2.5.

A Crisis of Confidence in Past Approaches

Modern Portfolio Theory, the core investment hypothesis of the past 50 years, seemed to suggest that diversification (among uncorrelated asset classes, regions, and securities) should be sufficient to ward off much of the extreme volatility and potential for catastrophic loss in a portfolio. But it became clear that, in our increasingly global and interconnected world, almost everything is correlated when investors all head for the exit at once.

Across the alternative asset class spectrum, there was little diversification to be had in the GFC, as many strategies had been productized and leveraged to the extent that they ended up showing high correlations to drops in the equity markets with little, if any, hedging or structured offset in their portfolios.

Investors now understand that risk could not simply be measured as volatility, but rather as the permanent loss of capital or exposure to "fat tail" events of substantial, and often unexpected, consequences.

Indeed, family investors have been dealt some heavy blows in the past decade. It is no wonder that many are chastened, confused, and fearful and are now acting differently as a result, as evidenced by a massive shift to safe assets like cash, gold, and high-quality fixed income, even if they provide little, if any, real yield.

There has been a very understandable loss of faith in the equity culture and portfolio tenets that underpinned many long-established approaches to family wealth management.

Many investors also no longer trust alternative investments to do the job in the creation of portfolio alpha—after fees and carry—they once did.

"More of the same" was clearly no longer enough.

After so many family portfolios took such a battering during the crisis, many legacy family chief investment officers (CIO) and family principals are now stepping back to determine what the future will look like, what will be the new rules of the game, and how they might move forward in this new world to achieve their investment objectives and longer-term visions.

By the nature of things, as we pass a significant tipping point, old plans become obsolete, a new environment needs to be taken into account, new factors must be considered, and decisions need to be made from a different point of view.

Differing Perspectives

In many ways, the nature of the investing environment will depend on where you stand. From the perspectives of family investors in Greece, Iran, Syria, Sudan, or other, more volatile regions, things may seem darker than at any time in living memory. From a Chinese, Indian, Asian, African, Emirati, Turkish, or Burmese perspective, the world may never have looked so rosy. It clearly is a "two-speed" world with radically different contexts and consequences for family investors.

Some aspects of the new world are here to stay. The geopolitical world will never revert to the once stable Pax Americana and U.S. global economic dominance that prevailed for half a century. Each continent—the Americas, Europe, Africa, and Asia—is undergoing fundamental political and economic change that will reshape the future forever, and increase both risk and opportunity along the way.

Short-, Medium-, and Long-Term Change

Although some of the environmental changes faced by families are cyclical and short term in nature, and others are normal parts of a typical five- to seven-year credit crisis, others are secular in nature, reflecting tectonic changes, which will be part of the future of family investing for many years to come.

Sourcing income for distribution solely from safe government and other fixed-income investments may need to be augmented by approaches to income generation with greater creativity, complexity, and inherent risk. Alternative assets may no longer be a reliable source of alpha without more investor hard work and engagement than in the past.

Relying on a traditional ecosystem of advisors for unbiased and cost-effective advice may not be, on deeper understanding, realistic.

Counting on a mean-reverting positive environment for equity market returns and a relatively benign tax environment are likely to fall away as core tenets of a family investing model.

The overall picture is, as ever, a balance of complex and interrelated elements of both a positive and negative nature. Permanent deficits in Western economies, an increasingly intrusive and demanding fiscal policy, and the more positive macro-themes set out in Chapter 13 are here to stay.

In addition, due to an increasing crisis in global warming and other aspects of the environment, and a growing sensitivity to environmental issues in families, a more principled and sustainable approach to investment may be called for.

These secular changes are only a few of the many reasons why things are different this time from other shallower, and less transitional, crises. These secular trends and patterns will carry through the eventual recovery and then onward into the inevitable waves of future economic cycles and crises yet to come.

The more challenging investment climate may also lead to an approach that is more conservative in expectation and more engaged in risk management to mirror the nature of the "new normal."

Some Old Investing Truths Remain Relevant in the New World Order

Despite any recent shortcomings, not all past approaches should be discarded; there has been much learned over an extended period that should be built into an applicable long-term model of family wealth management for the future.

- A wealth management strategy should be firmly rooted in each family's own objectives.
- Asset allocation should be based on portfolio objectives, reasonable expected risk and returns, and liquidity considerations.
- Portfolio diversification (based on uncorrelated assets) should be a central part of the investment strategy.
- A combination of top-down and bottom-up perspectives will add value to asset allocation and fundamental valuation analysis.
- Investing should be carried out in the context of an integrated approach, which includes an awareness of tax, noninvestment assets, and unique family issues.

- A focus on risk management provides critical protections to the investment portfolio.
- Requiring a margin of safety, using conservative forecasts, and not reaching too aggressively for yield are core principles that may keep investing families out of trouble.
- A written investment policy and a disciplined process will yield better results.
- Insights from behavioral finance on investment decision making will continue to help to avoid some of the major pitfalls of family and individual wealth management.
- A set of solid relationship-driven advisors will be valuable companions on the journey.

Resetting Best Practice—and "Next Practice"—in a World of Change

At the same time that these immutable principles of investment need to be respected, the changing nature of the investment climate and the uncertainties in many once stable dimensions of the investment universe suggest that investors pay equal attention to the elements of change.

Learning and applying the proven lessons of history will be a necessary, but no longer sufficient, set of guidelines for family investors.

Far-sighted investors are also looking to understand and apply family wealth management "next practices" as well as best practices, extracting and applying the lessons of the future to navigate successfully through the coming waves of economic cycles and difficult investing periods.

Wide Range of Potential Outcomes

Each new generation and each passing crisis carries with it opportunities for successful investment as well as the risk of catastrophic loss of wealth; each new fortune carries with it the possibility of preservation across decades and generations, despite the odds against such an enduring success.

Capital markets bought at low points, the acquisition of property or operating assets at distressed prices, and other opportunities created by dramatic changes in asset values and supply/demand imbalances in investment capital can go a long way to the creation of major enhancements to family wealth if understood, timed, and executed properly.

By determining the range of outcomes, developing a deep understanding of the requirements and consequences of each outcome, and acting according to these insights with a disciplined and diversified plan, families will be far better placed to shape the future to their liking.

Effective insight and action can only increase the odds of a desired outcome coming to pass. Equally, as Dietrich Bonhoeffer said so eloquently, "not to act is to act," and for families failing to engage with a more demanding approach to investment, "not to choose is to choose."

The Future Global Investment Context

by Dr. Thierry Malleret

The future global investment context will mirror the world of tomorrow: messy and bumpy, changing everywhere, radically, very rapidly and in multiple intersecting ways that will lend themselves to constant surprises.

It will be a world lurching from one global crisis to the next, ever more susceptible to shocks and dominated by sharp discontinuities.

New opportunities will abound for investors, but there will be no place to hide from the turbulence, the challenges, and the uncertainties.

From an investment standpoint, the fundamental problem is this: We are moving from a world of risks (which are generally well-known, understood, and measurable—meaning that probabilities can be assigned to them) to a world of uncertainties (unknown, hence misunderstood, and to which we cannot assign probabilities).

Investors like risk, but very much dislike uncertainties because, from a cognitive viewpoint, we are ill equipped to deal with them. What is not measurable makes us feel uneasy and uncertain about what decisions to make.

Over the next few decades, six global megatrends will dramatically affect the investment landscape. Their systemic connectivity

(*continued*)

(i.e., the fact that they criss-cross with each other all the time) will amplify risks and will create yet more uncertainty. They are as follows.

1. The *unfavorable demographic outlook*, characterized by unprecedented growth in population—from 7 billion today to more than 8 billion by 2030—and the time bomb of global aging, which will exacerbate both the fiscal strains in rich countries and the burden we impose on our planet.
2. *The scarcity of resources*, which in the decades ahead is bound to increase dramatically. It suggests that the provision of our three most critical resources—water, energy, and food—will come at a considerable cost.
3. The evidence of *climate change* is by now incontrovertible, and extreme weather events will soon become the norm. This will entail dramatic economic, financial, societal, and geopolitical consequences. Extreme volatility in food prices is almost a given in the future.
4. A *geopolitical rebalancing* away from the West is happening: The world will no longer be shaped by the United States and dominated by those institutions it modeled (such as the G7 and Bretton-Wood organizations). It may be a good thing not to have a global hegemon, but the world will be more disorderly and unstable. It will also probably be more dangerous.
5. *Indebtedness and fiscal issues* overwhelmingly affect the richest countries, but their knock-on effect can be felt worldwide. Public and private deleveraging will take many years of painful structural reforms that will ultimately entail a complete redefinition of the social contract.
6. *Rising inequalities* is one of the biggest threats to social stability around the world. It has also a debilitating effect on economic growth.

All this suggests that we'll be living in a "fat tail" world—a world in which "low probability–high impact" events will happen much more frequently than most investors currently assume. In such a context, it may be better for investors to go for subtractive rather than additive solutions.

The logic for this is quite straightforward: If we are destined to live in a world dominated by a stream of constant surprises, the best investment strategy may not be the one that chases the best results (by essence ephemeral), but rather the one that avoids the bad ones. The corollary of this simple idea is that successful investors will revert to simplicity by refusing to engage in anything they do not understand.

This may sound banal, but in an increasingly complex global context, sell-side institutions will often propose products obfuscated by complexity, the best way for them to benefit from asymmetrical information. What will the sensible investor do? He or she will only control the things that can be controlled, and only take the risks that are understood.

Dr. Thierry Malleret is the founder of the Monthly Barometer, an expert advisory business focused on risk and its application to wealthy families. Dr. Malleret is also a former director of the Global Risk Network at the World Economic Forum in Davos, Switzerland, a network that brings together top-end opinion and policy makers, CEOs, and academics to look at how global issues affect business and society in the short and long term.

CHAPTER 3

Addressing the Differences between Private and Institutional Investing

The total amount of private wealth is growing quickly around the world, yet much of the investment industry and most of the financial models are still oriented toward the institutional investor, primarily pension funds, insurance companies, endowments, mutual funds, and sovereign wealth funds.

Although there are many similarities between family and institutional investing when both are done well—good process, thorough review of each individual investment, and balanced asset allocation—there are some fundamental differences that can influence how a family works in the management of its financial wealth.

For many families, it is worthwhile to consider carefully the relevance of an institutional investment model for a wealthy family. In fact, private investors who are not aware of the important distinctions between traditional institutional investing and the special issues facing families, and who do not factor them into their planning, may be at more risk than they know.

Summary of the Differences

There are at least seven key differences between institutional investment management and the management of substantial private wealth:

1. Private and family investors are normally taxable, whereas institutions are not. This has a whole range of impacts beyond the obvious diminution of income.
2. Private investors also have very different patterns of fund flows from institutions, with family wealth often crystallized through a single, nonrepeatable liquidity event.
3. Families and individuals often have multiple goals, complex stakeholder relationships, and issues that must all factor into their decision-making processes at the same time. This requires them to take a more integrated, holistic approach to their wealth planning as opposed to an institution that normally has a narrowly defined investment mandate that is standardized across time and investor objectives.
4. Private investors generally have less sophistication and fewer resources available to them, including in the areas of asset allocation, financial modeling, investment analysis, and risk management, than their institutional counterparts; this may be particularly true for foreign or other unfamiliar markets.
5. Private investors are generally more susceptible to emotional biases that can affect wealth planning and investment management than professional investors.
6. Advisor selection and management are usually less objective and analytical than that carried out by institutions.
7. Many families have (or had) a family business as a large, single component of their wealth. Institutional investing usually focuses exclusively on financial asset management and does not usually have an investment in a large operating entity or need operating business expertise. In addition, the culture of an institutional investor tends to remain relatively constant, while that of a family may need to shift swiftly from a "business family" to an "investing family."

Private wealth management, then, is a field centered on investment management, but considers the client's complete financial picture in a well-integrated fashion that incorporates the dynamic nature of the client's explicit and implied assets and liabilities, the complexity of his or her tax profile, and the nuances of behavioral biases.

Source: William W. Jennings, Stephen Horan, and William Reichenstein, "Private Wealth Management: A Review," *CFA Research Foundation Literature Reviews* 5, no.1 (July 2010): 1.

Family Risk and Opportunity

In addition to this list of issues to understand and manage, one of the major differences between institutional and family investing that crosses over into many related areas is the different nature of the scope and scale of risk faced by the two.

While both face the implicit risks of financial investment common to all investors, families carry with them a whole series of other risks that can be separate from or linked to generic investment risks and can, either on their own or as they compound through interaction, pose greater threats to the continuing prosperity of the family than any pure investing concern.

The sources of catastrophic loss of family wealth, for example, may be more likely to be the result of fundamental issues and flaws within the family than errors in finance or investment.

In fact, investing families could face twice the risks faced by institutional investors, as they need to define and set priorities for action on family risks as well as those related to the portfolio and individual investment risks. It is not just catastrophic loss that is at risk, as all of the potential costs of human and family frailty can play out in the investment arena.

Such "soft" family risks can include unwarranted arrogance, inadequate self-knowledge or assessment, lack of education and preparation, inadequate succession planning or wealth transition, lack of formal governance or informal leadership, a dysfunctional culture and resulting conflict, personal and family branch disputes, competition for leadership positions in the family and in its business and investing activities, litigation and marital complexity, in-laws, and many more similar issues that can depress returns and interfere with the pure dispassionate pursuit of financial gain.

Similarly, families have a longer list of opportunities as well. Usually, they can be more patient and long term in orientation, can invest freely across a broader range of opportunities, can be bolder in their approach to new funds and investment opportunities, can be more creative in structuring and participation, can move faster (which can also be a disadvantage if not carefully managed), and can tailor investments to suit their own vision, values, and full set of investment objectives.

Taxation

Taxes obviously have a significant effect on family portfolio returns and will necessarily influence all of the wealth planning decisions of a family, including spending plans, long-term distribution strategy, asset allocation, and expected returns. Taxes also affect the structures in which assets are held, how wealth is transferred, and how decisions are made about the wealth. Families in jurisdictions with estate taxes or deemed distributions on death have an extra level of planning to do to ensure that wealth passes to the next generations as unscathed as possible.

There is much planning activity by tax and investment professionals to minimize taxes payable, which can add significant complexity to the family's affairs. This can lead to the concern about the "tax tail wagging the dog" as tax-saving structures trump investment choices and even override important family objectives.

Taxes can also have a significant effect on portfolio risk and hence create the need for an after-tax risk analysis across different investments and investment strategies. Interestingly, taxes can actually be seen to reduce portfolio risk when fully considered, since the government may share in an investor's losses.

Tax regimes and interpretations can also be changed by the relevant jurisdiction, which means that investors and their advisors must remain diligent so they will not miss any adjustments that will affect them. In general, taxes add an additional level of family wealth management complexity that institutions do not face.

Cash Flow Patterns

The patterns of inflows and distributions are usually different between family and institutional investors as well. Families may receive their wealth through the sale of a large single operating entity or property, a one-time liquidity event that creates a need to invest the wealth created all at once in one form or another, without a long experience in investing over time, and without a predictable flow of future income for reinvestment. Families may be tempted to rush into investment decisions with the advent of a liquidity event, purchasing what is available at the time rather than what is right for the portfolio on a more considered and carefully paced basis.

For example, given that "good vintage" private equity fund performance correlates with fund raising in bad years for the capital markets and relates primarily to top-decile managers, families who sell a business well at the top of the market may be looking to invest funds at the worst possible time to invest in this asset class, and may have access to only average, or worse, funds.

The newly liquid family may be coming into a market with high prices, no availability of investment in the best funds, and, in the future, facing a relatively tougher environment at the time of intended sale. If this is the case, newly liquid families should take extra care not to turn a successful family business sale into an unsuccessful family investment program.

Institutions, however, may have a flow of premium income or alumni donations that are far more regular over the years and more naturally lead to a more optimized portfolio spread over asset classes and economic cycles.

Although there are occasionally large bequests, often tied to a special purpose or building program, institutional investing is usually focused on the conversion of a steady stream of contributions or donations into funding for short-term operating expenses and for long-term investment to ensure the continuing viability of the school, university, or pension fund.

In some cases, notably Harvard, Yale, and Stanford, the alumni of these fabled academic institutions may include some of the best money managers and businessmen and women in the world. This unique global network can also provide a flow of advice, financial information, and investment opportunities not open to smaller investors without the institutional affiliations of these investment stars.

The impressive reputation and historical track record of these institutional investors may also allow them access to otherwise unavailable investments. Marquee names are always welcome additions to the list of investors for fund managers.

A family's cash needs may also vary significantly from those of their institutional peers year by year as funds are needed to acquire a substantial property, pay inheritance taxes, or fund a large divorce settlement.

The process of decision making may also be different. Family decisions tend to be less well-analyzed than those in an institutional context, and they are often more anecdotal, emotional, or intuitive than the data-driven processes of their institutional counterparts. In part, this is due to the large gap in scale of resource, training, and technology availability between all but the largest family offices and institutional asset managers of any reasonable size.

A multifamily office or set of integrated advisors can provide families with significant institutional-quality resources, experience, and professional process which can level the playing field with their institutional counterparts.

Family Complexity and Influence

A family, unlike an institution, will have an overall vision and objectives that go beyond systematic financial return and which can lead to different investment outcomes compared to a similarly sized institution.

These nonfinancial factors include balancing sources and uses of capital and income, accommodating different personal profiles, finding roles for key family members, balancing rights and responsibilities between branches and generations, ensuring family unity and harmony, planning for succession, integrating the contributions and demands of an operating company, adapting to the individual investment philosophies and needs of family members, and addressing the internal cultural needs of a family-owned and -run investment office.

The nature of the relationships between the leaders of a family and their staff or advisors will always have a more personal element to it than the relationship between the chief executive officer (CEO) or chief investment officer (CIO) of an institutional investor and their employees, beneficiaries, and shareholders. Because continuing employment, compensation, and the quality of the working environment are often determined by one or a small set of individuals, the family investment vehicle will always take on a personal and family tone—for better or worse—that is unique to that family and the key individuals within it.

Personal relationships may matter more in a family investment organization. It is not uncommon to find difficult relationships, family schisms, conflicting philosophies of wealth, differing investor profiles, leadership battles, unresolved conflict, and other problems in many wealthy families.

Although there are many successful family investors, the selection mechanism (DNA or marriage) for a family member differs dramatically from that of an asset management institution, which is typically run as a meritocracy. Even if the family's financial affairs are run in a highly professional manner, there will almost always be a flavor of individual choice and family preference in all major decisions.

Understanding, respecting, and managing these dynamics and idiosyncrasies of a family system lies at the heart of an effective family wealth plan.

Behavioral Biases

Families and individual investors are more subject to behavioral investing traps than institutional investors. This is true because there are generally fewer systems, processes, and disciplines in place than in professional institutional investment organizations.

Also, families are managing their own money, with all the emotional connections that entails. Although institutional managers can be among the most professional and dedicated of wealth managers, they are normally employees and are managing someone else's money. There can be very different attitudes toward risk and a deeply felt sense of personal and family failure if investments don't work out.

Yet, Modern Portfolio Theory assumes that people are rational and make the best decisions possible, even under pressure. But the reality of how people actually make investment decisions has proven to be very different. Behavioral scientists have long known that human beings can be irrational and can make repetitive errors in systematic and predictable ways.

An Honest View

There is substantial evidence to suggest that investors don't tell themselves the truth and consistently act in irrational ways.

> Research indicates that we tend to examine evidence in a biased, incomplete fashion, if at all; quickly reach a rushed decision before we even realize it; and then distort our perception of reality in order to support, justify, and rationalize that decision, in which we are over-confident.

Source: Nicholas Sordoni, *Decision-Making Processes in Equity Investing: The Case for Investment Frameworks* (New York: Lazard Freres, 2010).

Recurring patterns of dysfunctional investor behavior have been described and categorized by behavioral scientists over the past few decades, a list of which includes:

- *Overconfidence and excess optimism.* Research has shown that people think they have better information and expertise than they actually do, and are generally too optimistic about likely outcomes. This, in turn, can lead to investors taking bigger investment bets than they should, resulting in an underdiversified portfolio and greater risk than initially envisioned.

  This same overconfidence can also lead to paying too high a price for an investment relative to its fundamental value. It also leads to "intuitive investing" (i.e., trusting your gut), an approach that works well for a small number of brilliant individuals, but has led to far more big losses than big wins over time.
- *Representativeness.* This is the tendency to evaluate a situation by using mental shortcuts based on generalities or stereotypes. This false assumption can cause investors to assume, for example, that a dividend-paying stock is more conservative just because it pays a dividend. It can also cause investors to assume, wrongly, that an investment manager's excellent recent performance is a result of expertise, when a more complete analysis could reveal that it was more a matter of luck.
- *Herding.* Herding is when people who regularly communicate together tend to think similarly. This phenomenon can lead investors to follow the lead of others (who may have no more knowledge or skill than they do) or to buy an investment merely because a friend is doing it. Taken to a broad community level, this can lead to speculative bubbles well beyond the point of reasonable risk limits.

  A similar bias lies in chasing trends, which is associated with the fear of being left behind while others profit from what may appear superficially to be a very convincing proposition.
- *Friends.* Perhaps even more dangerous than "trend following" can be "friend following," in which a social or family relationship allows an idea to bypass the kind of rigorous scrutiny to which other deals are subject; this can all too often result in the loss of both funds and friends through the same situation.

- *Endowment effect.* The endowment effect reflects the fact that people overvalue the investments they already own. They often demand much more to give up an investment than acquire it, resulting in a temptation for unwary investors to hold on to an investment longer than they should.

Evidence shows that a well-designed investment plan and practical decision making framework can help families avoid some of these more common behavioral errors.

For instance, private investors can mitigate the endowment effect by having a specific sell discipline for each investment determined at the time of acquisition. A written investment policy with specific diversification requirements can also help to mute the over-optimism bias by ensuring that no single investment can dominate the portfolio. Similarly, an experienced, professional advisor can also help to mitigate these biases and bring objectivity and guidance to the management of family wealth.

Professional Advisors Can Mitigate Family Risk

An objective and trusted professional advisor can also help bring perspective and facts to the table, particularly during turbulent times—both positive and negative—when emotions are most likely to drive decisions better left to a more rational process.

Source: Dr. Marcus Schulmerich, "Behavioral Finance in Asset Management: A Primer," SSgA Capital Insights, 2011.

Identifying and Managing the Risks of the Family as a Social Unit

Some risks are similar between institutions and private investors. Others are very different. Some of the broader family risks not fully shared by professional institutions would include:

- *Culture, vision, and values.* Culture counts in families, and the framework of values, behaviors, and operating styles that make up a family culture can be either a great support or a dangerous handicap in investing. Culture is defined by the way we relate, operate, communicate, celebrate, retaliate, and pursue other aspects of social behavior. Each of these behaviors can carry with it risk as well as opportunity, and the elements of culture need to be carefully understood and managed.

For instance, a family who has had a domineering patriarch may have a poorly developed governance and investment decision-making framework. A family with a sense of stewardship of wealth for future generations may take a more conservative capital preservation approach to their funds regardless of the perceived level of valuation of capital markets.

- *Relationship breakdown.* It is said about family business that all problems in the executive suite begin in the sandbox. The competitive search for maternal affection or paternal approval can carry forward across entire lifetimes, and even leave vivid traces in the generations that follow.

  Allowing friction or frustration to boil over into familial conflict can carry with it the risk of great distraction, dysfunctional competition, intrusive disorder, and lingering resentment. It can also distract from the superior investment practice, unbiased decision making, or cool-headed logical analysis of investment decisions required for long-term financial success.
- *Interbranch or intergenerational conflict.* Often arising in a situation where formal family governance has yet to be established, or where the formal mechanisms of family organization and leadership are ignored, this kind of risk also arises in long-established families with a multigenerational history of harmonious relations and successful family investing. No one can take a conflict-free existence for granted. "People are messy," as one successful businessman once summed up as the essential observation of his stellar business career—an observation that we can all ignore only at our peril.
- *Competence risk.* This is one of the greatest risks families face: ensuring that their family members who are active on the investment side are as competent as their institutional

colleagues. This is difficult, as the requirements for family membership are not the same as the requirements for a successful career as a professional investor.

In addition, less competent family members are often kept in their positions despite a history of poor investment decisions due to a desire to avoid family strife. Having the courage to go outside for resources to bolster or replace less competent family leaders—who may be superb at other aspects of their job—may not come easily to families with a tradition of family-only leadership.

- *Succession risk.* Although institutions and families both face succession issues, the role of family leader or patriarch carries with it greater weight in many ways than an institutional investor CEO. Both the quality of the candidate and his or her preparation for the role may differ between the two investing entities. For instance, there is often a far narrower range of candidates available for leadership of a family entity, and few, if any, would have had experience as a successful leader of an independent investment business.
- *Process risk.* Because family decision makers are kings of the world they inhabit, it can be easier for them to override disciplines, skip essential steps in the process, and assert the value of "hunches" and "gut feelings" in the investment process. Partly because many institutional investors themselves are risk averse from a career perspective, thorough analysis and calculated assessment may come more easily to them than to investing family members who have fewer approvals to seek and lower due diligence requirements.
- *Resource risk.* Families can also be at risk of deploying too limited a set of resources, accessing too little information, or spreading limited resources too thinly, which can result in poor decision making. Families will often need to outsource part or all of the investment function to access a greater pool of ideas, information, and opportunities than a stand-alone operation might be able to mount.
- *Ecosystem risk.* Having the wrong advisors, or accepting the wrong advice, can be more of a risk for a family than an institution, especially if the family is relatively inexperienced. Selecting, assessing, and managing advisors require expertise and an objective view of performance. Sometimes advisors,

even those who have become friends, need to be fired. This can be difficult for many families, but it is essential that family members remember that their primary job as family wealth managers is to earn an acceptable rate of return and provide sufficient income to meet the family's objectives.

The Challenge and the Opportunity

Private investors and institutional investors each face the same capital markets, the same challenges of returns and volatility, and many of the same investing dilemmas. But private families shoulder added challenges that they should not underestimate, from taxation to relationship challenges to a unique set of risks.

An awareness of these issues is a good place to start, and the combination of a thoughtful wealth plan and a competent set of advisors will provide ample opportunities for increasing the odds of success.

CHAPTER 4

Reinforcing the Importance of a Disciplined Investment Process

Far too often, a family's investment decisions are made on a loosely defined, ad hoc basis, with heavy influence from sell-side investment brokers and banks, personal relationships, and a high degree of investor subjectivity. Over time, a well-defined and well-disciplined investment process is far more likely to lead to a good result than a random, intuitive, or relationship-driven approach.

There are four aspects of a wealth management plan that will help ensure its success: clear goals; a sound framework; an integrated approach; and a resilient, adaptable, and disciplined process.

Any well-conceived investment process should include excellent strategy; high-quality investment oversight; fully informed decision making; and rigorous attention to results, costs, risks, and the need for specific decision-making on the buy, hold, trim, manage, or sell tactics for each investment.

The result should be an investment process that is fully aligned with the family and also transparent, phased, analytical, systematically skeptical, and, importantly, subject to the discipline of documentation.

Each step needs to be subjected to an ultimate decision test: What is best for the portfolio, given the family objectives and the strategic framework?

Answers will be subject to comprehensive analysis, a determination of fit with the portfolio strategy, and careful monitoring through postinvestment reporting tools.

Given the significant impact of different outcomes to a family, it is often wise to find a qualified, objective, and experienced guide to help a family along the way, and also improve the odds of arriving at the selected destination with both family and fortune intact.

Start with the End in Mind

An effective family wealth planning process starts with the end in mind.

It states clearly the objectives of the family and sets out to achieve those goals with the highest possible probability of success and the least amount of risk. Most investors, prodded by the media and financial industry, still focus on the elusive search for the highest current return or try to beat a particular well-publicized benchmark.

The mistake most investors make is focusing solely on the asset side of the family balance sheet when their focus should be on the whole balance sheet—assets and liabilities, hard and soft elements—with particular attention to the most important goals they wish to achieve.

The Tyranny of the Urgent

The now ubiquitous "urgent and important matrix," shown in Figure 4.1, highlights the dilemma wealthy families face every day in setting priorities and providing the correct rigor and discipline to the true priorities in the wealth management process.

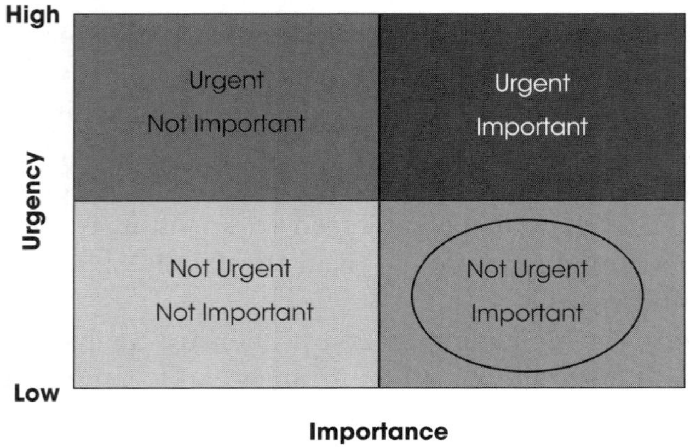

Figure 4.1 Eisenhower Matrix

The matrix is sometimes called the Eisenhower matrix, as it is allegedly based on Eisenhower's quote, "What is important is seldom urgent and what is urgent is seldom important."

The upper right-hand quadrant represents the tasks that are both urgent and important. The two quadrants on the left-hand side represent activities that are not important (whether urgent or not urgent) and can be addressed as appropriate—with the most urgent matters that need to be addressed first on the list.

The problem for investors often lies in allocating sufficient time to the activities in the bottom right-hand quadrant: not urgent but important. While important, these tasks may too often be deferred by the seemingly urgent issues (whether really important or not) despite the greater longer-term value they represent.

Getting a coordinated plan in place for a family's financial affairs with the right kind of advice and a regular review process clearly runs the risk of falling into this "important but not urgent" quadrant. The same is true of family education, governance, and succession planning.

It can be hard to move forward on these kinds of projects, but the positive impact can be enormous if appropriate time is allocated to initiatives.

Mastering the Phases of Family Wealth Strategy

While every family is different and will develop its own unique investment strategy, there is no substitute for a thoughtful, well-conceived, and well-executed plan.

Usually, that plan would incorporate seven imperatives, with each addressing a specific component and contributing to the completion of an integrated family and family wealth framework. While the order of tackling these issues may vary depending on the family, the key imperatives, and hence critical steps, in the planning process are:

1. Establish family vision, values, and goals.
2. Set a practical framework for family investment.
3. Set a long-term family wealth strategy and define the asset allocation model.
4. Refine investment tactics and draft the annual investment policy statement.
5. Monitor performance and respond to the need for change.
6. Select and manage an ecosystem of trusted financial advisors.
7. Engage and educate the family.

Imperative 1: Establish Family Vision, Values, and Goals

The first step in the journey forward is looking inward.

Each family will want to develop a clear understanding of its own past, present, and future. A look at the family's past provides perspective on their view of money, the operating principles and assumptions they have developed, and the culture that has been created.

It is valuable to identify both strengths and weaknesses in a family system. Some thinking about the family's current situation will reveal the values that are central to the family and the way they make decisions. And looking to the future, they will want to determine their vision for the family as a whole and for the wealth they wish to preserve or to spend.

This process will be doubly important if a family is using outside advisors to help, as they will require a strong understanding of the family history, culture, and philosophy of wealth to provide relevant advice.

Imperative 1 reviews these topics in more detail, and helps families to develop a solid understanding of the cultural and historical context that will have a significant impact on future decisions. It will address the following questions:

- What are the history and culture of the family, and how does that affect family relationships, goals, and decision-making processes?
- How do the current values and governance systems help or hinder the wealth management process for the family?
- What is the family's vision for the future? How can a family ensure that the vision is realistic, achievable, and aligned with the family ethos?
- How can leaders ensure that all family members are aligned? Is this necessary and even possible?
- What are the family's goals and which are the highest priority?

Imperative 2: Set a Practical Framework for Family Investment

As a result of evolution and change in both the content of investment models and the context in which they are now applied, families need to reconsider the required change in both content and application of their core investment models. Adaptability is the key to survival in a changing environment; continuing to flourish and prosper across time and multiple periods of change will require an even deeper capability to understand and act to respond as most appropriate to changes in both content and context of family investment.

Even long-held ideas and highly respected advisors will need to be tested for continuing relevance in the new world order.

The basic models of strategy and asset allocation will need to be assessed for continuing applicability, and many of the most basic of issues would benefit from a fresh view in the light of new evidence and new circumstances emerging over recent years.

- What is the most appropriate planning framework for the family to use?
- How can the family goals be best integrated into the wealth planning and investment process?
- How should the family think about risk?
- Which priority risks are the family likely to face, and how can these risks best be mitigated?

Imperative 3: Set a Long-Term Family Wealth Strategy and Define the Asset Allocation Model

A strategic wealth management plan is a holistic, forward-looking document called a *long-term strategy (LTS) document.* It lays out how the family's goals will be achieved, given the family's full balance sheet, along with their current and expected future financial situation.

The LTS takes into account all of the components that have an impact on the family's financial health and future prosperity.

Imperative 3 will answer the following questions:

- What are the key components of the family's strategic wealth plan?
- What are the other factors that must be taken into account along with investments (e.g., taxation, human capital, legal structures, cost bases, differing family objectives)?
- What are reasonable assumptions to use in crafting an investment plan (e.g., investment returns, inflation, number of generations to fund, market volatility, taxes)?

- What rate of return is required, and which asset classes should be included in the portfolio to help ensure that all the family's goals are met? How much loss, volatility, and illiquidity can the portfolio withstand?
- What factors are specific to each family and need to be addressed explicitly (e.g., global family members, multigenerational wealth plans, single stock concentration, overspending family members)?

Imperative 4: Draft the Investment Policy Statement and Refine Investment Tactics

Once the LTS wealth plan is developed, the next step is creating an investment policy statement (IPS) that captures the key elements of the family's investment policy and wealth management guidelines and turns them into actionable steps. The IPS is used to provide guidance for those actually managing the investment portfolio and focuses on the selection and management of investments within preset tactical ranges and with defined objectives and performance targets.

The IPS should be the key point of reference for all major decisions in the portfolio and will require answers to the following questions:

- What are the appropriate components of an IPS?
- Which asset classes should be included in the portfolio and in what proportions?
- What controls, prohibitions, and review process should the IPS contain?

Once the investment plan is developed, the tactics of execution need to be set to ensure that the high-level objectives are met, as well as possible.

Some of the questions family investors need to answer in the IPS include the following:

- What are the key components to successful implementation of the plan? What practices and governance structures can families use to make sound and effective decisions?
- What is the best timing for the execution of the plan (e.g., capital markets, liquidity needs of the family, experience of the family with investments)?

- How can the family minimize fees, taxes, and execution costs?
- Who is responsible for making sure the plan is properly executed?
- How can the family increase its chances of choosing good investments and investment managers?
- How should the process be managed?
- How can a family best ensure they stick with the plan, adapt it as needed, and make good choices under pressure?

Imperative 5: Monitor Performance and Respond to the Need for Change

Another key part of a successful family wealth management process is monitoring and evaluating progress and making changes where necessary, which include defining and managing risks associated with the family investments.

Imperative 5 reviews how best to monitor and evaluate a wealth management plan against appropriate benchmarks and how to make adjustments, if required, and addresses the following questions:

- What tools are available to define, monitor, and manage portfolio risk and the risk to the overall plan?
- What benchmarks should be used to measure the progress of the wealth management plan?
- Does the investment plan still make sense, given the changes in capital markets and family circumstances and goals? Do family goals need to be adjusted?
- Is the execution of the plan as effective it can be? Does it need to be recalibrated?
- If changes need to be made to the plan or the implementation of the plan, how should they be made?

Imperative 6: Select and Manage an Ecosystem of Trusted Financial Advisors

It is difficult for most affluent families to manage their affairs without at least some help. Wealth planning and investment management are not necessarily areas of expertise for all families.

The recent developments in financial markets have only exacerbated the complexity of the wealth management environment with the speed and interconnectedness of global capital markets, the array of investment options, and the changes in fiscal regimes.

A further step in developing and executing a family wealth plan will be to design, select, and manage the integrated ecosystem of advisors, service providers, and other influences on the family's wealth management plans. In Imperative 6, we answer the following questions about how families can effectively select and work with good advisors:

- How does a family determine what kind of advisors are needed?
- How can a family find the best available advisors?
- How can a family work most effectively with an advisor?
- What is the family's role in the advisor relationship?
- How should a family assess, evaluate, and manage the performance of advisors?
- When and how should a family consider changing advisors?

Imperative 7: Engage and Educate the Family

The sad fact is that the majority of wealth transfers across generations fail to achieve the full set of objectives of the transferring generation. One of the main reasons is the lack of preparation of heirs for inheritance or management of family wealth.

There is typically a great deal of attention paid to "preparing the money for the heirs" through tax and asset structures and investment selection and management.

However, there is usually far less preparation on the human side of the transition, with far less attention paid to "preparing the heirs for the money." The latter involves addressing the educational needs on family governance and wealth management, but also ensuring that there is sufficient engagement and motivation on the part of the inheritors.

Given the importance of this task, and the high rate of failure in successful maintenance and transfer of wealth across generations, one could argue that the current approach of most families reflects a significant underinvestment in one of the most critical areas for the preservation of family wealth.

Imperative 7 addresses the twin objectives of education and engagement of heirs with the goal of preparing them for the wealth they will inherit for their own use, or for which they will be called to hold as stewards for future generations.

Imperative 7 will require families to address the following questions:

- What skills do families need to develop within the younger generations?
- How much should families invest in educational activities relative to investment management functions?
- How can a family engage the next generation in the work of building and sustaining family wealth and relationships?
- What family structures are most appropriate?
- What are the costs of disengagement?
- Who is responsible for the success of the generational wealth transfer?

Process Objectives and the Definition of Success

As developed in some detail throughout the different sections of this book, and as summarized in the seven imperatives in Chapter 1, the framework needs to incorporate all of the elements of strategy for a family wealth management program in order to address and overcome a long list of issues and challenges.

All of these elements should be true to the central tenets of family wealth management, with the following outcomes proof that the process is working well:

- *Family-centric.* Based on a firm foundation of knowledge of what makes a family unique and guided by a specific family's unique vision, values, and goals.
  - Founded on a clearly articulated family philosophy of wealth, long-term vision, and values.
  - Fully integrated—addressing all long-term and current aspects of family wealth management, including family culture, governance, and other soft factors within the family itself.
  - Based on a practical approach to multigenerational and multipurpose family investment.
  - Avoiding past family investment mistakes and the classic behavioral errors of individual investors.
  - Taking a forward view of family roles, preparation, education, and succession planning.
  - Integrating family business considerations.

- Considering direct and coinvestment with other like-minded families.
- *Based on a sensible and thoughtful investment model.* Built on both "best practice" and "next practice."
  - Taking a goals-based and family balance sheet approach.
  - Reflecting strengths and addressing weaknesses of Modern Portfolio Theory and traditional models of asset allocation.
  - Reflecting a forward-thinking, scenario-based, and active asset allocation model.
  - Fully global in seeking current and future opportunities.
  - Surfacing and acting on "mega-theme" opportunities for the future.
  - Respecting the principles of long-term value investing.
  - Adopting strategies and tactics for effective application in turbulent and challenging times.
  - Principled and sustainable.
- *Well-structured and well-advised.* Aligning family and investment purpose, protecting wealth from tax and other risks.
  - Incorporating multiple purposes of wealth.
  - Aware of and responsive to state-of-the-art asset structuring options.
  - Fully integrated with family governance structures and principles.
  - Supported by a high-quality and fully aligned ecosystem of advisors.
  - More conservative in expectation and in compensation targets for advisors.
  - Lower cost on a see-through basis.
  - Includes a comprehensive approach to family and financial risk.
- *Pursued through a disciplined process.* Designed and implemented in the most effective process.
  - Right level of family engagement in the present and preparation for the future.
  - Rigorous process that is both disciplined and documented (LTS document and annual IPS).
  - Data-driven and analytical approach to decision making.
  - Fully defined investment strategy and tactics.
  - Formal risk management approach in place.

- Implemented in a manner that ensures the greatest likelihood of success.
- Well-monitored and subject to objective critical review versus benchmark and redirection as needed.

If a family can tick off each of these desired end states as having been considered carefully and integrated successfully into a program of family wealth management, then that program is far more likely to achieve its fundamental objectives and to act to support the family's broader long-term vision and aspirations.

Investment Discipline: An Undervalued Asset

H. F. "Rick" Pitcairn

Imagine that you decided to use $15 million of your personal wealth to create a trust for your children. Next, suppose that I told you that over the next 35 years you should expect this trust to pay out about $45 million in beneficiary distributions, investment-related fees, and tax expenditures. You'll likely be taken aback by that figure. Then, suppose that I told you that 35 years from now you could expect this trust to be valued at more than $200 million!

To be sure, it is an inspiring forecast that any family that creates trusts and other wealth-preserving financial entities would welcome. In fact, I have seen this exact scenario play out over the past 35 years in my own family. And it is not unreasonable to believe that any family can achieve similarly impressive returns over the coming decades. The vital component here is establishing and adhering to a disciplined investment strategy built for the long haul.

In fact, a goal like this may not be easy to achieve. The emotional confluence of love, power, self-interest, and money common to most affluent families makes it challenging to maintain the required discipline. The reality is that it takes strong family leadership built on a foundation of robust governance.

Succumbing to the temptation to react emotionally, spontaneously, and capriciously to the inevitable vicissitudes of the capital markets is the greatest destroyer of family wealth that I have witnessed during my long career in advising families of wealth. As the old, but insightful, saying goes: "All winds blow ill for a ship that knows no port." Think about the last three decades or so. Without a rigorous, disciplined investment plan, it would have been virtually impossible for a

(continued)

family to respond thoughtfully and strategically to the onerous and difficult market environments we experienced in 1987, 1999, and 2008.

Successful families identify the common values around which they establish and manage their ongoing governance processes. Strong leadership and proven outside counsel can help ensure that those values will be present in all of the family's investment philosophies and actions.

Steps to establishing and maintaining a disciplined investment process include:

1. *Align the family's values and goals regarding shared family assets.* This is often done with the assistance of investment professionals, but it is most effective when a family council (or similar governance entity) jointly develops a sense of ownership over the strategy.
2. *Document the agreed-upon strategy using a well-designed IPS.* For example, many families choose to employ a goals-based process in which multiple investment policies are used for each of the family's specific goals, such as liquidity, growth capital, or aspirational achievement. Each policy would have its own risk and return profile, and, of course, different kinds of investments would be used to achieve the different goals. The purpose of the goals-based policy is to allow families to measure their investments against the various goals rather than a set of market indices. This has the added benefit of helping sustain a disciplined process during turbulent market environments.
3. *Ensure consistency.* Once the policy, or policies, have been designed and documented, family leadership must also ensure fidelity to the strategy as well as effective implementation. Well-crafted investment plans don't usually require dramatic changes due to market conditions or a change in investment providers. Haste is not your ally. It is important to use the same governance process described earlier to evaluate possible new options for improving a policy or taking advantage of a short-term opportunity.
4. *Manage change as the family changes—not as the market changes.* No strategy is set in stone. All families change over time. They grow in number. Values and goals change from one generation to the next. New voices will insert themselves into the leadership structure. Successful families meet frequently and communicate effectively in an effort to manage change well.

True, the concept of a disciplined investment process has taken a beating over the past few years. The financial community has created hundreds—if not thousands—of new, high-fee products. The advent of the Internet, social media, the 24-hour news cycle, and a much more aggressive and competitive financial media have triggered ever more rapid cultural change. Many advisors espouse the benefit of knee-jerk tactical strategies while engaging in the same kind of market-timing activity that has contributed to the financial downfall of affluent family after family over the past decades.

Clearly, each extreme market environment presents us with a different set of investment dynamics and opportunities. Families that successfully employ long-term discipline in their investment processes are, by nature, better prepared to evaluate the asset classes and investment methodologies that have historically proven to be wealth creators. They understand that discipline does not equate to buy-and-hold. Nor does such discipline preclude thoughtful tactical positioning as opportunities present themselves. In fact, success lies in their ability to maintain strict parameters around those opportunities.

Leadership and governance, accordingly, are critically important if families desire to react wisely and profitably to a dynamic investment world. Happily, families that can demonstrate that leadership will not only achieve superior investment results, they will also have in place a mechanism for communication and transference of those values that will be a unifying, rather than divisive, force.

H. F. "Rick" Pitcairn II, CFA, serves as the CIO of Pitcairn, a 90-year-old multifamily offi ce based in Philadelphia, Pennsylvania. He has spent his career advising families of wealth regarding their investments and their governance structures.

THE SEVEN IMPERATIVES

IMPERATIVE 1

ESTABLISH FAMILY VISION, VALUES, AND GOALS

CHAPTER 5

Documenting Family Philosophy, Vision, and Values

Before setting out on the family wealth journey, it is essential to understand where a family has come from, and where it wants to go. In addition, defining the values it wishes to respect along the way will confirm who the family is and what its members stand for, as well as what they wish to accomplish through their investing activities.

Understanding Context and History

It is important to understand family history and culture when putting together a wealth plan. The sources of wealth, current assets and advisors, historic approaches to investment decision making, and the family's gallery of investment trophies and scars can inform a plan most likely to fit with a family's principles and objectives.

A family's cultural approach to risk, their investment time frame, liquidity preference, level of engagement, and capability with regard to financial wealth management are all critical parts of the foundation of a family wealth plan that will be best suited to align with a family's investing style, purpose of wealth, and specific performance objectives. Also, any limitations, impediments, or guidance to be provided by family trust deeds or governance principles needs to be understood at the outset of the process.

What Is Family Culture?

Recently, highlighted in one study as part of the academic research of Professor Heinrich Liechtenstein at the IESE Business School in Barcelona, family culture was ranked even higher than formal governance documentation or family leadership model in its importance to family legacy and unity. Family culture—the way families operate, integrate, separate, communicate, celebrate, and address similar social functions—will play a substantial role in determining where, how, and how successfully the family will invest.

Only by understanding a family's culture and the impact of history on the present and future can a realistic plan be developed.

There are also wide ranges of differing cultural attributes and essential complexity within families. Some families are relatively straightforward and generally cooperative. Other families have a history of complexity and difficulty. In the words of Leo Tolstoy, "All happy families resemble one another; each unhappy family is unhappy in its own way."

In general, complexity and discord add time, cost, and stress to family activities and, in some cases, requires more complex structures and administration to mitigate or protect against internal risks complexity can create.

No Single Approach

Because each family's history and culture are unique, there is a wide range of outcomes visible in differing portfolio constructions, risks undertaken, and the results achieved by different families.

Some invest only in traditional asset classes through third-party advisors, while others invest only in property using their own resources. Some families adopt a Swensen-esque endowment portfolio, embracing multiple managers in a multi-asset-class model, while others put all of their family wealth into a single operating business.

There are families that keep half—or even more—of their money in cash, while others use every possible source of leverage to accelerate and enhance return. Some portfolios are set to generate cash for distribution, for either personal or philanthropic purposes, while others are designed to keep capital intact and most income is reinvested for future generations.

Each of these choices has been made for the future, but with the hand of family history felt at each stage of the very different processes they went through to define that pathway forward.

Defining a Clear Philosophy of Family Wealth

Long before setting out to invest, spend, or give away wealth, it is essential to clarify the philosophy that a family holds toward that wealth, an approach set out most clearly by Sara Hamilton of the Family Office Exchange.

There are two very different attitudes that family members have toward inheriting family wealth, as shown in Figure 5.1. Some family members view themselves as "personal proprietors" of the wealth (also referred to as "owners" or "inheritors"). If the wealth was inherited, they view their inheritance as something passed on to them for their personal use. These proprietors see themselves as fortunate to have received an inheritance, but don't feel obliged to preserve the fortune for future generations or may not believe

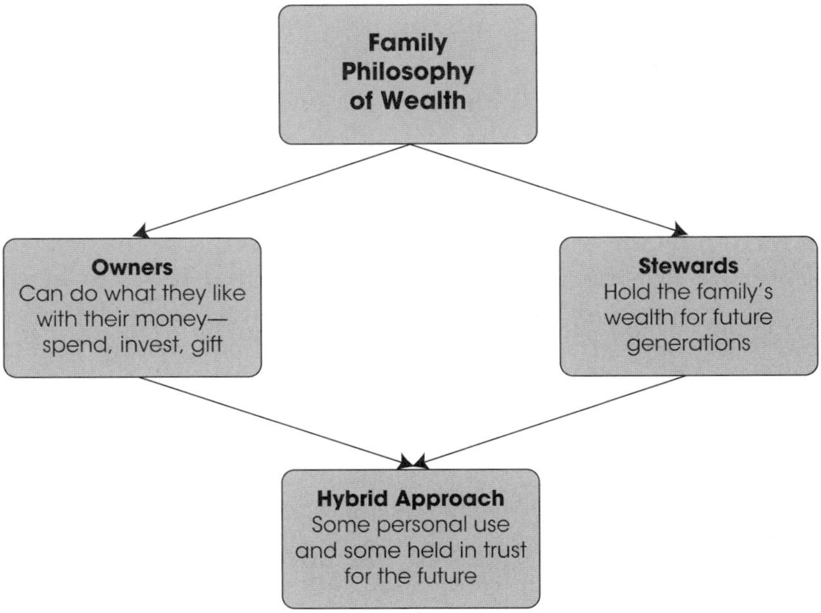

Figure 5.1 Philosophy of Wealth

that a common future enterprise is viable for their family. They are comfortable with the fact that the legacy may end with their generation, and they may spend down the assets. They see themselves as capable of making this decision without regrets or concerns about future generations.

For many others, a legacy of wealth is viewed as something to be cared for and passed to future generations. These owners feel a great responsibility to preserve the wealth during, and even after, their lifetime. These "stewards" of wealth have a broader definition of what they are passing on and a different attitude toward legacy, responsibility, risk, spending disciplines, and education of the next generation.

Obviously, a family that aspires to preserve family wealth for future generations and acts consistently with that view is more likely to create a long-term financial and family legacy than an individual who sees his or her wealth as a short-term resource to be spent or invested with only personal interests in mind.

Balancing Different Views

As experts and family counselors explain, there is no right or wrong about these philosophical differences, and most multigenerational families have both types of owners in their group. Each wealth owner needs to be comfortable with his or her own philosophy and not be judgmental about those who feel differently. The trouble surfaces when differences in philosophy are not discussed openly as a family.

Second-generation siblings who inherit wealth are almost always told by the founders that it is important to keep the family and the wealth together. They seldom feel that they are in control of the money, during their parent's lifetime, so their views on stewardship are typically mandated by their parents and are not challenged during the patriarch's lifetime. In the third generation or beyond, differing philosophies emerge. The siblings and cousins have more freedom to have different views on spending down or preserving wealth.

Immigrants and Natives to the Land of Wealth

An iconic article by wealth psychologists Drs. James Grubman and Dennis Jaffe ("Immigration to the Land of Wealth") describes the differences between newly arriving "immigrants" and the long-standing resident "natives" in the land of wealth, and the different choices they have to make, different attitudes toward their status, and different levels of experience to apply to the challenges of their citizenship.

Having the confidence and ability to define who one is and what one wants to become are the first stages of moving from untutored immigrant to comfortable long-term resident in this landscape. In addition, many of the stresses experienced by individuals, couples, and families of affluence are similar to other types of immigrant experience, including the strains between first-generation immigrant parents and their native-born children and grandchildren.

It is essential for families to have a conversation about their philosophies of wealth as they begin to think about legacy and leadership of the family. Failure to clarify each owner's basic view about stewardship versus proprietorship (personal inheritance) may otherwise lead to a series of misunderstandings or controversies as families struggle to reconcile beliefs.

Consensus and Coexistence

Proprietors and stewards of family wealth can coexist as long as they respect each other's beliefs and agree on the decisions and actions they need to take that can be mutually beneficial. There is no way to force all family members to adhere to one philosophy; since every family has a variety of owners, including proprietors, stewards, risk takers, risk avoiders, and consumers, the coexistence of different views is inevitable. Acceptance of these different views is essential for the family legacy to survive.

Most families of substantial wealth adopt a balanced approach. Some assets are considered to be personal or "proprietary," while others are treated as "heirloom" or "legacy" assets for a future generation. Different investment strategies and distribution policies are often in place for the different "buckets" of money. These sophisticated wealth owners see the choice of steward or proprietor as a false choice, since they comfortably embrace both roles and multiple pools of wealth with clarity and balance.

If there is a shared pool of family assets, and there are different philosophies about wealth ownership and legacy, there may never be an ability to reach perfect agreement about these matters. But setting up a family structure and process to support different philosophies allows diversity to thrive and the legacy to survive.

Investment Implications

In terms of investment objectives for family investment portfolios, stewards of wealth and wealth proprietors may well choose very different options for the management and disposition of their wealth.

Wealth stewards, by definition, have a longer-term investment horizon, a greater sensitivity to risk, and a view that looks for solid investments that will do well across many inevitable economic cycles and many generations of family circumstances. Wealth stewards may also have a greater propensity to professionalize the investment process, and to establish clear and disciplined investment guidelines.

To meet a balanced approach—with some money considered as personal inheritance or ownership and other as family (stewardship) funds—many families choose to have multiple investment portfolios or partnerships pursuing separate strategies. One portfolio designed for wealth preservation may have a more conservative orientation and be characterized by low liquidity, a selection of lower-risk investments (with lower expected return), a higher proportion of real (inflation-resistant) assets, and a longer-term investment horizon.

Another portfolio, aimed at meeting the spending needs of a proprietor, may be characterized by shorter investment periods, greater liquidity, more income generation, and, perhaps, a greater appetite for risk in the search for higher investment return to fund lifestyle expenses proportionately in the near future.

Creating a Family Vision

There is no easy way to set a vision for a family, just as there is no easy way to establish a corporate or organizational vision for a family business. Sometimes the most simple and brief of statements are the most difficult to get right.

Defining a family vision is as much art as science, requiring that the drafters combine a subtle blend of historical insight, precise language, and broad aspirational ideals. Finding the right content, the right tone, the right words, and even the right process by which a family defines a common goal are as important as the actual words themselves.

Example of a Vision Statement

Vision statements set out the overarching multigenerational and enduring objective for a family. Supporting values, specific investment principles, and investment strategies will come later, but need to reinforce the pursuit of the overall goal.

One specific family vision reads:

"The family will strive to become one of England's most highly respected business families, pursuing, with humility and modesty at all times, true and demonstrable excellence in our core family affairs, including our family business, wealth management, community engagement, and philanthropic contribution.

Throughout all of our endeavors we shall respect the highest standards of business ethics and family integrity—building on our historic reputation as "capitalists with a conscience."

Family Values

A family vision will establish what a family wants to be and where it wants to go. Family values will establish how the family will act on the way toward that long-term goal. Life is as much a journey as a destiny or destination, and the principles we live by contribute substantially toward the determination of our value as individuals and as members of a greater family.

Family values establish the limits, standards, and rules its members live by. In great part, the people they are, the families they create, and the legacy they leave behind are deeply influenced by the values they adopt in their personal and business lives. These values may include humility and modesty, generosity to the community, and adherence to the principles of a religion or community. A family may also espouse a sense of both rights and responsibilities among its members. They are entitled to receive benefits by being family members, but are expected to be accountable and perhaps contribute in some way to the betterment of the family.

Values Relevant for Investing

In some families, values may translate into investment negative screens (prohibitions against tobacco, alcohol, gaming, for example) or limitations on areas where questionable practices (e.g., child labor) may be employed. Similarly, families may provide positive guidance to search for investments that promote health or wellness or that reflect other fundamental values and shared beliefs.

Attitudes toward risk, leverage, concentration, and distribution policies may also be shaped by values aimed at preserving family wealth, giving freedom to family members and generations, or reinforcing family unity and joint activity.

Not all family values will carry forward comfortably across generational lines. Younger generations may have a greater interest in tougher negative screens, or in allocating more funds to philanthropic purposes, creating a need for more income generation than a long-term family-only philosophy might imply. Younger generations might also be more risk averse than their predecessors, especially common in second-generation family members, who may not have the skills or confidence of their parents.

What is important is that the relevant vision and values are understood and communicated with sufficient clarity to provide the guidance needed for the family wealth plan.

Determining an Investment Profile

Each wealthy family will have a different history, asset base, investment profile, set of investment objectives, and approach to the investment process.

The investor profile, comprising attitudes toward risk, return targets, geographic markets, classes of assets, liquidity needs, and investment horizon, will vary substantially between families, even if these families are of the same wealth category and have similar experience with inherited wealth.

Each wealthy family will have unique investment objectives. Some may need income to support a family foundation. Others may be seeking long-term capital gains to fund future generations through a second set of investment and inheritance vehicles with low income-generating characteristics.

Multiple Profiles

There are also multiple investor profiles in any one family. Even if the money is managed as one pool (e.g., in a trust), there will be different investor profiles embedded in that single pool.

It can be a continuing challenge for the family and its advisors to manage the funds with not only differing stakeholder needs, but also with a wide range of investment experience, sophistication, and comfort level with risk. Typically, where there is a single pool of funds for multiple stakeholders, there will be a board of trustees, an investment committee, or someone appointed as the manager who can make decisions about the investments. Otherwise, it can be difficult to make good decisions on a consistent basis.

Distribution and Growth Requirements

Client goals and objectives, reviewed in the context of the family balance sheet, must ultimately be translated into investment terms and managed accordingly. The central goal of an investment plan is to meet the specific distribution and growth aspects of the portfolio. The balance between income and growth is the classic trade-off in investing and must be managed with care and must be in tune with the objectives of the wealth owners and other stakeholders.

Investment Time Frame

The length of time over which investments are held is very important in portfolio management. Returns are usually correlated to the time frame available for investment. Long-term investments in, say, a private equity fund or a development property may pay off better than short-term investments such as money market certificates. However, a long-term private equity investment involves higher risk and may not satisfy the investor's shorter-term liquidity needs, as it is often difficult to sell an investment that may not yet have a proven return and may carry substantial fees and future capital commitments.

Liquidity Preference

An investor's preference for the capability to buy or sell an investment quickly will also affect potential returns. The liquidity preference can be high, medium, or low, and the ability to avoid short-term needs for cash can have a broadening effect on the investments available and a positive impact on long-term returns.

Risk Appetite

There is no gain without risk. Without risk, there is also no chance of loss of capital and income. An investor's appetite for real risk (and not just for potential gains) is one of the major determinants of the portfolio's construction and its potential returns. An investor's interest in exposing the portfolio to varying degrees of risk will have a major influence on the category of investment, the potential return, and the potential for permanent capital loss through an investment that goes bad.

There is a hierarchy of risk between asset classes. Junk bonds, some speculative hedge funds, highly levered private equity transactions, portfolios of derivatives, and highly levered property deals can lead to a high return or to a total loss of capital invested. The same is true for direct investments in businesses, especially those just starting up or in their early stages.

Unmanaged or misunderstood risk can have very harmful results. In the Lloyd's syndicate of the past, many wealthy investors took on unlimited personal liability—and eventually lost everything—for a seemingly attractive investment that carried an apparent risk (but not the true risk exposure) that was only a fraction of their full net worth.

At the other end of the scale, there are virtually risk-free and highly liquid instruments in the form of developed market government bonds and near risk-free assets such as federally guaranteed deposits in healthy banks. The return on these lower-risk assets will, of course, be far lower than the potential return on more speculative and higher-risk investments.

Capabilities and Constraints

The other key area the family needs to assess (in addition to their current balance sheet goals and funding sources) is the family's own human capabilities and constraints. Does the family have the tools, skills, emotional wherewithal, and advice to manage their wealth effectively? What factors might limit their ability to manage their funds or achieve their goals?

These factors include the family's investment profile (their needs, preferences, and attitudes toward risk), their level of financial sophistication and portfolio size, any trust terms or other limitations that might restrict certain investment options, and the integration of other financial components of the total family wealth.

Taking an inventory of the skills-based and emotional capabilities of the family is a key step in the wealth management process because it identifies the likelihood of the family's meeting its goals and filling the necessary gaps in order to achieve success.

Financial Scale, Sophistication, and Experience

The scale of family wealth may also influence the investor profile and investor objectives in significant ways. In the higher categories of family wealth, new investment strategies may subdivide the portfolio into a set of differing strategic portfolios with differing profiles, objectives, and managers; at the lower end of the wealth categories, there may be a single portfolio with a single profile and set of objectives.

There are varying degrees of financial sophistication demonstrated by wealthy families and their representatives. Some invest only in high-quality corporate and government bonds, avoiding risk, investing for the short term, and preferring to have a high degree of liquidity (and freedom from concern) at all times. Others are highly sophisticated, investing across all asset classes in many currencies and geographies, achieving far higher returns and remaining comfortable with managing the risk that comes with a more complex portfolio.

Improving the level of sophistication and the investment capability may be an important part of a family's forward strategy, as most wealthy families, sooner or later, end up with a substantial portfolio of investments to manage either alongside, or coming from the sale of, a family operating business. At the very least, it is useful to understand what the current capabilities are and tailor the wealth management plan so that the family is able to handle the information they will receive and the decisions they will be required to make.

In addition, it is important to understand the family's interest and willingness to engage in the wealth management and investment process. This will determine the type of investments they can own, the vehicles they choose, and the type of relationship they have with their advisors.

Trusts' Terms and Letters of Wishes

Regardless of an individual family member's personal investor profile, some family trusts may also contain specific investment proscriptions or mandate a set category of assets in which the trustees are allowed to invest. These directions may be embedded in the trust deeds themselves or spelled out in an accompanying (but not legally binding) letter of wishes from the settlor to the trustee, in which is spelled out the guidance the settlor would like the trustee to consider in making decisions on behalf of the beneficiaries.

Some trusts may accumulate all value and income, while others may require a defined approach to the distribution of dividends, income, or sales proceeds. Others might confine investments to a narrow range of low-risk (and potentially low-return) investments, such as government and municipal bonds or triple-A-rated corporate bonds.

Some family trusts may carry prohibitions against excessive concentration in any one holding or under the control of any one manager. Since diversification is one of the many answers to risk management in a portfolio, such prohibitions need to be understood to determine the best approach consistent with the documented limitations.

The Importance of Clarifying Values in a Family Wealth Plan

Dr. James Grubman and Dr. Dennis Jaffe

Families successful in creating wealth rarely pause to step back and think about what the wealth means or can accomplish for them as a family, now and in the future. There is a golden opportunity to look inward at these questions when the family revises its wealth planning, whether in proactively upgrading its wealth management services or in having to react under time pressure to a stressful change in generational leadership. Too often, families begin with technical questions about tax planning, portfolio management, estate planning, and the like. Yet, the best planning occurs when the family anchors itself in knowing the purpose and goals for their wealth.

These are questions less about managing a portfolio's value than about cultivating and preserving the family's values. These questions cannot be answered by one person alone, but require engagement and dialogue within the family where members likely hold different values and experiences.

There are two main reasons why a family must ensure that its wealth management is integrated with its values. The first is that families of wealth must learn how to *work together in the sharing of assets*. Most successful families originally come from modest financial circumstances, arising from working- or middle-class lives to make the journey to wealth. Their values, skills, and culture stem from the much less affluent world from which they emerged. Financial resources were typically scarce, with most decisions based on the needs of individuals or nuclear families.

In new circumstances where resources are abundant and blended across generations or family branches, the family as a whole must learn new decision-making skills and strategies. This requires a process for open sharing of differences that can lead to resolution of problems, rather than bitterness or estrangement. The adult children must be included in this dialogue, as they have their own perspectives on wealth, what wealth can do, and the direction of their futures. Working together on sharing assets amicably and effectively means the family must know its culture and its values. Otherwise, risk to the family grows over time from excessive conflict or unresolved differences.

The second reason is that affluent families must learn how to *raise the next generation responsibly with wealth*. Wise parenting and grandparenting with wealth requires adapting the family's middle-class orientation to add new strategies where solid values are taught and demonstrated. These are crucial for raising responsible, strong, and purposeful children and grandchildren.

Research has demonstrated that families must do the following:

- Communicate effectively about money and wealth, rather than stay silent or leave things to chance.
- Actively prepare the next generation with skills and knowledge for living with affluence.
- Develop clear agreements, policies, and procedures for working together to pass on assets and control across generations.

Most successful families, for example, hold regular family meetings where information can be discussed and pending issues figured out collaboratively. Family leaders relate the story of how the wealth was built, including the risks that were taken and how those risks were managed. In turn, they learn from their children who have become adults with their own families.

The elder generation listens to the next generation's life goals and plans, with a willingness to discuss how the family wealth can make a difference in the lives of everyone. The family also develops consistent,

(*continued*)

transparent policies so decisions about financial support, gifting, or the family business remain equitable over time. Effective, clear communication within the family; effective preparation of heirs as good stewards of wealth; and effective processes for governing the family justly are the core processes. Taking the time to develop these processes ensures the successful transfer of wealth, whether through inheritance, lifetime transfers, or both.

Few families who come to wealth have been prepared for these tasks. They often don't know these new strategies are even necessary. Truly successful wealth management is best when grounded in the family's very nature—its story, its culture, its values. Those families who make the effort to know themselves can develop a wealth plan that is thoughtful, integrated, fair, and deeply satisfying. By investing in this process seriously, they plan well and develop responsible communication and decision making.

Values-based wealth planning then leads to the most wonderful payoff: family members who can manage the power of wealth and use it effectively for themselves and for society.

Dr. Jim Grubman is a consultant to multigenerational families of wealth and their advisors. He provides guidance about family communication, affluent parenting, estate planning, and financial education, among other issues. He is the author of an upcoming book about the different perspectives of those who come to wealth from modest economic circumstances compared to those who come from wealth as inheritors. Dr. Dennis Jaffe is a professor of organizational systems and psychology at Saybrook University in San Francisco, and an advisor to families about family business, governance, wealth, and philanthropy. He is the author of *Stewardship in Your Family Enterprise: Developing Responsible Family Leadership across Generations* (Pioneer Imprints, 2009).

CHAPTER 6

Determining the Purpose of Wealth and Setting High-Level Financial Goals

Clear financial goals and good investment plans are critical to successful wealth management. A solid, well-thought-out investment process will contribute immeasurably to the management of a wealthy family's financial affairs and the simultaneous accomplishment of nonfinancial goals as well.

Clarifying family goals helps to determine clear priorities and a way forward. It also helps make choices and allocate priorities to specific decisions. A clear sense of goals also helps families stay on track and not be blown off course by the vagaries of the economy, markets, and family issues.

Family investments are usually required to serve a multiplicity of purposes such as providing cash for short-term distributions, preserving wealth in lower-risk growth instruments, taking some higher-risk investments to pursue capital growth for the next generation, funding a charitable program, and setting aside the financial assets necessary to respond to unforeseen contingencies and family emergencies.

For most wealthy families, objectives may vary across different portfolios or across different parts of a single investment portfolio.

However it is constituted, the following questions need to be asked and answered:

- What does the family want to accomplish?
- What is the relative priority of their various goals?
- Is the priority on capital preservation, capital growth, income generation, or some form of balanced return?
- Do the decision makers want to take the risks required to, say, double their family wealth within a set time frame? If so, do they recognize that doing so requires a very ambitious annual return and high levels of investment risk?
- Will there be different portfolios or portfolio objectives (e.g., a charity that requires income or a long-term capital gain preference for future generations) that need to be managed separately?
- Are there different family groups, perhaps representing different generations, that require a separate set of investment objectives for their investments?
- Are there specific requirements regarding risks, time frames, or objectives that need special consideration?

Sample Family Goals

Family goals that have been part of various family investment philosophies include:

High-Level

- Maintain family unity.
- Encourage an entrepreneurial spirit in the family.
- Develop a sense of personal responsibility and independence among family members.
- Ensure that our children have solid values and strong financial literacy skills, and are prepared to receive their inheritance when the time comes.
- Ensure that our employees and staff are fairly treated and well looked after.
- Keep things simple.
- Be remembered in the community as a hardworking, fair-minded, and generous family.

- Ensure that the family estate and business stay in the family.
- Give the bulk of our charitable gifts during our lifetime so we will be able to ensure we achieve the results we want from our philanthropy.
- Manage our money in a manner to ensure a balance of a continuing family legacy and reasonable lifetime benefits for our descendants.
- Ensure that our handicapped daughter is comfortable and has the best care available as long as she lives.

Specific

- Maintain our current standard of living (e.g., annual lifestyle spending of $1 million) throughout our lifetime.
- Donate $1 million per year from the company to charitable causes.
- Retain $20 million in liquidity over the next several years to fund the purchase of a business acquisition.
- Fund all education expenses for as many future generations of family members as possible.
- Leave $10 million to each of our four children on our death.
- Sell the business within five years, unless the next generation decides to take up meaningful roles therein.

It is always helpful to confirm that the stated goals make sense for that particular family. One of the first tests is to ensure that the goals are congruent with the family culture, vision, and values. If not, they will cause tension, stress, and frustration—and be far less likely to be achieved.

Another question to ask is whether the goals are realistic and achievable. Do some of the goals conflict with one another? Are they likely to cause family tension and disagreement? Are they affordable? Can they all be achieved at the same time or do they have to be pursued based on priority or phased over time?

Families can benefit from building a specific plan to accomplish each goal whether it relates to next-generation education, creating a family mission statement, or planning a significant family event. As a part of a sensible plan, it should have a leader or point person, specific measurable objectives, and, where appropriate, a budget.

In the cases where a goal needs significant funding, there are additional financial issues that must be taken into account to ensure that the goal is accomplished. As a starting point, it is helpful to think of wealth not as the value of the total capital, but rather as the generator of future cash flow to meet the family's objectives.

Hierarchy of Goals

One classical way to think about family goals is reflected in a "hierarchy of needs" framework. There are basic financial needs that all families must meet in one way or another. These include basic necessities, emergency needs, and other lifestyle spending. For most wealthy families, these goals are achievable based on their income or availability of capital (see Figure 6.1).

Beyond the basic needs, there are optional goals that families will try to meet based on the degree of surplus capacity in their wealth and the relative priority of the objectives. These can include discretionary spending, legacy, and charitable goals, among others.

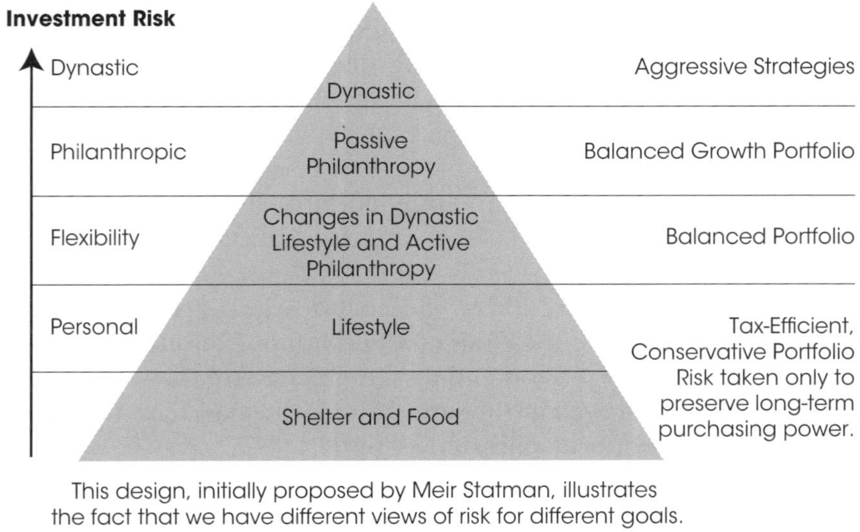

Figure 6.1 Investment Risk Pyramid

Source: Jean Brunel, Brunel Associates, "Goals-Based Wealth Management in Practice, CFA Institute Wealth Management Conference, March 2012.

Lifetime-Legacy Approach

Another valuable goals-based approach is the lifetime-legacy framework. This is a method of identifying goals, evaluating risk, and determining appropriate investment policies based on the unique needs and financial circumstances of each family. Here, we categorize families' objectives (and the assets required to meet those goals) into two broad categories: lifetime and legacy. In an essay entitled "The Why of Wealth Management" planning pioneer Ross Levin uses the illustration in Figure 6.2 to show the distinction.

Lifetime Requirements

Lifetime financial needs are those that will need to be funded during the lifetime of the wealth owners. Typically, they will also be the highest-priority and most near-term goals and can include maintaining current lifestyle needs, keeping an emergency fund or "dry powder" liquidity, funding children's activities, and the like. Normally, these commitments are ones that the family has decided they do not want to put at risk. As such, many families will choose to assign relatively safe assets to meet these very certain commitments.

A present-value calculation of net lifetime expenditures will generate an estimated amount of capital that will be required to

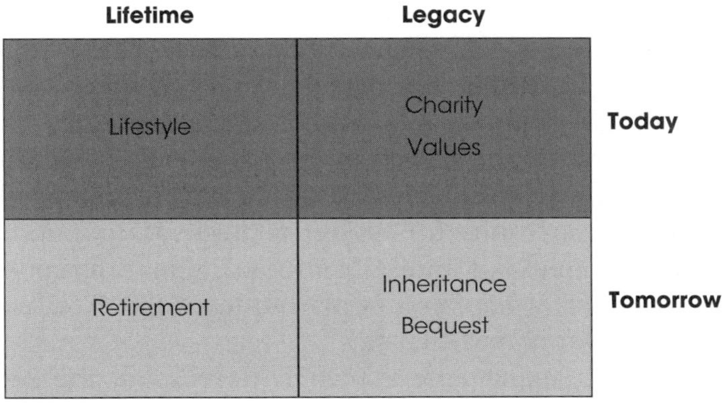

Figure 6.2 Lifetime and Legacy Requirements
Source: Ross Levin, "The Why of Wealth Management," in *The Investment Think Tank*, ed. Harold Evensky and Deena Katz (Princeton, NJ: Bloomberg Press, 2004), 357–364.

fund them. While this is an inexact science because of the difficulties in forecasting expected future cash flows (and potential investment returns), it does provide some guidance for the family on the order of magnitude of capital that will be required to fund the highest-priority and nearest-term objectives.

It also allows families to set aside funds (physically or notionally) to ensure that specific objectives are looked after, reducing the worry that they will have to compromise their spending during their lifetime.

Lifetime assets (allocated to funding the lifetime needs of the family) will typically have a lower risk profile because at least some of the planned spending will be relatively near term and probably quite high priority for the family. The assets a family has to set aside to fund all lifetime requirements will depend on how much the family plans to spend, for how many years they plan to keep spending, and what kind of risk they are willing to accept to achieve the targeted rate of return.

In fact, the more conservative assumptions a family uses in terms of both expected spending and investment returns, the higher the probability that they will meet their lifetime goals.

Legacy Goals

Once the lifetime objectives have been provided for, the balance of the capital is available to be used for other purposes, even to meet needs arising after the lifetime of the wealth owner. These legacy goals are designated as such because the money is no longer solely for the wealth owner but rather for someone else or something other than current or planned personal use. Legacy goals typically include funding future generations and charities.

Assets designated for legacy purposes typically have very long-term horizons and can be invested with a higher risk profile and the potential opportunity for higher returns. Many families also think of legacy goals as more "optional" than lifetime obligations. For instance, some families plan to leave the *balance* of their wealth to the children and charities.

As the wealth management plan is developed, the next step in goal setting is estimating how much the various goals will cost, to see if the goals are all in fact financially achievable given the

Matching Lifetime and Legacy Goals and Investments

Most investors have lifetime needs and legacy plans. But many investors are tilted in one direction or another. Lifetime investors are primarily focused on managing their assets to fund their own lifestyles and those of their immediate families and/or to fund charitable and gifting goals within their lifetime. Legacy investors have a much longer term orientation. They may have more than sufficient funds for their lifetime and are investing with the intention of funding multiple generations.

Lifetime and legacy investors are divergent in investor profile, and generally have different attitudes toward risk, liquidity, and term of investing, the three core tenets of an approach to investment. Here are the various elements:

Element of Investor Profile	Lifetime Investor	Legacy Investor
Term of investment	Short	Long
Liquidity preference	High	Low
Risk appetite—tolerance of short-term volatility	Low	High
Risk appetite—tolerance of long-term capital loss	Low	Low
Income need	High	Low
Growth focus	Low	High
Target return	High	Range

While both types of investors may have a more balanced portfolio, their principal purpose and selection criteria may differ substantially, resulting in quite different portfolios in the end.

family's asset base, investment capability, spending plans, and distribution policies.

Some of these factors are easier to estimate than others.

Less predictable factors will also need to be considered, such as investment returns, expected inflation, changes in asset values, and how long an income stream or expense requirement will last.

Combining Lifetime and Legacy Assets in a Single Portfolio

Although the two concepts of lifetime and legacy purpose may be fundamentally different, the resulting portfolios may have some overlap. Both may include a mix of traditional, real, and alternative assets, albeit in different proportions.

Families have a choice of either managing the portfolios separately, through separate accounts or different legal entities, or managing the combined set of assets on an integrated basis. For purposes of simplicity and overall risk clarity, the dual-purpose portfolio can be managed on a consolidated basis, simplifying interactions with brokers, tax authorities, and the like, so long as the requisite separation is preserved where needed to achieve the defined purposes.

If one were to consolidate the two portfolios, the illustration in Figure 6.3 shows how the two portfolios might look on their own, and on a combined basis.

Determine the Family Balance Sheet and Range of Potential Options

Once the family's goals are well understood and have been calibrated, the next step is taking an inventory of the family's overall financial affairs and the capacity to manage the wealth to fulfill current and future purposes.

Most corporations and institutions use a balance sheet to assess their current financial position and test the likelihood of the achievement of their future objectives. A family can benefit from using the same analytical and assessment tools, adapted for the family context, as part of a robust and effective wealth plan. Just as each company has a balance sheet and "balanced scorecard" with both tangible and intangible assets and liabilities, so does a family have its own balance sheet of financial and nonfinancial assets and liabilities. For the family, assets are relatively straightforward, liabilities less so.

The Family Balance Sheet

On the left side of the balance sheet, the family lists their assets (see Figure 6.4). A private wealth balance sheet includes tangible assets (investments, personal assets, and family business) as well as

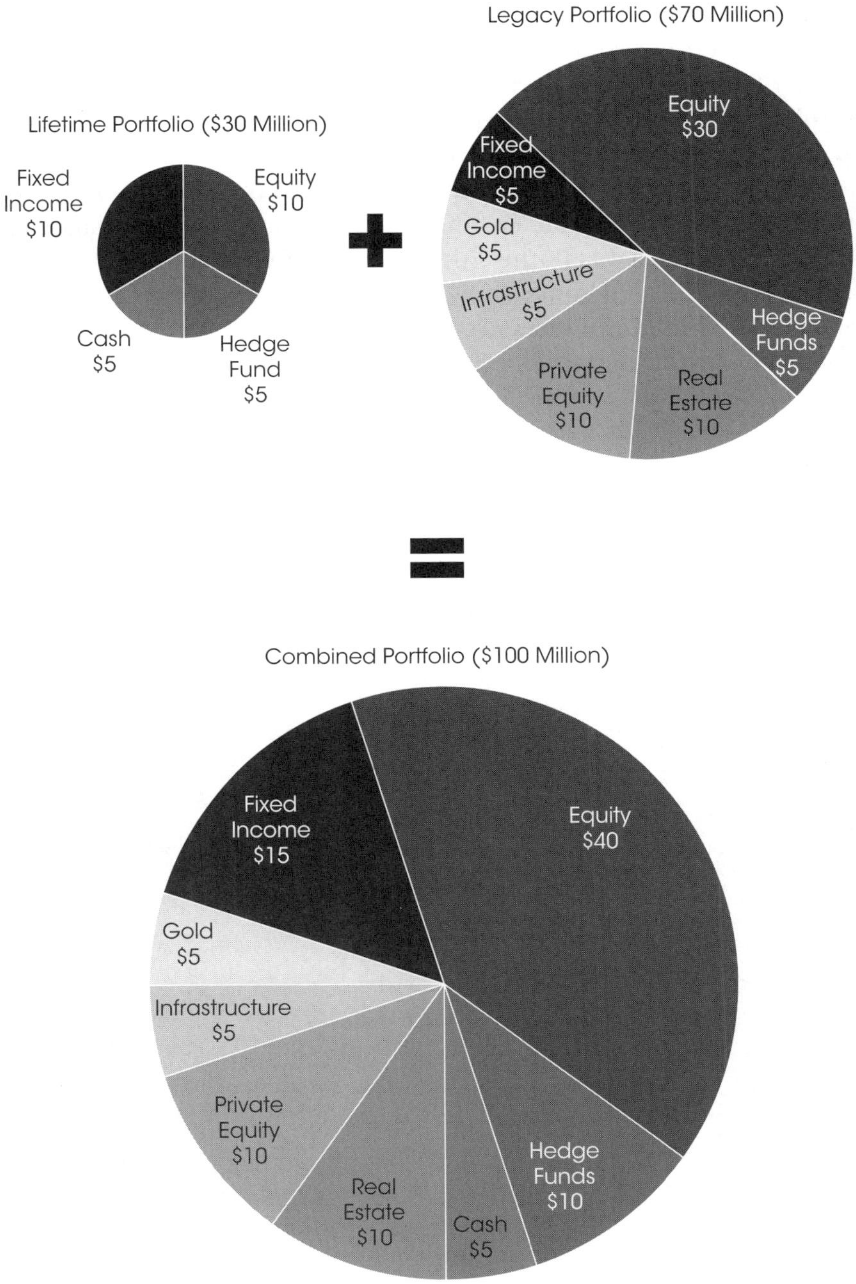

Figure 6.3 Sample Lifetime and Legacy Portfolios

intangible or "soft" assets (human capital, deferred compensation, and expected inheritances). Human capital represents the present value of the expected earnings stream and capital creation from employment or entrepreneurial activity, as well as the skills the family has to manage and grow their wealth.

On the right side of the balance sheet are the current liabilities and future commitments. For most wealthy families, their liabilities are not actually debt. Rather, they are funding plans for goals the family has set or, in some cases, financial commitments they have made. These commitments are normally self-imposed, but must be funded by income or assets nonetheless.

Implied liabilities typically include the following categories:

- *Lifetime spending.* This is simply the cumulative annual spending plans of the family over the lifetimes of the relevant

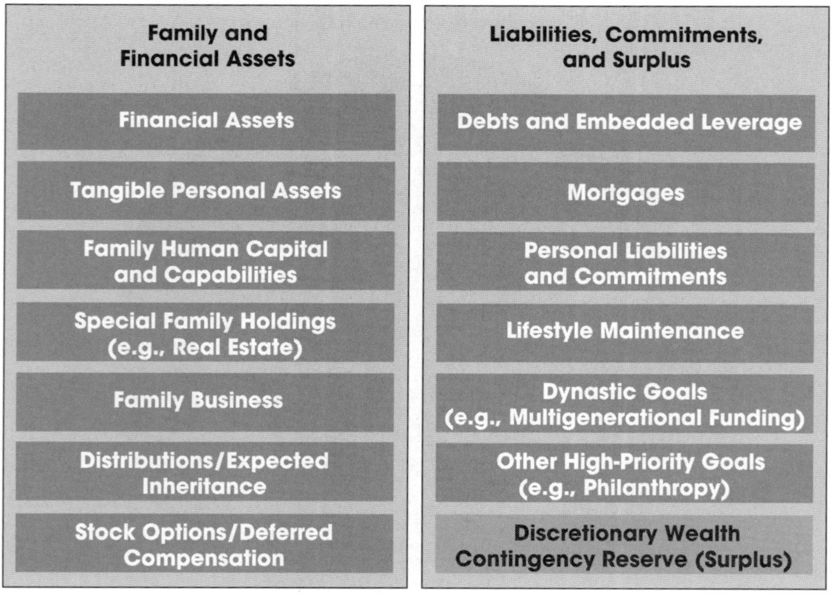

Figure 6.4 Family Balance Sheet

Source: Stephen Horan, "Asset-Liability Management for the Private Client: Lessons from Pension Plan Managers," CFA Institute, Canadian Private Family Office Invitational, Banff, Alberta, June 15, 2012, 5 (authors' additions).

family members. An appropriate amount of capital, assuming a reasonable discount rate on the future spending and consideration for inflation, should be notionally allocated to cover this planned spending.

- *Bequests and gifts to heirs.* The wealth owners may wish to identify a certain minimum or target amount of funds that will be allocated to their current and/or future heirs. The liability is the current amount of capital (based on reasonable growth assumptions) that will need to be allocated to fund this liability. Some families will choose to identify only specific liabilities to fund and then will bequeath "whatever is left" (i.e., the surplus of assets over implied liabilities).
- *Generational funding.* Some families want to fund many generations of family members for a certain lifestyle or level of wealth. The decision as to how many generations they want to fund and how much each beneficiary will receive will have a significant impact on the liability they need to fund. The capital that would be needed to fund 10 generations as opposed to one single generation would be enormously different in obligation and required capital commitment.
- *Charitable donations and bequests.* Similarly, plans to fund philanthropic projects or a foundation, either during the family members' lifetimes or upon their deaths, must be taken into account and funded. In some cases, these are explicit commitments (such as a charitable bequest in a will) and in other cases they are simply the implied liabilities of an intended donation.
- *Large investments or purchases.* Any anticipated large purchase or investment must also be planned for and ultimately funded by assets. This could include plans to fund a business, buy a recreational property, or fund a family bank.

It is important for each family to determine the relative importance and priority of its goals and commitments and notionally (or, in some cases, explicitly) assign existing investment capital to fund these amounts.

Lifetime spending is normally viewed as nonnegotiable and so will require the first assignment of capital. The relative importance of other goals will depend on each family's own preferences and

Different Goals May Need Different Types of Funding

It goes without saying that the goals families set are not static and can change (sometimes dramatically) over time. A wealthy family will often have substantial flexibility to defer, reprioritize, or even eliminate one of their optional goals if circumstances change. It is important to reassess the family goals on a regular basis and readjust the family balance sheet as needed.

The Calderon Example

Jose and Maria Calderon own a produce distribution business. They have two adult children and four grandchildren. The business has recently been valued at $200 million, net of all expected taxes payable on a sale of the company. They own three homes worth a combined $20 million. Their investments are worth $130 million—$30 million in cash and fixed income, $50 million in listed equities, $15 million in real estate, and $35 million in private equity.

Jose and Maria spend $1 million per year, which they want to continue to do throughout their lifetime. Based on a reasonable assumption of inflation and modest investment returns (from a low-risk asset class), a capital allocation of $25 million of capital would fund this particular liability. This lifetime spending plan is a very high-priority goal for the family, so it will receive the first "notional" capital allocation and the capital will be invested with low risk.

The couple wants to leave a legacy to future generations upon their death and would also like to leave significant funds to charities, if possible. Again, based on reasonable investment return and inflation assumptions, the present value of these goals are $200 million and $50 million, respectively.

On the basis of this information, the family balance sheet looks like Figure 6.5.

As you can see in this example, the family should be able to fund all of these liabilities. However, these calculations rely on assumptions of returns and inflation, and such forecasts can, of course, be unreliable, making the achievement of the goals uncertain. (Conservative assumptions for investment returns and the ability to contain spending will help prevent disappointment.)

Also, in the example, there is a surplus of assets over liabilities that can act as a buffer against poor returns or higher spending or inflation than forecasted. In some cases, however, the implied liabilities can be larger than the family's assets, so the goals (or liabilities) must be prioritized. If, for instance, the family was keen to fund many more generations and the present value cost was calculated as $300 million (vs. $200 million), there would be a deficit of $25 million in the discretionary funds account.

The family might reset priorities on their goals as follows, to ensure that the top-priority goals are funded:

Living expenses	Top priority
Bequests	High priority
Philanthropic	Optional

A balance sheet is a helpful construct here to evaluate families' current and future financial health. In particular, the asset-liability matching framework puts the focus clearly on the family's goals and helps to ensure that there will be funding available to meet the objectives when the time comes.

Assets ($mln)		**Goals and Commitments/ Surplus ($mln)**	
Homes	$20	Living expenses	$25
Cash/FI	$30	Bequests	$200
Equities	$50	Philanthropic	$50
Real eatate	$15	Total goals and commitments	$275
Private equity	$35		
Business	$200	Surplus	$75
Total assets	**$350**	**Total goals and commitments surplus**	**$350**

Figure 6.5 Calderon Family Balance Sheet

priorities. The more goals a family puts in the "high-priority" category, the more "liabilities" they will have and the less discretionary wealth they will have for other purposes. This may reduce the amount of risk the family will be able to withstand in their overall portfolio.

This balance sheet approach is a helpful method by which to determine investor goals and then build an asset mix that is most likely to meet these goals, depending on their relative priority.

Key Questions for Family Investors

Following are some of the questions family members will want to ask themselves as they create their family balance sheet:

- What are the family goals? Can they be afforded given current and expected assets and liabilities? What cash flow funding will they require?
- How much certainty does the family want that those goals will be met? How far into the future will they need to be met?
- What are the family's assets? What cash flow can they generate? How likely are the assets to be able to fund plans and commitments when needed?
- Will there be sufficient cash flow to fund all of the objectives and aspirations?
- Is there a gap between liabilities and assets? How will the gap be addressed? Or will goals have to be prioritized or deferred?
- Does the family have surplus assets? What is the purpose of those surplus assets?
- How is the family balance sheet likely to change over time and over generations?

The Implications of Differing Investment Philosophies: "Egg Farmers" versus "Chicken Farmers"

James Garland

An amusing metaphor for different investment goals and their practical implications can be seen in the comparison of "chicken-farmer investors" and the other "egg-farmer investors."

On the farm, chicken farmers own chickens to sell them. They care very much about the market value of chickens. However, egg farmers own chickens for the eggs those chickens will lay. Egg farmers care very much about the quantity of eggs.

Now move from farm to finance. Chicken-farmer investors buy securities with the intention of selling them, and they care very much about the value of their "chickens" (i.e., their securities). However, egg-farmer investors own securities in order to enjoy the dividends and interest (i.e., the "eggs") that those securities will produce. Simply put, chicken-farmer investors spend income and principal, while egg-farmer investors spend only income.

Most investors are chicken-farmer investors—they're investing typically for retirement and may spend everything by the time they die. Only a few fortunate ones have sufficient capital to become egg-farmer investors (i.e., to live off just their income). While each type of investing requires a very different mind-set, the media and Wall Street both ignore egg-farmer investors, perhaps because their numbers are so small. The media and Wall Street give investors a one-size-fits-all package of advice and products designed just for chicken-farmer investors. As a result, many egg-farmer investors are confused and think they are chicken farmers.

These two groups of investors differ in many important ways.

- *Market values.* While chicken-farmer investors care very much about market values, egg-farmer investors care very little. The first group wants market values to rise. The second group is happy when market values fall. When prices fall, the capital gains tax cost of making changes, as a fraction of the capital involved, falls as well. Furthermore, many investment managers charge fees based on market values. When market values fall, managers receive less, and the investors keep more.
- *Risk.* For obvious reasons, "risk" for chicken-farmer investors means market declines—and market values are both volatile and unpredictable. On an annual basis, the Standard & Poor's (S&P) 500 market value has declined in 17 of the past 60 years, and in 11 of those years the declines were more than 10 percent. However, for egg-farmer investors, "risk" means a decline in income. On an annual basis, S&P 500 dividends have declined in only 6 of the past 60 years, and in only one year was the decline greater than 5 percent.
- *Capital gains taxes.* Chicken-farmer investors have no option—they'll face capital gains taxes (or even ordinary income taxes, for capital held in retirement accounts) as they sell securities. However, for egg-farmer investors, paying capital gains taxes is to some extent optional. Egg-farmer investors can be buy-and-hold investors if they so choose. Chicken-farmer investors consider capital gains taxes an inevitable cost of doing business. Egg-farmer investors consider capital gains taxes an avoidable (or at least optional) expense. Each time an egg farmer pays capital

(*continued*)

gains taxes, he or she surrenders income-generating capital. He or she loses some egg-laying hens.

- *Asset allocation.* For chicken-farmer investors, for whom price volatility equals risk, cash is the safest asset, followed by bonds and finally by stocks. For egg-farmer investors, whose risk is related to uncertain income streams, just the opposite is true. The S&P 500's dividend stream historically has been far more stable and predictable than its market value. Stocks are low-risk investments for egg-farmer investors. Not so for chicken-farmer investors.

The mind-sets of chicken-farmer and egg-farmer investors are very different. Consider the following widely held beliefs:

Chicken Farmer's Adage	Egg Farmer's Response
Watch stock prices.	Don't bother.
Price volatility equals risk.	Not for us.
Taxes are inevitable.	Taxes are controllable and sometimes even avoidable.
Up markets are good markets.	Not for us.
Cash is a low-risk investment.	Not for us.
Stocks are high-risk investments.	Not for us.

Egg-farmer investors can ignore what they read in the press and on Wall Street. It's mostly noise anyway—and what's more, for egg-farmer investors, it's irrelevant noise.

James Garland recently retired as president of the Jeffrey Company, a private family investment firm in Columbus, Ohio, and now serves as chairman emeritus. Earlier, he worked for a money management firm in Portland, Maine, and before that at NASA's Goddard Space Flight Center in Greenbelt, Maryland.

CHAPTER 7

Structuring Assets and Aligning Investments to Serve Multiple Purposes

Family wealth almost always has multiple purposes, and substantial wealth carries with it the potential to serve multiple generations as well. As such, the structuring and oversight of family wealth should clearly reflect these different purposes and support the realization of a family's long-term financial objectives.

Asset structuring can be employed to serve multiple purposes: institutionalizing family values, limiting risk and distribution to allow wealth to endure across multiple generations, and creating an opportunity to fund nonfamily philanthropic ventures.

Multiple Nonfinancial Purposes to Consider as Well

Financial capital can be invested for lifetime use or legacy purposes, for income or capital preservation, for family or philanthropy, or for one individual or group within the family or another.

The financial factors in generational planning are key considerations, but there are many other factors to consider as well. Equally important are the personal issues of avoiding loss through litigation, marital disputes, profligate or incapable heirs, family discord, economic upheaval, and even expropriation due to political or other unforeseen events. Careful planning can help ensure that family wealth is successfully protected and preserved across many generations and through many economic challenges.

While not all risks and disasters can be anticipated and managed in advance, a sound approach to the structuring and administration of family assets can provide protection from many of the established patterns and risks that have brought down wealthy families over time. Effective structuring can thus enhance both an individual life and the collective future of the family.

Dividing the Pool

Whatever the purpose and division, many forward-thinking families are now allocating their assets into separate groupings, managed accounts, or separate legal entities. These distinct pools of family wealth are all managed to achieve a specific set of objectives and are accounted for separately. This can lead to informal allocations within existing pools of financial assets, or the establishment and maintenance of a coordinated set of specific accounts, corporate entities, trusts, partnerships, limited liability companies (LLCs), and other entities.

The various "buckets" of assets within the pool of family wealth need to be identified and can be addressed, based on the following steps:

- *Divide wealth into meaningful separate pools, each with a defined purpose and specific beneficiary.* These may include business versus financial assets, income versus. wealth preservation, personal versus family assets, income and distribution needs, lifetime versus legacy, family versus philanthropy, siblings or children, living beneficiaries versus future generations, branch versus generational allocation, and any other aspect relevant to the overall approach.
- *Allocate the family capital into the buckets.* Families then need to determine how much goes where and how high a priority each objective represents. Unfortunately, there is not much science to the answer. It depends very much on each family's goals and an estimate of the future cash flow (and current net present value of capital) required to fund the defined goals.

- *Outline the appropriate investment strategy for each goal/category.* Investors need to determine what the best investment strategy is to their overall goals for each pool, based on the current and anticipated capital market environment.
- *Ensure the various individual portfolios are optimized at the family level.* Investors need to ensure that the overall portfolio makes sense from a risk, return, and diversification standpoint once the various buckets are totaled up.
- *Decide on appropriate structures to serve family, tax, reporting, and control issues.* In the context of overall portfolio and family objectives, minimizing current and future taxes is one of the major traditional purposes of family asset structuring, although not the only one.

The list of structuring objectives is long, and the practical opportunities available for structuring to achieve those objectives—trust, foundation, corporate, will, custodial account—varies enormously by country and the nature of its fiscal, legal, and judicial systems.

Institutionalizing Values and Opportunities across Generations

Some families employ these structures to achieve specific objectives linked to family values or cultural standards across generations.

By linking access to family wealth to a defined set of behaviors or accomplishments (e.g., finishing college, demonstrating a "work ethic" lifestyle, or maintaining certain family traditions or assets), family leaders can channel some or even all of their wealth to preserving valuable assets, and do their best to help to protect future generations from the "dark side of wealth" that can be so destructive.

Also, in a world of ever more "unknowns," characterized by events and risks that cannot be predicted, placing some money into a safe harbor to be applied only for the health, education, and welfare of individual descendants can ensure that, no matter what happens to the rest of the family wealth, future generations will always be able to be safe, well-housed, and receive a good education—the first steps on the ladder back upward in every society—no matter how far the family's other fortunes have fallen.

The "HEW Trust": A Practical Model of Legacy Planning and Values in Action

A few families, currently wealthy but also gazing thoughtfully into an uncertain future, have taken a very far-sighted approach that both preserves opportunities for future generations and enshrines their values in a formal asset structure to hold a defined set of long-term assets.

The approach they have taken is to carve out a certain portion of current family assets, say 10 percent, and put the resources into a perpetuity trust or similar vehicle in order to provide funding for the health, education, and welfare needs—hence the "HEW" title—of future generations whose parents or other family members may have lost the money that ordinarily would have come to them in a direct bloodline transfer or inheritance.

The bulk of the family wealth may stay in branch or generational trusts, or in a single pooled portfolio, but the availability of increasingly expensive health care, private education, and other needs specific to each family member are guaranteed from this carved-out sum of money, structured, and managed separately from the main body of the wealth. The investment strategy for such a trust or managed account is often more conservative than that of a main portfolio, perhaps more in line with the investment parameters of a philanthropic foundation than a more adventurous family trust corpus.

Thus, patriarchs, matriarchs, and their families know that no matter how profligate or unfortunate any one branch or generation may be, their descendants will be safe from the financial costs of an economic or personal health-related disaster, can always count on a high-quality education, and may access funds to address special needs, drug counseling, and any other unpredictable problem life throws in the path of members of future generations.

See Figure 7.1 for a sample asset structure with an HEW trust.

Similarly, providing funds for the continuing ownership and upkeep of a family home, or funds to cover travel to and from an annual family meeting, can ensure that a family's sense of place, harmony, and unity can be carried forward over time as well.

A brief summary of common vehicles and approaches follows.

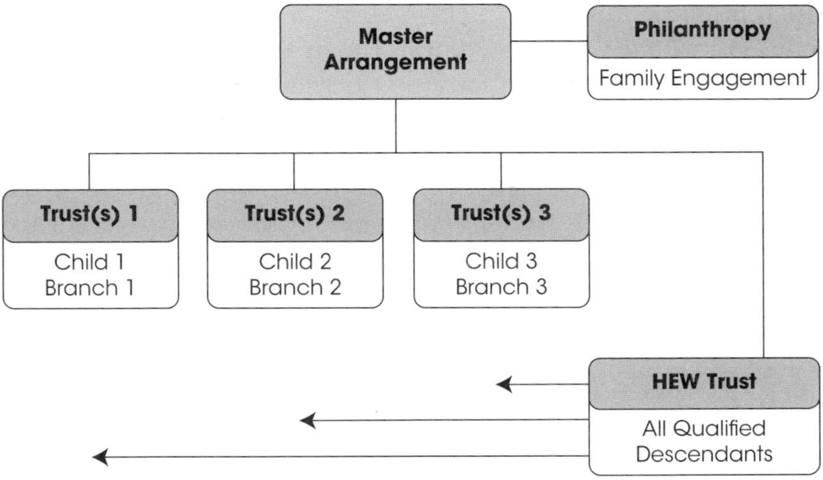

Figure 7.1 Health, Education, and Welfare (HEW) Trust

Trusts

Essentially, trusts can be thought of as three-way contracts that regulate the relationships among the settlor, the trustee, and the beneficiary.

One of the mainstays of Anglo-Saxon tax and estate planning, the trust is a well-established approach to long-term wealth structuring, where each trust has a set life and operates to a set of general principles and specific documents, usually including a deed of settlement (establishing the trust) and a letter of wishes (guiding its operation).

Trusts are well-suited to manage tax and transfer wealth effectively, build in future distribution of funds in line with the specific wishes of an individual, delay transfer of funds if certain conditions are not met, and achieve a whole host of other purposes. A typical trust with multiple objectives could, for example, transfer available funds (after taxes, portfolio costs, and inflation) to an intended beneficiary only upon that person's reaching the age of 25 or 35 and completing a degree from an accredited university.

Matching Form to Purpose

Trusts can take many forms. They can be onshore, offshore, special purpose, foreign grantor, revocable (allowing the settlor to cancel the trust at his or her discretion), or irrevocable. Many favorable tax treatments require a trust to be irrevocable to qualify for tax exemptions.

There are other variations on the theme: contingent trusts, incentive trusts, charitable trusts, blind trusts (about which the beneficiaries have no detailed knowledge of investments or control over fund management), a rabbi trust (which has been used to defer U.S. taxation under certain circumstances), a freezer trust (which specifies a preset maximum value of assets, beyond which another vehicle is required to capture any excess value), and other creative approaches.

One of the major purposes of a trust structure is to provide vehicles to skip ownership of assets in every other generation in order to avoid inheritance tax and other fiscal liabilities. For example, by leaving his assets to a grandchild, a grandfather in some jurisdictions can still avoid one generation of death duties or trust restructuring costs.

Treatment of generation skipping varies enormously from one country to another. In the United States, for example, transfers into a trust are subject to a gift tax, and any subsequent generation skipping may be subject to a "generation-skipping tax"—a very costly double whammy.

An example of a traditional trust structure, with a master trust and subsidiary individual trusts, is illustrated in Figure 7.2.

Anstalts and *stiftungs,* Germanic speaking countries' equivalent of the Anglo-Saxon trust, function in much the same way as a trust, but are regulated by different bodies and according to rules specific to the low-tax jurisdictions adopting these structures.

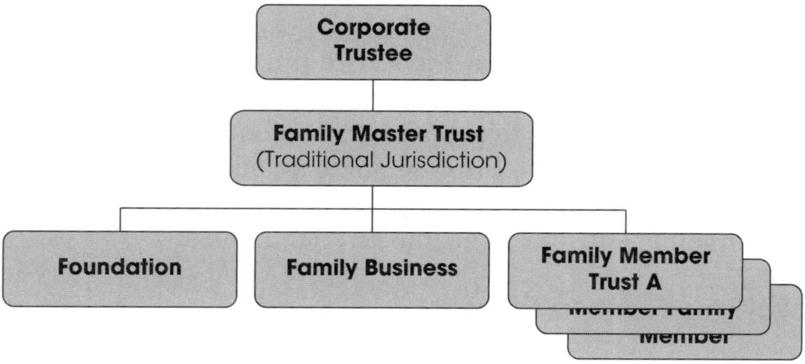

Figure 7.2 Traditional Trust Structure

Corporations and Companies

Corporations in various jurisdictions can also play an important role in tax and legal plans for families of substantial worth. Many families will have a corporation in one jurisdiction underneath a trust from another, with a private trust company incorporated in yet another jurisdiction.

Corporations have the advantage of protecting owners against liability, are not constrained by trust deeds and documents, and are not subject to the imprecise rules of trustee stewardship. They do have disadvantages, however, including directors having fiduciary duties, and a requirement for audits and disclosures on an annual basis.

Partnerships and Dedicated Fund Structures

Partnerships, either general or limited, can also be employed to achieve specific structuring purposes related to tax, liability, and disclosure. Many private equity investments, for example, are structured as partnerships, with the managers being the general partners (GPs) who operate the fund, and financial investors being the limited partners (LPs) who receive their economic benefits without the full set of broader rights and responsibilities of the partnership GPs.

LLCs and LLPs

Limited liability companies (LLCs), often used in the United States for tax planning and risk management, are legal corporate entities with limited liability that provide for much of the benefit of a corporate entity without the unlimited liability on the part of the directors. Limited liability partnerships (LLPs) have the same liability protection, along with the additional advantages and disadvantages of a partnership vehicle.

Other Vehicles

The list of asset structuring options does not end with these traditional vehicles. Captive insurance companies, fully owned fund companies, segregated portfolio companies, protected cell companies, family investment holding companies, and other such exotic vehicles may also play a role in a family's structuring plans.

As many trust and incorporation jurisdictions are now actively competing for business, offering different supervisory regimes and registration requirements, it can be worth shopping around to find the best terms and the most suitable jurisdictions.

It is also advisable to employ an expert lawyer, accountant, or tax practitioner, as the opportunities and risks of different jurisdictions can change rapidly. The full benefits of such new and attractive opportunities as Singapore and New Zealand trusts, which can come along with embedded private trust companies, may not be fully visible to any but the most up-to-date professionals. Similarly, in the United States, Nevada and New Hampshire may provide attractive options as their rules evolve and as they invest to create particularly welcoming jurisdictional characteristics for both trust settlors and beneficiaries.

Multijurisdictional Approaches

Although all trusts, corporations, and partnerships are registered and "resident" in a single jurisdiction, most asset structuring approaches for very wealthy families, especially those outside the United States, are multijurisdictional in nature. This provides the benefit of general asset structuring by itself and the risk management benefit of diversification as well.

For families seeking to avoid undue scrutiny and preserve family privacy, a multijurisdictional approach has many advantages. In addition to sheltering income and assets from taxes, litigation, and other risks, a multilayered approach can make it very difficult for corporate rivals, journalists, or other unauthorized parties to discover the extent and nature of a family's wealth and businesses.

A number of countries offer significant immigration tax incentives to entice wealthy individuals to come to that jurisdiction. For instance, Canada targets educated, high-net-worth immigrants. It has an immigration trust structure, which can result in an immigrant's paying no Canadian income tax for five years after becoming a Canadian resident, and provides a "step up" on the cost base of an asset upon immigration, such that capital gains made prior to arrival will never be taxed in Canada. Canada also offers a dynasty trust (or "granny trust"), wherein if a non-Canadian relative contributes all of the assets to a trust and the trust remains nonresident, the trust can distribute capital tax free to Canadian beneficiaries, effectively forever.

In setting up an international asset structure, or even a complex domestic approach, members of wealthy families would be well-advised to think through the benefits of a diversified approach

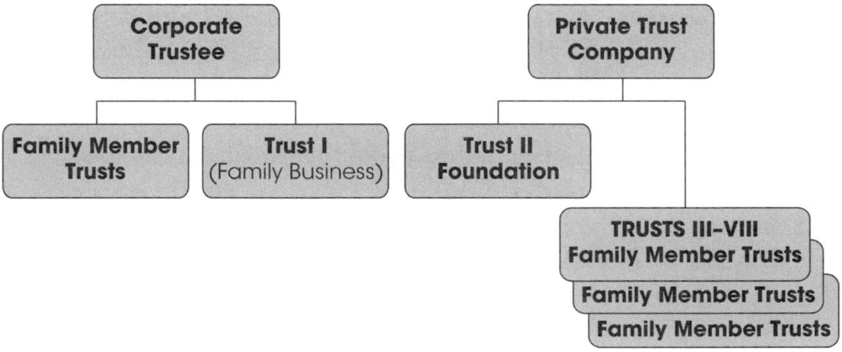

Figure 7.3 Diversified Structure

to asset structuring and trustee or director roles. Although setting up more than one system of interlocking companies and structures is more expensive and cumbersome than working under a single structure and trustee, the longer-term benefits of multiple trust and jurisdictions may well be worth the incremental setup and operating costs.

A more diversified approach to a wealthy family's affairs could look as shown in Figure 7.3.

It should also be pointed out that the increasingly prevalent GAAR (general anti-avoidance rules) legislation (which is coming into effect in the United Kingdom, and already present in Australia, Canada, and other jurisdictions) may eventually reduce the value of many traditional structuring approaches. Essentially driven by a notion that any asset structuring approach that is done for "tax purposes" may be considered abusive and no longer effective, GAAR principles may reduce the value of many formerly acceptable approaches to asset protection and wealth planning.

Tax Obligations and Options

One of the primary purposes of a structured approach to family asset and wealth management is to minimize taxes wherever possible. This objective, adopted in virtually all countries around the world by wealthy families, may involve both onshore and offshore asset structuring.

Although periodically criticized by governments, politicians, and economists, the world of effective asset structuring is entirely legal, correct, and even blessed by one of the greatest legal minds in the history of American jurisprudence.

Judge Learned Hand specifically encouraged individuals and families to undertake advantageous tax planning in his famous words:

> Anyone may arrange his affairs so that his taxes shall be as low as possible; he is not bound to choose that pattern which best pays the treasury. There is not even a patriotic duty to increase one's taxes . . ., for **nobody owes any public duty to pay more than the law demands.**[1] [bold added]

Taking advantage of all opportunities to manage wealth on an after-tax basis across multiple generations is an essential part of long-term wealth preservation for every family in virtually every country.

Types of Taxes

On the tax front, income, gift, and capital gains tax; inheritance tax or death duties; property taxes; and wealth tax can play different roles in tax management depending on the nationality, residence, domicile, and asset profile of the family. Figure 7.4 shows the history of top inheritance tax rates in three major countries over time.

Figure 7.4 U.S., UK, and German Inheritance Tax Rates, 1900–2010
Source: Thomas Piketty, "Inequality in America," Columbia University, Lecture, September 27, 2012, 29.

---

[1]Marvin A. Chirelstein, "Learned Hand's Contribution to the Law of Tax Avoidance," *Yale Law Journal* 77, no. 3 (January 1968): 440–74.

Citizenship as a Risk Management Decision and Wealth Management Tool

Wealthy global families are becoming increasingly aware of their need for a well-thought-out citizenship and residency strategy to protect their wealth and to safeguard their freedom of movement. In the uncertain world facing us today, prudent families understand the importance of keeping their options open and having multiple passport choices.

Those who have started to examine this complex subject will have found that the problem is not the lack of options. Rather, it is identifying the right ones and, probably more important, avoiding the wrong ones. For instance, how do you find a place that is safe, stable, and free? That is livable, accessible, and cosmopolitan? That offers "first-world" health care, education, culture, and services? That is business friendly, family friendly, and privacy friendly? That offers tax advantages and the opportunity to preserve family wealth? And, just as important, is likely to retain all these features in the future—both in the near term and over the many ensuing generations?

As the world's economies continue to globalize and integrate, more and more wealthy families are recognizing that citizenship is more than just a nationality inherited at birth. In fact, citizenship and residency are powerful, strategic assets that can be acquired or given up in order to create a better life for themselves and their families. Citizenship is really about family, safety, and choices.

Threat 1: Restrictions on Mobility

All over the world, affluent businesspeople who thought they had the freedom to travel have found themselves facing unexpected restrictions. If you look at the first page of your own passport, you'll see that it's not yours—it belongs to the government.

The government and its courts (even in civil or matrimonial litigation) reserve the right to take it away at any time. How would your life be affected right now if they did? Today, wealthy families treasure mobility. Prudent high-net-worth individuals and families are increasingly seeing the value of a second passport and a second home and a strategy to ensure they have the right combination of citizenships and residencies to meet their needs and give themselves the ability to "make the world their oyster."

(*continued*)

Threat 2: Increasing Taxation

After a number of years of tax reductions in many countries, including the United States and the United Kingdom, the drums of significant tax increases are beating again, particularly in the wake of significant government spending to bolster their financial institutions and economies in the latest credit crisis. The wealthy are likely to be the targets of the tax increases as populist sentiment continues to take hold in economies around the world.

Threat 3: Family Law and Divorce Settlements

Prenuptial agreements can be attacked in many jurisdictions. The best way to preserve a family's wealth is to make sure they have residency or domicile in a country that takes a hands-off approach to divorce and upholds legitimate prenuptial and trust arrangements, so they can make appropriate and sustainable decisions regarding marriage and divorce.

Of course, it takes time and specialized expertise to identify which countries provide the best combination of security and opportunity for each client. And once families do identify the most likely jurisdictions, it's not always easy or cheap to get the citizenship or residence they are seeking; qualifying for those citizenships can take years. Selecting the right portfolio of passports for each family is a job for experts who understand the tax, financial, and mobility needs of business families. To maximize their security and freedom, they also need advisors who know the pros and cons of multiple citizenship and residency opportunities around the world.

In fact, getting this right may be the most important factor in determining whether wealthy families maintain and grow their wealth over their lifetime and future generations. It is worth remembering that the decisions made by our own ancestors to move from their country of origin had a profound effect on the course of not only their own lives, but those of the generations that followed them.

Source: Tom McCullough, Scott Hayman, Jonathan Garbutt, and David Lesperance, "Canadian Citizenship: The Wealthy Global Family's Safe and Tax-Efficient Alternative," Northwood Family Office white paper, October 2009.

Marital Issues

Marriage and the nuclear family, the basic building blocks of every society and civilization, can also provide a great source of discord and threat to family wealth and well-being if they do not work out as planned.

With national divorce rates surpassing 40 percent in some European countries and in the United States, family leaders would be well-advised to think through in advance the various options available to protect family wealth from any future marital complications.

Even if there is no divorce or difficulty in a marriage, the addition of in-laws can be, for some families, a great source of aggravation and difficulty.

Many family structures are put in place with a potential divorce in mind at a later date. Hopefully never needed, anticipating ever more likely events can be a sound investment in the long-term protection and preservation of family wealth.

Aligning Investment with the Purpose of Structure

As each structure is set up, there is an opportunity to align the investment content with its broad purpose.

Trusts in need of income can best benefit from income-generating assets such as corporate bonds, dividend stocks, property, infrastructure investments, energy projects, and other similar financial and real assets.

However, entities set up for multigenerational wealth preservation and growth could focus more on long-term investing, with a portfolio of different stocks or manager styles (or market exchange-traded funds), longer-term (and hence higher-yielding) bonds, and adding a larger portion of alternative assets and property investments, creating a portfolio that takes on more risk and is characterized by less liquidity.

Examples of different approaches to investment to achieve different purposes can be found throughout this book, and family investors would be well counseled to review the purpose of a trust or bequest and ensure that the structure, process of administration, risk management, and portfolio of assets are all fully up to date and aligned with the fundamental purpose of the family involved.

CHAPTER 8

Integrating the Family Business into Wealth Management Strategy

Many family leaders and family office chief investment officers (CIOs) make the mistake of leaving the family business out of their thinking about family wealth management.

This may be due to a separation of responsibilities within the family, or because the focus of the family office is solely on the investment of liquid wealth, or the family keeps the main business aside as a single entity subject to a different ownership structure, governance participation, and management approach.

In most cases this is a mistake, despite the good intentions of the leaders and advisors involved. To optimize family wealth over time, it is crucial that the family business be included in financial and wealth planning strategies. Of course, it is also vital that the family business is well run, that the leadership is smoothly transitioned from one leader to another, that its value is enhanced, and, if appropriate, that its value is realized through a sale, partial sale, or listing of the company.

At the same time, a family business can play an integrated role in the family wealth portfolio, bringing with it such issues as capital and income contributions, cash and debt drawdowns, risk, cash flow, leverage, currency, sale timing, family role definition, and other considerations common to all assets in the portfolio.

For many families, the vast bulk of their wealth may be tied up in a family business. The sheer magnitude of the value at hand makes it impossible to leave out any financial calculation or consideration.

Definition of a Family Firm

Although there is no fixed definition of a family business, academic literature would define a family business as "a venture in which the majority of the ownership lies within a family (and its branches) and where two or more family members are directly involved in the management." A stricter definition would be that the business "has experienced a transfer at least once to the succeeding generation of family owner-managers."

This is different from a private or entrepreneurial business, in which one person controls an enterprise, but it does not involve the "family" in the wider sense.

Evolving Role Across Generations

Although some families keep their core businesses operating successfully across multiple generations (the Antinori wine family in Italy is celebrating 26 generations of family ownership of the business, for example), many family businesses are wound down or sold by the third generation. This reduction in importance of the operating business as an economic asset can be matched by a resulting increase in liquid fund generation and portfolio investment opportunities.

As such, the family business, which may be the single source of a nonrepeatable liquidity event, needs to be integrated into family wealth plans as both a source and use of cash at different times in the life of the enterprise.

Another part of the evolution is the challenging shift from a "business family" in the first generation to an "investing family" by the second, third, or fourth generation, which brings with it a whole host of economic, cultural, and individual issues to address.

Three Pathways to Evolutionary Survival

Dr. Dennis Jaffe and Jane Flanagan

Successful multigenerational family enterprises invest a lot of time and energy monitoring their investment performance. What would happen if a similar investment were made to track the family's efforts related to governance, family connection, and next-generation personal development?

Creating a successful family business that generates substantial family wealth across generations is a rare and special event. The Family Firm Institute reports that less than one-third of family businesses are able to survive as they cross generations. Of those, less than 10 percent survive into the third generation. How do these remarkable exceptions to the rule do it? What are the secrets of their success?

A study of 192 of the world's largest and most successful multi-generational families shows that these families recognize the need for balance when it comes to:

- The desire for family harmony and effective communication.
- The needs of the business.
- Personal fulfillment for all family members.

In the fall of 2011, we surveyed members of the Family Business Network and Family Office Exchange to learn about their current use of 15 key practices that have been linked to cross-generational sustainability. We also asked about their views of the importance of adopting these practices in the future. The practices of family relationship and governance that we identified are not business and financial practices. Rather, they span the interconnected worlds of family, business/finance, and personal development and are organized into three distinct pathways.

Pathway I: Nurture the Family

The first-generation business founder accumulates substantial wealth that is passed on within the family. While the second-generation heirs grow up together, each second-generation sibling begins his or her own family. The third-generation cousins live separately and may not share the family heritage as deeply or clearly.

Yet, to remain a family enterprise, the members of several families in several generations must believe that there is a good reason to be business partners. They must have a common vision as an extended family that makes them want to work together. In addition, as partners and shared owners, they need to develop trust in each other, spend time together, develop personal relationships across families, and share common values. The practices in this pathway help the family actively build connection and shared purpose over generations, fighting the natural tendency for family members to move into separate worlds and become more disconnected.

(*continued*)

Practices in Pathway I: Nurture the Family

- Clear, compelling family purpose and direction.
- Regular extended family gatherings and interaction.
- Climate of family openness, trust, and communication.
- Sharing and respect for family history and legacy.
- Shared family philanthropic and community service.

Pathway II: Steward the Family Enterprises

The extended family shares not only a family legacy but also a family business and/or several family financial enterprises they own together. The business may be large and public and have a high profile in the community. As owners, family members are identified with the business and have personal expectations of what the business will provide and their role and relationship to it.

As more and more family members are, or expect to become, owners, there must be clear rules for how to make decisions and work together to operate their financial and business entities. The family needs a plan for how they will grow and diversify, and how the rewards and resources of their family enterprises will be distributed. The roles, responsibilities, and authority of each person need to be clear so that each family member feels that he or she is treated fairly.

The family must organize itself for the business of the family and develop strategies to manage conflict. The practices in this pathway help the family make decisions that preserve both family harmony and financial returns.

Practices in Pathway II: Steward the Family Enterprises

- Strategic plan for family wealth and/or enterprise development.
- Active, diverse, empowered board guiding each enterprise.
- Transparency about financial information and business decisions.
- Explicit and shared shareholder agreements about family assets.
- Exit and distribution policies for individual shareholder liquidity.

Pathway III: Cultivate Human Capital in the Next Generation

A unique element of a multigenerational family enterprise is that a new generation of young people grows up in the family, feeling a connection to and an expectation to share in its legacy. The young people are the future. They need to be prepared for their role within the family and the business and to learn how to work with each other. The successful multigenerational family enterprise must actively develop the next generation. The practices in Pathway III encourage the personal development and preparation of each and every next-generation family member through governance and family activities.

Practices in Pathway III: Cultivate Human Capital in the Next Generation

- Employment policies for family members working in the family enterprises.
- Agreement on values about family money and wealth.
- Support for development of next-generation leadership.
- Encouragement for all family members to seek personal fulfillment and life purpose, regardless of personal or financial involvement in family enterprises.
- Age-appropriate education to teach financial skills to young family members.

Study Findings

We were delighted to learn that families in the study use nearly all of the practices to a significant degree, and all families expect their use of these practices to rise in the future.

The most prevalent current practices are related to nurturing the family (Pathway I). The least prevalent are practices related to cultivating human capital for the next generation (Pathway III). However, there is widespread recognition of the importance of preparing the next generation and a clear intention to increase the use of these practices in the future.

We were surprised to learn that reliance on these practices is consistent and significant to a similar degree in every region of the world. Similarly, there were only minor differences between the use of these practices by business-owning families versus non–business owners.

This study opens a window on the behavior of some of the oldest and largest family enterprises in the world. We asked them some simple questions about practices for sustaining family connection, governance of their family enterprises, and developing the next generation

(*continued*)

of family leaders. We found, not surprisingly, that these successful families use these practices regularly and plan to use more of them in the future.

Dr. Dennis Jaffe is a professor of organizational systems and psychology at Saybrook University in San Francisco, and an advisor to families about family business, governance, wealth, and philanthropy. He is author of *Stewardship in your Family Enterprise: Developing Responsible Family Leadership across Generations* (Pioneer Imprints, 2009). Jane Flanagan is a senior consultant at the Family Office Exchange (FOX) where she works as a developer, writer, and editor on industry whitepapers and research studies for FOX members.

Differing Risk Profiles

Within the segment of family business are many variations on the theme: from 100 percent single family-owned private businesses to large, publicly listed businesses with a legacy minority family position. Different roles in ownership, governance, and management can be seen in the different models.

A long-established national family business with substantial barriers to entry can be a solid low-risk source of cash flow and reliable repository, as can a diversified property portfolio made up of core holdings.

At the other end of the risk spectrum, an entrepreneur-led highly leveraged first-generation business may be a highly volatile global trading platform or new technology business characterized by high growth, loss-making operations, and a great deal of expert competition.

In all cases, the risk aspect of a family business should be taken into account. Some businesses will act as a stable income generator (a bit like a bond) and others will seem more like a potential growth capital holding (like a venture capital or emerging market investment).

Businesses, like other investments, may require investment, leveraging, bridging finance, restructuring, and other options for development that can have an impact on family fund's availability.

Businesses can also carry concentration risks, key man and succession risk, leverage risk, and counterparty risk.

Emotional Ownership

One of the major nonfinancial aspects of owning and operating a family business is an engagement by the family members, even younger ones, in the emotional ownership of the business. The family "brand" may also be far more affected by association with a business than with a portfolio of deliberately diversified and relatively anonymous family assets. Whether or not the family name is on the front door, there is a unique pride of association and personal identification with an operating business that is not usually present in a portfolio of deliberately diversified and relatively anonymous family assets.

A family business can also play a distinctive role in family governance, engagement, and identity. In some cases, the role of the family business is so important that experts have posed the question: "Is the family keeping the business together, or is the business keeping the family together?"

A family business can also play a significant role in determining the allocation of a family's human capital—providing opportunities for employment, salary, bonus, and contribution to family wealth and stature. Emotional ownership by individuals and family bonding within and across generations can be enhanced in the context of an active engagement in the ownership, governance, and management of a family business.

Another function of family business growth or direct investing into companies in which the family has an active management or strategic role is the incubation possibility of what could become the next-scale family enterprise. One successful American family makes it an objective to grow and sell at least one large business every generation, using their direct and coinvestment platform as a way to source and invest in these potential "home run" transactions.

Buying a New Family Business to Replace the Old

One seventh-generation family, the Bembergs, sold their large brewing business, Quilmes, in Argentina, to InBev Group in 2006. With a clear understanding of the importance of a family business, within 24 months the family had purchased another business, this time the leading wine company in Argentina, Peñaflor, and were soon united as a family and fully engaged in the ownership and management of a new family business enterprise.

Family Business Performance and Portfolio Consequences

Interestingly, family businesses evidence some of the same characteristics as family wealth, with a decline over three generations. From a *BusinessWeek* analysis, first-generation (publicly listed) family businesses outperform nonfamily businesses in the first generation, slightly outperform or achieve average results in the second, and begin to underperform by the third.

Other measures also throw up some challenging statistics. In one survey of family business chief executive officers (CEOs) expecting to retire in five years, only 45 percent had selected a successor. Few family businesses have effective feedback systems for family members in the business, and in another survey only 3 percent of family business leaders had a written succession plan.

The family business must also be considered in the context of the family's other wealth. For instance, if the business is taken into consideration, it can have a meaningful impact on the way the family thinks about its asset mix, as can be seen in the Marmot family example.

Considering the Family Business in the Asset Mix

The Marmot Family Example

The incorporation of a family business into the asset allocation model can have a fundamental impact on decisions made on behalf of the family's overall wealth strategy. The question to ask is how to incorporate the family business into the investment asset mix.

The Marmot family provides a good case in point. The family has a net worth of $175 million, including $50 million in liquid investments (stocks, bonds, etc.) and a family business that they believe is worth about $125 million (after tax).

They are comfortable with an asset mix of 25 percent bonds and 75 percent stocks (considering just two asset classes for simplicity).

The liquid portfolio looks as follows:

Asset Mix (considering only the liquid investments)

	Target Mix	**Investment Allocation (million)**
Bonds	25 percent	$12.5
Stocks	75 percent	$37.5
Total investments	100 percent	$50

Convinced to reconsider their asset mix *with* the family business in the mix, the family determined that the business enterprise actually had a risk profile more akin to a stock than a bond. In fact, it probably had an even riskier profile than a balanced portfolio of stocks since it was one single, undiversified asset.

This changed the perspective entirely:

Asset Mix (considering the entire net worth)

	Target Mix (percent of net worth)	**Net Worth (million)**	**Business (million)**	**Investments (million)**	**Target Mix (percent of investments)**
Bonds	25 percent	$43.75	$0	$43.75	87.5 percent
Stocks	75 percent	$131.25	$125	$6.25	12.5 percent
Total	100 percent	$175	$125	$50	100 percent

If the business is properly considered as a stock in the portfolio, then the family already has $125 million (i.e., its business) of its target allocation of $131.25 million to stocks, so it only needs to allocate $6.25 million of its $50 million liquid investment capital to stocks and the balance ($43.75 million) to bonds.

Taking the business into account actually switched the original investment allocation from 25 percent bonds and 75 percent stocks to 87.5 percent bonds and 12.5 percent stocks, which allowed the family to achieve the target family net worth allocation of 25 percent bonds and 75 percent stocks.

Creating Liquid Family Wealth through Sale of a Family Business

The decision to sell a family business can be a wrenching one. While less emotionally burdensome if a family retains some degree of management control or active participation, or even a significant ownership stake and a visible role in governance, the decision to move on from a pure family business to one managing liquid wealth is one that will have consequences that last for generations.

For a successful sale to take place—both sale of the business on optimal economic terms, and successful in the sense of a family's adapting to the new world—the family and financial issues, yet again, need to be pursued in tandem.

On the family front, this can mean determining new roles and activities for those engaged actively in the family. For others, it may be to begin the search for a new family business, perhaps of a lesser scale, but of equal emotional importance to those involved in the decision.

And, of course, the pool of liquid wealth created will need careful management, with a well-thought-out plan in place to ensure that the professionalism that characterized the management of the operating business will be carried forward seamlessly into the management of the pool of liquid assets created by the sale.

The Family Business and the Family Portfolio: Another Relationship to Consider

Dr. Stephen Horan

The Davenport family and the Wu family have some things in common. They both run family businesses. They have both amassed about $200 million in wealth, including $175 million stakes in their respective family businesses. The remaining wealth for both families is invested in real estate and other financial assets. Moreover, they are both relatively risk averse when it comes to financial investments.

Their businesses are different, however. The Davenports have been running their lumber business for four generations. The Wu family, however, runs a first-generation specialty semiconductor company. Their similar entrepreneurial success and risk tolerance might suggest that their financial portfolios should look pretty similar. But let's take a closer look.

A Broader Perspective

When investors and financial professionals think about asset allocation, they typically think about how the assets on their brokerage account statements and other financial statements are invested. The value of most investors' human capital, however, far outstrips the value of their financial assets. Human capital represents the value of our lifetime labor if it were expressed in today's dollars. In the United States, for example, it represents 90 percent of total assets for investors under 30 years of age (see Figure 8.1).

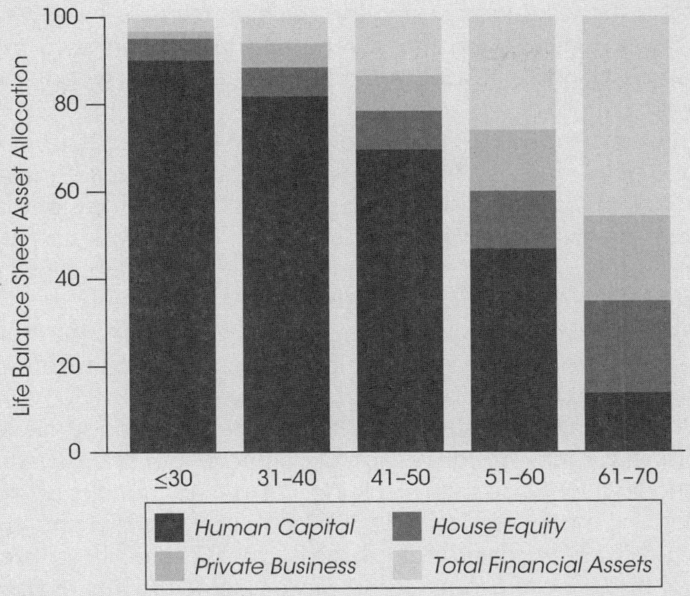

Figure 8.1 Magnitude of Human Capital
Source: Vladyslav Kyrychenko, "Optimal Asset Allocation in the Presence of Nonfinancial Assets," *Financial Services Review* 17, no. 1 (Spring 2008): 69–86.

Because human capital is so large, investors should think more broadly about the assets in their "portfolios." This fact is especially true for families with significant holdings in an operating company, which has some distinct implications that vary from investor to investor.

For business owners, human capital is largely represented by the value of their equity stake in the company and is usually the single largest asset by far for most families. It represents 87.5 percent of wealth for the Davenport and Wu families. It stands to reason that changes in its value and the nature of its character would dramatically influence how a family's remaining financial assets are invested. In fact, the operating business is the single most important factor in customizing a financial portfolio to meet a family's unique needs.

Four Factors of Family Business to Consider

At least four factors of the family business influence the optimal composition of the remaining financial assets. The first factor is risk of the business. One of the most important differences between the human

(*continued*)

capital of the wage earner and the business owner is the risk of the cash flows. Human capital for a tenured university professor is very stable and bondlike. In fact, human capital for many wage earners is bondlike.

Owners of family businesses, however, are equity holders by definition and have much riskier positions in their human capital. Therefore, business owners should approach the allocation of their remaining financial assets very differently than wage earners. All else being equal, they can absorb less risk in their remaining financial assets and should be more risk averse with financial assets.*

Business owners should also consider how correlated the fortunes of the business are to the market. The Wus' specialty semiconductor business, for example, may be more sensitive to market fluctuations than the Davenports' timber business. If so, the Wus already inherently have more risk through the operating company than the Davenports and should think twice before adding to it in their financial portfolio.

Third, no matter how sensitive the family business is to changes in the value of the overall market, private businesses are inherently undiversified and expose a family to industry or sector risks that most investors would sensibly diversify away. Entrepreneurs understandably balk at the idea of diversification and gladly accept the concentrated risk of the business because they can create value through control and management of the company. This is certainly true in many cases. Neither the Davenport nor the Wu family controls the industries in which they operate, however. So, although they might be comfortable with excess industry or sector exposure to the business, it seems foolhardy to add to that risk through the financial portfolio, especially when they cannot control it.

Even a seemingly diversified equity portfolio contains significant commodity and technology exposure that does little to diversify the Davenport and Wu holdings, respectively. A more sensible strategy is to build a financial portfolio that is diversified in the context of the family business—one that at least avoids additional industry exposure. A more compelling solution is to build a portfolio that is negatively correlated with industry and sector fluctuations associated with the business and that is outside the family's control.

---

*All else is rarely equal, however, and a family's investment goals have a strong influence on risk tolerance. A discussion of investment goals and risk tolerance is beyond the scope of our discussion here.

Finally, and perhaps most important, the sheer size of the family business relative to financial assets profoundly influences how financial assets are optimally invested. Because the stake in the business is large and inflexible, all rebalancing and adapting to changes in family or business circumstances need to be accounted for in the relatively small financial portfolio. Therefore, even modest changes in family or business circumstances can lead to dramatic changes in the financial portfolio. The sensitivity of the financial portfolio to changes in the operating company or other family circumstances highlights the importance of considering the size and character of the family business when constructing financial portfolios.

It is difficult to overstate the importance of the family-owned business on asset allocation and portfolio construction. Investors and advisors miss valuable opportunities to create custom portfolio solutions that meet investors' unique needs and reflect their unique circumstances by overlooking the magnitude and character of a wealth owner's business.

Dr. Stephen Horan is the head of University Relations and Private Wealth at CFA Institute in Charlottesville, Virginia. He has authored, coauthored, or edited a number of books, including *The New Wealth Management: A Financial Advisor's Guide to Managing and Investing Client Assets* (Hoboken, NJ: John Wiley & Sons, 2011) and *Private Wealth: Wealth Management in Practice* (Hoboken, NJ: John Wiley & Sons, 2009).

IMPERATIVE 2

SET A PRACTICAL FRAMEWORK FOR FAMILY INVESTMENT

CHAPTER 9

Rethinking Modern Portfolio Theory, Considering Goals-Based Wealth Management

Few professional investors would argue with the premise that asset allocation is one of the most important decisions an investor has to make. They may disagree, however, on what is the most effective model to make that asset allocation decision.

The most common asset allocation framework investors have used for many years is based on Modern Portfolio Theory (MPT). Developed by Harry Markowitz in the 1950s, MPT suggests that investors should attempt to maximize the amount of return they can achieve for a given level of risk or, conversely, to minimize the amount of risk required for a given level of return.

One of the central ways to accomplish these goals, the theory says, is diversification among various asset classes and securities.

Historic Background to Asset Allocation

Classic asset allocation models are traditionally driven by three major conceptual elements—portfolio theory, scientific asset allocation, and the efficient frontier—which combine to provide the foundation for modern asset allocation.

- *Portfolio theory.* The first element of an asset allocation model is the perspective that a portfolio of different asset classes will perform better than any individual asset class, on a risk-adjusted basis. A blend of asset classes can (theoretically) weather the inevitable economic storms better and protect long-term value more reliably in the overall investment portfolio.

  MPT argues that the risk for individual stock returns has two components: systematic risk (market risks that cannot be diversified away, such as big picture economic issues) and unsystematic risk (that is specific to individual stocks and is not correlated with the overall market, so can be diversified away by increasing the number of stocks in the portfolio, assuming those stocks are not correlated with each other).
- *Scientific asset allocation.* Once an investor has decided to invest across more than one asset class, the question arises as to how best to allocate capital between so many "classes" of investments. Asset allocation will be driven, in large part, by the investor's scale of wealth, investor profile, and investment objectives. The final model will reflect a unique appetite for risk and preferences for liquidity, term of investment, currency strategy, and other factors. No single portfolio approach will serve all masters equally well, but a scientific, data-driven approach to investment allocation is a common element in almost every high-performing portfolio.
- *The efficient frontier.* Within portfolio theory, the efficient frontier—which appears as a line on a risk/return graph—provides guidance on the various optimal combinations of investment assets an investor can choose from, depending on their risk tolerance.

  The concept is also related to the Sharpe ratio, first calculated by Professor William Sharpe at Stanford, who, along with Harry Markowitz, won the Nobel Prize in 1990 for their work on modern portfolio management. The Sharpe ratio provides insight into how different investments perform on a risk-adjusted basis, taking into account the volatility of the investment and the risk-free rate underlying the market. It allows portfolio managers to determine, with mathematical precision, how much of their investment return is driven by excess portfolio risk.

What Is the Essence of Modern Portfolio Theory?

Essentially, MPT revolves around a number of assumptions and observations. Originally posited as a work-in-progress idea expected to evolve with further research and experimentation, the original tenets actually remained largely in place from the original work onward.

Key observations and assumptions included:

- People like to make money and do not like to lose it.
- As potential return increases, so does risk.
- Risk is the variability of returns around the mean.
- Diversification among different types of assets can reduce risk in a portfolio.
- There is an infinite number of possible combinations of assets that are efficient (i.e., maximum reward for a given level of risk).
- Which one you choose depends on your own tolerance for risk or your required return.

A Popular Choice While MPT was initially developed in the 1950s, it did not come into common usage until the late 1970s. Once accepted as a standard "best practice" approach, it was heralded as a significant breakthrough in the field of portfolio management. MPT has been a popular tool, in both practical and academic circles, in part because it is relatively easy to use. Its ease of use comes partly from its simplifying assumptions and practical rules of thumb. As it turns out, these assumptions, while indeed simplifying, actually make the theory less robust when faced with real-world events. Some of those assumptions include:

- Standard deviation is the accepted definition of risk by all investors.
- Investment returns are "normally distributed" (i.e., distributed predictably around an average return).
- Observed values in the past are the best available assumptions for future values.
- Investors are rational.
- Markets are efficient and investors have the same information at the same time.

- Correlations between asset-class returns are fixed and constant.
- Investors feel as good about investment gains as they feel bad about investment losses.
- There are no taxes or transaction costs.

Even Harry Markowitz, the founder of the theory, agreed that there were probably better assumptions (e.g., other than observed values from the past of expected return, volatility, and correlation) and he hoped that better methods would be uncovered in subsequent work.

However, 50 years later, not much has changed. The same assumptions and data streams Harry Markowitz started with are still used to calculate efficient frontiers today.

A paper from the Brandes Institute opines: "Perhaps this helps explain the common tendency to rely on the past as a guide, despite its limitations. After all, in the absence of other tangible information, historical numbers might not be much, but they are something."*

In his classic book on risk, *Against the Gods,* Peter Bernstein retells a story of Kenneth Arrow, a Nobel laureate statistician who had served as an Air Force weather forecaster during World War II, that underscores the limits of the past as prologue to a predictable future. Some of the meteorological officers had been assigned the task of regularly forecasting the weather a month ahead:

> But Arrow and his statisticians found that their long-range forecasts were no better than numbers pulled out of a hat. [They] asked their superiors to be relieved of this duty. The reply was: *"The Commanding General is well aware that the forecasts are no good. However, he needs them for planning purposes."*† [Italics added]

In the same way, it may be argued that MPT has also been popular because there have been few other robust asset allocation models developed in the past several decades. And that, in turn, may be true because MPT was never sorely tested in the 1980s and 1990s

*"The Past, the Future, and Modern Portfolio Theory," Brandes Institute, 2004, 6.
†Peter Bernstein, *Against the Gods: The Remarkable Story of Risk* (New York: John Wiley & Sons, 1996), 203.

because markets were generally strong and correlations across asset classes were low.

In other words, it still seemed to "work," so there was little in the way of testing studies or alternative models developed.

An Alternative View With increasing confidence over the past few decades, behavioral finance adherents have taken issue with all of the assumptions underlying MPT cited earlier. They claim that human behavior is normal, but certainly not purely rational, pointing to many examples of overconfidence, overoptimism, herding, and irrational loss aversion.

Research also shows that returns are not "normally distributed," and, in fact, there are many more abnormal or unexpectedly large movements in securities pricing than normal distribution would suggest. That same body of research also suggests that real risk, certainly for private investors, is more related to permanent loss of capital and the inability to achieve their goals than simply the degree of variability of returns around an average.

There is also substantial behavioral evidence to suggest that investors actually feel worse about losses than they feel good about gains, which leads to a stronger desire to protect capital from permanent loss.

Behavioral finance suggests that markets are not efficient and that investors as individuals are normal, not rational. It argues that investors take into account other factors beyond risk-return analysis in designing their portfolios, including actions that increase their comfort level, reduce taxes, and reflect differing priorities within their overall goals.

This does not mean that MPT is entirely without merit (diversification among uncorrelated assets still makes sense, and lower risk to get the same return is desirable), but simply that it needs to be modified to take into account the realities of investor behavior, other relevant factors in investors' lives, and the way the world actually operates.

Post-Modern Portfolio Theory While a fixture in the investment management arena for many years, in recent years MPT has come under further scrutiny by behavioral scientists for its failures, as clearly exemplified in the 2008–2009 financial crisis.

MPT failed to account for the extreme movements in security prices and the high levels of correlation that drove virtually all asset classes down in unison. The failure to foresee the correlations in an adverse environment may have been rooted in the assumptions that underlie the core MPT hypothesis.

A revised theory—what we might call Post-Modern Portfolio Theory (PMPT)—would assume that investors:

- Are normal, not rational.
- Have multiple goals and multiple time frames.
- Don't have easy and free access to all information.
- Measure risk as loss.
- Are unhappier with losses than they are happy with gains.
- Are subject to decision risk.
- Are path dependent.

The Risk of Underestimating Risk

It is important to note that the use of historic "static" return, volatility, and correlation measurements, embedded in MPT and its economic brethren, does not factor in some potential (even if unlikely) macroeconomic scenarios such as war or terrorism, deep recessions, and a return to stagflation. Using a more active, forward-looking approach to portfolio allocation, extra dimensions to portfolio modeling and asset allocation can be added.

Typically, the data set used in efficient frontier analysis does not include such event risk and "fat tail" incidents (a technical reference to an event with a low likelihood of occurrence, but with a significant impact on the financial markets should it occur). This has led to the increased use of scenario-based planning to better understand capital allocations across a wider spectrum of investment environments.

The addition of a more forward-thinking perspective and a more comprehensive view of risk can have a major impact on the value of financial investments for a wealthy family.

Anticipating significant negative events can play a valuable role in securing future family fortunes in times of economic turbulence.

The Traditional "60–40"

The classical expression of the MPT portfolio for most institutional investors and many wealthy families has been a calculated combination of stocks and bonds, with the most common iteration being the traditional "60–40" mix of 60 percent stocks and 40 percent bonds. For years, this asset allocation model yielded reasonable results for pension funds and private investors alike.

However, over the past decade, the poor performance of stocks, falling bond yields, the increased correlation among most risk assets, and increased volatility have pressed investors to find new ways to think about asset allocation and portfolio construction. The improvements in technology and the dramatic increase in the number, breadth, and accessibility of new financial instruments have made it practically possible to move beyond the traditional 60–40 portfolio into other asset classes and portfolio constructs.

In addition, the intended purposes of many asset classes to provide asset protection, capital growth, portfolio alpha, and income or portfolio risk management were not fulfilled during the global financial crisis (GFC) and are also under review and reconsideration by many families.

Even those investors experimenting with new asset classes and products found many of them wanting in this environment. Liquidity dried up as alternative asset funds continued to draw down against commitments with significantly reduced distributions, high fees became more visible in a low-growth (and/or loss-making) environment, and the failure of many hedge funds to hedge against negative scenarios reduced their effectiveness in fulfilling their intended portfolio role.

The importance of absolute return in investing also gained more credence and popularity, given the volatile and often negative investment environment, based on the observation that "no family ever created its second fortune by losing less money than the market."

Absolute return is the actual rate of return achieved, independent of benchmark or market performance overall. Simply beating a negative benchmark may no longer be sufficient for families having been promised consistent positive absolute returns by the expensive managers to whom the families have entrusted their wealth.

Firmly Focused on Family Goals

The key question facing each investing family is which mix of assets is most likely to achieve the family's financial objectives for capital protection and growth, income generation, portfolio efficiency, and investment effectiveness.

The GFC, the disappointment of MPT, and the experimentation with new PMPT portfolio approaches has spawned a whole new range of asset allocation models and a brand new discussion about the best ways to build portfolios and meet the needs of private investors in the colder climate of the new world order.

One of the outcomes of the last decade of investment mayhem and frustration with overly simplistic assumptions has been a refocusing of the goals on the family as the central determinant of investment policy and objective of risk management.

Goals-based wealth management and an amended approach to asset allocation flow directly out of recent experience and the observations of behavioral finance, and put the focus where it should always have been on a practical approach to serve the goals of the family and private investor as adapted to the realities of the markets.

The Rise of Goals-Based Wealth Management

Goals-based wealth management (GBWM) does not necessarily replace the other capital market–based models, but can be a helpful addition and, one could argue, provides a far better starting point for family wealth management.

GBWM begins with the premise that the aim of the entire investment process is to meet specific client goals, which could include funding a family's lifestyle, maintaining a contingency fund, funding multiple generations of family members, starting a new business, or endowing a chair at a university.

The development of the behavioral finance field in recent years has demonstrated that investors use what is called *mental accounting* and commonly hold multiple goals at the same time. That does not fit well with the concept of a total portfolio, but rather better reflects the real-world approach of breaking an entire portfolio down into smaller subsections, with each designed to meet a specific family goal.

Families may want to create different "pools" of capital to serve different family purposes. Distinctions can be by specific purpose of the funds, preferences of a branch or generation of the family, foundation needs, or other specific family objectives. The result is a set of defined pools of capital, with each serving a specific purpose with separate objectives, but also finding a way to manage all of the separate vehicles and managed accounts in a coordinated and coherent manner to achieve the overall objectives of the family or private investor.

Similarly, GBWM assumes that the true definition of risk is the potential inability of a family to achieve its goals, and not simply how volatile are the current investments. It also suggests that, in private investors' minds, risk is more related to events (i.e., not meeting a goal) than a time interval (i.e., annual volatility measures).

GBWM advocates separate risk tolerance estimates by each goal as opposed to trying to determine an overall risk tolerance for an investor. For instance, funding family expenses from the portfolio over the next five years might be a low-risk-tolerance (i.e., high-priority) objective, whereas buying a second private plane might be a higher-risk-tolerance (i.e., low-priority or even optional) objective.

Real Risk

Investment managers talk about risk as volatility. Individual [investors], however, are much less focused on volatility. Their perceptions of risk are often driven by emotions and, therefore, are easily misunderstood or ignored by managers. . . . In order to be successful, managers must identify how clients actually perceive risk.

Source: Leslie Kiefer, "Investment Policy Best Practices: Communication, Creation and Commitment," *CFA Institute Conference Proceedings Quarterly*, March 2007.

One example of a goals-based asset allocation model is the "bucketing approach" modeled on the behavioral finance concept of mental accounting. Families actually segregate their goals into different categories and think about the risk of each in quite different ways.

Ashvin Chhabra developed a useful model called the Wealth Allocation Framework (Figure 9.1), which helps families identify different types of goals that have different risk profiles and priority levels. He suggests that there are three buckets to which families allocate, based on their perceived needs. Assets are allocated to each of these buckets based on their ability to fulfill the goal at the appropriate level of risk:

- The *personal risk bucket* is focused on protecting the investor from the anxiety of a dramatic decrease in his or her lifestyle. It contains those assets that provide some degree of stability

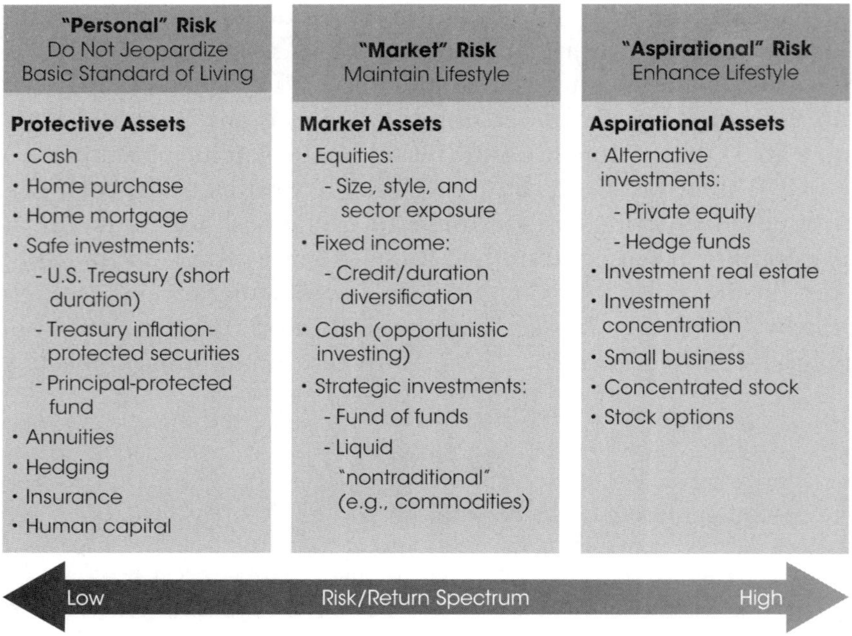

Figure 9.1 Classification of Assets and Liabilities Using the Wealth Allocation Framework
Source: Ashvin Chhabra, "Beyond Markowitz: A Comprehensive Wealth Allocation Framework," *Journal of Wealth Management* (Spring 2005): 17.

and principal protection. Allocations to the personal wealth bucket will limit the loss of wealth but will typically yield below-market returns.

- The *market risk bucket* allows the investor to maintain the family's lifestyle in the face of inflation and spending growth. The objectives of the assets in this bucket are to balance risk and return and to earn a higher rate of return than inflation, usually from a broadly diversified portfolio. (This bucket reflects the Markowitz MPT framework.)
- The *aspirational risk bucket* provides an opportunity for the investor to increase his or her wealth substantially and meet the family's aspirational goals. The assets in this bucket are intended to provide higher-than-market returns that enhance the family's lifestyle, but they will also carry the risk of substantial loss of capital.

Note that hedge funds are often placed in the aspirational bucket because of the risks associated with any single partnership regardless of an investment strategy. A properly diversified portfolio of hedge funds would normally be placed in the market bucket.

Suitable, but Is It Optimal?

The goals-based asset allocation approach divides the portfolio into discrete units that are designed to fund specific goals.

Some academics have challenged these models on the basis that they do not provide an *optimal* overall portfolio (i.e., a model that provides the best possible overall return for a given level of risk). Several recent academic papers have demonstrated that goals-based approaches can indeed produce optimal portfolios, even if they do so in different ways.

No single framework can meet every financial challenge or work for every family. And there is no "perfectly right" way of determining appropriate asset allocation.

What is clear is the need to start and end with family goals in any investment theory or practice. Many families get caught up in forecasting capital markets and tracking complex financial and risk indicators and lose sight of the achievement of their own, more personal objectives.

Investors who have a clear perspective on why they are investing, what the money is for, when they need it, and how high a priority it is may be better served no matter what asset allocation approach they ultimately choose to employ.

Integrated Goals-Based Wealth Management

Jean Brunel

Over the past 10 years, many families have had the opportunity to revisit their strategic financial asset allocation. Historically, the goals-based approach had been criticized as potentially suboptimal (i.e., does not provide enough return for the level of risk or has a higher level of risk for the defined rate of return). Yet the market meltdown of 2008 and the publication of the seminal academic paper on the optimality of mental account portfolios changed these perceptions.

Until 2008, many investors had been used to minor discomfort or disappointment with markets when these did poorly, but not to the

(*continued*)

wholesale fear that the world had changed, and traditional financial tenets with it. Diversification did not seem to work as advertised, and certain strategies hitherto perceived to be liquid proved not to be. People became willing to start considering that the framework and approach they had been using might need some revisiting.

At the same time, Das, Markowitz, Scheid, and Statman (in "Portfolio Optimization with Mental Accounts") demonstrated that creating individual subportfolios to deal with each of their multiple goals actually did not give rise to suboptimality, if the definition of risk was shifted from the academic "volatility of returns" to the much more real probability of "not achieving a goal." There are several issues that families now need to face when they adopt this new framework.

The first fundamental element of this goals-based framework is that any analysis must be totally integrated into the family's overall wealth management program. Indeed, though one must at times be prepared to disentangle issues relating to asset management from those that affect other dimensions of the wealth management effort, it is essential that a goals-based strategic asset allocation should integrate financial, estate, philanthropy, and tax management goals. A simple example illustrates such a need: If some part of the assets is meant to help me meet my lifestyle spending needs, I must make sure that these assets either belong to me or are held in a structure of which I am a rightful beneficiary.

The second challenge is to draw up a list of the family's goals that is as comprehensive as possible. Over the years, I have found that the use of words such as *goal* or *risk* may obscure rather than enlighten the process. I thus prefer the terms *dreams* and *nightmares*. Families respond much more comprehensively—and thoughtfully—when they are asked to formulate their dreams.

The list of such dreams is typically much longer and more multidimensional than any prosaic summary of my financial goals. Similarly, risk is something that is an amorphous concept for many families, particularly when you are speaking to an entrepreneur who has recently sold her business. By contrast, nightmares are much more real, in that they are the fears that the individual is working to manage as far away as possible.

Compiling such a list, however, is only the beginning of the process. The family and its advisors need to know more than that. For instance, how should we prioritize these goals? Ostensibly, a few will be viewed as crucial, while others might be superfluous. Over the years, I have found that the biggest nightmare for affluent families is to be forced to change their lifestyle, at least in a way that neighbors might notice. Thus, lifestyle goals tend to have very low tolerances for error.

By contrast, goals that might involve creating some form of a legacy, such as the creation of some collection to be bequeathed to a museum, for instance, are viewed as less critical. Having prioritized these goals, the next challenge is to determine the amount of financial assets needed for the goal to be achieved with a risk profile consistent with its degree of priority.

The current frontier relates to families that have "excess assets." These are families who can achieve all of their goals with only some of their current assets. Tradition in the asset management industry has been to assume that any "unneeded asset" should be invested in a way that seeks maximum return, the theory being that you will not miss assets that you did not need in the first place.

While this may be a perfectly acceptable assumption, I do not believe it to be universally correct. In fact, there are instances where families would prefer to invest any surplus asset in a real—or even at times nominal—capital preservation mode. Their logic is often just as straightforward: taking investment risk will expose me to occasional losses, which, though not permanent, may still upset me. Further, how do I know that I will not compound the error of having taken too much risk by bailing out at the point of maximum pain? Thus, quite a few families are opting for some form of capital preservation for their surplus assets. More specifically, I have seen families choose to invest the surplus assets of the current generation in a capital preservation mode, while opting for growth for the surplus assets of future generations.

Two main challenges still remain, and the industry would do well to focus on them. The first relates to incorporating tax-efficiency considerations into the mix. The second relates to the need to be able to report performance at both the total portfolio and each individual goal level. While complex in practice, it is a crucial element of the overall framework, as one of the main rationales for GBWM is the ability to benefit from the feedback loop associated with the realization that goals are being met with the probability that was initially required.

Jean Brunel, CFA, is one of the world leaders in integrated wealth management and goals-based investing. He is the managing principal, Brunel Associates, Bonita Springs, Florida; the founding editor of the *Journal of Wealth Management;* and author of *Integrated Wealth Management* (London: Euromoney Institutional Investor, 2006).

CHAPTER 10

Reviewing Different Approaches to Asset Allocation

There is a wide range of approaches taken by families to allocating assets to suit their needs, level of sophistication, and scale of wealth.

This range has increased substantially over the past decade as investors have rejected simplistic models that were not able to deliver what they promised, or moved on from more complex models that did not work out in the real world.

Each of the models discussed in this chapter has some benefits and some drawbacks. It is clear, as outlined in the previous chapter, than any model will be most effective if the family's longer-term goals are at the forefront of thinking and the final model chosen is specifically designed to meet those objectives.

The Evolution of Asset Allocation

The early days of asset allocation consisted mostly of balanced mandates of multiple assets based on income and growth needs of a portfolio (see Figure 10.1).

Modern Portfolio Theory brought more science and precision to the determination of the optimal level of the mix of assets. Further evolution followed.

Employee Retirement Income Security Act (ERISA) legislation in the United States in 1974 changed the fiduciary requirements of pension funds and drove the development of multimanager and

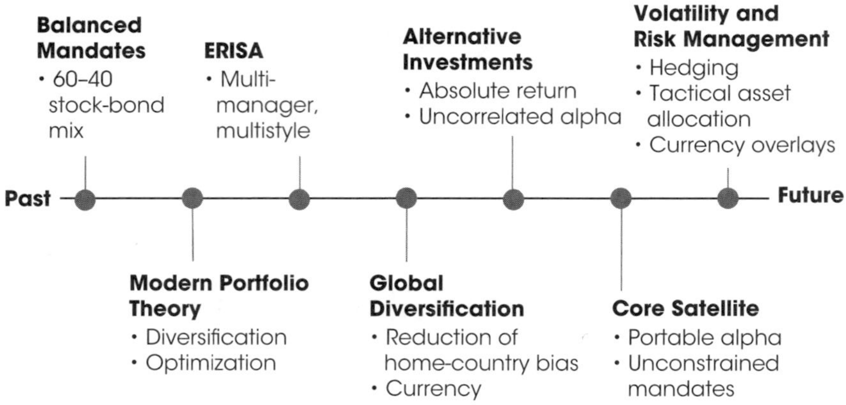

Figure 10.1 Evolution of Asset Allocation
Source: "The Evolving Nature of Global Asset Allocation," Lazard Freres, July 26, 2010, 1.

multistyle investing, followed by diversification outside the investor's home country to spread risk and boost potential reward.

Later came the discovery of new ways to produce different return streams that were more stable, less correlated to the core asset classes, and had the potential to provide "absolute return" regardless of the general market environment. This discovery, along with significant technology developments and growth in exchange-traded funds (ETFs), spawned the separation of alpha and beta in the portfolio and the assumption of different cost models for each segment of return (i.e., high for alpha, low for beta).

With the assistance of technological innovation, the recent asset allocation trends have included more complex hedging and currency overlay techniques.

Core and Satellite

Families frustrated with the cost and lack of value added from active management strategies have increasingly employed a "core and satellite" strategy, which combines actively managed funds with index funds in a single portfolio. The appeal of this approach is that it seeks to establish a risk-controlled portfolio at low cost, while also securing some prospects of outperformance (alpha), with the alpha component forming the primary focus of manager and family attentions.

It is interesting to note that passively managed ETFs and actively managed hedge funds have both grown substantially over the past

10 years, even if the latter had a massive decline in assets under management after the crisis—declining by nearly 50 percent before recovering, albeit only in part, in the 5 years following the crisis.

It is increasingly difficult for active investment managers managing large-cap stocks and government bonds to generate alpha (i.e., outperform the broader markets), which makes those managers an expensive vehicle to deliver market-related performance. Investors have therefore been looking for cheaper ways just to access beta (i.e., market performance), which ETFs have been well-suited to provide.

At the same time, many investors believe that an unconstrained and talented manager in almost any asset class, motivated by the right incentive compensation structure, can generate significant unique, non-market-related alpha performance using innovative techniques and asset classes—and they are willing to pay for it.

Core and satellite investing allows investors get their core exposure to long-term increases in market (beta) very cheaply through ETFs, and get their outperformance (alpha) from targeted, specialized, and generally more expensive satellite managers who are able to generate true net-of-fees-and-carry alpha.

The model argues that investors should neither pay high fees nor performance fees for easy-to-achieve beta. This would then allow them to reallocate the fees they save to the more rewarding task of finding and engaging active managers who have a much greater likelihood of alpha generation.

Some investors use this approach to provide a stable, benchmark-oriented, lower-cost way to get exposures to the major asset classes, and then fill in the satellite slots with allocations to riskier, higher-return-potential investments such as sector funds, frontier markets, strategic bets, and alternative alpha funds.

The S-Curve: Balancing Risk and Return, Short and Long Term

For a family with a single asset pool, living in a single jurisdiction with little need for complex family or tax planning, issues may focus simply on risk and return parameters. This simplified model of asset allocation is captured in a display called an *investment S-curve.*

The S-curve (shown in Figure 10.2), is perhaps most valuable in translating a family's or individual's real risk appetite or time frame for investing into a meaningful guide to asset allocation, based on

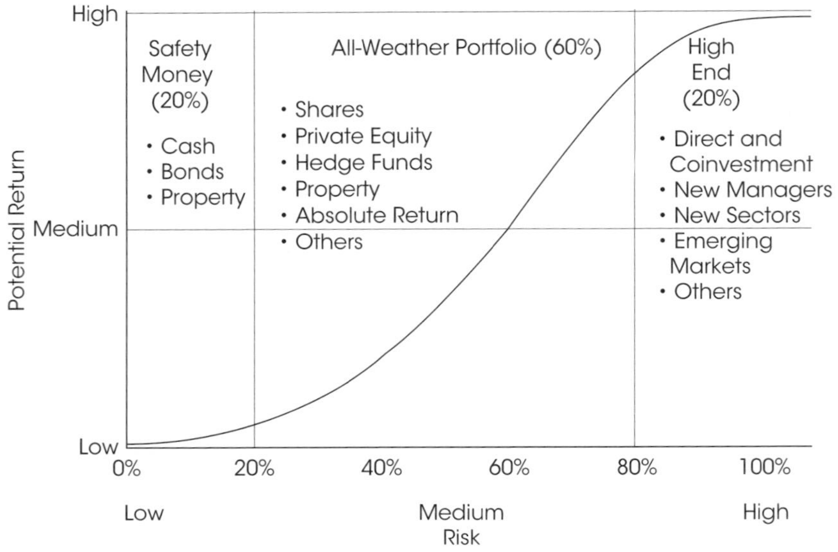

Figure 10.2 The Investment S-Curve
Source: Mark Daniell, *Strategy for the Wealthy Family* (Singapore: John Wiley & Sons, 2008).

risk and potential return or taking into consideration the relevant time frame for the investment holding period (the two may often be the same in the end).

The classic investment S-curve plots investment alternatives on an upward-sloping curve, with low-risk, low-return investments in the developed markets in the lower left, and higher-risk, higher-return opportunities as in emerging markets, emerging sectors, emerging managers, direct investments, highly levered transactions, and other similar areas of potential exploitable inefficiency in the right side sector.

The following is a typical breakdown of asset classes in the S-curve:

Low Risk

- Core fixed income
- Noncore fixed income
- Preferred shares
- Life insurance
- Real estate rental properties

- Infrastructure
- Family business (if long established and stable cash generator)

Medium Risk

- Domestic equities
- Dividend-paying equities
- Global equities
- Emerging markets equities
- Absolute return
- Hedge funds
- Family business (if medium risk)

High Risk

- Private equity
- Hard assets
- Energy and commodities
- Distressed investment
- Real estate development
- Private debt
- High-yield debt
- Emerging markets
- Direct investment
- Family business (if highly levered, start-up, or risky)

One of the purposes of the S-curve is to highlight the nature of a total portfolio's allocated exposure to risk and potential return, which serves as an easy-to-understand visual supplement to the traditional asset class allocations driven by the efficient frontier displays of Modern Portfolio Theory (MPT).

A second purpose of the S-curve is to highlight the allocation of funds to the most interesting (and highest-risk) investments in the high end of the S-curve, or "the innovative end of the market" as described by one United Kingdom–based billionaire.

Timing participation in different S-curve segments is critical; one of the pathways to the highest returns is to select investments in emerging areas before a period of rapid growth in global interest and investment, and hence growth in sector prices, takes place.

Successfully investing ahead of an economic "tipping point" can achieve exceptionally high returns through all growth phases of an asset class or sector opportunity.

Implicit in any more complete S-curve investment strategy is the broader consideration of multiple markets, currencies, and geographies, and a need for a more sophisticated understanding of selected markets, asset classes, global trends, and the management skills of professional fund managers.

The (Alternative) Time Dimension

The dimensions of risk and return are not the only ones that can be applied to a custom-tailored S-curve as a key part of a family's investment strategy development.

The S-curve may also be a useful device as well to ensure that an investing family exploits its inherent advantage to be both longer term in outlook and less sensitive to interim volatility. In addition, opportunities for creative structures and participation can be explored to create an approach best suited to a particular investment opportunity. Equally, the display can be adapted to reflect liquidity characteristics or other dimensions of grouped investments.

A broader set of S-curve displays can ensure that the ultimate portfolio tightly matches the family's investor profile:

Investor Profile Element	Custom-Tailored S-Curve to Show
Risk appetite	Risk and return
Investment time frame	Short-, medium-, and long-term investments
Liquidity preference	Liquidity profile: high, medium, low liquidity
Investor capability	Complexity of investment: low, medium, high

In many cases, these different S-curves will appear in similar form, as some longer-term investments, such as an investment in an operating company, will also be complex, high risk, and low liquidity, and thus appear on the extreme right side of the curve in all cases. Similarly, cash and some government bonds will be highly liquid, low risk, simple, and short term, and thus appear consistently on the left side in all four versions of the displays.

Opportunity and Choice

There are far more investment choices available to the wealthy family today for tactical selection within an overall strategic model than for any preceding generation. It is important to understand this "endless buffet," as one investor has dubbed it, and to pick very carefully—and at the right time—only the items that fit the family's overall strategy and add specific value to the portfolio.

There is no "right" answer as to the correct quantum of assets in each area, nor is there any single answer on the specific strategy and tactics within each asset class along the curve. This will depend on the family concerned, but seeing it in graphical form can help to identify whether the correct balance of risk and return is being targeted, and whether there is undue concentration in any one area of exposure.

It can also provide a high-level snapshot of the portfolio that can inform open discussion within the family about objectives, increasing the odds of the outcome actually aligning with a family's overall risk/return appetite.

Ivy League Lessons

Over the past two decades, much of the more refined science and practice of asset allocation has come from the chief investment officers of the Harvard and Yale University endowments. Their models have a number of attributes that mark significant departures from past models, most notably a dramatic increase in the use of alternative asset classes, minimal cash holdings, a greater exposure to equities in emerging markets, and more creative financing schemes, as shown in Figures 10.3 and 10.4.

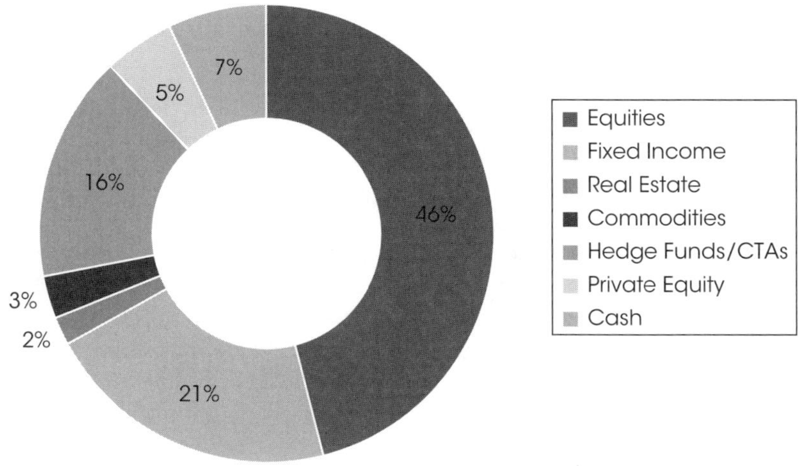

Figure 10.3 Average Endowment Asset Allocation
Source: Various U.S. endowment funds annual reports.

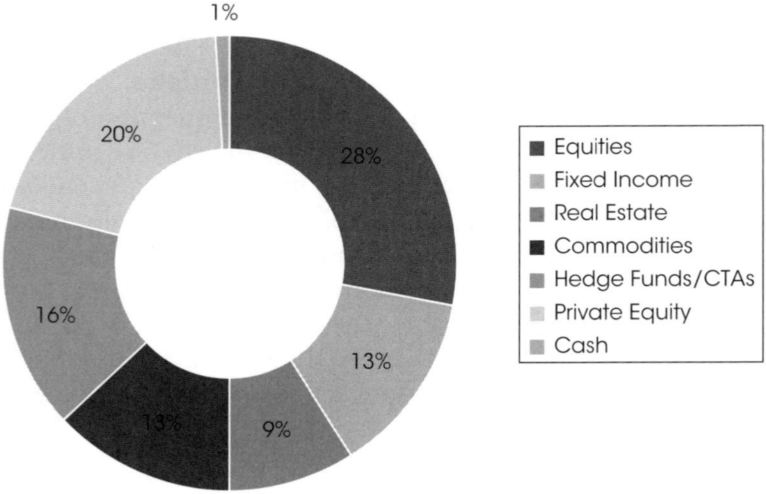

Figure 10.4 Large ($1+ billion) Endowment Asset Allocation
Source: Various U.S. endowment funds annual reports.

Their strategy emphasized two key factors. They targeted assets that were *actually* uncorrelated, so they received some of the benefits of diversification that traditional stock and bond investors found increasingly difficult to sustain. And they also bought asset classes that were relatively illiquid, with the view that the long-term nature of their portfolio could tolerate the illiquidity for a defined portion of the portfolio.

In return, they would capture the higher rate of return that illiquid asset classes typically offer.

What Is the Endowment Model?

The term *endowment model* is often used to describe a theory and practice of investing, first used by major endowments including Harvard, Yale, and others starting in the 1990s. The model is characterized by highly diversified, long-term portfolios that differ from a traditional stock-bond mix, in that they include allocations to less traditional and less liquid asset categories, such as private equity and real estate, as well as absolute return strategies.

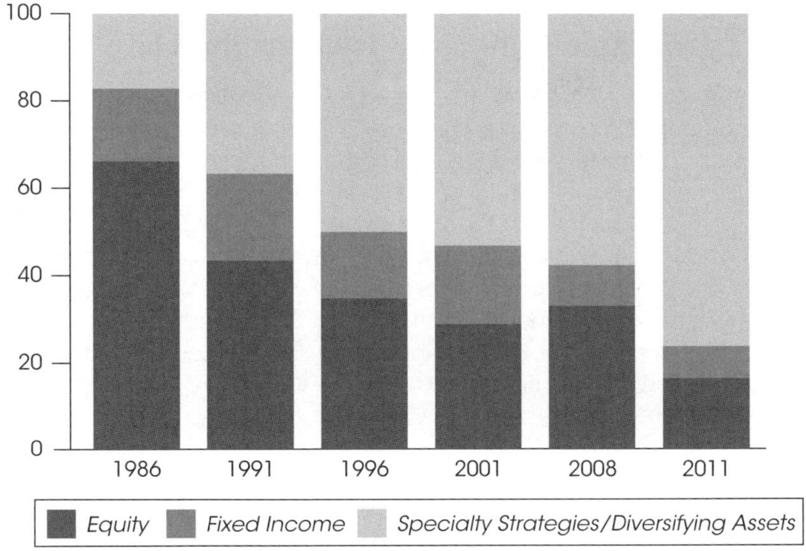

Figure 10.5 Yale Endowment Asset Allocation, 1986–2011
Target asset allocation as of June 30 for each year. Excludes cash.
Source: Yale Endowment Report, 2012.

Their balanced approach has led to portfolios divided roughly equally among equities, fixed income, timber, commodities, private equity, hedge funds, property, and some cash/liquidity positions. And because of their size and early entry into some of the more esoteric asset classes, the endowments were able to secure access to some of the highest-caliber fund managers available.

The largest endowments have made the most aggressive moves into the nontraditional, endowment model space. As can be seen in Figure 10.5, Yale has been steadily reducing its exposure to traditional asset classes and upping its concentration in alternatives. As a result, for several decades, the Yale and Harvard endowment portfolios posted returns exceeding 15 percent.

For many other endowments, this strategy also worked well for some time, although it suffered in the 2008–2009 market crisis when the large declines in their liquid portfolios required them to sell some of their illiquid holdings at bargain basement prices and raise cash through bond offerings and other creative approaches to fund university operating budgets.

Shining a Light on Endowment Investing

Although a few uber-performing university endowments like Harvard (12.5 percent per year over the past 20 years) and Yale have set a new standard for institutional investing, their success has not been easy to replicate. An article in the *New York Times* highlighted that data compiled for the 2011 fiscal year "show that large, medium and small endowments all underperformed a simple mix of 60 percent stocks and 40 percent bonds over one, three and five year periods. The 91 percent of endowments with less than $1 billion in assets underperformed in every time period since records have been maintained."

The same compilation for 2012, once figures are available, may be even worse.

Taken as a group, smaller endowments and many families have difficulty gaining access to the best-performing managers, and are relegated to second-tier (or worse) performers with first-tier costs.

Source: New York Times, October 12, 2012.

The Role of Scenario Planning

Many forecasting and planning groups, from Shell to the World Economic Forum to some of the world's largest and most successful investing family offices, use scenario modeling as an essential part of their forward planning exercises for investment and risk management purposes.

Probability-adjusted scenario analysis is not about guessing at a single outcome. Rather, it is about defining different future states of affairs and assessing, given present trends and influences, what are the probabilities of each occurring.

Performing a scenario analysis will help wealth owners to determine how achievable their goals are under differing financial states of affairs and how reasonable their assumptions. It can also provide families with input to the various options they will have at their disposal to meet their wealth objectives.

This testing phase can employ a simple set of alternative scenarios for investors to consider, or it can use more sophisticated techniques, such as Monte Carlo simulation, which runs thousands of different scenarios with different variables to predict potential portfolio outcomes, and seeks to find the optimal mix of assets for the range of outcomes.

Holistic and Active Portfolio Management

It is important to understand each individual asset class selection and the investments within it. It is equally, if not more, important to understand how a family's overall investment portfolio will behave in different economic environments.

This will require stress testing and risk management assessments to provide an understanding of how a particular portfolio will behave if interest rates, energy prices, consumer demand, or a particular currency or stock market rises or falls within the investment horizon.

One investment guru in the United States described a portfolio as being like a cake, where individual ingredients, such as butter, sugar, flour, and eggs, behave very differently when combined together in different proportions under different thermal conditions.

Best (and Next) Practice: The Expert Family Office's Approach to Investing

One of the most sophisticated chief investment officers (CIOs) in the family office world has been developing and refining an approach to a large family portfolio for one family for many years, aligning investment strategy and action plans with the support and guidance of the family's very insightful and engaged G2 leader.

His approach is comprehensive and addresses all of the issues inherent in an ambitious multipurpose, multi–asset class, multimanager approach, which also includes scenario planning, direct investing, and a parallel set of activities for family education and involvement.

The approach is well-documented so that any unexpected succession issues within the family can be dealt with smoothly, with next generation members being prepared through a structured program of education and practical experience to step into a leadership role when the time comes.

There are seven steps in their approach to asset allocation.

Step 1: Adapting to the Macroeconomic Context through Scenario Planning

This family's asset allocation approach outlines seven basic global scenarios, ranging from "Meltdown" to "Muddle Through" to "Big Boom" based on the family office team's expectations and long-term observed history and probabilities.

Scenario	Description	Real GDP	Fed Funds Rate	1930-p	1970-p	Current Probability
Scenario 1	Total collapse and anarchy	NA	NA	0%	0%	1%
Scenario 2	Worldwide economic collapse	<−1.5%	0%	8%	0%	4%
Scenario 3	World recession	−1.5	1%	9%	5%	8%
Scenario 4	Low growth and low demand	1.5–2.5%	2–3%	9%	11%	34%
Scenario 5	Trend growth	2.5–4.0%	3–4%	30%	46%	28%
Scenario 6	Economic boom	5.0%+	4–5%	34%	16%	10%
Scenario 7	Stagflation	<2.0%	4–6%	10%	22%	15%

Figure 10.6 Sample Global Scenarios

A sample scenario spreadsheet is illustrated in Figure 10.6.

Historical results do not on their own drive recommended future asset allocation. However, they do provide important context from which to see relevant patterns.

Step 2: Redefining Asset Classes and Identifying Long-Term Megatrends

By thinking out of the box, this family office has developed an attractive blend of long-term investment perspectives that allows them to look and act afresh in a world driven by group thinking and hamstrung by conventional asset-class definitions.

Qualitative and quantitative overlays include a consideration of underappreciated and sustainable "megatrends" in a range of asset classes, regions, and industries.

Step 3: Incorporating Selected Quantitative Inputs

As a final step in their asset allocation process, this family office incorporates a range of quantitative and qualitative analyses that include fundamental valuation, credit cycles, corporate earnings, structural changes in asset classes and economies, as well as conventional mean-variance tests, one of the most valuable parts of MPT.

These inputs are designed to help gain additional insights into asset allocation results and identify opportunities for active management of asset exposures within preset policy ranges.

Step 4: Incorporating the Implications of the Global Context

One of the most important aspects of the expert family office model is its formal incorporation of perspectives of the global macroeconomic situation, an essential component in an interconnected world with global systemic risk, correlated global asset classes, and geographically proximate capital markets.

Step 5: Identifying and Managing Strategic Risk

Risk is addressed in the family portfolio at two levels: strategic risk and tactical risk.

Strategic risk is made up of those long-term or market trends that can have a substantial impact on the fundamental value of the portfolio, such as dramatic changes in market trends, regulatory or tax change, counterparty and systemic risk, family business risk, and other family wealth-threatening events.

Tactical risk is played out at a lower level. It may apply to a smaller part of the portfolio or is related to individual investments, trades and transactional issues, execution risk, timing, hedging strategies, insurance, and other such performance-determining factors. These factors can be extremely important for a family's financial well-being, but may not have the fortune-threatening impact that strategic risk can have on a portfolio.

Step 6: Seeking Alpha

The practice of alpha identification and capture, like asset allocation and investment management broadly, is a combination of art and science. Large markets are enormously liquid, highly informed, and fast moving. They are, if anything, overcrowded with intelligent investors.

The clever strategies, niche opportunities, inefficient markets, and price/value arbitrage opportunities that can lead to alpha generation are hard to find in any such environment.

Alpha is more easily found in less efficient markets and in alternative asset classes that are accurately described as "less crowded airspace" in which to seek and find unexploited opportunities and investment advantage.

By being creative, by adhering to the policies of an asset allocation model, but also abjuring the conventional and the crowded investment theses, family investors can be well-placed to harvest more of those rare opportunities to benefit from real alpha and absolute return in a far colder climate than anyone we have seen in our investing lifetimes.

Step 7: Rolling All of the Elements Above into a Single Global Capital Allocation Strategy

Appropriate, global, and diversified strategic asset allocation planning should produce a "true north" portfolio that accounts for low probability but high impact fat tail and event risks—modulated between "defensive/safe" and "growth/risk."

Such a portfolio can be focused on capital preservation and capable of enduring though negative and downside markets as well as more positive growth periods.

An Expert's Allocation 2012

With so many variables and choices to process, how did sophisticated investors allocate capital at the end of, for example, 2012?

One major portfolio manager ended up with the following model for his clients who were focused exclusively on liquid and real investments:

Controlled Risk

Cash	2%
Investment-grade fixed income	3%
Treasury inflation-protected securities (TIPS; short duration 3–5 years)	4%
High yield (income)	5%

Equity Risk (via ETFs, managers, and hedge funds)

U.S. equities	
Large-cap	15%
Small- and mid-cap	10%
Foreign developed markets	10% (also provides foreign currency exposure)
Emerging markets	10%

Real Assets	
Commodities	10%
Property	
U.S. (including "Agland")	20%
Foreign	6%
Gold	5%
Total	100%

Choosing a Framework That Is Right for Each Family

There is a wide range of asset management frameworks available for family investors to choose from. Each has its pros and cons; some are more complex and others less so. Many investment frameworks can also be adapted for effective use by an investing family who is willing to put in the time and effort. But it is most important that the family chooses an approach with which they are comfortable, that suits their own style, and that aligns with the scope, size, and makeup of their investment portfolio. In this way, the framework is most likely to be useful for the family and able to endure through the inevitable challenging times.

Complexity Does Not Equal Sophistication

It has become almost an accepted truth that to be a "sophisticated" investor in a complex, interactive, tightly coupled, and adaptive world, one has to adopt a complex, interactive, tightly coupled, and opportunistic investment model (and organization) tied to that world.

In my opinion, that conclusion is simply wrong; a simpler, transparent, and focused approach is a very viable alternative. The goal should be to survive comfortably with the highest odds over the very long term. As long as an institution enjoys long-term stability, produces returns comparable to the market, and produces returns at least in the pack of institutional investors, there should be no reason to be jealous of the few that hit home runs.

The endowment model relies too heavily on a false sense of diversification, on too many strategies, on selecting exceptional managers where the odds are heavily against that exercise, and on an

(*continued*)

underlying view of the market that has been demonstrated to be severely compromised. To use a cliché, it tries to pick up hundreds of nickels (often using excessive leverage or severely restricted liquidity), while underestimating the speed and acceleration of the steamrollers coming its way. Not only is the achievement of additional return over longer periods problematic, but also when turbulent markets arise, additional issues of liquidity and lack of transparency can devastate the portfolio.

A complex investment world does not require a complex response, either in the nature of the investment organization or the particular investment strategies chosen. The cockroach lives in a very, very complex environment with one of the best long-term success rates of any creature. Yet it has only one defense mechanism—running in the opposite direction from a puff of air. The equivalent for the investment world is, at the core, a very simple structure founded upon public market diversification with one basic defense mechanism: see a volatile movement, and react in the opposite direction (i.e., rebalance into it). A simple structure and strategy, if adhered to, has one of the best chances of surviving for many decades.

Source: Robert Maynard, "Conventional Investing in a Complex World," *Journal of Investing*, Spring 2013.

CHAPTER 11

Comprehensive Risk Management

The economic environment over the past decade provided most wealthy families with an unwelcome education about risk.

The global financial crisis, financial setbacks, the destabilization within many countries and currencies, terrorism, and natural disasters have all served to remind investors of the uncertainties and risks for which they need to be prepared.

Following the capital market and economic events of 2000–2001 and 2008–2009 in the United States, and the following euro crisis in 2011–2012, risk has become a major concern for family investors. Even many hedge funds, which were specifically designed to resist correlation with equity markets and protect against downside risk (by having a short component), got caught up in the upside zeitgeist and performed poorly during the most recent market downturn.

In addition to recent damage to family portfolios, there are three major reasons for the current attention being paid to the identification and management of risk to family wealth and well-being.

1. Global risks and volatility seem to be larger than ever and risk profiles seem more likely to increase than decrease in the future.
2. The tools used in the past to manage those risks have not been working, leaving investors to try to find new ways to understand and mitigate risk.

3. There is good reason to believe that the nature of risk is changing and that the probability of occurrence of negative outcomes will increase and the scale of potential impact will become even more pronounced over time as the world becomes more interdependent and the speed of interaction increases.

Old Tools Not Sharp Enough for New Challenges

The set of risk management tools we have used in the past, particularly for investment management, did not do the job in the last financial crisis for many reasons.

Modern Portfolio Theory (MPT) previously has provided the most common approaches to risk management for many years. Its advocacy of diversification of asset classes and securities as a way to reduce investment volatility seemed to work for a long time at least to some degree, but failed to deliver acceptable results for many portfolio investors following its passive allocate-buy-and-hold message in the global financial crisis (GFC).

In this latest (but far from last) crisis, however, the correlation of most asset classes (bonds being an exception) went to 1.0 (i.e., proved to be highly correlated and all trending in the same direction at the same time) so there was, unfortunately, almost nowhere for investors to hide.

MPT also didn't predict the magnitude of the potential losses in a diversified and, theoretically, optimized risk-return portfolio under different extreme scenarios. In fact, because of its normal distribution probability model, it probably provided false comfort that a large drop in markets was so improbable as to be nearly impossible. But the nearly impossible happened, and many families paid dearly for their unfounded assumptions.

Some portfolios were ravaged by broad market declines and the failure of risk management systems, such as they were.

In many countries, these problems were exacerbated by plunges in housing prices and commodity prices. At the time of writing, the major economies' stock markets are just now reaching the peaks of 2007 again and the return on equities over the decade in many major markets was close to zero. Depending on the country, it was the worst decade since the 1930s.

Black Swan Events

The recent crisis also highlights that not all changes are predictable and that no simple model of investment works in all seasons and circumstances.

Nassim Nicholas Taleb, author of *The Black Swan: The Impact of the Highly Improbable*, similarly rejects a simple reliance on traditional investing models and a limited definition of risk as volatility.

Taleb's thesis is that "black swan" events are likely to occur with increasing regularity, due to the global financial integration of today's world. Black swan events in the economic arena are rare, like the bird itself, but exert a significant impact; despite their importance, their rarity and unique nature make them difficult to predict in advance. He believes that these types of catastrophic events have a much greater impact on financial markets and the broader world of human affairs than we usually suppose.

The challenge of wealth preservation for a wealthy family is, at its core, the successful management of risk. A good plan is a good start, but an expanded awareness of risk in the investing environment, tight performance monitoring, and effective risk management are important disciplines to ensure that the plan stays on track and the desired results are in fact achieved over the long term.

What Is Risk?

There are many different definitions of risk: volatility, permanent impairment of capital, underperformance, absolute loss, loss of purchasing power, failure to meet a specific objective or protect capital, and other variations referring to goals both absolute and relative.

Volatility is the most common definition of risk in the investment industry, but volatility is actually not always the principal risk factor or concern for wealthy families. For example, if a family knows it has enough money on hand to meet all of its shorter-term objectives and the luxury of time to allow assets to grow to meet the family's longer-term objectives, then the volatility of prices of publicly traded assets will not be a major concern.

Private investors are thus rightly searching for a new way to think about risk and ways to protect themselves and their capital going forward. Investors have paid a steep price to learn that it is not just volatility that should be a signal for concern, but rather the real possibility of permanent impairment of capital.

The definition of risk for a family is a very personal and specific exercise, and for many families of different levels of wealth, the best definition of risk may simply be "not being able to meet your goals" or "not having the money to do what you want to do, when you want to do it."

Because of recent experience and resulting dissatisfaction with volatility as a sole risk measure, some investors have started to reset priorities on their goals and redefine their concept of risk. Examples might include:

- Not losing more than 10 percent of liquid wealth.
- Not risking the loss of a family estate or legacy assets.
- Not losing the business.
- Not having to reduce family lifestyle.

Many families will also allocate capital to safer assets to protect their highest-priority goals.

For other families, lower-priority goals become optional. Achieving those goals may depend on the growth of the business or of the investment assets. In fact, investors emerging bruised from the GFC are realizing that investment management and risk management are, in fact, one and the same thing.

The Evolution of Risk

Most entrepreneurs and business owners took significant risk to start or build their business. They may have used substantial leverage and their net worth was likely highly concentrated in one place (the business), both of which would have made them vulnerable to adverse market and economic conditions if pursued in the capital markets as an investment strategy; but that concentration and leverage was what helped them create substantial wealth in the first place.

Wealth management is different. The goal of wealth management is usually to preserve and manage assets to ensure that they meet family goals and objectives, and are not unduly vulnerable to undue risk of any kind. There is normally a significant capital preservation element in liquid wealth management, since the family probably does not want to have to start the wealth creation process all over again, realizing how rare are the successes in business that can generate a substantial fortune.

As such, concentrated and high levels of risk, which were the companion of the entrepreneur, become the adversary of the investor.

Financial Risks

Investors face a wide range of risks, all of which must be managed based on the investor objectives, risk tolerance, and investment policy. Key risks include:

- *Systemic risk.* The risk of the banking system or monetary system "melting down," or at least allowing a number of major financial institutions to fail, could raise major issues of economic survival under the most extreme of assumptions.
- *Macroeconomic and currency risk.* Recent years have shown how linked national and international macroeconomics (including currency) are. Understanding and acting on these high-priority risks is an important part of risk management.
- *Concentration risk.* One of the major issues faced by entrepreneurs and following generations arises when an operating business, property asset, or concentrated single stock position plays such an enormous role in a family portfolio that it dominates the family balance sheet and requires the special attention of both family and advisors to appropriately manage it.
- *Business risk.* This includes basic business operational risks, family dynamics related to the business, business succession, taxation, and other strategic and technical risks.
- *Leverage risk.* Portfolio leverage, whether at a family holding level, in fund positions, or in related financial structures, can be a major source of unmanaged risk. Leverage can enhance returns dramatically but does so only at the cost of creating risk.
- *Reporting and control risk.* A failure to capture the full set of relevant economics and act on information received can also create substantial risks. Uncontrolled trading losses at investment banks and similar episodes in other areas show how a risk policy, even if somewhat onerous at times, can preserve a fortune that might otherwise have fallen prey to traders or managers acting outside of risk guidance and investment parameters.
- *Settlement risks.* Risks associated with closing a transaction and receiving payment.

- *Custodial risk.* Potential loss due to inadequate safeguards of assets and documents.
- *Liquidity risk.* The possibility, all too real for many investors in the GFC, of an inability to sell an asset when desired.
- *Counterparty risk.* The risk that the party on the other side of a transaction may default on a contract or agreement or be unable to fulfill its obligations.
- *Fragmentation or complexity risk.* In some ways the counterbalance to concentration risk mentioned above, having too many investments also carries risk and causes distraction, often spreading management time and capital too thinly.
- *Interconnection and interaction.* One of the major risks that has brought down more than one property empire is the threat posed by cross-collateralization, in which all the assets within a portfolio are interconnected by debt terms, operating agreements, or shared systems so that a shortfall in any one area can bring down the entire group.
- *Tax burdens.* Taxes, whether on income, wealth, capital gains, or inheritance, are one of the greatest sources of loss of family wealth. While always remaining fully compliant, families will need to identify current and future tax policies and stay "ahead of the curve" to avoid paying an enormous penalty for their inattention.

Family Risks

Financial risks are just one component of the risks that wealthy families face. There is a long list of other risks that wealthy families need to integrate into their planning.

- *Family harmony, continuity, and risk.* Any threats to family harmony, unity, and integrated family wealth, such as a potential schism or dispute, marital issue, or litigation, should also be given the utmost and urgent attention due to the degree of risk to the family as a whole.
- *Physical security risk.* Personal safety and freedom from harm, and protection from the potential loss of physical assets to fire or theft, are of increasing concern to families, especially those in higher-risk urban environments. This includes risks

to health, privacy, residential security, contagions, food shortages, kidnapping, and information theft, among others.

- *Ecosystem risk.* Hiring the wrong staff members or advisors can also be a recipe for disaster and a significant risk. "Predators in the ecosystem" are one of the most common causes of catastrophic loss of family wealth, as the clients of Bernie Madoff now know all too well. Ensuring that all selected participants in the ecosystem have a high degree of integrity as well as capability should be a key part of any family's risk management policy and procedures.
- *Longevity and mortality risk.* Outliving your money or dying without a current will and estate plan is a risk to any family and fortune.
- *Key person risk.* The degree of risk will vary depending on the degree of capability, control, and influence the key person has, and how many others have been trained as successors if and when needed.

Having identified and set priorities on expected risks, family leadership must design and put into effect appropriate risk reduction and impact mitigation to ensure that the many potential risks are not allowed to blossom into real disasters for the family.

Figure 11.1 shows a risk matrix provided by the Family Office Exchange, the world's leading network of family offices and their advisors. The four quadrants clearly reflect both the range of risks and the diversity within any one category. Setting priorities on this long list of risk factors is an important element in a successful long-term program to protect, preserve, and enhance family wealth.

Less Stability in the New World Order

This past half-century has been, according to experts, the most peaceful period in the past 140 years. It has also been a period of great abundance and prosperity, supported by the relatively benign political, economic, and even military environment. Now, however, simmering conflicts in southern and eastern Asia, the Middle East, and northern Africa are pushing up the risk indicators dramatically.

Business Ownership and Control
- Family Control
- Family Leadership of Business
- Family Dynamics
- Alignment of Interests
- Business Strategy
- Business Governance
- Business Operations

Wealth Preservation and Enhancement
- Investment Goals and Objectives
- Asset Diversification
- Manager Selection
- Investment Performance
- Public Equity Concentration
- Private Equity Control
- Private Equity Distressed Situations

Shared Risk

Financial Reporting and Compliance
- Legal Exposure
- Fiduciary Roles and Responsibilities
- Wealth Transfer Protection
- Physical Asset Protection
- Financial Leverage
- Financial Oversight
- Financial Reporting/Compliance
- Family Office Oversight

Family Unity and Governance
- Family Legacy
- Philanthropic Legacy
- Family Governance and Decision Making
- Family Relationships
- Family Reputation and Public Image
- Personal Security and Privacy
- Personal Health and Wellness
- Personal Ownership Responsibilities

Figure 11.1 Key Risks Faced by Wealthy Families
Source: Family Office Exchange, 2007.

With more flashpoints surfacing around the world, and a declining Pax Americana to impose order on a more chaotic world, the risk of an event's spilling over into the more negative range of potential outcomes is rising far more than in the past.

A multipolar world, with new actors and institutional roles, will be, by its very nature, less stable and predictable than that prevailing in recent decades.

Government Overspending

The fact that global government spending is out of control will come as no surprise to the intelligent economic observer. Long-term trends of growing government spending as a percentage of gross domestic product (GDP) have been visible for 50 years, and recent patterns only accelerate that long-standing drift.

Implications for investors are many: interest rates, inflation, currency pair movements, tax rates, infrastructure development

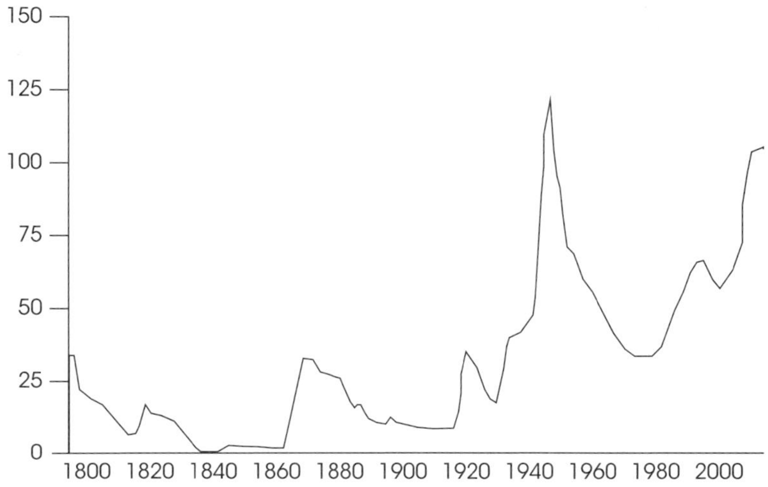

Figure 11.2 U.S. Gross Federal Debt as a Percent of GDP
Source: Office of Management and Budget, U.S. Government.

(employment creation), health care burdens, and other factors will be deeply affected by this seemingly irreversible pattern of near-permanent deficits.

The United States, as but one example, currently taxes at 17 percent of GDP and spends at 23 percent, with little evidence of meaningful deceleration or decline in long-term spending rates. Total U.S. debt (as shown in Figure 11.2) currently amounts to $16 trillion, close to 100 percent of GDP, an astounding number that rises even further to above $60 trillion once off-balance-sheet liabilities for Medicare, Medicaid, and Social Security are taken into account.

In western Europe, Japan, and many other regions, governments have reached—and even exceeded—the normal limits of borrowing. They are now having to scale back social programs, restructure sovereign debt, and review the sustainability of their economic models going forward.

Tax Climate Heating Up

Taxes will, in all likelihood, need to increase and may target the rich more aggressively as the wealth gap widens and the concentration of wealth becomes more visible (Figure 11.3).

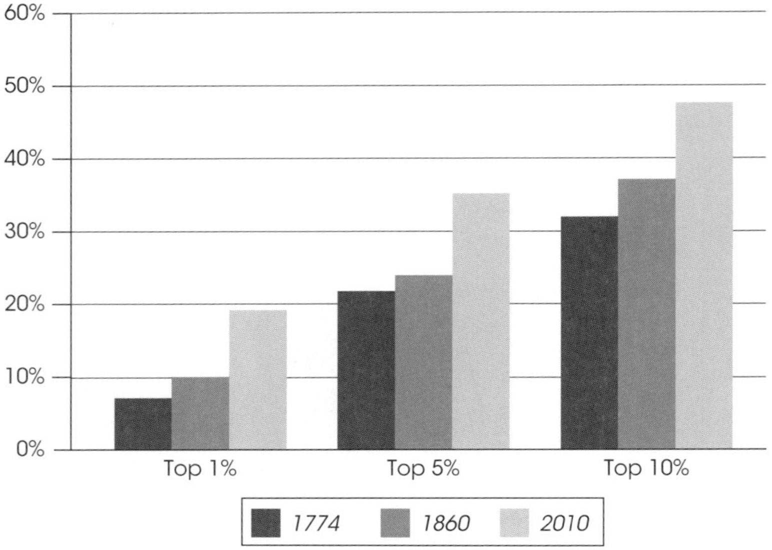

Figure 11.3 U.S. Income Distribution, 1774, 1860, and 2010
Sources: Peter H. Lindert and Jeffrey G. Williamson, "American Incomes 1774-1860," NBER Working Paper No. 18396, September 2012 (Cambridge, MA: National Bureau of Economic Research); Piketty and Saez, 2012.

More stringent enforcement, along with higher rates, is appearing on the horizon, as governments target avoidance (legal planning) as well as evasion (illegal nonpayment of taxes) as moral hazards in their strained economy.

The growing adoption of GAAR (general anti-avoidance rules) also casts a wider net for tax revenues.

French marginal tax rates on the wealthy proposed to be boosted by the new government to 75 percent in 2012, triggering an exodus of a few of its wealthier citizens to more welcoming tax jurisdictions.

Other countries in Europe have recently set, or are already imposing, a top band of 50 percent on worldwide income, which is supplemented by the value-added tax (VAT), fuel tax, property taxes, and local community charges, among others.

While many long-term trends and their attendant risks can be understood and prepared for, others, such as rising taxes and physical security concerns, will need to be managed in an environment of growing instability, unpredictability, and constantly evolving risk.

The Ultimate Safety Strategy

The New Zealand (or Equivalent) "Bolthole"

Over the years, and accelerated in times of crisis, the more concerned (some would say paranoid) investors prepare carefully for worst-case economic and political scenarios.

This means moving some portion of assets to safe jurisdictions and safe physical locations, being prepared to continue to operate in the wake of a banking system collapse, and providing easy access to food, water, and shelter in a place far from likely areas of political, military, or civil conflict.

The elements of this strategy can be made up of positions as follows:

- *A safe and accessible place.* Residence in a neutral country distant from potential conflict. This could include New Zealand, a Pacific island, or, somewhat creatively, northern Canada or Scandinavia. This strategy is sometimes referred to as a "bolthole" or "a place of escape or refuge." Safe shelters from nuclear blast, environmental disasters, chemical or biological warfare, and other such unpleasant future events may also be required for maximum safety.
- *Well-stocked for survival.* Needless to say, any special shelter will need to have its own supply of food and water for an extended stay by a defined set of family members and support team. Larger crises will require access to an operating farm with abundant reserves of its own water, and with a capability to farm livestock and provide adequate grain, fruit, and vegetable crops.
- *Cash and gold.* Keeping some reserves of cash in the local currency, in dollars and in Swiss francs, provides a back-up reserve in case of a banking system failure or inability to access wealth held by banks or similar institutions. Gold for bolthole purposes should be in coin form, not bullion (as it is hard to go to the supermarket in a dire post-meltdown apocalyptic scenario and shave off a bit of a bullion bar to pay for groceries). Gold as an ultimate fallback reserve of monetary value should be kept in a safe storage facility, available 24/7 in a location entirely independent of the banking system.
- *Multiple locations.* One of the main principles of risk management boils down to the old adage "do not put all of your eggs

(*continued*)

in one basket." While expensive and onerous to set up, having more than one bolthole may make sense in case there is an unexpected problem in accessing or protecting one particular space. One billionaire, particularly sensitive to global risks of all kinds, has five such locations scattered around the earth.

- *Multiple citizenships.* Prudent wealthy families may want to keep their options open by having multiple passports. Restrictions on freedom or capital may cause a family to move from a home jurisdiction. It may be helpful to have another jurisdiction and/or home to go to on a moment's notice. Other factors such as location, tax regimes, livability, ease of access, and the ability to acquire a passport will play into these decisions as well. Countries like Canada, Singapore, New Zealand, and some Caribbean islands often stack up well, depending on the priority factors of a given family and its members.
- *Luck and human limitation.* Although not part of the specific elements of this strategy, luck can, as ever, determine the outcome of any strategy no matter how well a plan is designed and implemented. An apocryphal story describes the result achieved by one far-sighted risk-managing individual. Having foreseen the darkening clouds of war gathering over Europe and Asia in the 1930s, he analyzed all of the options for likely safety and picked what seemed to be the ideal location to avoid the coming wars. Unfortunately, his choice of a tiny remote Pacific island as his refuge—Iwo Jima—was not, in the end, the best choice.

As they say, "Man plans, God laughs. . . ."

The Starter Kit: Four Basic Principles of Risk Management

While the management of risk can be highly complex, it is instructive to start with the basic principles that underlie all risk-management related activities before venturing into the inevitable intricacies of execution. The four seminal tenets are as follows:

1. *Have a realistic plan and stick to it.* One of the most effective ways for wealthy families to manage and mitigate risk is to

have a realistic plan and stick to it. For many families, developing realistic goals and how much is "enough" is one of the most powerful risk management tools. Once a plan has been put in place, it requires a strong framework, along with discipline and good counsel to stick with it when investor emotions are tested. When there are no specific investment goals in place, most investors are simply tempted to reach for "more." This can push them further out the risk spectrum, often at exactly the wrong time.

2. *Diversify*. The successful long-term investor John Templeton called diversification the "cornerstone" of every investment and risk management program. Diversification is a central element in risk management because it spreads the risk among many different asset classes and securities on the assumption that if one declines, at least some of the others will not, and an overall portfolio will buffer the downturn in one area by more solid performance elsewhere. Many families hold very undiversified portfolios, given the relative size and location of their operating business and the concentration of other investments they hold, often focused in the same industry or even geographic region.

> *More money has been lost reaching for yield than at the point of a gun.*
>
> *Investment manager Raymond DeVoe*

   It is worth mentioning that investors should be careful not to diversify beyond what is necessary for proper risk management, as this may create diversification into mediocrity, increase complexity, and provide a false sense of real diversification away from general market risks that can cause permanent capital loss.

   For instance, many real estate business owners also buy real estate investments, and many resource entrepreneurs buy primarily resource stocks. It is important for families to diversify their portfolio exposures into multiple asset classes, economic and financial markets, and geographic regions.

   Bonds, despite their low current returns, have also been beneficial to portfolio diversification and are particularly important to fund near-term family goals but, given the low current yields, are not the portfolio staple they have been in the past. Real estate, private equity, timber, and emerging markets have all at various times provided some level of diversification. Diversification for a global investor can also include diversifying the type and location of asset structures, currencies, counterparties, advisors, and other essential elements of a family's wealth.

Different styles of management (e.g., value, growth, momentum) can also help increase diversification as can investing in various regions around the world (e.g., developed vs. emerging and frontier markets).

Diversification is much more difficult in today's world, with the extreme correlation of securities and asset classes in adverse markets and the strong linkages among global markets. This simply increases the challenges for family investors and requires new and creative approaches to find diversification in nontraditional ways.

3. *Plan for multiple scenarios.* While a good plan will provide valuable guidance, all will never go entirely according to that plan. Changes in the family and the financial world are continuous and unpredictable; new risks and unforeseen challenges are inevitable. What wealthy families need to know is what the implications of the inevitable setbacks are likely to be under differing scenarios, how severe the impact will be, how much flexibility they will have, how they will be able to respond, and at what point their goals will be in jeopardy.

   Monte Carlo simulations and other scenario-based models can be used to lay out a wide range of potential investment return scenarios and to incorporate low-probability, high-impact events (fat tails and black swans) into the core asset allocation and investment model.

   One of the key pieces of information gleaned from a scenario-planning exercise is the degree of flexibility (i.e., risk capacity) a family has. In other words, how close to the line are they living? If one significant assumption changes, what other options will they have to meet their goals, or will they have to defer and abandon one or more of their goals?

   The factors that add flexibility to an investor's situation include a large amount of surplus capital, some of their goals being categorized as optional, and intentionally conservative assumptions (which should lead to fewer negative surprises).

Scenario planning is one of the important tools in the risk management toolbox. It helps families to envision and plan for the future and not be caught off-guard by the changes and hazards that will inevitably emerge over time.

4. *Control what an investor can control and conservatively estimate the rest.* Investors face a world full of unknowns that can play havoc with their plans and aspirations. Investment returns are unknown, future trends in inflation are uncertain, correlation among asset classes is a moving target, and the level of market volatility is, well, volatile.

> *The essence of risk management lies in maximizing the areas where we have some control over the outcomes, while minimizing the areas where we have absolutely no control over the outcomes.*
>
> *Peter Bernstein,* Against the Gods

Obviously, some investments are more predictable than others. A five-year bond ladder is more predictable than a portfolio of equities. Dividends are more predictable than capital gains. This does not mean that investors should not have expectations for their investments. All investment plans will require some element of forecasting, with the proviso that many asset classes and individual investments are notably difficult to assess in determining when and how returns are delivered.

Importantly, however, if the timing of the expected returns does not match with the timing of the family's spending needs, there may be a significant problem as a result of the mismatch.

What Cannot Be Controlled?

There are many factors investors cannot control. They include:

- *Investment returns.* A large percentage of the activities of the investment and wealth management industry focus on forecasting near-term investment returns despite substantial evidence that this is difficult, if not impossible, to do consistently.

- *Black swans and major disasters.* These "one off" and big-impact negative events can have significant implications for families and investors, but they usually come as a surprise.
- *Inflation and economic growth.* Investors have no control whatsoever over inflation (which affects the costs of things they buy) and economic growth (which can affect the success of their business and investments), both of which can have a significant impact on their wealth management plans and achievement of their goals.

> *Investors are hopeless at forecasting, yet it remains at the heart of the investment process.*
>
> *James Montier, Grantham Mayor Otterloo*

- *Tax rates and regimes.* Investors know what current tax rates are but cannot control what the tax regimes and enforcement protocols will be in the future.
- *Longevity.* While actuarial tables can tell how long the average person will live, it is very rare for anyone to know the specific longevity of any living individual with certainty.

Logic dictates that that the wise risk management route is to use conservative estimates in planning models for the factors that cannot be controlled. Positive surprises are rarely a problem, but negative surprises can wreak havoc on family plans.

What Can Be Controlled?

There are also factors investors can control. They include:

- *Tax management.* Every dollar saved in taxes goes into the pocket of the investor; in that way, it is a "certain" additional return with no added risk (an infinite Sharpe ratio). There are a number of ways to save taxes depending on the family's jurisdiction and tax regime, including income splitting, trust and other tax structuring, deferral of taxable gains, and the use of tax-effective products, among others.
- *Costs.* Every dollar saved in costs also goes into the pocket of the investor; it pays to minimize costs wherever it makes sense. This may include reducing investment management fees, trading, custodial and advisory costs, and transaction fees.

In a low-investment-return environment, managing taxes, costs, and risks can have a significantly positive impact on the net investment return available to the family. Other, at least somewhat controllable, factors include the following:

- *Family expenses and distributions.* Some expenses are completely optional; other expenses can be cut back as needed or assets (like personal residences) that require constant maintenance costs and tax payments can be sold. While not pleasant, expense and distribution control is a risk management tool families can, and may even be forced, to employ.
- *Asset allocation.* Investors are able to control how they invest their portfolios and what expected risk they take on.
- *Conservative assumptions.* As mentioned above, investors can make conservative assumptions on the noncontrollable aspects of their lives. This knowledge and management can reduce the risk of negative surprises.
- *Diversification.* A diversified portfolio is an important risk mitigation tool and is another factor the investor can control.
- *Behavioral risk management disciplines.* While investors cannot control the returns their investments provide, they can exercise some control over the way they themselves respond. Tools such as a written wealth plan and an investment policy can provide much-needed self-discipline that can help save the portfolio from the effects of rash and unwise reactions, as can the objectivity of a qualified, independent advisor.
- *Tactical tools.* Similarly, the many tactical tools to manage risk—puts, calls, insurance, synthetic puts, stop losses, rising floors, floors, sales triggers, and other approaches—can help to manage a risk once identified and quantified.
- *Years of work or timing of business sale.* Families normally have some control over how long they work and bring in income or when they sell the family business. The timing of cash flows can be an important risk management tool for any investor and can usually be controlled, at least to some extent.
- *Leverage.* Families can control the level of debt they take on. Debt can provide important leverage for growth but can also restrict investors' options in difficult times when liquidity and flexibility are required.
- *Complexity and illiquidity.* While complex and illiquid investments can provide additional returns where the investor understands the investment details and is comfortable not

having access to the cash, complexity also has costs. These include additional fees, extra due diligence, distraction, and an inability to make high-quality decisions when required under time pressure.

Investors almost always have some degree of control over these and other key decisions, and can set their risk levels according to their risk definition, family goals, and their investment and risk policies.

Welcome to Risk Management 2.0

Dr. Erwann Michel-Kerjan

As recently as a few years ago, few world leaders would have pegged the accelerating rhythm of large-scale catastrophes as one of the biggest economic challenges in the foreseeable future. But one of the hallmarks of this new century will be more and more such unthinkable events, previously unseen contexts, and pressure for individuals, private companies, and government authorities to react extremely quickly, even when they cannot predict the cascading impact their actions will have. The GFC is just the latest—and perhaps most devastating—illustration of incredible consequences of myopic behaviors.

Don't think only financial crisis, but also food and energy security, intercontinental pandemics, megaterrorism, and new war type; think worldwide global warming and large-scale natural disasters, to name just a few. In the first few years of the twenty-first century, the world has faced a string of catastrophes of a totally new dimension. For instance, if you consider the 20 most costly insured catastrophes in the world since 1970, more than half of them have occurred in the last decade.

And this trend toward more catastrophes will continue, in large part because of hyperconcentration of population/value in high-risk areas, climate change, and because globalization is making the world much more interconnected than ever before.

In order to do a better job at preventing or mitigating the cost of future disasters, there is an urgent need to better understand the new risk architecture. There are six defining features of the new world of risk we live in:

1. *Extreme cost/extreme benefits.* There will be a much wider variance in possible losses and gains. The events in the past decade in the United States have translated into

unprecedented economic consequences. It might be difficult to imagine that when Hurricane Hugo hit the country in 1989, it was the first catastrophe to inflict more than $1 billion of insured losses. But times have changed. Hurricane Katrina in 2005 killed 1,300 people and forced 1.5 million people to evacuate the affected area—a historic record for the nation. Economic damages are estimated in the range of $150 billion.

With increasing urbanization and concentration of social and economic activities in high-risk areas, costs of catastrophes will continue to increase. It is also no wonder that new business opportunities around catastrophes are proliferating with a huge growth in catastrophe bonds (cat bonds), which are financial instruments transferring catastrophe exposure to investors in the financial markets.

2. *Confusing distribution of the roles and responsibilities of the public and private sectors.* In almost all catastrophes that occurred in the past 10 years, it has been almost impossible to dissociate the economics of catastrophe management from politics, which contributes to a fuzzy distribution of the roles in preparing against future disasters.
3. *Growing interdependencies/globalization.* We are becoming more dependent on each other. At the annual meeting of the World Economic Forum in Davos in 2007, former British prime minister Tony Blair stated that "interdependency is the defining element of the twenty-first century." While this is not totally new, we have reached a degree of interdependence that no other society has experienced before us. What happens on one continent today can affect those on another continent tomorrow. Certainly the most illustrating example is the Pan Am 103 catastrophe, where an uninspected bag containing a bomb was placed on Malta Airlines at a small unsecured airport in Malta, transferred in Frankfurt to a Pan Am feeder line, and then loaded onto Pan Am 103 in London's Heathrow Airport. Pan Am 103 crashed over Lockerbie, Scotland.
4. *Change in scale from local to global risks.* One of the consequences of these increasing interdependencies is that disasters and crises are likely to affect a higher number of people. Dealing with large-scale disasters is much more challenging than dealing with a series of local small accidents. Resources and collaborative effort needed simultaneously are not simply

(*continued*)

cumulative but exponential. Furthermore, global response and global reaction capacity are needed. Multinational coordination becomes critical. Another important element is how information is shared on a larger scale and among many more stakeholders whose actions are ultimately likely to affect the level of loss.

5. *Speed/just-in-time society.* The development of rapid transportation and cheap communication has created a "just-in-time" society. People and products are moving faster and faster from one part of the globe to the other. While this provides a wide range of positive returns, there is also a flip side: Risks are more likely to spread across the globe very rapidly. Thanks to jet travel, for instance, viruses now fly business class, too, so a pandemic starting in Asia today might very well spread extremely rapidly. The just-in-time society also puts pressure on us to make decisions faster than before, without necessarily taking the time to adequately measure the possible effects these actions will have on others and in the long run.
6. *Uncertainty, if not ignorance.* A lot of research has been devoted in the past decades to decisions under uncertainty, and the preceding features create an unprecedented environment in which assessing risks becomes more difficult. We were trained to solve problems with clear questions and clear scientific knowledge. Knowing the risk profile, we made investment decisions. But historic data does not shape the future any more, given how rapidly the world is changing. We move from risk to uncertainty or even pure ignorance. This is, of course, a major challenge.

The general surprise that came with the series of catastrophes and crises that have unfolded one after another over the past few years—including the GFC—reminded me of excerpts of *The Plague*, the famous novel written some 60 years ago by French author, journalist, and Nobel laureate Albert Camus: "There have been as many plagues as wars in history, yet always plagues and wars take people equally by surprise."

Welcome to Risk Management 2.0.

Dr. Erwann O. Michel-Kerjan is the managing director of the Wharton Risk Management and Decision Processes Center at the University of Pennsylvania, and he teaches Value Creation in the Wharton MBA program in Philadelphia, Pennsylvania. He is an authority on managing the risks, financial impact, and public policy challenges associated with catastrophic events.

IMPERATIVE 3

SET A LONG-TERM FAMILY WEALTH STRATEGY AND DEFINE THE ASSET ALLOCATION MODEL

CHAPTER 12

The Elements of Long-Term Strategy

A long-term strategic wealth plan is the map for the family's investing journey. Such a plan helps the family think through the reasons for the structure and allocation of its wealth, provides clear guidance and direction for the future, offers protection from the behavioral biases that challenge all investors (especially during a crisis), and is a valuable tool for keeping a wealth management plan on track.

Yet that long-term plan also needs to be flexible and adaptable; it needs to be reviewed and adjusted regularly based on changes in the external environment and as needed as the family evolves. Nothing is fixed forever. The realities of the world as they unfold are often different from the ones envisaged when the plan was conceived.

Focused yet flexible may be the watchwords of long-term family investment success.

Components of the Plan

While there are many ways to approach wealth planning, regardless of the actual framework employed, the following components should be present in almost any wealth plan:

- The family context, including philosophy, vision, and values.
- Family goals and financial objectives.
- Family balance sheet analysis.
- Definition of risk and approach to risk management.

- Cash flow forecast and scenario analysis.
- Family elements of long-term strategy.
- Economic and financial market perspectives.
- Asset allocation and investment policy.
- Asset classes and investment tactics.
- Operational considerations.
- Tax and structure elements.
- Family financial ecosystem and advisor selection.
- Performance reporting and cost management.

An Integrated Framework

Managing money is a complex task. It requires mastery of a process that begins with an understanding of the investor's personal profile and overall investment objectives, and ends with disciplined investing, tight reporting, and control to ensure that the original objectives are being met throughout all stages of that process.

Successful family wealth management also requires an understanding of asset allocation, the behavioral characteristics of all asset classes under different market scenarios, investment selection, advisor management, and the addressing of a whole set of integrated elements including tax issues, estate plans, spending and distribution strategies, and risk management.

Pursuit of a predetermined set of investment goals, within the policies and parameters established by the family, can best take place in a framework, which systematically addresses every stage of the investment process and keeps the process on track to accomplish its original objectives.

A well-conceived family wealth framework embraces both family and financial matters, including an allocation model that is family-centric, goals-based, both top-down and bottom-up, and balances historical learning, and combines all of these factors to form a sensible forward-looking risk and return perspective.

The integrated framework described earlier creates a structure that can highlight the areas of long-term strategy (LTS) to be addressed in the LTS document. The illustration of this concept can be found in Chapter 1, where it shows the multiple components that need to be included in an integrated family framework.

The framework must make sense in the near term but also be positioned for the very long term, and even multigenerational time frames. It also has to be robust enough to hold firm through various challenges the family will face, yet flexible enough to adapt as the world changes. As such, it needs to be reviewed and adjusted on a regular basis to take into account changing objectives, shifts in capital markets, and reflect new developments and understandings.

Integrated Wealth Management

Integrated wealth management ensures that decisions are not made in isolation, but rather are made with the full knowledge of the family's overall perspective and all of the individual components that could influence their financial situation. Components of integrated wealth planning include:

- *Family goals.* Determination of family goals and objectives, across a range of stakeholders and generations.
- *Tax planning.* Structuring the family's financial affairs to ensure that they are tax effective.
- *Estate planning issues.* Passing wealth across generations in a tax-efficient manner that meets the family's dynastic objectives.
- *Financial planning.* Ensuring that the family's cash flow needs will be met both on a current and future basis.
- *Investment management.* Building and managing an investment portfolio that will the meet objectives of the family for income, growth, and preservation of wealth.
- *Family governance, education, and harmony.* Ensuring that the family is properly structured and has the skills to meet its objectives and to preserve strong family bonds.

Starting with High-Level Family Objectives

The first step in the plan lies in understanding the family's context and specifically calculating investment goals and cash flow needs. The lifetime-legacy approach, discussed earlier, may be a helpful tool for allocating and setting priorities on the goals the family wants to fund.

A family's lifetime requirements include funds that are intended to be spent during a current lifetime. Normally, these commitments are ones that the family has decided that they do not want to put at risk. As such, many families will choose to assign relatively safe assets to meet these very certain commitments.

The balance of the wealth, after all lifetime commitments have been looked after, is essentially legacy money—assets that will usually serve the purpose of funding the needs of children, charities, and future generations.

Legacy goals are the longer-term objectives, normally enduring after the deaths of the patriarch and matriarch. They can more often be funded with riskier, more growth-oriented assets due both to the long time periods until the funds are needed and the optional nature of many legacy goals.

Any long-term plan will require families to assign priorities to both lifetime and legacy objectives and then determine how much and what types of assets should be used to fund the particular goals in question.

For instance, if a family is planning to pay for a generation of education for all grandchildren in the next five years, or are planning to have capital available to fund a daughter's new business, it would not be appropriate to have too many assets locked up in illiquid, no-yield private equity investments.

The asset liquidity and income generation should be appropriate to the family's liabilities and commitments or spending intentions. Near-term and high-priority lifetime requirements should be matched with near-term and certain assets. For very near-term liabilities, families may want to allocate assets that are both liquid and safe, such as cash and treasuries.

For longer-term lifetime commitments that are still high priority, but not imminent, high-quality developed market dividend-paying stocks that will build value over a long time period might be the most appropriate investment. Because they will not be needed to fund a specific commitment in the short term, the investor can weather the volatility that typically comes with a higher-return/higher-risk asset like equities.

Some families will choose to immunize completely all of the lifetime assets with a laddered bond portfolio. In that way, they can reduce worry substantially, knowing that all of their most important lifetime commitments will be met. A family with $1 billion net worth may choose to allocate "just" $75 million to fixed income to ensure that all of their lifestyle, housing, education, and charitable expenses are covered during their lifetime.

An Engineering Issue

Portfolio management is neither art nor science.

It is instead a very special problem in engineering, of determining the most reliable and efficient way of reaching a specific goal, given a set of policy constraints, and working within a remarkably uncertain, probabilistic, always changing world of partial information and misinformation, all filtered through the inexact prism of human interpretation.

Source: Charles D. Ellis, "Investment Policy: How to Win the Loser's Game," Association for Investment Management and Research, 1994.

Legacy Assets

Legacy assets can be thought of differently from lifetime assets. They generally have a much longer time frame and can therefore be invested with expectations of relatively higher return, depending on what the family's legacy goals are and how much risk they are willing to accept.

The family will then need to decide how much of their funds should be allocated to legacy assets in trust for future generations and what should be considered as a lifetime pool of assets available for the use of the current generation. The decisions and allocations within the framework will vary depending on the market conditions and changes in the family circumstances, but the framework itself will be appropriate for all seasons, as it is based on and consistent with the fulfilment of the full set of the family's articulated goals.

Cash Flow Forecast

A cash flow forecast is the next step in the development of the plan. It puts meat on the bones of the family's goals and calculates where, how, and when they are likely to generate and deploy their cash flow in the future. Because the future is never clear, any forecast needs to make use of assumptions and those assumptions need to be reasonable.

Expectations will typically include such factors as anticipated inflation (particularly on the goods and services the family is most likely to consume), changes in spending levels, potential large inflows or outflows of capital, tax rates, future family size, retirement ages, and mortality dates. Unless all of the family's goals are to be funded out of employment income, investments will normally be called upon to carry some of the burden of funding the family goals and commitments over time.

The cash flow analysis will demonstrate what rate of return the family will require on its capital to fund the family's various objectives—described as the required rate of return (RRR). This iterative process will also give rise to other investment issues that need to be addressed in the portfolio, including the degree of liquidity required, the amount of regular income expected from the portfolio, the timing of the distribution needs, and degree of focus on capital preservation and risk.

It is important to start with realistic family income and expense projections. This kind of fact-based decision making will help to determine the needs of the family and ultimately the required asset mix.

The Core Role Played by Cash Flow

It is not always the absolute amount of wealth that should be the family's sole target. Rather, the focus may also be on net cash flow available, and what the money can do for family members.

In that context, there are only four factors that can impact cash flow:

1. Income, from employment, investment, or other sources.
2. Assets that can be sold and converted into cash-flow-generating assets (e.g., sale of a residential property).
3. Expenses.
4. Time (e.g., how long an individual plans to work to generate income or how long the family investment portfolio has to produce returns, and how long the family members will live and require funding).

There are trade-offs among and within the four factors. Employment income diminishes as a working career comes to a close, so investments will be called upon to contribute a higher proportion of the cash flow. If investment income falls, expenses may have to be reduced, or assets may have to be sold to meet commitments.

Other Factors

Of course, there are a number of noninvestment factors that must be taken into account in the development of the investment plan, such as multiple goals with various time frames, tax management, family law issues, residency and citizenship realities, cost bases of specific securities, trust and corporate structures, and investor preferences.

Any of these issues can suggest a change to the investment policy from what might otherwise be expected. For instance, in a jurisdiction with capital gains tax, a family might continue to hold a large position in shares with a low cost base longer than might otherwise be assumed when building a diversified portfolio, due to the large amount of tax payable upon disposition of the shares.

Family investment plans are regularly built to meet the needs of multiple owners, inheritors, and stakeholders, so they will typically try to balance all of those needs as best they can, such as managing the trade-off between the need for income from the portfolio and growth in capital.

Asset Allocation and Long-Term Strategy

Once the asset class universe and the expected returns are determined, the next step is making the allocation decisions among these various asset classes. This will, in large part, determine the return the investor receives on his or her investments and the risk he or she must take to achieve these returns. The more uncorrelated the asset classes are, the lower will be the volatility of the overall portfolio.

Typically, each asset class is assigned a strategic target as a percentage of the portfolio, but the investment manager will also be free to adopt tactical asset allocation ranges and work within the preset range during the year. These ranges provide necessary flexibility in managing the assets for increases or decreases due to:

- Investment performance
- Rebalancing and timing
- Cash and asset inflows and outflows
- Investment ramp-in models
- Flexibility for near-term opportunities to overweight or underweight a particular asset class or individual investment

The output of this phase is a multiyear statement of guidance and direction, within whose parameters and principles the actual investment strategy will be drafted and implemented each year.

Indicative Allocation

The decision to allocate capital to the various asset classes is an important one. The portfolio must be constructed to achieve the RRR for the portfolio, based on the cash flow and growth needs of the family.

Although the precise annual allocations and tactics of investment are covered in the investment policy statement (IPS), the LTS may provide an example or some guidance as to how actual asset allocations may be made over time.

If the investor is taxable, he or she will want to focus on the expected after-tax returns. The RRR also must be accomplished within the risk parameters determined by the family and its advisors, so volatility and quality measures must be considered as well.

Following is an example of the Macdonald family, in which the required rate of return has been calculated as 7 percent nominal and 4.5 percent after expected inflation of 2.5 percent. They and their advisors have estimated the expected rate of return on each of the individual asset classes; the combination of asset classes is built to ensure that target rate of return is likely to be met.

Table 12.1 shows how that weighting allocation among the asset classes translates into the targeted nominal and real returns for the overall portfolio.

Scenario planning models a wide variety of potential capital market and asset class return scenarios, and calculates the expected performance of the portfolio under each of those events. Alternatively, another simpler approach is to assess the impact on the family's goals of various levels of returns (e.g., a 5 percent or 6 percent targeted portfolio return vs. the expected 7 percent).

The goal of scenario planning is to help determine whether the family's priority objectives can still be met under each of those scenarios, and if they need to take other steps to ensure the attainment of their goals.

Those "other" steps family investors can take to manage through the uncertain world of capital markets includes: resetting priorities on goals, allocating safe capital (e.g., fixed income) to fund some of the most important goals, and reducing the potential risk (and likely expected return) of the portfolio to boost the certainty of portfolio return outcomes.

Table 12.1 The Macdonald Family

Asset Class	Weighting	Range	Expected Return	Expected Real Return
Fixed Income	15%	10%–20%	3.5%	1.0%
Dividend Equities	10%	10%–20%	7.5%	5.0%
Equities	10%	0%–10%	8.0%	5.5%
Real Estate	5%	0%–10%	6.0%	3.5%
Infrastructure	5%	0%–10%	8.0%	5.5%
Natural Resources	5%	0%–10%	6.0%	3.5%
Managed Private Equity	0%	10%–20%	10.0%	7.5%
Direct Private Equity	15%	NA	10.0%	7.5%
Family Business	35%	NA	7.0%	4.5%
Total	**100%**		**7.0%**	**4.5%**

Table 12.2 The Bardali Family

Asset Class	Weighting	Expected Return	Current Interest or Dividend Cash Flow	Capital Growth
Fixed Income	20%	2.5%	2.5%	0.0%
Dividend Equities	20%	7.5%	3.5%	4.0%
Global Equities	25%	8.0%	2.0%	6.0%
Real Estate	10%	6.0%	5.0%	1.0%
Infrastructure	10%	8.0%	6.0%	2.0%
Natural Resources	5%	6.0%	0.0%	6.0%
Managed Private Equity	10%	10.0%	0.0%	10.0%
Total	**100%**	**6.7%**	**2.8%**	**3.9%**

Also, the form of the returns can be important. If the family needs a certain level of recurring income, it can be helpful for the portfolio to include assets that spin off regular cash flow, such as fixed income, dividends, or real estate income.

Table 12.2 shows the expected cash flow from a *different* family portfolio (the Bardali family), based on the intended asset allocation, and compares it with the actual cash flow needs of the family. In this family's case, the actual cash flow produced is more than enough to fund the annual family cash flow needs of $500,000.

Most Plans Are Obsolete

When So Much Has Changed, Why Haven't Most Plans?

Even before the recent financial crisis, many financial plans and investment policy statements, even those of the wealthiest, were unrealistic. The problem is now compounded by the combination of a transformed investment world, changing rules of the investing game, shifting risk/return calculations, along with higher tax and operating costs.

Consequently, many plans are not only obsolete when compared to the external environment, but also incapable of meeting investors' most basic and important internal goals.

At stake is whether people will have enough money to live on for the rest of their lives and/or to leave a legacy for future generations and philanthropic causes.

Source: "2020 Vision: The Most Critical Decade." BNY Mellon, 2010, 21.

Keeping Up with the Changes

Things change and so must even the best-laid plans of family investors. For many families, the new lower-return environment has not yet been fully taken into account. Similarly, inflation, even though relatively benign in most of the developed world following the crisis, can still have a deleterious effect on family wealth over the long term.

Planning Constraints

Most families will rely on their investments to meet some or perhaps even all of their spending and capital growth needs. It is usually possible to forecast with some degree of accuracy (using reasonable and conservative assumptions) what the family's cash flow requirements are likely to be and what returns will be required from the portfolio to meet those needs. As mentioned earlier, families may need to set priorities on their goals and focus investments in support of those goals, which is especially relevant in the event that there is insufficient capital to fund them all.

While expected returns on investments are among the most important inputs into investment decisions, they are unfortunately one of the most difficult for investors to forecast. Even professional investors cannot do it with much consistency, as shown in numerous academic papers and studies. Yet it must be attempted (even if the result is a range of expected returns) for investors to have any serious ability to plan for the future.

Many investors use flawed and ineffective methods to determine their investment expectations, including extrapolating current trends, relying on consensus forecasts, and employing historical averages. These approaches, while common, can lead to disaster if the family's investment plan relies too heavily on the accuracy of the forecast.

It may be true that stocks have earned a long-term (80-year) average annual return of 10 percent, but that does not help the family who actually needed the money in the decade of the 2000s when the average annual return was closer to zero (at least in the United States).

CHAPTER 13

Investing for the Future: Mega-Themes and Principled Investment Management

Families have a unique advantage in their ability to invest with greater flexibility for the longer term, compounding returns and taking valuable positions not justifiable by short-term investors held to quarterly performance reporting.

Long-term investing plays a key role in the investment plans of many families, where patient capital can buy opportunistically and wait through cycles to take full advantage of the secular opportunities on offer. One of the target long-term investment areas is "mega-theme" investing in opportunities created by visible patterns and trends in demographics, markets, and sectors.

The list of long-term strategic opportunities in this chapter may help investors to start to think about where and why to invest for the future. There are opportunities to invest in a different manner from the past as well, investing with a sustainable or principled approach that aims at creating results in both the financial and nonfinancial arenas.

Trends and Opportunities

Identifying key global challenges is one thing. Investing in them profitably is another.

There are a number of long-term investment themes that may make sense for investors with the appropriate time frame and staying power. The best opportunities are secular trends, set to run for years, which are not cyclical in nature, not likely to be reversed, and equally unlikely to revert to some past lower mean level of performance.

Even negative societal trends, such as the rise of conflict over water rights, and environmental challenges can provide great investment opportunities. As the trends, emerge and become the subject of regulation (necessitating investment in compliance), and result in targeted government spending or private initiatives, an attractive set of investment opportunities can emerge.

It is not only the areas of concern, such as the environment, obesity, and aging, to cite but a few, but also the areas of natural growth or positive development that can create a situation in which long-term "mega-theme" investing is likely to find fertile ground.

While each sector requires a separate strategy and tactics of participation—geography, asset class, instrument, and timing of investment, for example—selecting certain areas for investment is the first practical step in developing a family's long-term portfolio asset allocation, which address and includes these opportunities.

There is a wide range of potential approaches to each mega-theme area, where the "how" of investing can be as important as the "where" and "why." As with investment in emerging markets or growth economies, there are options to participate directly or through coinvesting in operating companies, through shares and bonds of publicly listed entities, funds, mutual funds, and alternative assets (private equity and hedge funds).

Property investments linked to hospitals, clinics, fitness facilities, nursing homes, and assisted living are also available.

Mega-Theme Opportunities

Although there is a long and interesting list of macroinvestment themes that family wealth managers may consider, there is usually a common set of broad headings within which most families would start in some fashion:

- Asia and the emerging markets.
- Climate change and the environment.
- Resources and energy (including scarce resources such as water).
- Agricultural land.

- Health care, wellness, aging, and obesity.
- Education.
- Direct and coinvesting opportunities.

Asia

Asia, for many good reasons, is one of the mega-themes shared by most family investors around the world.

Asia is home to 60 percent of the world's population, including its two largest countries (by far)—China and India. Asia is also home to over 50 percent of the world's youth, is the destination (mostly China) of a large percentage of emerging market foreign direct investment, and has accounted for a large share of world economic growth over the past decade.

The mission of many investors is to capture, through a variety of vehicles, the consumer growth and infrastructure development opportunities in China and India. Although a sensible position at one level, there is much more to Asia than this strategy might suggest, and there is a broader range of options to be considered than just those presented in these two large markets.

- *A balanced long-term portfolio.* Given the long-term nature of the opportunity, and the lack of large liquid markets in some of the highest-growth countries, a blend of countries (and hence currencies), sectors, and investment classes embracing marketable and nonmarketable positions may be the best way forward.
- *Direct deals.* Although not a part of every portfolio, direct investments in operating companies, or coinvestments with partners into these companies, can be a useful way of investing without paying a stack of fees and participating in the asset classes (property companies, operating businesses, and banks) where the greatest Asian family fortunes have been made.

Asia As an Asset Class?

One family in the United States thinks of Asia as being so important to the future wealth of the family that it merits a relatively large role in their multi-asset-class allocation model, describing it as a special category of attractive "risk-on" growth capital opportunities.

(*continued*)

Asia can also play a distinctive role in a family's nonfinancial activities as well, providing a platform from which a Western family could visit the growing region and "see the future" as an example of economic growth and business success.

By linking investment to an on-the-ground visit at least once per year, if not more frequently, family members of all generations can have a multiple-purpose sharing, informative, and investment-focused experience together.

The Other Emerging Markets

The brightest macroeconomic growth rates, and hence some of the more attractive future investment prospects of the world, are captured in the emerging markets and the commodity markets they serve, or in the manufacture and distribution of products they consume. These trends are likely to continue as countries new and old proceed in their relentless march out of poverty and on to larger roles on the world's economic stage, as shown in Figure 13.1.

Of the world's fastest-growing economies, nearly all were from the emerging markets, also now called "growth economies," with

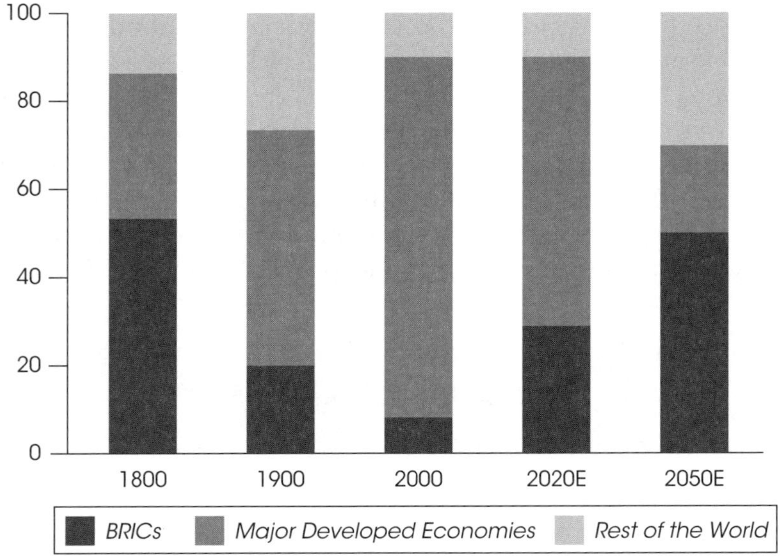

Figure 13.1 Share of Global GDP
Source: OECD, Goldman Sachs Global ECS Research, 2010.

these markets accounting for the majority of world growth and far more than half of the world's population of young people under the age of 25.

Per-capita income gains of the emerging markets also far outstrip the traditional developed countries (see Figures 13.2 and 13.3).

The potential for consumer and infrastructure investments, educational investment, telecoms, transport and logistics, resources, and others are substantial, as are the challenges of getting the right set of markets, individual investments, tactics, and timing. In addition to Asia (economic and population growth, consumption, increased sophistication in most industries), the Middle East (population growth and energy), and Latin America (resources and market development) offer some of the greatest opportunities.

Even more future-oriented investors are looking beyond the rise of the current emerging giants into a future where the youngest populations make up an ever-greater share of the global demand landscape. Countries like Nigeria, Egypt, India, Indonesia, and Ethiopia may be tomorrow's most interesting demand-driven markets, while resource-rich and the agriculturally led countries, some located in a rising African continent, may play a lead role in tomorrow's supply picture.

The African Renaissance Africa, long avoided by international investors as too risky, corrupt, politically unstable, complex and volatile for foreign investment, has become an area of great investor interest. Resource discoveries and developments, coupled with infrastructure investment, education, a reduction in gross corruption, and growing populations have combined to create a situation in which five out of eight of the fastest-growing world economies in 2010 were African.

Its underdeveloped economies and equity markets, where they exist, have provided some exceptional returns in recent years and may continue to do so in the years ahead.

Climate Change and the Environment

As a consequence of this emerging market boom in population and urbanization, the resulting pollution and generation of waste will continue to place great demands on virtually every facet of the environment. Land use, air quality, water availability and quality, and access to other natural resources such as oil, gas, and food supplies,

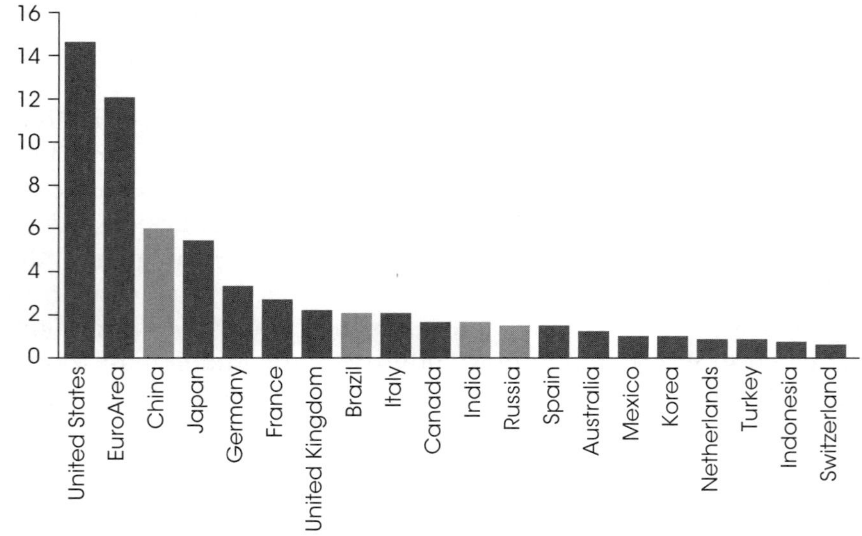

Figure 13.2 GDP by Country, 2010
Source: IMF, GS Global ECS Research.

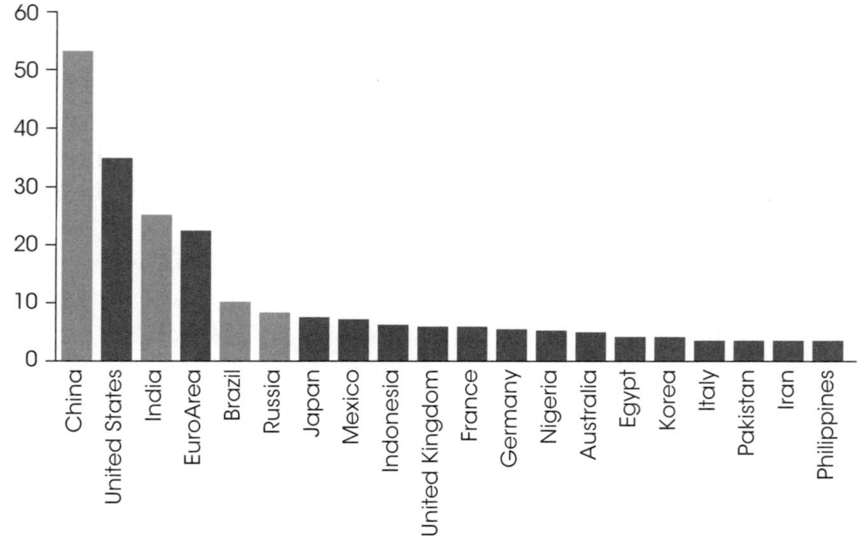

Figure 13.3 GDP by Country, 2050
Source: IMF, GS Global ECS Research.

will rise in importance as demand growth outstrips supply for many scarce resources.

Environmental pressures will only increase as the global population continues to add 100 million new people (net) per year.

As regulatory environmental standards rise and traditional sources of energy become increasingly expensive and dirty, many opportunities emerge in water, alternative energy, air, and other areas.

These investment opportunities, found across the world, can take the form of transportation, packaging, recycling, efficiency equipment, assessment and advisory businesses, engineering services firms, and other facets of the overall theme.

Resources and Energy

World economic growth creates demand for all sorts of commodities—their identification, extraction, processing and transport—across the globe. Oil, gas, iron ore, copper, water, rare earth minerals, hard and soft commodities, and other "factor inputs" are all in demand to fuel current and future demand.

In order to provide domestic heating, air conditioning, and transportation, and to support industrial activity, world energy consumption continues to grow ahead of both population and gross domestic product (GDP).

With increasing scarcity, both natural and politically created, oil, gas, water, essential manufacturing inputs, and other resources are a source of potentially profitable investment in many countries.

For instance, clean water, only available to a privileged segment of the world's population, is already in scarce supply as urbanization, industrialization, and irrigation use place contending claims on water needed for human consumption and efficient management.

Water, hard commodities, and "soft" agricultural commodities are in short supply in many industrial sectors and geographic areas. The so-called CAARB countries/continents (Canada, Australia, Africa, Russia, and Brazil), along with Indonesia and a few other countries, are rich in resources and can present attractive opportunities within the resources theme.

Agricultural Land

As the world's population grows and increasingly wealthier people in the emerging markets join their developed-world counterparts in demanding a greater daily caloric intake and a more resource-intensive diet, the value of agricultural land seems set to increase steadily over time.

While total arable acreage is shrinking, the pressure for higher efficiency in production rises apace, as more and more citizens aspire to an Organisation for Economic Cooperation and Development (OECD) diet characterized by the consumption of more animal protein and packaged foods.

There are many factors contributing to the expectation that agricultural land will increase in value: greater demand for basic products to feed an increasing population, increasing per-capita consumption, inflation-resistant value (even benefiting from inflation as products prices are rising faster than the general rate), secondary demand for many ethanol and biofuel inputs to relieve environmental pressures arising from the continued use of carbon fuels, and other factors.

Opportunities for agricultural sector participation include straightforward land ownership and farming, but also extend into infrastructure (chilled, frozen, and ambient storage and transport), processing, packaging, logistics, and distribution, all of which offer interesting areas for consideration.

Education and Related Activities

Education, particularly in emerging markets, has been in a growth phase for many years. With Asian cultures in particular prizing education highly, commercial educational opportunities in degree-granting schools and institutions of higher learning, tutoring, language schools, online classes, test preparation, technical training, executive education, skills refreshment and certification, and a full range of complementary services from exam grading to outsourced physical education classes will continue to be in demand.

In educationally related sectors, student housing, sports facilities, online learning aids, tutoring, retail, school supplies, testing preparation, catering services, medical services, record keeping, information technology (IT) support, security, and a long list of other areas of profitable growth, businesses also combine to create an interesting global opportunity for themed investment.

Health Care, Wellness, Aging, and Obesity

Along with unfunded pensions and excessive government expenditure above revenues received, the future health care crisis will be a major factor in government obligations, tax demands, economic policy, and investment opportunity (and risk) for decades to come.

Global health care is a growing market of $6.5 trillion, with the family food "health and wellness" budget estimated to reach $663 billion on a full potential basis.*

The health care budget expenditure in the United States is now forecast to grow from 15 percent of GDP in 2000 to over 20 percent by 2020. Global growth is also positive, with forecasts showing an estimated growth from 8.8 percent of OECD GDPs in 2000 to 16 percent by 2020. With advances in medical care, increasing life expectancy, and new models of care for the aged, opportunities can be found in many sectors of the health care market for technologies, products, services, and infrastructure.

Aging and obesity are no longer only a concern for the older Western OECD markets. An epidemic of obesity is increasing health care costs even further; its associated social and other economic impact will also be extraordinary.

Of all countries, to date the United States has the highest rate of obesity. From 12 percent obesity in 1990, estimates have steadily increased, reaching 23 percent in 2005 and 36 percent in 2010.† But obesity is also now a major concern in Europe, the Middle East, and parts of the emerging markets as well. Russia, Japan, China, and India (due to social changes rather than demographic decline) also have dual concerns over rising obesity and the extensive costs related to the care of the aged.

With a global population of obese individuals of 500 million, which has doubled since 1980, Sarbjit Nahal of Bank of America Merrill Lynch Global Research says obesity is "a mega-investment theme for the next 25 years and beyond."‡

The health care and wellness theme is not limited to the care of the ill, overweight, and aged. Healthy lifestyles; fitness facilities; healthy foods and drinks; preventive care; food supplements; "active foods" that, for example, lower cholesterol; monitoring equipment; and other products and services designed to support a healthy and fit lifestyle can also form part of a mega-theme portfolio focus.

---

*Sarbjit Nahal, "Globesity—The Global Fight Against Obesity," Bank of America Merrill Lynch, June 2012, 5.

†"F as in Fat: How Obesity Threatens America's Future," Trust for America's Health, 2012, 3.

‡Nahal, 1.

The New New Thing: Direct and Coinvesting

For a number of reasons, direct transactions by, and coinvestment transactions between, families are becoming increasingly attractive avenues for wealthy families to put some of their money to work.

Direct investment is defined as taking a direct ownership share of an operating company (not through a fund). It may or may not include board representation, and the ownership stake could be either majority or minority.

If such a transaction is taken up in a public company and is arranged through a separate transaction, it would qualify as a PIPE transaction—a private investment in a public equity. Other transactions could take place with unlisted entities for example, in the form of a pre–initial public offering stake in a to-be-listed entity.

Other Opportunities

There is no fixed number of investment macro-themes that can be explored profitably by family investors. "New" opportunities from the past go mainstream, peter out, or evolve beyond recognition. New themes and opportunities will continue to rise and fall in the future, just as they have in the past.

The list and examples presented earlier should thus be considered as only part of a much longer and ever-changing list of potential investment themes and ideas that presents itself at any given moment in time.

This world of new ideas and opportunities is indeed a moveable feast, with attractive ideas and geographies appearing quickly for consideration. Yesterday's BRIC countries are today's MIST: Mexico, Indonesia, South Africa, and Turkey.

Families with particular expertise in, say, property, may find subthemes of particular interest: multigenerational homes in the United States for Asian families or the many variations on the assisted care theme in virtually every market.

Setting Priorities, Exploring Synergies

Identifying the most interesting sectors for family investment is a first step in mega-theme investing, but must be followed by an equal if not more important stage of determining how and when to best participate in the chosen area of activity.

Not all opportunities can be pursued, no matter how attractive they seem, and setting priorities—and possibly grouping investment ideas with synergy or common issues—can make the use of time more efficient and any required analysis more effective.

Principled and Sustainable Investing

One of the major themes in the new world of family investing is a conscious effort to align a family's investment principles with a broader set of values and an engaged societal agenda.

One of the most eloquent summaries of family values that provides a useful high-level guidance for investment, as well as family behavior, comes from Dave Werklund, a thoughtful Canadian businessman and investor whose simple credo states:

> We must respect
> the air that we breathe,
> the water that we drink, and
> the earth that we walk upon.

Redefining Return

In essence, a more principled approach redefines "return" to embrace more inclusive measures of investment performance for both family businesses and family investments, going beyond the financial to embrace impact on the environment, community, and broad societal issues.

This effort to embed a broader agenda in family investment assessment and management, which has been variously defined and described as sustainable investing, venture philanthropy, ethical investing, principled investment management, and philanthrocapitalism, usually incorporates financial, environmental, and community impact in its selection and return criteria.

In some cases, investors are willing to adjust expected financial return to meet more exacting standards of environmental impact or local community engagement. In other cases, investing families stipulate that the broader criteria are not to be allowed to dampen return, insisting both full financial performance and a more principled approach to investment.

Negative Screens

One of the more typical historic approaches to principled investing has been to establish a "negative screen" that automatically excludes investment in sectors considered harmful for the environment, damaging to the community, or dangerous to the consumers of a particular product. The usual exclusions include tobacco, firearms, alcohol, gaming, environmentally damaging extraction or manufacturing businesses, and those businesses dependent on child or enforced labor, or those oppressive to indigenous people.

The standard adopted for private sector investment by the International Finance Corporation (IFC), part of the World Bank organization, provides one set of comprehensive standards, adapted for each industrial sector, which are available for viewing in their current form on the IFC website (www.ifc.org).

Ironically, nuclear energy, once a bugbear of nongovernmental organizations and environmentalists, is now considered by some to be a "clean" energy alternative and an attractive destination for some environmentally sensitive investing families.

In any family, the range of exclusions and standards on investment will be a personal one. Actual approaches vary from full and unfettered *laissez faire* capitalism, to an intermediate "do no harm" policy that excludes a few defined sectors, to a robust "green and sustainable" approach that embraces stringent standards on sustainability and responsibility in every phase of investment and operation.

Beyond the Negative Today, while still using negative screens, many families are embracing a more comprehensive set of values, practices, and approaches that contribute to a more holistic and proactive approach to principled investing, which also aligns a family's investment practices more firmly with its core values and beliefs.

The most advanced thinkers in this space, both family and institutional, take an integrated approach to principled investment. They incorporate ethics and principles in their brand, hiring practices, internal documents and processes, selection frameworks and evaluation criteria, due diligence priorities, monitoring criteria, and governance.

They may insist, for example, on an environmental audit for each direct investment or the establishment and effective operation of a board-level corporate social responsibility committee.

The approach is both quantitative and qualitative, providing actual numbers on a more comprehensive set of metrics and a broader dialogue on issues and ideas not captured in those metrics. Principled investment is thus as much about how a company operates as it is about what it produces, how it sells its products, and with whom it works.

Some businesses, such as those promoting energy recycling, sustainable water use, or farming efficiency in poor countries, can have a direct benefit from the nature of their products and services. Yet principled investing can also include forward-thinking companies in traditionally "dirty" business sectors. Chemical companies, once the arch eco-villains of the business world, are now among some of the most admired businesses in the world on the environmental front.

Green Investing

There are also simple and direct investment vehicles that allow access to green technologies, assets, and services for the concerned family investor. There are many businesses springing up to take advantage of the opportunities presented by global problems in the environment and regulations related to environmental protection. Opportunities include investment in environmental engineering firms that can clean up some of the messes of the past, along with technology businesses and infrastructure projects that can profit from addressing the major environmental risk issues of the future.

Broadly, sustainable or green investment can be divided into two sectors. The first is the technology and service area, populated by companies operating from a lower capital base and profiting from demand growth for consulting services, filter and other technologies, clean air and water products, and other high-growth product and service sectors.

The second area encompasses the large infrastructure projects such as municipal water treatment systems, solar and wind farms, land reclamation and clean up, steel, chemical, automotive, and power plant refitting, and similar major capital-intensive activities.

While many green operating businesses have had a mixed track record from a financial perspective, the additional opportunities, rising demand, more developed industry, and private equity rigors are expected to improve future returns in the sector.

Financial Ethics

In selecting financial advisors, lenders, or asset managers, principle-driven family offices are looking at the financial ethics and values of their advisors as well as their clients and investment practices. The way firms manage their own employees, the clients they select, the products and services they offer, the partners they work with, their reporting and ethical compliance models, and other similar criteria can help to select an appropriate set of advisors.

Although not wishing to be "moral policemen" in the investment world, these families have been able to have a substantial impact by working with, and promoting, those managers and financial institutions with whom they share the greatest overlap of values and approaches.

Rewarding good practice with continuing mandates and relationships is another way of aligning practice in a way to both do well and do good on a larger stage.

There are now many indices and rankings of companies for their ethical behavior. Although not perfect, this new source of information reflects a growing and important trend toward a more ethical way of doing business for all companies, not just those with a specific priority on principled practices.

Stock exchange and regulatory bodies are also falling in line as reporting requirements are moving inexorably toward what used to be known as *triple-bottom-line reporting*, covering financial, environmental, and social elements. This is increasingly adopted by major companies under the Global Reporting Initiative, and is now known more succinctly as *sustainability reporting*.

Broader Definition of Success

A number of family offices have been paving the way at a global level on investment policies that are both financially focused and have a sustainable impact on the environment or local community. The uniquely personal nature of family investment and family organizations, coupled with a natural longer-term concern for future generations rather than a fixation on quarterly investment performance, have led to the development and implementation of sustainable investment strategies by some of the more insightful wealthy families and their family office organizations.

Historically, the approaches to a more sensitive program of investment have embraced *sustainability*, usually related to environmental impact; *responsibility*, usually related to the practices of a business in its markets; and *ethical* investment, limited to a defined set of sectors and specifically precluding investment in others.

Although a number of labels are available to describe such an approach, the term that best captures the sentiment underlying active investment is *principled investment*, which reflects a sound commercial approach plus good business ethics, corporate governance, environmental standards and community impact.

Delivering the Promise of Alternative Investing through Principled Strategies

Stephen J. George

Over the past 30 years, for a generation of investors, most alternative assets have become more efficient and it has become more difficult to invest in traditional assets. Since their genesis as an organized asset class, private equity generated consistent mid-teen returns and distributed capital to investors at a fast pace from 1982 to 2000. Hedge fund strategies generated equity-level returns with lower volatility and muted equity correlations until the Global Financial Crisis of 2008. As more capital flowed into both asset classes, the easy-to-access returns and diversification benefits have dissipated.

Concurrently, in America we have just come through a 30-year period where U.S. interest rates have declined steadily from 14 percent to 1.5 percent, so a major component of diversified portfolios has dwindled down to a negative real (postinflation) return level that will be followed by a phase of rising interest rates, which will produce mark-to-market losses on bond portfolios.

The other major traditional asset class, equities, has seen valuations rise from eight times price-to-earnings in 1982 to more than double that rate. So while equities can be attractive to allocate capital to from time to time, there are fewer tailwinds in the form of expanding price-to-earning and rising profit margins than for the past generation of investors.

Sources of Alpha

The most appropriate investment strategy in this milieu is to focus resources and capital on a range of alternative investments that recognize these constraints. There are several key characteristics that are

(*continued*)

critical in alternative investments in order to deliver on the promise of higher returns than traditional asset classes:

- Theme-based and fundamentally attractive market seams.
- Smaller funds in the range of $150 million to $750 million.
- Flexible mandates that focus on the most attractive risk-reward security in the capital structure.
- High alignment of interest between managers and investors.
- Active and cost-effective coinvestment opportunities.
- Integration of the major themes driving society and our world in the next decades.
- Lower fee structures oriented toward capital growth
- High transparency.

Currently, we believe that there are attractive investment opportunities across several major thematic areas. These themes are less "asset-class" driven and rather more driven by compelling secular and social fundamentals, which create opportunities for investors to provide capital to well-managed companies or assets in the bull's-eye of actual demand by customers.

Some of these themes are set up most appropriately for venture and private equity, while others are well-matched for public strategies; some can be invested in on both the public and private side. In any allocation of capital to alternative investments, it is important to integrate the preferred investment characteristics described earlier with a wider and longer perspective on key societal issues driving global trends, combining a sharp investment eye with a panoramic perspective on the world—through principled investing. By so doing, I believe that investors can identify attractive themes for investment and provide the basis for generating superior long-term returns in alternative investments such as the following:

- Private debt
- Health care and wellness
- Technology
- Energy, efficiency, and sustainability
- Real estate
- Agriculture and renewable resources
- Emerging markets

Favorable Factors

The probability of superior returns is higher when the investment strategy is more nimble and the supply-to-demand of capital ratio is in the investors' (rather than the investees') favor. While there are clearly strong-performing fund managers with many billions under management, the most attractive size for manager allocations appears to be in the $150 million to $750 million range generally, as this is where capital can be deployed to truly proprietary opportunities that are privately negotiated—the essence of private investment markets.

In very large private equity or real estate deals, the process has become efficient and competitive, with capital providers competing on razor-thin elements of differentiation. When deals are smaller, there are fewer capital providers with which to compete, and smaller, nimble funds can find the sweet spot of best return for the risk.

To provide a bit more detail on how to consider principled investing in an investment strategy, here are a few factors that could be included:

- The people, processes, and investments seek to be of uncompromising quality, deeply aligned, ethical, fair, long-term oriented, and not harmful to our world or people.
- Where possible, seek to make investments that are aligned with creating solutions to "big" problems in the world, which can often lead to fundamentally sound, excellent investment opportunities.
- We embrace the belief that the most passionate, committed, and sustainably successful fund managers, companies, and investors consider the wider mission of their activities beyond financial returns alone.
- To be clear, the financial return thresholds during underwriting should not be lowered due to the principled investing objectives; the best investments meet both high financial and principled return and risk standards.
- In its investment process, apply a principled philosophy from sourcing through to all phases and filters in the due diligence phase.
- Beyond the objectives of achieving organizational and financial alignment, specifically investigate the fund manager and their investment thought process on any relevant issues or concerns.

  Examples can include environmental or climate change issues that may exist in an underlying fund and how the managers factor these important societal considerations into investment decisions.
- Investigation of a fund manager or operating team's philosophy and sensitivity to issues of principled investing provides an

(*continued*)

investor with valuable up-front information as to how they are likely to handle future decisions, which is critical in making 10-year-plus financial commitments.

Stephen J. George, CFA, is founder and managing partner of Panorama Point Partners, LLC, an investment firm that specializes in unique alternative investment strategies that integrate some of the most important global mega-themes and principled investment strategies. Stephen has over two decades of investment experience and was the cofounder and chief investment officer over the past decade for Capricorn Investment Group, LLC, a respected private investment firm based in Palo Alto, California.

CHAPTER 14

Long-Term Strategy Document (Example)

Long-Term Strategy (LTS): The Reynolds Family

For the period [Year 1] to [Year 3], but also addressing the next three generations of the family.

The LTS sets out the plan for the management of the family wealth and investments of the Reynolds family and its entities.

- The family context
- Family goals and objectives
- Family balance sheet and SWOT analysis
- Long-term strategy
- Family elements of LTS
- Family financial ecosystem and advisor selection
- Economic and financial market perspectives
- Asset allocation and investment policy
- Asset classes and strategies
- Operational considerations
- Performance reporting and risk and cost management

The Family Context

History

The Reynolds family history stretches back over 350 years in this country. Arriving as early settlors and landowners, the family has grown and spread across the country, with branches now on both the East and West coasts.

Shaped by a Protestant work ethic and a low-key approach to public profile, the family has had a long history of substantial wealth, although rising and falling across various generations, and with the original property and investment wealth spread increasingly broadly across the various branches and members of the family.

With the Reynolds family's passion for aviation and the post-war founding investment in the Reynolds Aviation Group (RAG), the stage was set for the dramatic increase in the family fortune. After an investment by two major private equity houses, an initial public offering, and subsequent recapitalization, the family's holding fell to 22 percent of the business, but leaving a substantial corpus of financial wealth to invest for the purposes of the current and future generations of the family, along with a large philanthropic foundation.

The family asset management business, Artorius Capital, was established in 1996 in order to allow family members to pursue their own interests while ensuring that their very substantial family funds were well-structured and invested wisely in line with long-term family values, principles, goals, and objectives.

Culture

As a result of James's personality and the family's history, the family has benefited from a culture that is hardworking, ambitious, humble, and professional.

Perhaps the most striking element of family culture is a strong value placed on Protestant religious values derived from the family's Unitarian Universalist traditions (honesty, faith, and service to others), formal education, and the arts. This educational tradition and balanced model of life has helped to provide family members with both a balanced and ambitious view of what is possible, both financially and personally.

While the culture is very positive, this plan period will need to focus on embedding that culture more deeply in areas that involve the family, and also in areas that are led by investment professionals.

Values

The family values of central importance are spelled out in James and Susan's letter of wishes. They include personal humility, family unity, perseverance and adaptability, discretion, financial conservatism, philanthropy, social responsibility, and the value of education.

Vision

The key elements of the vision for the Reynolds family and its supporting organizations are listed below. The family wants to have a world-class family wealth management process to ensure that they can achieve an ambitious set of goals over the next five years and beyond.

- To secure the health, education, and financial welfare of members of the Reynolds family indefinitely.
- To make a valuable contribution in selected areas of philanthropy, sustainable investment, and environmentally focused "clean" technology.
- To create a process to protect, enhance, distribute, and share Reynolds family capital, both financial and human, across generations in a manner that increases the choices, promotes independence and self-motivation, and enhances the quality of life of Reynolds family descendants and their families.

The realization of the vision will result in the achievement of:

- Wealth protection
- Wealth enhancement
- Stability and continuity beyond current generation
- Positive family relationships and development
- Personal engagement and motivation for the family members
- State of the art modern global approach
- Flexible and creative approach that meets lifestyle and geographic preferences of key family members

Philosophy of Wealth

The family's philosophy of wealth has been carefully reviewed and principles have been established that are designed to both preserve family capital and create the right degree of individual freedom within the family context.

We will thus act as both owners of our own smaller pools of assets and stewards for the main pool of assets for the benefit of future generations in the family and future beneficiaries of our philanthropic activity.

The bulk of the family's financial capital is kept within a coordinated set of trust and other asset vehicles and is formally divided into two major pools of wealth—one to support the family, the other to fund the activities of the family's philanthropic foundation.

The family is committed to "doing no harm" in all of our investment activities. As a result, we shall not invest in firearms, tobacco, or other similar activities. Further, a minimum of 5 percent of the portfolio shall be invested in "clean tech" enterprises, and a further 5 percent in enterprises characterized as sustainable, without sacrificing or reducing the financial returns on those investments when compared with the rest of the portfolio.

Distributions

Each generation shall be entitled to a capital distribution of 10 percent of the total corpus, calculated at the time the first member of the generation reaches his or her 35th birthday. That distribution shall be spread evenly among all members of the generation and paid out as family members reach 35, 40, and 45 years of age.

Annual distributions shall be restricted to 50 percent of income generation and value increase above the rate of inflation, after taking into account all relevant costs and taxes. This calculation shall be made on a five-year trailing average basis.

Family Goals and Objectives

- *Lifestyle maintenance.* We want to fund a comfortable lifestyle for ourselves (James and Susan) with the ability to provide substantial support to our children and grandchildren, as needed. Included in this goal will be funding for annual family meetings, educational programs, and other governance and development activities.
- *Capital preservation and growth.* While not having a fixed investment goal, our long-term expectation is to make 6 to 8 percent in an environment of 3 percent inflation. This leaves

1 percent for costs and 2 to 4 percent percent real appreciation to grow our family capital over time.

While accumulating funds well above the needs for personal capital distributions required by the current family members, we are aware that many families grow rapidly in numbers over time, requiring far more substantial payments in the future. In order to fund those personal capital obligations, we have set a principle at each generation of not depleting the quantum of family capital—in real terms—from the original settlements of the trusts.

- *Other high-priority goals (philanthropy).* Our philanthropic goal is to fund worthy projects, using the income generated from the family foundation. The foundation is focused on child and maternal health care in the world's 20 poorest countries, the restoration of sight through cataract operations in India and Africa, and investment in libraries and the education of gifted underprivileged children in our home city. Capital has already been assigned to the family foundation, and it will be managed separately by a designated group of trustees.
- *Discretionary wealth contingency reserve (HEW trust).* A portion of the family's financial capital will be set aside to fund a health, education, and welfare trust aimed at ensuring that all bloodline descendants can receive support to ensure that needs are met for health, education, and welfare. This can cover special needs, emergencies, and other uses of income for members of the family whose parents may have lost their personal capital or have lost access to their capital and its associated income. In addition, if wealth taxes or other confiscatory tax policies are adopted in our home country or elsewhere that affect our wealth, this separate offshore trust structure should remain as a source of capital protection and life enhancement for future family members.
- *Personal liabilities and commitments.* No family member or generation shall use family capital as collateral for any loan or other liability, or encumber family capital in any manner that shall diminish its value or limit its access by members of any future generation.
- *Personal use real estate.* The Reynolds country hunting lodge and beachfront home are both legacy family assets that are not to be sold.

- *Family business.* While there are no plans to reduce further our holdings in RAG, it is part of our long-term asset allocation model to continue to diversify away from our historic concentration in RAG and other aviation sector–related investments. This may lead us to divest some of these shares if the conditions are right.
- *Pending foundation donations.* As two of the foundation initiatives were held up by wars in the countries for which the funds were intended, we have accumulated those funds and held them in a separate account for distribution when conditions are more conducive for our team to work in those countries.
- *Family human capital.* We think of our family and its members as our greatest asset and will invest to build and protect our family and its individual members. During this plan period, we would like to determine the nonfinancial family capital metrics we should use. While addressing the collective pool of family human capital above, we also wish to address the individual members of the family and look at their assets and capabilities, while the family human capital concept looks at the consolidated capital within and across the family.
- *Portfolio debt and embedded leverage.* The Reynolds Aviation Group carries with it a medium level of debt as a result of the recent recapitalization exercise. The current portfolio contains within it substantial leverage in the private equity and hedge funds, property funds, and selected direct investments, but all of these are netted out against assets on the balance sheet. As a result of this embedded debt, coupled with an overall objective of wealth preservation, we do not have and do not expect to have any explicit additional portfolio debt.
- *Mortgages.* Our property portfolio has a low to medium level of debt, with no cross-collateralization and income from rents and leases at least two times debt service obligations and loan-to-value ratios relatively conservative when compared to market norms.
- *Operating costs and lifestyle maintenance.* Since the family's wealth is substantial when compared to the number of members, and personal capital distributions are made in lieu of individual annual expenditure distributions, the family expenses are relatively low relative to net worth. We have notionally assigned $50 million to fund our long-term family lifestyle costs, until the death of James and Susan.

- *Family office costs.* The major expense items are related to the offices and teams operating within the family office, Artorius Capital, and the Reynolds Family Foundation. These costs are to be capped at 1 percent of total assets under management, with substantial room for variation based on the nature and demands of the investments made and overseen. They are expected to be funded by the return on assets in the portfolio and do not show up on the family balance sheet.
- *Expected distributions.* Until the exact amount for G3 distributions is set, we have notionally assigned a present value capital value of $30 million to fund these commitments.

Family Balance Sheet

The family balance sheet has grown with time, achieving the levels described below with increasing consistency over time:

Assets	**Assets (in millions)**
Personal use real estate	
City	$10
Lodge	$5
Beachfront	$5
Investments	$200
Family business (Reynolds Aviation)	$100
Due to foundation	$5
Family human capital	n/a
Total assets	$325
Liabilities/Discretionary Capital	
Net portfolio debt and embedded leverage	$0
Mortgages	$10
Operating costs and lifestyle maintenance	$50
Distribution goals	$30
Pending foundation donation	$5
Planned charitable bequest	$20
Wealth contingency reserve (HEW)	$20
Total liabilities and commitments	$135
Excess/discretionary capital	$190
Total	$325

SWOT Analysis

The following lists the key strengths and weaknesses of the family and our financial management, as well as the key opportunities and threats we face today.

Strengths

- Highly capable, forward-thinking, and entrepreneurial principal.
- Global view and reach.
- Good internal people in the family office, private equity, investment committee, and sustainable investment, with growing capability.
- Growing network of platforms, strategic funds, and contacts around the world.
- Liquidity and potential for growth from current position.

Weaknesses

- No central vision and inconsistent values.
- Organizational inefficiency and gaps.
- Undermanagement of people and investments.
- Insularity.
- Poor hiring history.

Opportunities

- Asset values low.
- Good people available.
- Growth capital scarce.
- Organizational change possible.

Threats

- Increasing tax risk.
- Outdated investment model.
- Poor execution: quality and timeliness.
- Insufficient resources (analyst and financial modeling).

Long-Term Strategy

A long-term strategy will be put in place every three years and will review the current environment and its future consequences for the management of Reynolds family wealth and in the structuring and investment of funds. The strategy must address all discrete elements of the Artorius Capital, Reynolds Aviation Group, and Reynolds family (family, family services, family businesses, philanthropy, wealth structuring, wealth management, and reporting/control).

That plan should cover the coming three years in detail, but also project forward across multiple generations, ensuring that all necessary is being done in the planning period to ensure the long-term health, wealth, and welfare of our family.

The plan should address the following areas:

- An organizational review to address weaknesses in the execution of strategy, people quality, and the design and implementation of the family leadership model. In part, this is due to poor communication and a lack of a central vision.
- Cost management will be a continuing priority. Budgets for all of the major family and business entities should be developed for the directors' or trustees' approval.
- A review of offshore and jurisdictional strategies for the family.
- A comprehensive review and action plan to adapt the family and family investment model to a new environment.
- An improvement in the asset allocation and investment process model.
- An objective assessment of the reasons to continue with in-house family office staff versus outsourcing to a multifamily office or an outsourced chief investment officer (CIO).

Family Elements of Long-Term Strategy

- *Family vision, values, and investment principles.* We will continue to test the activities and investments of the family to ensure that they align with the family's vision and values. Specifically, we will clarify the new principles of investment related to sustainability and build a network of opportunities in the area of environmentally sound clean tech.
- *Family wealth purposes and asset structures.* We will continue to align asset structures, family office resources, and investment processes to improve execution, reduce costs, and prepare for increased tax pressures. Work has begun on a private trust company (PTC) structure and jurisdictional diversification.

- *Family governance, engagement, and education.* We will formalize the family organization (family council formation and operation), continue clarification of next-generation family rights and responsibilities (in family and financial affairs), increase engagement and level of knowledge of the children, continue the upgrade in family services, and ensure family and family support functions all have clear succession and handover plans.

  We understand that a proper governance system can help a family gain a sense of direction and communicate its shared values, mission, and vision to both family members and the community at large. We also understand that family governance takes on increasing importance as the family grows in size and complexity (e.g., spouses, children, grandchildren).

Family Financial Ecosystem and Advisor Selection

- *Family office organization.* We urgently need to determine the best model for the family office (in-house, outsourced, or combination) and agree on the structure, scale, and budget of the organization. We have also decided to investigate the hiring of an outsourced CIO to professionalize asset allocation, improve reporting, provide access to selected funds, and to provide improved risk-adjusted performance through a more effective strategy, investment manager selection, and tactical management.

  The CIO's tasks will include a wholesale review and restructuring (if required) of the existing portfolio, divesting weak funds and adding high-performance managers, imposition of concentration risk parameters, and other portfolio disciplines to upgrade the family's management of risk, asset allocation, and individual funds.
- *Investment committee (IC).* The IC needs to be reconstituted. The IC will be composed of five to six members chosen from our roster of key advisors, directors or trustees, friends, and other specially invited members.

Economic and Market Perspectives

We need to plan to operate in a low-growth (in OECD markets), low-interest-rate (and hence low yield and income) environment for the foreseeable future.

It is obvious that we are now in a different world than that of the long boom period. As a result, strategies need to be adjusted to respond appropriately to a volatile, uncertain, and negative (for some time to come) operating environment. There is no longer a rising tide to lift all boats. Strategies now need to be more flexible, faster to adapt, more sensitive to cost, less dependent on financing opportunities, and fully aware of all of the interconnected problems unfolding around the world.

The lack of credit, tougher terms demanded by lenders, low consumer confidence, and increasing desire to save and invest in lower-risk assets will slow the real gross domestic product (GDP) recovery for some time to come. We believe it will be some time before OECD countries return to non-deficit-funded growth, with expected low returns on portfolios a characteristic of the "new normal" for some time to come. Emerging markets will continue to offer far brighter prospects during the same period.

Our estimates for the global economy for the coming three years are:

- Fifty percent likelihood of slow/no growth.
- Twenty-five percent return to recession.
- Twenty-five percent moderate growth, primarily due to stimulus packages.

In addition, we are moving into an era of enormous tax revenue shortfalls and a likely targeting of ultra-high-net-worth families by tax authorities. In this environment, we must ensure that our asset structures and investment processes provide solutions to current and likely future tax demands.

Asset Allocation and Investment Policy

The overall asset model needs to be developed in the context of a clearly defined set of objectives for the total family wealth, including supporting objectives for all asset classes and investments. This model will set out guidelines for target return, type of return (income vs. capital gain), liquidity preference, leverage parameters, risk tolerance, and the time frame for investment. Each portfolio attribute can and will vary by class and change over time, as will the precise portfolio allocation. The asset-class targets in the model will be range driven and will flex in response to external events and internal developments.

An investment policy statement (IPS) will be developed and updated each year that reflects the long-term strategy as well as the current investing environment.

- *Lifetime and legacy portfolios.* We remain comfortable with the structure of two separate notional endowment portfolios. One portfolio carries low risk to capital, a higher degree of liquidity, and a focus on income generation. The quantum of this portfolio will be set by the forecast lifestyle costs of the family.

  A second portfolio, focused on the family's legacy objectives, could carry a higher risk to capital, but with a greater expectation of capital appreciation over time. This portfolio could be lower liquidity and longer in investment time frame.

  Within these two broad categories, the following portfolios (or buckets) will be recognized:
  - A lifestyle portfolio to cover the family living expenses and operating costs for the houses
  - A conservatively managed HEW trust for broader family needs
  - The central "stewardship" portfolio focused on capital preservation and enhancement
  - Philanthropic foundation with predictable annual income needs
  - A fund notionally targeted for personal capital payouts to individual family members
  - Funding for annual family meetings, educational programs, and other governance and development activities requiring income for expenses
  - Allocation of funds for clean tech and sustainable investments meeting overall portfolio criteria
- *Adopt S-curve approach to family wealth.* We will look at a range of asset allocation models, using each to provide a different perspective on our portfolio, and acting on relevant insights from more than one model. An S-curve driven model of investment may be the most useful for our current purposes, with the allocation within the simple areas of targeted risk and return matched to the various components of our family liabilities and commitments.

- *Investment return target.* The combined family portfolio will target a 6 to 8 percent long-term investment return to allow for spending, inflation impact, and capital growth. While we also desire capital preservation, our horizon is sufficiently long term (and our discretionary capital sufficiently large) that we can afford some illiquidity and volatility in our portfolio. This will translate into different annual targets and focus on the creation of long-term value independent of inflationary growth.

  While 7 percent still remains the long-term mid-range target, expectations may be reduced for particular periods to reflect the exceptionally low yields available in the fixed-income markets and the risks inherent in volatile equity markets, while in other, more positive times we may seek a higher return on our funds.
- *Type of return.* The balance of income and capital growth objectives will need to be set with input on spending and capital needs from the family, the family office, and investment advisors. Income should be generated to cover lifestyle and operating costs, subject to an annual review.
- *Time frame for investing.* Each component of the portfolio will need to have a different time frame for investment, ranging from a lifetime (or more than one lifetime) for some family residences to instant liquidity for cash and short-term investments. Each time frame will need to be specified as part of the overall portfolio strategic and tactical approach.
- *Liquidity preference.* Recent events have highlighted the value of liquidity in a turbulent environment. Although carrying cost as well as benefit, the liquidity of the portfolio may need to be increased from past levels to create flexibility, both to exit unprofitable volatility and to shift assets to better opportunities as and when they arise.
- *Risk policy.* The overall risk philosophy is expected to be one of low to moderate risk within the portfolio, with a focus on a broader set of risks surrounding the portfolio and its operation. Each asset class will have a different risk profile, which will need to be spelled out for discussion and consideration by the investment committee.

  Risk can be defined here as the risk of permanent loss of capital or substantial reduction in income from or value of the portfolio.

Given long-term trends in the environment, we want to give particular attention to three risks: tax risk (offshore planning), institutional risk (diversify custodians and jurisdictions, establish back-up banks, improve financial security due diligence), and operating risk in the portfolio (review RAG risk strategy, reviewing underperforming or at-risk funds in the portfolio).

A "bolt-hole" strategy may also merit revisiting in every planning cycle. The idea of a small amount of ultimately safe money (invested in cash, highly liquid securities, and gold coins in a separate trust structure) to mitigate the effects of a meltdown scenario could provide additional comfort and security to the family over the long term.

- *Currency.* We shall also begin to measure our financial capital in both dollars and our own currency unit made up of one third dollars, one third euros, and one third other strong currencies, a category whose membership may vary over the years but may include resource-backed currencies and currencies representing low-debt economies.

Asset Classes and Investment Strategies

- *Target investment strategies.* The primary focus in the investment area has been to move to a more conservative approach to the management of family wealth. In particular, this has meant continued delevering of the portfolio, a search for new sources of income across all asset classes, a diversification of the number and nationality of banks selected to hold family cash in safe (government-insured) jurisdictions in a diversified basket of currencies, a systematic effort to identify and exit high-fee hedge funds and private equity funds with strategies performing below benchmark, a focus on better management of existing direct investments, and a deceleration in the rate of new investments.

  We plan on making fewer, better investment decisions and moving toward being a long-term value investor with the capability of making successful direct and coinvestments, along with an element of sustainable and clean tech investing added on.
- *Cash and treasury management.* Cash and equivalents (including gilts and liquid money market certificates) should have

virtually no risk to capital. This implies holding very secure assets in a diversified set of solid banks (no more than 20 percent in any one bank, with a preference for state-owned or guaranteed banks) in insured jurisdictions (as were Singapore and Hong Kong during the crisis) and in a diversified basket of currencies (currently one third each: dollar, pound, euro), with the currency balance achieved through actual currency holdings or via forwards.

- *Fixed income.* While retaining an allocation to fixed income, we expect to position our portfolio at the low end of our range. We are concerned about the medium-term returns in this market due to low interest rates (stock dividends are above bond yields for comparable risk in some markets), overfunding, negative real rates over the long term, and little opportunity for fund alpha (after fees and carry) in the current environment. As most of our funds are taxable, fixed-income returns are further reduced by the impact of taxation of interest.
- *Equity.* We will continue our focus on dividend-paying equities to grow our income over time. Access to equity markets will primarily be through exchange-traded funds (ETFs) in large efficient markets, with a parallel search for managers in emerging markets who can consistently outperform their market indices. This approach will provide low-cost beta, with investment in alpha targeted on less efficient market spaces and proprietary investment theses.
- *Hedge funds.* Many hedge fund investments proved to be disappointing in the crisis. Some absolute return funds lost more than they should have given their stated strategies, liquidity was more restricted than anticipated, overall returns were lower than expected, and hedging did not seem to be as common as speculation in the portfolio. Since there is no particular need to hedge any one single investment, the objective in the hedge fund area is to select the best performers in the most attractive categories and thus obtain a return equal to the best performers in the best hedge fund category—long/short, arbitrage, momentum, and so on.
- *Private equity (PE).* Large PE funds dependent on leverage to achieve targeted returns are unlikely to prosper in the new world order as much as they did in the past. Earlier stage

investments, growth capital, new funds, income-generating funds, distressed, and other strategies may require a greater role in the portfolio.

- *Property.* At present, the direct real estate portfolio is spread across residential, commercial, and industrial properties, with nearly 75 percent in high-end commercial in capital cities. Other activities include property funds in OECD markets and some speculative development activity in eastern Europe and Asia with partners. As high-end city properties have not exhibited distressed pricing trends, we are holding off on aggressive investment until there are greater dislocations in the property markets of long-term interest.
- *Real assets.* Real assets may also play a larger role in the portfolio to protect the after-inflation-adjusted real value of the portfolio. Global population growth, food and water shortages, GDP growth in emerging markets, and other long-term secular trends are expected to keep upward pressure on demand and prices for scarce goods and services in the hard and soft commodity space. Growth in investments in related areas such as agricultural land, contract farming, solar energy, and other areas may also be attractive, although cyclicality can curtail expected value in any one time period. We will want to have some exposure to this asset class, but will look to our advisors to determine the best timing.
- *Direct investments.* We will also look at more direct investments, which carry the longest time frames, are nonliquid, and are higher risk but have the expectation of the highest return. Where possible, high-risk investments should be derisked through partnering, careful use of leverage, strategic payouts and recapitalizations, and other approaches that return invested capital quickly or provide income.
- *Sustainable investment.* This type of investment is defined as achieving financial, environmental, and community goals at the same time. Substantial progress is envisioned for this year as we continue our development of this sector, as our network in the space grows, and as more investments are made in the portfolio. We like this category for the investment opportunity and social impact and because it fits with our family values. We will seek to grow our expertise and investment in this area over the plan period.

Operational Considerations

- *Speed and quality of execution.* The current system and procedures will need to continue to improve, with an emphasis on high-quality (speed and timing) execution. Past opportunities to sell down the portfolio, hedge currencies, diversify banks, and take advantage of trading opportunities have not always been captured in a timely or effective manner.
- *Better manage current investments.* Each investment should have a defined strategy, a set of operating and financial targets, and a review (possibly two or four times per year, based on the size of the investment) on strategy and performance.
- *Develop a list of reliable coinvestors.* Expanding the (very limited) set of reliable coinvestors we currently work with will be an explicit part of our building process. This will require a conscious broadening of the network of contacts and intermediaries to geographies beyond our home region.

Performance Reporting and Risk and Cost Management

- *Dashboard.* We want to develop a simple strategic dashboard that reports on performance against benchmarks, costs against plan and industry norms, and nonfinancial risks as we define them ourselves. Measurement of performance may be complex due to different national and currency zone inflation rates, but annual valuation exercises should take into account only real asset growth and its implications for investment strategy. The overall risk-return balance will need to be set, monitored, and amended over time.
- *Technology.* We plan to review technology vendors regularly to acquire the best platform for real-time reporting to show total family wealth, asset allocation with and without the family business included, individual manager performance net of fees and carry, cash on hand, and currency exposures.
- *Improve reporting and finance.* Improved reporting on bank balances, cash flows, currencies, and portfolio progress has recently been implemented. An initiative has begun to broaden the number of banks with whom we do business. Specific ideas for currency options, leverage, transactional finance, and deposit management have been tabled,

examples of an active policy in this area we would like to continue.

- *Relevant benchmarks* will be selected for each asset class and mandate, with like-for-like historical and current performance specified. This performance will be assessed against both plans and the most appropriate benchmark indicator or series of benchmark indicators.

IMPERATIVE 4

DRAFT THE ANNUAL INVESTMENT POLICY STATEMENT AND REFINE INVESTMENT TACTICS

CHAPTER 15

Drafting the Annual Investment Policy Statement and Refining Investment Tactics

Following the determination of high-level family objectives and investment strategy, a practical plan of action must be developed, drafted, and implemented. The investment policy statement (IPS) is perhaps one of the most important documents investing families will create as they manage their wealth.

Investment Universe and the Role of Asset Classes

Once the family and their advisors feel comfortable with the long-term strategy plan, they can start to determine how this plan will be achieved during the coming year—specifically which asset classes they will use to meet their investment return targets within their specified risk levels.

This decision will also be influenced by the family's experience, income needs, and their ability to handle volatility, complexity, and illiquidity, along with the interests and skill sets of the advisors with whom they choose to work.

Changing Role of Asset Classes

In the new normal, not only has the context and expectation for investment return changed, but the individual asset classes themselves may have an actively evolving role in a portfolio.

Cash, while being nothing more than negative debt in some ways, also plays an additional role as the source of liquidity to meet collateral obligations and loan repayments as well as distributions. As such, cash can be a key component in asset/liability matching calculations, and can play a role as designated collateral as well.

Similarly, Treasury inflation-protected securities (TIPS), according to some investors, should actually be considered as real assets, as they are both inflation resistant and income generating. While fitting in the fixed-income asset allocation bucket, TIPS, like cash, can also serve a variety of purposes.

Set out in Table 15.1 are some traditional and new roles played by different asset classes.

Table 15.1 Old and New Purposes of Asset Classes in a Portfolio

Primary Asset Class	Traditional Approach	New Purpose/Attributes
Cash	Standby funds	Value preservation
	Local currency	Multiple currencies
	Single local jurisdiction	Multiple international jurisdictions
	Presumption of bank safety	Value of national deposit guarantees
	Low risk	Counterparty risk
	Low (but some) return	No/negative real return
	Small allocation	Larger allocation
	Collateral	Collateral
Core fixed income	Low/no risk	All at some risk
	Source of income	Yield below dividend rates
	Laddered for diversification	Quality of concern
TIPS	Income	Income
	Inflation protection	Inflation protection
		Liquidity
Credit strategies	Bank-led syndications	Direct loans plus pools
	CLO channel	Source of income and upside
Global public equities	Reliable long-term growth	No expectation of growth
	Yield	Source of income
Alternative assets	Multiple exposures (hedge, private equity, VC)	Less hedge, less expensive
	Low correlations with other asset classes	More correlated than previously thought

Primary Asset Class	Traditional Approach	New Purpose/Attributes
Private equity	Growth above market beta	Declining return expectations
	Uncorrelated with equities	Highly correlated
	Return sensitive	Cash flow and fee sensitive
	Difficult to access best managers	Easier to access
Hedge funds	Speculative return	Hedge
	High return	Variable/volatile
Direct and coinvest	Small role	Greater role
Absolute return	Reliable returns	Hard-to-predict return
Property	Value growth	Volatile pricing and greater risk
	Inflation hedge	Inflation hedge
	Area for leverage	Reduced leverage available
	Income	Income
	Tax efficient investing	Generational transfer at relatively low tax
	Growth sector	Distress opportunity sector (in some areas)
Real assets (nonproperty)	Value growth	Volatility and growth
	Inflation hedge	Price cyclicality
	China-led "super cycle"	Slowing demand
	Fear hedge (gold)	Speculative/fear hedge
Hard commodities	Inflation hedge	Surrogate currency
	Cyclical opportunity	Secular opportunity
Emerging markets	Small allocation	Larger allocation
	High risk	Declining relative risk
	Growth	Growth
	Currency risk	Currency upside
	Systemic and high political risk	Lower risk (than before)

Not all changed roles are positive. As private equity funds grew in size and the industry spilled over into the mega-deal (and therefore mega-fund) era, correlations to public markets increased dramatically, as much as doubling over the past 10 years by some calculations.

Alternative assets are thus not so alternative anymore; the small, lean, and highly selective private equity and hedge fund managers exploiting a big arbitrage gap between private and public sector pricing are now few and far between.

There are few areas of uncrowded airspace left, leaving a large group of investors now to jostle in a teeming field, which has pushed returns down and pushed risk up in the search for some alpha (and therefore fee justification) in a more difficult capital world.

Similarly, cash has become expensive to hold, with substantially negative real rates of return on deposits, or even fees for holding cash, possibly for many years to come.

In the rosier past, 4.5 percent returns were easily available across the board from OECD cash rates alone. Now we see these same rates for emerging market bonds, a similar yield for somewhat different risk exposure.

Sovereign debt, once the bellwether risk-free asset class, has also changed. Organisation for Economic Cooperation and Development (OECD) government bond haircuts, rerating of some of the world's largest economies, and the arrival of blue-chip companies (think Nestlé) with a higher rating than the financial instruments of developed market governments in the West, may reposition the relative attractiveness of this asset class relative to its past portfolio roles.

The purpose of fixed income is still to generate regular and reliable income, but this task is far more difficult in an environment where a $10 million deposit might yield annual income of $50,000 or less.

Generally, because of the need for an asset-liability match, and sometimes due to its anchoring role as collateral as well, there is a sensible domestic currency matching between fixed income and local liabilities.

In the new world order, "unrepeatable six sigma combinations" and "thousand-year events" seem to pop up with some regularity every few years. Markets lurched from the emerging markets crisis in 1997–1998 to the Tech Wreck in the early 2000s to the global financial crisis (GFC) in 2008, with little equity market upside in between, creating a volatile context in which the role of investment assets changed far more rapidly than in the past.

Drafting the Investment Policy Statement

Drafting an IPS can provide the opportunity to determine the role, appropriate allocation, and expectation of all asset classes and individual investments.

As the practical short-term guide to action, the IPS will pull together all policies, principles, and thoughts on family wealth management and turn those thoughts into practical and measurable action.

The Purpose of an Investment Policy Statement

1. *Setting objectives.* This includes establishing and defining client expectations concerning risk and return, and providing guidelines on how the assets are to be invested.
2. *Defining the asset allocation policy.* This requires identifying various asset classes that will be used to achieve the investor's objectives, and determining how best to allocate the assets to achieve a diversified portfolio.
3. *Establishing management procedures.* A guide needs to be put in place for selecting and monitoring investments, and making changes as necessary. There also needs to be a way to evaluate the performance of whoever is in charge of the investment process.
4. *Determining communication procedures.* A concise method of communication needs to be in place so that all parties involved are aware of the process and objectives, and responsibility must be assigned for implementation.

Source: Norman Boone and Linda Lubitz, *Investors, Policy and Change* (Greenwood Village, CO: College of Financial Planning), 2010.

Just as important, an IPS, reviewed retrospectively, can also identify where and why mistakes were made and how to make the required midcourse corrections. The IPS came into more common usage for private investors after the Tech Wreck in the early 2000s, when many investors had dramatically overweighted the technology sector in their portfolios and then rode the sector down as it crashed.

Many investors had no written guidelines that might have provided an early warning system of the dangers of extreme and undiversified investing.

IPS as a Key Source of Success

The single most important thing we see that has led to [investment] success is having an investment policy and sticking to it. The purpose of the IPS is to help define the investment and financial goals and objectives of the [pool of capital] and to describe which investments will be used to meet those goals and objectives—far and away the most critical part of the investment policy.

The policy statement is also a tool for managing portfolio risk.

Source: Leslie Kiefer, "Investment Policy Best Practices: Communication, Creation and Commitment," *CFA Institute Conference Proceedings Quarterly*, March 2007.

The IPS provides a structured, disciplined process to guide decision making for the investing family. More specifically, the IPS is designed to help define the family's financial objectives and identify which individual investments will be employed to meet those goals.

The IPS acts as the link between the family's goals and the capital markets. It should cover the full range of issues relevant to the professional management of the investment portfolio.

The process of developing an IPS is an excellent educational journey for a wealthy family. The requirement to think about all aspects of an investment plan ahead of time can expose weaknesses in the risk management system, decision-making process, spending policies, or investment return assumptions. It can help families understand the choices and trade-offs they have to make between risk and return, between income and growth, and between lifetime and legacy spending.

It also helps define roles and responsibilities of all the various actors on the investment stage, including family leaders, beneficiaries, the family office, external advisors, and investment managers. It is very important that the wealth owner, trustee, and/or the family participate actively in the development of the IPS. It is not something that can be delegated wholly to advisors. It is the expression of the family goals and objectives in financial terms and is the main lever of influence and control the family has over the investment program that will (or will not) deliver the results they require.

The investment policy is a living document and should be updated and adjusted as circumstances and/or the objectives of the family change. It will need to be cognizant of and flexible to adapt to shorter-term views of the economy and capital markets, with specific attention paid to specific investments, taxes, distributions, and financial considerations relevant for the coming year.

It needs to reflect which asset classes to consider, and how the macro environment will affect the choice of those asset classes. It must consider how much of each asset class the investor should hold, as well as how much those asset-class weightings should vary based on market conditions. And it should address both the returns expected from various asset classes and how other factors, like correlation among the asset classes, should be taken into account.

It should be a formal written document and should include all of the following components:

- *Purpose and scope.* The policy should clearly state whom the funds are for and the ultimate purpose of the investment. This helps provide clarity and context for how the funds will be managed. It is also important to specifically address the legal owners (individual, trust, or foundation) as well as the beneficial owners or family group that controls the funds or will benefit from them.

  The IPS will typically specify which and how much of the family's assets are covered by a particular policy. It should also put these assets in the context of the overall family wealth. It is important for everyone involved with the investments to know whether this is the bulk of the family assets with broad objectives or a small portion of the total wealth with a very specific mandate.
- *Objectives.* In this section, the IPS should detail the objectives of the investment program. It should cover such items as the goals the assets are intended to fund, and the reinvestment or distribution rate desired. This is the place where the investment policy links to the overall strategic plan. The clearer this statement of objectives can be, the better it can serve its overall purpose.

- *Investment principles.* It can be helpful for a family to outline its investment principles and assumptions so that all the parties involved will be clear on the way they want the assets to be managed. This could include their views on active (vs. passive) management, fees, illiquid assets, margin of safety, and simplicity.
- *Expected rate of return.* The IPS should specify the rate of return or income each part of the portfolio is expected to generate. This could be expressed as an absolute annual average return, a return above inflation or a risk-free rate, an absolute dollar return, or capital preservation target.

  It may also include an itemization of the investment performance expectations from each of the key asset classes included in the portfolio along with a target asset mix.
- *Income and liquidity needs.* The IPS should specifically address the spending plans (and related income requirements) and the liquidity needs from the portfolio, to ensure the funds will be available when needed without resorting to tapping the capital at an inopportune time.
- *Risk tolerance.* In addition to return expectations, the IPS should also address the risk tolerance and capacity of the investor and the resultant risk policies of the portfolio. In some cases it will specify a maximum loss or volatility the portfolio should expect. Some investors will be comfortable with large short- and medium-term fluctuations or significant illiquidity if they have a long-term horizon and are looking for above-average returns.

  It is valuable to specify the extent of losses that can be expected with the given portfolio strategy so families can be prepared in advance, which may reduce the chances for fear-based emotional reactions. Drafters of the policy should include the possibility of "black swans" in their risk calculations and not just rely on normal distribution projections. Risk capacity—that is, the financial ability of the family to withstand a loss to the portfolio (as distinct from risk tolerance)—should also be addressed.

  The IPS may also set out a particular investment philosophy or approach that the investor is or is not comfortable with. Risk will also be managed at a tactical level and specific actions taken to identify and mitigate high-priority risks as they occur.

- *Planning horizon.* The IPS should specify the investment time horizons. This should relate to the time horizon of the "liability" the assets are intended to fund (e.g., a desire to fund multiple generations over 100-plus years), the time frame of the investment cycle over which the portfolio will be managed and assets will be evaluated (e.g., 10 years or two cycles), and the frequency with which the investment policy will be reviewed (e.g., annually).
- *Asset-class universe.* The IPS should list which asset classes can be considered for use in the portfolio and which should be excluded. If a manager or investment committee wants to add an asset class that is not listed, it should be reviewed, agreed upon, and then added to the IPS before any investment is made.
- *Investment strategy allocation and target ranges.* In this section, the policy should specify what the target asset mix will be and how much it is allowed to vary from that target before it must be rebalanced or, if the investment management is fully outsourced, when the wealth holder must be consulted. The target asset allocation is set based on the expected returns and risks from the portfolio and is intended to keep a focus on long-term outcomes and remove emotions during times of stress and crisis.

  The portfolio must stay within the target range or, if it strays, must be adjusted back so it is in compliance with the investment policy or the IPS updated. The discipline of staying within the boundaries can help keep the portfolio safe from knee-jerk reactions to the investment environment and ensure it stays appropriately diversified.
- *Rebalancing.* Strategic rebalancing is a tool investors can use regularly to rebalance the portfolio back to the target weighting when portfolios stray from their targets. The policy should specify that the portfolio should be rebalanced back to the target weights on a regular basis, or if they get too far out of line for too long. It should address whether rebalancing should be done at the manager's discretion or on some more regular basis, such as quarterly or annually.
- *Tactical ranges and discretion.* Some investment policies will allow for tactical investment strategies within the established asset-class ranges. The typical practice is to define the strategic asset mix for each asset class within a target range and give the

investment manager or chief investment officer the latitude to operate within those ranges, depending on the realities in the marketplace. The IPS may specify the type of tactical activity the investment manager is allowed (or specifically not allowed) to undertake.

When the portfolio is first established, allocations will necessarily start with a set amount of funds and percentage of the portfolio. However, the exposure to that asset class will change due to increases or decreases in the value of that asset class, new perspectives on the outlook for the investment category, or changes to the family's investment policy.

Again, there is an important balance to be found in making tactical portfolio decisions. On the one hand, the emotional and volatile nature of capital markets means that there will be opportunities in particular asset classes for investors to take advantage of from time to time. On the other hand, there are few investors who can reliably and consistently profit from shorter-term trading.

- *Quality guidelines and portfolio constraints.* Every portfolio will have a different set of quality guidelines and portfolio constraints and these should be laid out in the IPS. These may include liquidity guidelines; legal requirements based on the structure of the fund; investment limitations based on quality, geography, or type; tax restrictions; or currency constraints. They may also include investment preferences (e.g., socially responsible investing) and investment manager fee limitations.
- *Tax issues.* The IPS should reflect any relevant tax issues the family faces and the potential tax effect of purchase or sale of a particular asset class or security. Some entities within the family system may be taxable and others not. This may be an important decision factor in the ultimate "location" of the family's assets in one entity or another. It is important that investment advisors and managers are fully aware of these constraints.
- *Investment selection.* The IPS should also outline the criteria for the selection of investments and investment managers. It may specify a due diligence process, fee structures, track record, and manager experience.

- *Governance.* The IPS should identify clearly who is responsible and permitted to make and implement investment policy with regard to family funds. It should address explicitly the division of duties and the specific roles and responsibilities of anyone involved in the investment process. It should also specify all of the costs and fees associated with managing the portfolio.
- *Family roles and responsibilities.* Each investment should also carry with it a specific understanding of the roles and responsibilities of any family members engaged in the initiative. It should also clearly state how the family is able to exert its control and influence over the investment process.
- *Manager roles and responsibilities.* The policy should address the ways investments are managed. They may be managed by an advisory firm on a discretionary basis, or decisions may be made by the wealth owner with the assistance of an advisor. Family office staff, portfolio advisors, and asset managers should also have their roles specified so it is clear who is monitoring the investment, who is taking any required corrective actions, and what should be the reporting obligations and milestones achieved for the life of the investment.

  The IPS should also set out a standard of care for advisors involved in the management of the assets which, depending on the jurisdiction, will normally require compliance with fiduciary standards. Advisors are required to act in the best interests of their clients at all times and put their clients' interests ahead of their own.
- *Monitoring and review.* Once the investment plan and policy are built, they will need to be well-executed and managed along the way. The investment program should also be monitored regularly against its original goals and adjusted as needed. This includes establishing and enforcing policies and schedules to rebalance the portfolio to reflect changing markets, to respect specific risk measurement criteria, and to track and report on the investment performance of the portfolio. This will include the selection of appropriate benchmarks against which to assess the portfolio's progress.

  Each year the IPS should be reassessed to review its appropriateness for the current environment. Target returns for the portfolio and for individual asset classes should be specified each year in advance, as well as expected drawdowns, distributions, and realizations; changes should be made as needed.

- *Acknowledgment.* The IPS should be signed by the wealth owner and the portfolio manager to acknowledge their agreement with the financial goals, investment policy, and their intention to live by it. Any subsequent changes to the policy must be fully understood and also signed by all relevant parties.

The Value of Simplicity

Even though capital markets are complex, and the execution of investment management requires full-time attention and expertise, investors often confuse complexity with sophistication. Nothing could be further from the truth. An investment policy, and indeed an entire investment program, should be straightforward and understandable to most members of the family.

It should focus visibly on the family's objectives, it should use clear language, the investments and strategies should be understandable (not simplistic), and the outcomes should be able to be tracked without difficulty.

Complexity and lack of transparency actually add costs to the portfolio, sometimes in higher fees, but also in the amount of due diligence and monitoring required, the risk controls that must be put in place, and the time and energy expended for questionable benefit. It can also encourage investors to overfocus on the trees (i.e., the details of complex strategies) rather than the forest (i.e., the overall long-term objectives of the family).

IPS as the Bridge between Insight and Action

The investment policy is the vital bridge between the family goals and long-term wealth strategy, and the actual investment implementation of that plan.

As such, it requires careful construction and deserves considerable time and attention by family investors and their key advisors in order to make sure that it fills its important role in bridging strategic insight from the planning phases with practical implementation on the ground.

CHAPTER 16

Rethinking the Role of Traditional Asset Classes

Before setting out to draft an investment policy statement (IPS), allocate assets on a strategic basis, or select specific assets for investment, it is important to establish the overall purpose of the family's portfolio and to determine the role and financial purpose of each asset class within the overall portfolio: capital growth, wealth preservation, income generation, and diversification, among others. Over time, and in response to changes in the environment, the purpose of asset classes can evolve, thus creating an opportunity to rethink the role each plays in the overall portfolio.

Before allocating assets, and to provide a bit more background to the repurposing of assets in the current climate, the traditional role of each asset class is thus worth revisiting. Some observations on the asset classes and their role in different portfolios may help to guide investors in defining and implementing a family investment plan.

Cash and Fixed Income

Cash and fixed income typically play three roles in an investment portfolio: capital preservation, liquidity, and income.

Capital Preservation

These are typically the safest assets in a portfolio since the borrower is expected to repay the principal value of these assets in a specified time period. Often, the borrower is of a very high quality such as reliable governments and their agencies or high-quality corporations and can usually be relied upon to pay back the principal borrowed.

Governments in particular, assuming they are sound, can raise taxes or print money to cover the debt liability. Corporate bonds are higher security in a corporate capital structure and, in the event of bankruptcy, must be satisfied before equity shareholders. As a result, high-quality bonds can normally be used to both generate income and protect capital in a portfolio.

However, even sovereign bonds can now carry more default and currency risk than in most prior periods, and investors need to account for this evolution in the historic "risk-free" role played by government bonds in some family portfolios.

There are exceptions to every rule. There are also lower-quality (or high-yield) bonds, issued by entities with a higher risk of default, which do not contribute to the capital preservation objective in the portfolio. It is also worth noting that bonds generally do not keep far ahead of inflation, thus their contribution to postinflation real capital preservation can also be poor over the long term.

Even with lower yield than in past periods, fixed income continues to serve the purposes of providing stability and liquidity to portfolios, which has become especially important as some other asset classes have become more volatile and less liquid than expected.

Liquidity

Bonds and cash also play an important role in the portfolio as providers of liquidity. Cash is the most obvious form of liquidity since it can be put to use immediately. Liquidity from fixed-income investments comes in two forms:

- Interest payments from bonds are typically made on an annual or semiannual basis.
- The marketability of the securities provides the remaining liquidity. Most public securities are typically very liquid in today's market. Bonds, under normal circumstances, are easily sold and can provide cash in relatively short order.

Some investors will employ a laddered approach in which bonds are purchased across the maturity spectrum. Laddering attempts to capture the current coupon and add to portfolio yield when rates go up and protect portfolio yield when rates go down by averaging the yield across multiple bond maturities.

For instance, a "five-year ladder" would include bonds with one-year, two-year, three-year, four-year, and five-year maturities. After a period of one year, the one-year bond would mature, providing cash to the portfolio, which would then be invested back into a five-year bond. This would provide liquidity each year that could be available to the investor on demand for reinvestment or spending.

Income

Cash normally provides very minimal income, if any at all. Bonds typically offer some yield to investors, in addition to the promise to return the initial principal. The level of income is normally related to the prevailing level of interest rates, the investing term to which the investor is willing to commit (i.e., normally fixed-income investors have to receive higher yields to commit to longer terms), and the quality of the bond issuer as investors require higher yields to be compensated for the risk of owning a lower-quality bond.

The "income" purpose of fixed income has almost completely disappeared in the low-rate environment prevailing from 2008 onward. After inflation and investment management fees, investors are currently losing capital by investing in fixed income in such a low-rate market.

In some jurisdictions, particular bonds (e.g., municipal bonds in the United States) may carry tax advantages as well, providing a stream of steady, if not spectacular, after-tax income.

As a result of this limited income potential with high-quality fixed-income investments, investors have had to look elsewhere for portfolio yield. Unfortunately, that search has required many to move out of the risk curve to try to pick up extra income, either through lower-quality bonds or riskier (or at least more volatile) securities such as common shares. These income-seeking families may also pursue alternative investments, which use more complex trading strategies to replicate a more stable return, and in some cases they even target bondlike income.

Absolute return strategies can be helpful, but investors must realize that they carry their own risk and typically much higher fees to managers of up to 2 percent per year of the capital committed, and 20 percent of the gain, normally above a certain hurdle rate over the life of the fund.

Expected Returns from Fixed Income

The current low fixed-income return environment is a significant challenge for all investors, especially those who rely on portfolios for income such as insurance companies, pension funds, retirees, and wealthy families.

Forecasting the expected returns on cash and equivalents is highly certain in the short term, but longer term it is subject to prevailing interest rates and can vary dramatically. Over a period of 112 years (1900–2011), the return on U.S. T-bills has averaged 3.9 percent per year. At the end of this period, rates on cash were substantially lower than the long-term average.

Longer-term bonds tend to provide a higher yield than cash in a normal, upwardly sloped yield curve environment, when long-term interest rates are higher than short-term rates. Bond issuers have to provide borrowers with some incentive to lock up their money for longer periods of time than required by cash holdings.

The average return on global developed world government bonds over the long term has been 4.8 percent. Again, yields on government bonds in the United States at the end of the period cited above, and other relatively stable developed world economies, are much lower than long-term averages.

Given the extraordinary set of circumstances emerging after the global financial crisis, the average dividend yield on equities (2 percent) now exceeds the income generated by a 10-year Treasury bond (1.7 percent). And the bond yield is 70 basis points below the expected rate of inflation over the same period, a substantially negative real return and an expensive price to pay for some security and erosion in capital value over such a long time frame.

Range of Strategies

Fixed income strategies are numerous. However, in any low-return environment, significant risks must be taken to achieve above-benchmark return. Most fixed-income strategies typically focus on a combination of two variables—credit risk and interest rate risk over a set time horizon.

Corporate bonds will normally tend to provide somewhat higher yields than government bonds, all other things being equal, as a corporate credit is riskier than a high-quality government credit. It is interesting to note that corporate bonds in the United States have outperformed government bonds only marginally (0.2 to 0.5 percent) over their long histories, offering relatively poor compensation for the additional risk and liquidity.

It is very difficult to create excess returns in these asset classes, and they are traditionally viewed as a store of value, producing income streams and acting as ballast to the portfolio.

Past and Future Returns

It is interesting to note that bonds have been one of the best-performing assets over the past 20 years due to the substantial decline in interest rates. This return has been much higher than the traditional returns from fixed income. In fact, over this period, the returns from fixed-income investments have been better than equities and have carried less than half the volatility.

When investors are attempting to forecast future bond returns, history shows clearly that they should pay very little attention to past returns. In general, the current yield is a better guide for to future returns. In fact, studies show that there is a 0.96 (i.e., almost perfect) correlation between the entry yield on U.S. Treasury bonds and the subsequent 10-year return on the bond, as shown in Figure 16.1.

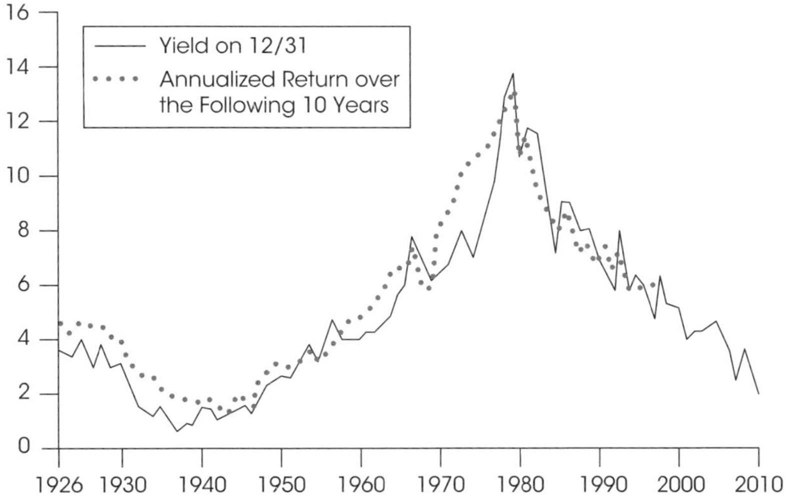

Figure 16.1 10-Year Treasury Entry Yield and Subsequent 10-Year Return

Source: John Bogle, "The Lessons of History: Endowment and Foundation Investing Today," Conference remarks, *The NMS Investment Management Forum*, Washington, DC, September 2011.

Due to the current low level of rates and low current yield, it is difficult to imagine a scenario in which bonds will provide an attractive return in the current forecast period, except on a relative basis if other asset classes decline substantially. In most stable developed countries, interest rates cannot fall much further. If they stay at current levels, investors will receive only the coupon; if they rise, the price of the bonds they hold will decline.

On top of these challenges, interest income is, in most jurisdictions, the most heavily taxed type of investment return, which further erodes the potential return on bonds.

The Real After-Tax Return on Bonds

10-Year U.S. Treasury Bond

Nominal yield	1.7 percent
Tax at 30 percent	-0.5 percent
Subtotal	
After-tax yield	1.2 percent
Inflation (est.)	-2.0 percent
Real after-tax yield	-0.8 percent

This real, after-tax return will be even lower if interest rates rise and the value of the bond declines. Holding a laddered bond portfolio can mitigate the risk of a potential rise in interest rates as the older, lower-yielding bonds drop off the ladder to be replaced with higher-yielding longer-dated bonds.

Why Hold Bonds at All?

Given the low level of yields, why would anyone hold bonds at all? The reason usually has more to do with the fear of the alternatives and the needs of the investing family. Low, zero, or even slightly negative returns on bonds may end up looking very attractive relative to large value declines that some investors fear from equities and other risky assets in an unstable global financial situation. Overall, bonds can act as a counterbalancing force to equity market and other risk exposures.

Families who choose to rely on equities or another, higher-volatility asset class may find that the portfolio is at a low point precisely at the moment when they need funds for their own purposes.

A family with $200 million in assets being willing to allocate *just* $20 million of their capital to bonds at the low current rates of return may only guarantee a modest annual $500,000 of family spending over the next 10 years (assuming they deplete the capital). Other families will eschew the low expected returns from fixed income, and simply use the income and/or capital from their diversified portfolio to fund their expenses along the way.

Investors who held a significant exposure to fixed income during the equity market crash of 2008–2009 enjoyed the protection that bonds afforded the portfolio. Not only did bonds not drop in sympathy with equity markets, they actually rose in price and protected the overall value of the portfolio.

This lack of correlation between bonds and stocks is a relatively recent development. For much of the 1980s and 1990s, bonds were not a diversifying asset but had positive correlation with equities.*

The other factor influencing bond allocations is the emotional preferences of the family. Some families will prefer to have large amounts of cash and bonds because they do not want to worry about the volatility of equities and other risk assets. Similarly, families who do not plan to have their money last multiple generations may prefer the stability of bonds and may not need the growth and inflation protection typically offered by equities.

Bonds and cash can also be thought of as a reserve from which to purchase equities when equity prices decline. Specifically allocated cash reserves also fulfill the role as an offset against future capital requirements, both internal and external. The forward commitments for all private equity–type drawdown investments are often placed in the reserves account and are drawn upon as needed.

Using a conservative reserves approach will cause portfolio returns to lag in positive markets, but materially reduces risk in negative markets and avoids the need for hastily arranged financing packages or distressed assets sales prices in negative market

---

*Richard Bernstein, "An Alternative to Alternatives," Richard Bernstein Advisors, May 2012, 1–2.

environments where there are few distributions and a continuing flow of drawdown commitments, loan-to-value covenant calls, or broker margin calls.

Equities

Equities represent a share of the ownership of a company and play three main roles in a portfolio: capital growth, income growth, and inflation protection.

In the short term, high-priority family requirements are normally met by fixed income because of the stability, certainty, and liquidity it offers. The role of equities or other growth assets in most family portfolios is typically to provide growth to fund longer-term family obligations.

Over the long run, equities have offered investors a return superior to fixed-income investments. But to benefit from that return, investors had to endure the anxiety of some swings in the stock market along the way. The volatility of the equity market has historically averaged 20 percent versus 5 to 10 percent for fixed income.

One of the ways to reduce the volatility of an equity portfolio is to diversify. The more uncorrelated the assets, the more beneficial is the diversification. Diversification can be achieved on many levels, including holding a number of stocks in a portfolio and diversifying across industry groups.

A globally oriented portfolio of equities can also offer local investors further diversification to markets and currencies as well as sectors that are not available in their home countries. Large global companies like Apple, IBM, Coca-Cola, and Nestlé are really global proxies as their sales, profits, and operating assets reflect a mix of current global positions and future global opportunities. They can also provide portfolio diversification.

Another diversification approach is using multiple styles and approaches to equity investing, which normally reflects managers' stock selection criteria. Examples of the most common styles include value (stocks that are very inexpensive relative to their perceived value), growth (stocks with high expected earnings growth), GARP (growth at a reasonable price, that is, halfway between value and growth), concentrated (a much smaller number of stocks in the portfolio), and momentum (capitalizing on the continuity of existing trends in the market).

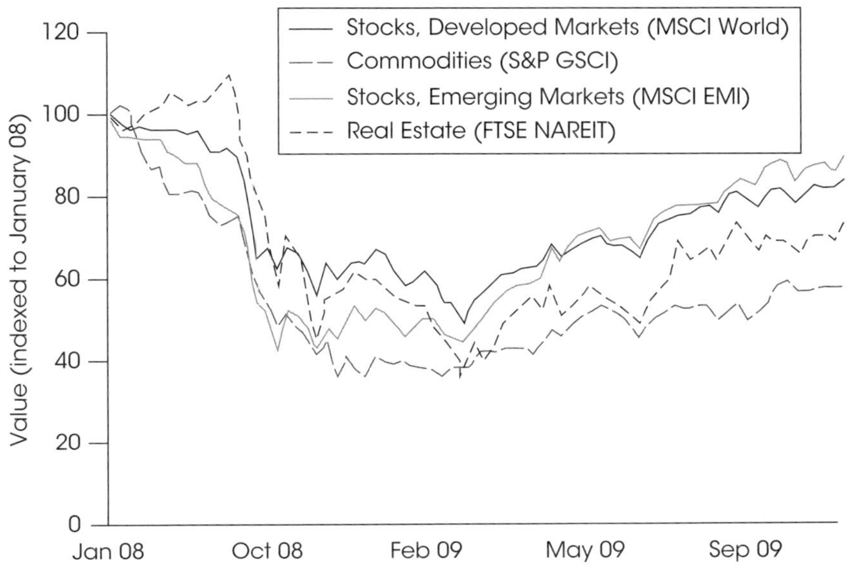

Figure 16.2 Correlation among Key Asset Classes During the Crisis
Source: "The Future of Long-Term Investing." World Economic Forum, 2011, 50.

Unfortunately, the correlation within equity markets (and among risk assets generally) has been increasing, which reduces the benefits of diversification. For instance, during the global financial crisis (GFC), the diversification benefit evaporated (see Figure 16.2).

Investors can also choose between large-cap and small-cap stocks. Most studies show that small-cap stocks outperform large-cap over the long term, albeit with higher volatility. Capitalization size is another category of opportunity for investors to diversify their holdings.

Equities can also be an important source of portfolio income. Dividend equity strategies offer current income, as well as growth in dividends over time. There is some evidence to suggest that dividend portfolios typically have lower volatility than the overall stock market. Depending on the portfolio strategy selected, the dividend focus can reduce volatility by up to 40 percent. In a low-interest-rate environment, dividends have appeared even more attractive than they have been historically, as seen in Figure 16.3.

In most major jurisdictions, the returns from equities (capital gain and dividend) are taxed more favorably than interest income.

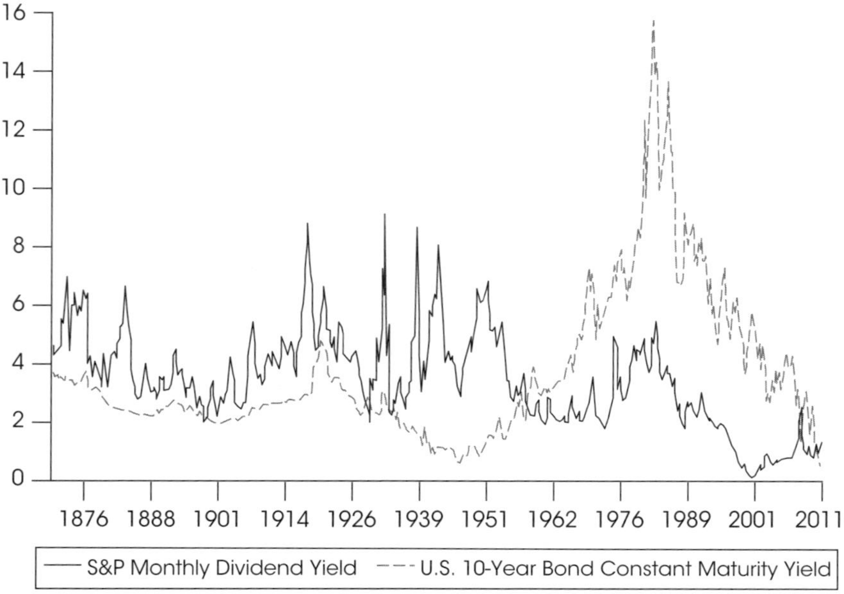

Figure 16.3 S&P Dividend Yield and 10-Year Treasury Yield
Source: Global Financial Data.

Expected Return from Equities

What return should an investor assume equities will provide? In most studies, the long-term nominal returns from stocks in the United States have averaged around 9 to 10 percent. But that return varied dramatically depending on the decade and time frame selected. In the decades of the 1950s, 1980s, and 1990s, the annual average returns from U.S. stocks were above 17 percent. In the 1920s and 2000s, average returns were negative (see Figure 16.4.) That makes it challenging, and maybe even counterproductive, for families to plan their investing over a very long time period on a rigid basis, a concern that carries with it guidance for avoiding overly constrictive investment mandates in trust deeds and other long-term documents.

In trying to understand investment returns, industry veteran John Bogle builds on a helpful concept introduced by economist John Maynard Keynes. They suggest that stock returns are actually a combination of two factors—the *investment return* (the initial dividend yield and the subsequent annual rate of earnings growth) and the *speculative return* (the change in price investors are willing to pay for each dollar of earnings, or the price-to-earnings [P/E] ratio).

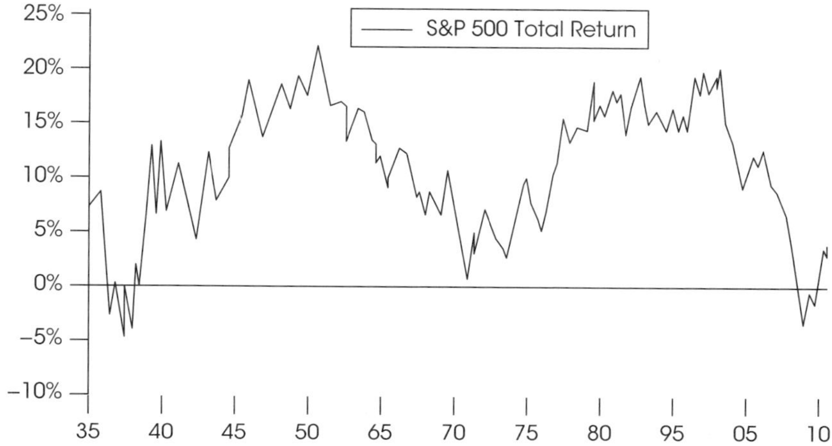

Figure 16.4 S&P 500 Rolling 10-Year Average Annual Total Return
Source: Blackhorse Analytics, Standard & Poor's.

As Figure 16.5 shows, the investment return (bottom graph) has been remarkably stable over time, averaging almost 9 percent, with only two decades being less than 6 percent. The dividend yield is a known factor, and earnings growth, while hardly certain, has always been positive (except for the 1930s)—typically in the 4 to 7 percent range (top graph).

The speculative return (middle graph), however, has been very volatile, alternating from positive to negative over the decades, averaging out near zero.

The encouraging lesson is this: Despite the swings in the stock market, driven mostly by speculation, the actual returns from equities over the long run have been derived primarily from real economic factors that have produced real results. For families with very long-term orientations and good staying power, equities may have reasonably predictable returns. Unfortunately, shorter time periods are subject to much more variability in returns, and families need to take this into account in their planning.

In another analysis of the U.S. market using a slightly different time frame, equity returns are deconstructed as in the following list:

S&P Returns (1926–2009)

4.10 percent—earnings growth

1.31 percent—P/E increase (10.2–25.1)

4.34 percent—dividend yield
9.75 percent—nominal equity return
3.00 percent—inflation
6.75 percent—real equity return

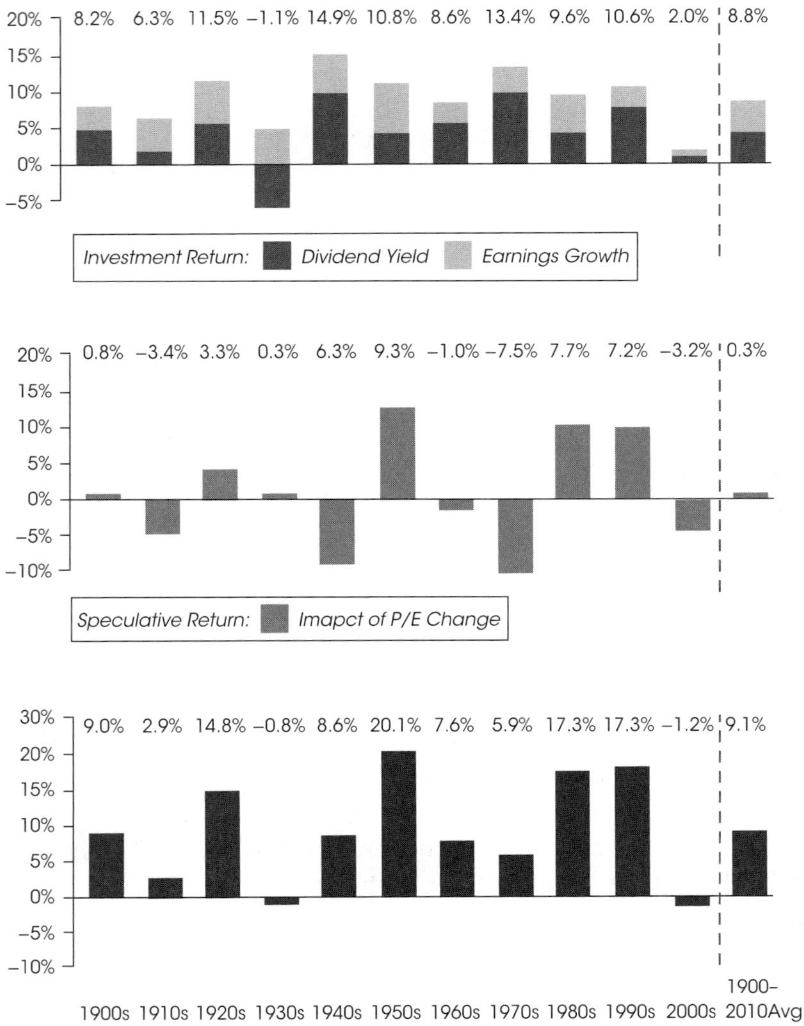

Figure 16.5 Eleven Decades of Returns on U.S. Stocks
Source: John Bogle, "The Lessons of History: Endowment and Foundation Investing Today," conference remarks, *NMS Investment Management Forum*, Washington, DC, September 2011.

Using the same math today to forecast future equity returns would, not surprisingly, produce a lower outcome than historical averages. For the purpose of this example, we simply assumed the same historical earnings growth rate, no P/E increase (most measures show the price/earnings ratio at an average level of valuation), and the current inflation rate:

4.00 percent—earnings growth
0.00 percent—P/E increase
2.00 percent—dividend yield
6.00 percent—nominal equity return
2.50 percent—inflation
4.50 percent—real equity return

These types of assessments need to be carried out on a regular basis since the market environment changes so rapidly, but the frameworks can be helpful in making a reasonable assessment of how much an investor should expect to achieve from each asset class over the foreseeable future.

In any case, sharp changes in equity price levels may provide opportunities to reassess valuations and the appropriate tactical response.

Reversion to the Mean

There is also a strong argument that says equity and other investment returns show strong evidence of mean reversion. In other words, if returns are well above or below the mean return for a period of time, then there is pressure to revert to the long-term average. Figure 16.6 shows how, over the past century, following periods in which the S&P lagged the 10-year Treasury return on a 10-year rolling basis, the return in the next decade was strongly positive, bringing the returns back closer to the long-term average.

Can Investors Outperform the Indices?

The answer is actually quite simple: a few can, but most do not.

Annual competitions between fund managers and, for example, monkeys throwing darts at the pages of stock listings in newspapers, do not always favor the human competitor.

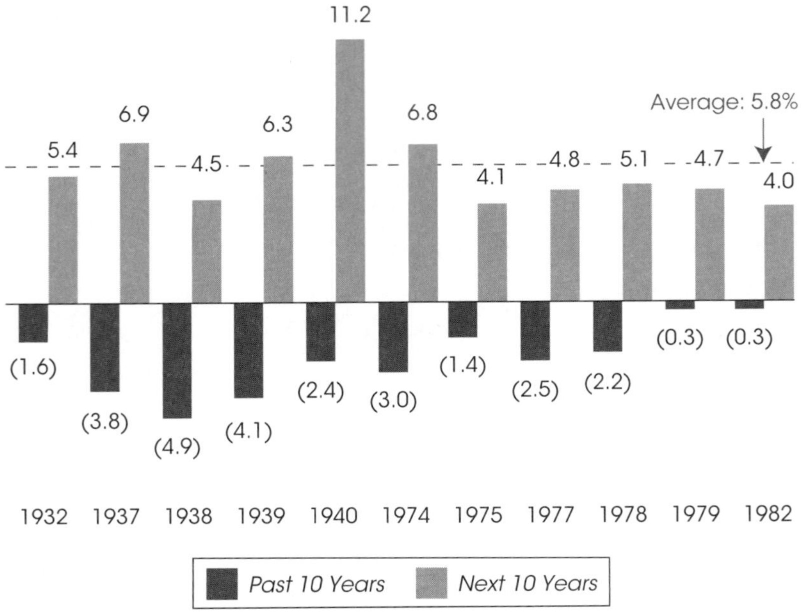

Figure 16.6 Mean Reversion Following Poor Equity Performance
S&P 500 return minus 10-year Treasury return (percent) Includes all 10-year rolling periods when the S&P 500 lagged 10-year Treasury bonds from 1901 to 2008.
Source: Global Financial Data, S&P, AllianceBernstein.

There is good evidence that the average investment manager underperforms the index by the amount of their fees. The same is true of mutual funds, which David Swensen criticized harshly as an industry for adding little value to their active management mandates and charging high fees for their poor performance.*

Some managers do, however, outperform the averages and their peers. That then raises three questions:

1. How easy is it to find those special managers who will outperform in the future?
2. By how much do they outperform relative to their fees and risk?
3. Once found, will they continue to outperform over time?

---

*David F. Swensen, "The Mutual Fund Merry-Go-Round, *New York Times,* August 13, 2011.

There are data to suggest that it is a very difficult task to produce consistently above-average results, at least for highly liquid, large-cap, public equities. Also, the dispersion of returns between the top and bottom tier of managers is relatively small. Yet there is quite a bit of anecdotal evidence that shows such managers do exist and can be found.

Believers in efficient markets argue that investors cannot outperform the averages long term, and those investors tend to choose low-cost exchange-traded funds (ETFs) for equity exposure. Believers in active investing are willing to pay extra fees in the hopes of above-average returns or below-average risk.

The Value of Value Investing

One of the most thoughtful, time-honored, and successful investment approaches is referred to as value investing. While there are many definitions, most practitioners will agree that value investors focus on buying securities that are priced substantially below their intrinsic value. The intrinsic value is determined by deep fundamental analysis on the company and the evaluation of key ratios such as price-to-book value and price-to-earnings.

This gap between perceived and real value is a function of the emotions of investors and the related volatility of the stock market. Benjamin Graham, one of the fathers of value investing, suggested, "Most of the time common stocks are subject to irrational and excessive price fluctuations in both directions, as the consequence of the ingrained tendency of most people to speculate or gamble."

Over time, value investors believe, the market will ultimately recognize the true value of the company and the stock price will rise to meet the intrinsic value. The lower the price the investor pays for the stock (relative to the intrinsic value), the higher the "margin of safety" the investor receives, and the more "room for error" the investor has in case his or her estimate of the real value is incorrect.

Value investing requires substantial patience because investors have no idea what will drive the market to recognize the actual value of a security or when that will happen. Warren Buffett, one of the modern-day practitioners of value investing, says, "We don't get paid for activity just for being right. As to how long we'll wait, we'll wait indefinitely."

There is substantial evidence to suggest that value investing is an effective long-term strategy, but there are clear periods when it underperforms a growth or momentum strategy. Investors need to have the flexibility (and ability) to shift styles at the appropriate time or the staying power to wait out the dry spells until value investing starts to outperform again.

Warren Buffett has built up one of the largest family fortunes in the world through shrewd equity investment over an extended time frame. Through disciplined investing, he drove the value of Berkshire Hathaway to such an extent that he created a personal fortune valued at over US$40 billion. Buffett's investments reflected a consistent philosophy that includes the following principles:

- Pursue a disciplined approach to asset allocation and investment decision making.
- Invest in companies an investor understands.
- Make fewer, better investments.
- Avoid losses in the portfolio.
- Look for strong cash flow and a strong management team.
- Hold for the long term.
- Understand, and benefit from, the psychology of markets.

There is a practicality to what Buffett has done consistently and successfully over a long time. It relates to anticipating how human beings react to the concept of risk. Most people instinctively seek to protect assets against further downside when the investment environment causes assets to fall. Top investors are programmed differently in how they approach rising and falling asset valuations.

The real challenge in family wealth management is that it is hard to be a buyer when markets are falling, and a seller when markets are rising. However, as Buffet has suggested, an investor wants to buy when the sky is thundering and lightning is striking, and an investor wants to sell when the sky is clear blue. His advice to investors is clear and succinct: "Be greedy when others are fearful."

In the midst of extraordinarily volatile public markets, screaming headlines in the financial press, and a growing interest in the seemingly sedate private equity asset class, one experienced value manager explained why he loves the public markets. "I would never buy private equity. I don't want to sit around the table and have a rational discussion with a small group of experts about the value of a company. I want to take advantage of the price swings that come with the irrationality of the public markets."

These tactical aspects of successful investment may be more palatable if a comprehensive strategic framework, a sensible process, and a decision-making committee are in place. Then the wealthy family, fully informed, is prepared to use downside volatility as an opportunity to buy and upside volatility as a time to sell.

Tough Wisdom from the Past

Having the information, expertise, and wisdom to act boldly in troubled times is a key to successful long-term family investing. Warren Buffett's famous exhortation to invest when markets are fearful is reinforced by insights and comments from families that have invested well through many great, and even cataclysmic, historical events.

An early member of the extraordinary European Rothschild family summed up this approach when advising an investor: "Buy property when there is blood in the streets, even when it is your own."

Alternatives to Traditional Assets

For many family investors, the traditional assets of cash, bonds, and stocks are still at the core of their investment portfolios based on their familiarity, liquidity, and transparency.

There is good evidence to suggest that these asset classes still have the potential to play important roles in wealth management plans. But the massive decline in interest rates and the volatility in equity markets over the past decade have sent investors searching for alternatives and a redefined role of these asset classes in their family investment portfolios.

CHAPTER 17

Assessing Alternative Assets and the Search for Recurring Alpha

Alternative assets provide an alternative to the more traditional classes of cash, stocks, and bonds. For years, these alternative asset classes were open only to ultra-high-net-worth individuals and sophisticated institutional investors.

For many years in the past, and likely to be for many years yet to come, effective strategies in the alternatives space have been the source of portfolio alpha for many wealthy families. In the "core and satellite" model described previously, it was often alternatives that provided portfolio alpha from the smaller "satellite" investing.

Over the past 10 to 15 years, alternative assets have come into more common usage as the traditional asset classes, equities in particular, have lagged historic performance and yields on bond investments have steadily declined.

Although alternatives, or at least selected asset classes in selected time frames and some elite managers, have proven themselves capable of producing consistent and recurring alpha for their investors, not all alternative asset classes and not all alternative asset managers have been so successful.

In this area, as in so many others, the rules of the game are changing as investment theses, leverage strategies (and availability), and fee arrangements (which can have a significant impact on after-fees-and-carry returns to investors) have all been tested in the global financial crisis (GFC), and many have been found wanting.

While still playing a key role in many portfolios, the novice alternatives investor needs to look at both sides of the coin—good and bad—of alternative investing before deciding on his or her investment strategy and tactics.

Interest in Alternatives

The interest in alternatives by families has risen substantially in the past two decades. The reasons are many. One driving factor has been the low returns available in traditional asset classes. Equity returns have been the worst since the 1930s, and bond yields dropped to all-time lows, so investors have been forced to look elsewhere for alternative sources of income, capital growth, and portfolio alpha.

Also, the increased correlation among and within traditional assets has driven investors further afield to find assets that are less correlated and therefore offer the joint benefits of alpha, diversification, and volatility reduction.

From the supply side, there has been a significant increase in the number of boutique fund managers cropping up. Many smart fund managers left the larger investment banks and investment management companies and set up their own firms, usually with a 2 and 20 fee model and focusing their attention on familiar areas where they had been active before. The advent of the Internet and improvements in access to capital market information has made this kind of boutique proliferation possible. It might not have been so easy a few decades ago.

The idea of separating alpha and beta has also fueled the growth of alternatives. Investors have realized that beta (market-related performance) could be attained easily and cheaply via index funds, leaving excess management fee room to purchase pure alpha (non-market-related performance).

Finally, the growth was exacerbated in the United States in many alternative investment categories because activities in these areas were unregulated, unlike the traditional investment managers, and allowed alternative managers to set up relatively easily and to operate in an unfettered manner.

Expanded interest in and use of alternatives was led by some of the largest U.S. endowments, including Harvard and Yale. They reasoned that their very long-term time frames, large size, and need for higher returns to meet rising educational costs would make them perfect candidates for alternatives. They could, in theory, absorb the illiquidity of alternatives and benefit from the uncorrelated nature of the assets and the higher returns they offered.

They began diversifying in earnest from the traditional stock-bond portfolios to include a wide range of asset classes, many of them illiquid, including hedge funds, private equity, commodities, precious metals, infrastructure, and real estate.

Following the early success of these large endowments, many private clients embraced alternatives as well, as did smaller endowments and some leading-edge asset management institutions. The early positive experience continued for some time, but then ran into problems of poor returns and limited liquidity in the 2008–2009 market collapse.

Alternate Views about Alternative Assets

Looking forward, many of the traditional assumptions about alternative assets may need to be reconsidered. Although still positive in many ways, recent events have revealed some unexpected characteristics about these assets.

First, many assets thought to be uncorrelated were indeed correlated in times of crisis, when diversification was most needed. The main goal of some alternatives, in addition to providing superior return, was volatility reduction, and many failed that test in the first big market decline since the advent of their widespread use.

Second, the illiquidity factor became a problem for organizations and families who had committed to deliver a certain level of income from the investment portfolio to fund capital calls, school operations, or family expenses. Investors learned the painful lesson that in times of great stress, liquidity disappears. With the alternative portfolios frozen, via straight illiquidity, gates, side pockets, or lock-ups, investors were obliged to sell their liquid securities at low prices or borrow at high rates to meet other obligations.

It is interesting to note that illiquidity can actually reduce the benefits of diversification by requiring intensive active management and thus adding "diversifiable" risk back into the portfolio that *cannot* be diversified away. It also does not allow rebalancing among asset classes, which is a key component to true diversification.*

*Robert Maynard, "Back to the Future: Conventional Investing in a Complex World," Brandes Institute, 2010, 22.

The early adopters (the largest endowments) ended up doing well over the period despite the setbacks, primarily because they had the experience and access to the very best funds given their contacts and early-stage investing.

The dispersion between the best and worst managers is much wider in alternative investments, as is the persistence, defined as the ability of a high-performing manager to continue to produce high returns. Some of the best managers have now closed their funds, leaving new investors to the asset class to select from less attractive, but more available, managers.

In the end, there was a large gap in the performance between the largest endowments and virtually everyone else who adopted the alternatives/endowment approach.

Performance Shortfalls

A careful and thoughtful use of alternative investments has the potential to add alpha performance and real long-term value to a family portfolio. But they must be approached with the same care, respect, and skeptical objective investigation that any less familiar and unrated opportunity should be afforded.

For many families, the recent net performance of their alternative investments, despite the positive publicity, has not been particularly attractive. From 1992 onward, the average hedge fund did about as well as an average diversified public portfolio.

Much of the data on alternatives is tainted by the so-called survivor bias, which presents a consolidated picture of, say, hedge funds with a 10-year track record, but in so doing, statisticians leave out all those that failed or closed over that period. If all of the firms that started at the beginning of a period were to be included in the summary statistics, winners and losers alike, then average returns would be far lower than those usually reported.

Publicly cited hedge fund return statistics may also include performance numbers before the funds actually started, adding to the positive overlay on reporting. These return-enhancing calculations apply to traditional managers as well, but the rate of start-up and failure is much greater in the hedge fund world than in these traditional asset classes.

In the recent crisis period, the endowment model struggled significantly even though this was just the type of turbulent environment it was designed to weather. Between June 30, 2008, and June 30, 2009 (the most common fiscal year for endowments), conventional stock and bond portfolios lost 14 to 17 percent. Sophisticated pension and endowment funds that followed the endowment model lost between 22 percent and 27 percent, based on information available for various plans at their respective websites.*

This underperformance also focused attention on the high fee model of most alternative investment vehicles. Many investors wondered whether the fees were fully justified given that the expected extra performance was not achieved and the goals of uncorrelated performance and volatility reduction were not realized.

A New Alternative

Asset-Backed Income and Its Emerging Role for Family Investors

Asset-backed income (ABI) sources may become a new cross-asset class area for family investment, as they serve multiple objectives through one investment.

ABI can include property-based investments in rental or leasehold payment yielding assets (possibly in the form of real estate investment trusts [REITs] for smaller investors), energy-producing assets (traditional carbon and clean tech), credit strategies where collateralized direct loans may be made to companies or individuals, agricultural land, or other actively operated commodities assets, and other nontraditional combinations of asset strength and income-generating capacity.

ABI can provide the following for family investors:

- Income.
- Inflation protection.
- Exposure to capital growth opportunities.
- Underlying asset exposure, which may be available for hedging.
- Tax-advantaged return in some jurisdictions (based on the asset involved).
- Liquidity (based on the contractual terms).

(*continued*)

*Robert Maynard, "Back to the Future: Conventional Investing in a Complex World," Brandes Institute, 2010, 22.

- Capital protection (for credit-based investments, based on collateral received)
- Low or no fees and carry

In addition, depending on the asset class involved, there may be an ability to structure assets effectively, allocating the asset to a trust and the income arising to a specified beneficiary. Finding or creating these products can be challenging, with a long history of a rise and fall in performance of collateralized loan obligations (CLOs), collateralized debt obligations (CDOs), and similar asset bubbles, providing many sad tales that reinforce the importance of alternative strategies on a firm foundation of strong underlying asset values.

Real Estate

Almost every wealthy family has a portfolio of property assets, most probably in a local or domestic national market, and possibly in foreign markets as well. Although cyclical in pricing, property investment has been the source of many great fortunes and a mainstay of many more.

Real estate has been an important feature of investment portfolios for centuries, so, in that sense, it is hardly an "alternative" asset class. Real estate typically serves three primary roles in a portfolio: income through cash flow received from rental income, capital growth via building improvements and rising property values, and inflation protection since, over time, landlords have the ability to increase rents or sell at higher prices if inflation rises. Property ownership can also be effective in cross-generational transfers and may offer tax advantages and leverage, reflect family traditions, and serve other family investment purposes, not to mention providing housing for individual members and their own families.

Real estate is a cyclical asset class with return and risk profiles heavily driven by interest rates, the availability of credit, and in some areas underpinned by long-term secular drivers such as housing supply/demand balances, government policies, and local market pricing.

Exposure to real estate can take many forms that range from very secure to speculative, including existing stable assets on long-term leases with blue-chip clients, raw land, shares in large companies, partnerships in individual projects, core retail, and residential and office buildings. The asset class should be considered relatively illiquid from a capital perspective and with relatively high sale and purchase costs. When selling a property, it may take months or years to generate the desired value from the asset sale and the process can be complex and costly.

Direct real estate holdings should be considered long term in most cases. Pooled investments offer an increased level of liquidity, as investors can benefit from the entry or exit of other investors in the pool and not force the sale of portfolio assets.

The Role of Property in a Family Portfolio

Basil Demeroutis

When we talk about investing in real estate, it seems sensible to start with how we invest and why, and how this reflects the values of the family. An obvious place to begin, perhaps, but in practice it is hard to steal time away from the day-to-day drumbeat of evaluating investments to pause and reflect.

For centuries, property has acted as a long-term store of value and a mechanism of wealth transfer between generations. It is, perhaps, the oldest and most resilient such instrument that we as investors know. Specifically for stewards of private wealth, we use property not only to preserve capital in a tangible way (think of the term *real estate*) but also as a reliable generator of income. At its most basic level, that's what is asked of our real property investments: to preserve wealth and provide a regular cash flow. This, of course, has relevance for private families in particular.

In addition to being a long-term store of value and income generator, direct private real estate exposure has specific characteristics that are difficult to replicate: inflation-hedging qualities, relatively low correlation to public equities and other asset classes, enhanced risk-adjusted returns, regularity, and predictability of cash flow streams.

Away from purely financial qualities, property is a physical and tangible investment as compared to a fiat asset. Not only does this provide real security, but it also allows investors to do things to it physically to improve its value, and investors have a much higher degree of control over its performance. In this, real estate is unique.

It is for these reasons, in a return to first principles, that the right kind of real estate exposure belongs in balanced investment portfolios.

(*continued*)

In the past two decades, iterations of successive innovations like CMBs, structured investment vehicles (SIVs), CDOs, and CLOs tried to get real estate to do more. By carving up risk and adding leverage (financial and operational), investors managed to take a building and squeeze additional return from it. But beneath it all, that same building was creaking under the pressure, as it could only do so much.

Of course, modern finance and capital markets have important roles to play in an investment strategy, but one cannot disconnect the asset underpinning it all, and we should remember that these assets particularly have unique characteristics and embedded risks and that they demand hands-on management. I believe one should not confuse the above and other indirect strategies with real estate exposure; they are quite different.

When investors invest in these alternative "real estate" exposures, they're not just buying pure real estate risk anymore; they're buying risk that behaves more in line with interest rates, general economic risks, operational execution, and so on. And the asset plays less and less the role we want real estate to play and more like something else.

I remember having a conversation with one real estate fund manager who invested 40 percent of his fund in a bank (yes, a bank). "But it has a substantial mortgage book and we see this as an undervalued investment," he said. Yes, but it is leveraged 33:1. And it is a bank.

That was 2007, and an investor can guess the outcome.

We've done a lot of work looking at long-term returns from property. In the United States, over 80 years from 1926 to 2006, nominal returns for commercial property averaged 6 to 8 percent, about half from income and half from capital appreciation. There have only been six years of total negative returns over those eight decades.

The data are remarkably similar across markets and time. It is an incredibly powerful bit of ballast to have in the portfolio.

One can be tempted by the promise of higher returns of property-related investments, be they direct or indirect. It is certainly okay to include these kinds of deals in the portfolio, but not as a substitute for properly managed, bricks-and-mortar property. This can be opportunistic, core, value-add; it can be offices, industrial, retail.

But it should be *real* estate.

Basil Demeroutis is managing partner of FORE Partnership, a private investment office in London focused on U.K. and European commercial real estate, designed and operated exclusively for family offices. Set up as a multifamily office for property, FORE provides families with direct exposure to real estate in a structure aligned with the principles and values of private wealth holders.

Private Equity

Private equity funds have played an increasingly large role in some of the world's most sophisticated and successful institutional portfolios over recent decades, including the Harvard and Yale endowments, and more recently for smaller private investors as well. Historically, good private equity funds managed by top-quality fund managers have systematically outperformed the public markets by large margins.

The primary role of private equity in a portfolio is capital growth. Most private equity investments provide no income, but investors receive returns of capital when investments are sold. Investors generally require higher returns than in public equity portfolios due to the increased risk and lower levels of liquidity.

Private equity funds traditionally invest directly in private businesses with the expectation of selling the business at a higher value in the future. They also develop value-added strategies including merger and acquisitions, operational efficiency, and market expansion.

The asset class still operates in a less efficient market than public equity, as there are fewer buyers and sellers of each business, and not all information is disclosed publicly. Private equity investors must also be willing to bear substantial illiquidity, costs, and inflexibility in exchange for the higher expected return. Individual investment liquidity can range from 5 years for direct investments to 12 years or more for fund-of-fund vehicles, with a J-curve characteristic of returns in which early years are net drawdowns, followed by distributions in later years.

There are two other major characteristics that need to be taken into consideration when selecting private equity as an investment. The first is that private equity is a cyclical business. Most funds are raised during peak years of capital market performance, and so they yield returns that are far less than satisfactory. Timing this market, or at least diversifying over multiple cycles, is essential to achieving good returns.

Current fund return targets tend to be in the low double digits, and have declined significantly from pre-2008 levels when the better funds often exceeded 20 percent returns for many consecutive years. A large portion of previous returns came from financial engineering and the use of leverage in investments, which has declined in the more credit-constrained post-GFC environment.

Second, family investors should be aware that private equity, while performing better than public equity markets over many years, is in fact a two-tier market. The top quartile—and even more noticeably the top decile—of private equity managers make high returns, while most others (i.e., the large majority of the market) make returns below public equities benchmarks and charge significant fees to do so.

If a family is seeking diversification by investing in a number of private equity funds that are not in the top quartile, they may well find themselves paying high fees for high-volatility and below-average, or even negative, returns.

There is a wide range of private equity funds available, including venture capital, growth capital, leveraged buyout, distressed asset funds, secondary funds (which buy investments from existing or defunct funds), themed funds (technology, energy, etc.), and a whole host of other investment strategies. Private equity can be accessed directly, through funds, or even via funds-of-funds, depending on the diversification the investor wants and fees they are willing to pay.

Private equity investing, once focused mostly on the United States, is now a global sector, and can provide an attractive avenue for investment in emerging markets as well as the more developed global economies.

Infrastructure

The infrastructure asset class provides investment exposure to large projects that generate income from large portions of the population such as airports, highways, bridges, power-generation plants, and parking lots. Infrastructure assets are very long term in nature and typically have very large capital requirements for initial investment and recurring operating costs to monitor and maintain the asset.

Infrastructure is a scarce asset that offers a meaningful opportunity to diversify a portion of a family's assets outside of public markets, albeit at traditionally lower rates of return than other asset classes. It serves two primary roles in a portfolio: income generated from the project and inflation protection for the projects that have the ability to increase prices in an inflationary environment.

For Islamic investors, the non-interest-bearing nature of these investments and a regular flow of income (e.g., toll road revenues, hydroelectric revenue streams, or port fees) can make them particularly attractive as part of a *sharia*-compliant portfolio.

Credit Strategies

In the absence of equity-fueled growth opportunities, a range of opportunistic credit strategies have been launched to fill the supply/demand gaps in the capital markets. They include broad credit strategies, loan syndicate participations, direct credit provision and other opportunities. A number of these strategies have been developed and implemented successfully by investing families.

Although they can provide attractive returns, these creative strategies are only for the most sophisticated investors, as they carry both market and execution risk. Understanding the inherent cyclical drivers of return and managing credit strategies according to these cycles is critical for success.

Hedge and Absolute Return Funds

Traditionally, hedge funds were quiet pools of money, raised from endowments, institutions, and wealthy families, which tried to achieve the specific investment objectives of their investors, usually focused on capturing a high percentage of upside return, while hedging out an equally high percentage of downside risk. In the early days, the few hedge funds that did hit the headlines were the "arb funds," which took aggressive arbitrage positions in mergers and acquisitions transactions or global currencies to make substantial, and highly visible, short-term gains with their investors' funds.

Now, hedge funds are regular front-page news, having initially raised and deployed funds exceeding US$4 trillion until suffering in the crisis and receding to an aggregate pool of capital at its low point falling to about half of what it was at the peak. These funds, even if diminished in scale, have now spread their ambit of activity to cover emerging markets and a full range of asset classes.

As a result, many families have concluded that hedge funds are not, in fact, an asset class at all. They are now seen as a means to access equity or fixed-income markets on a value-added basis. More specifically, their statistically driven approach is meant to provide an equity substitute with a defensive downside profile and simultaneously to generate growth in the portfolio.

In the view of many others, hedge funds are nothing more than a compensation model, often commanding a 2 percent annual management fee on assets, plus 20 percent of the upside above a rising portfolio "high water mark." There is pressure for fee reductions in the wake of poor performance of the category and the generally low absolute rates of returns available in the marketplace, but the best managers can still command the same high fees as they have in the past.

One active family investor pointed out that, from his perspective, only the weaker funds were reducing fees, leaving his interest, ironically, only in those hedge fund managers who were not cutting fees or reducing carry/high water mark compensation.

Very broadly, hedge funds fall into two overall categories in their pursuit of this shared goal: market neutral and opportunistic.

Market neutral includes fixed-income, event-driven (including distressed assets), and market-neutral multistrategy. They tend to be replacements for fixed income, targeting stability of return and capital. They are designed to provide the portfolio with diversification and low correlation, while generating attractive long-term returns by exploiting market inefficiencies and differentiated strategies.

Opportunistic strategies include equity long/short, sector long/short, macro-funds, directional multistrategy, and market-neutral multistrategy. They tend to provide the growth-oriented features of equity, but with either hedging strategies added on to reduce risk or leverage strategies to amplify positive returns.

It is critically important to select the best-in-class investment managers in this asset class, and a savvy family will focus its efforts on creating long-term relationships with a deep understanding of the team, strategy, and returns achieved. As in the private equity asset class, there is a wide spread between the best and worst-performing hedge fund managers.

Swaps, Derivatives, and Structured Notes

There is an ever-lengthening list of investment products emerging and evolving to suit the needs of sophisticated family investors, and often to generate substantial profits for the issuing or placing bankers or brokers.

Rather than delve into the high-level definitions and details on such instruments as swaps, derivatives, repos, structured notes, and other products of all kinds, which could take many volumes to address in full, we would only like to note that families should be aware of the full menu of items on the "endless buffet" of investment opportunities and select only those that fit their needs, that are fully understood, and that can sit comfortably within the limits of their appetite for risk.

Commodities

Natural resources include investments in materials that can be found in the natural environment including precious metals, base metals, oil and gas, timber, and water. They commonly serve two primary roles in a portfolio: value growth generated from changes in the underlying commodity price and expected world demand, and inflation protection, since commodities are typically highly correlated with inflation.

Given that resource supplies are finite, investment in the asset class represents a long-term expectation that society will continue to place high value on the resource, and/or that the supply of the resource will deplete over time. Investment in natural resources is often viewed as a proxy for investing directly in emerging markets such as China, as the largest portion of demand growth will continue to come from these markets as they industrialize, urbanize, and build their industrial, commercial, and consumer markets.

There are a number of ways to access the asset class, including direct exposure through purchase of the commodity, an investment in companies that harvest/produce/mine the resource or service the industry, exploration companies, and managed futures or commodity trading advisors (CTAs), to name but a few.

Most strategies of traded commodities or stocks offer good liquidity; however, some, such as managed futures and development of a portfolio of private exploration or resource technology companies, may provide significantly less liquidity. Natural resources are a very cyclical investment, and depending on the time of the investment in the cycle, returns can vary greatly.

Foreign Exchange

Foreign exchange strategies are often twofold: On the one hand, they address currency risk in a portfolio, providing a hedging function back into a home market currency, or back to a preset basket of currencies. On the other hand, "forex" can be seen as a speculative asset class on its own, offering investment opportunities where currency prices—always in relation to another currency or commodity—rise and fall. This is true for all currency pairs, with the exception of those pegged to a fixed exchange rate for economic policy reasons. For example, the Hong Kong dollar is fixed against the U.S. dollar, as is the Chinese yuan.

Traditional approaches in the United States, for example, include using forex overlays through the forward markets, with the objective of adding currency diversification and risk protections against a fall in the value of the U.S. dollar. Through this diversification and application of market trading skills, many families also hope to generate profits as targeted currencies increase in value.

Currencies, it should be noted, are subject to government intervention (or at least their Treasury printing presses) and are influenced by many factors and often move in a different manner than what the fundamentals may "normally" prescribe. Currencies are highly volatile, move in cycles, and are not attractive return providers for buy-and-hold investors. They require, like most financial assets, the right buy price and sell discipline in order to generate sustainable profits.

Direct Strategies

Direct investments are those in which more than one family and/or asset manager invest together in a set opportunity. This can provide attractive returns and even, on rare occasions, provide the foundations for the next major family business.

Direct investments are gaining in popularity; however, it is critical to appreciate that direct investments:

- Are much less scalable than funds
- Are hard to execute successfully on a consistent basis
- Place important responsibilities on the family's investment and business teams, in the area of governance and reporting

Operationally oriented families may believe that the benefits far outweigh the burdens of having a direct investment program, and invest a substantial quantum of their funds accordingly. Other families avoid all but liquid securities in large capital markets. A separate set of principles and guidelines needs to be established for direct investing, in particular when it may involve the engagement of family members in ownership, governance, or management.

Islamic and Other Religious Products

Although the Islamic products market is still in its early days of development and global expansion, it is already a multibillion-dollar market that is growing rapidly as a result of the boom in oil prices and consequent rise in Middle Eastern wealth.

Islamic bonds, in particular, are a new area that is proving particularly attractive to Middle Eastern and Asian Islamic and non-Islamic investing families alike.

Collectibles

One of the great benefits of accumulating wealth is the ability to acquire and enjoy assets that are both aesthetically pleasing and that increase in value at the same time.

Some of the great fortunes of history have been associated with the collection of art and antiques. John Pierpont Morgan and the Getty Foundation in the United States, the baronial Thyssen-Bornemiszas of Europe, and the reigning family of the principality of Liechtenstein were or are great collectors of art whose collections have skyrocketed in value over time.

The addition of hedge fund managers, along with newly wealthy Asian families, as active investors in collectibles is accelerating the increase in value in many sectors.

Exotica and Passion Investing

The exotic asset classes—fine art, classic silver, porcelain and the decorative arts, vintage and racing automobiles, jewelry and watches, planes, guns, sporting memorabilia, athletic and sporting teams and venues, and passionately assembled collections of all kinds—carry with them great personal satisfaction, but also distinct investment risks that need to be assessed and managed. Families may also decide simply to remove their collecting passion from their wealth process, seeing it more as a lifestyle spend than a financial investment.

The risks are fourfold:

1. *Poor investment judgment despite expertise.* On the one hand, passion for one or more of these asset classes creates a deep understanding of the market and even the role and value of each piece under consideration. On the other hand, research shows that passion collecting can often be characterized by clouded judgment from an investment perspective. A seasoned expert advisor may help in tamping down irrational exuberance and balance a collector's enthusiasm (or even obsession) with the disciplines of rational investment.
2. *High friction costs.* The auction houses, such as Sotheby's and Christie's, are the logical place for the presentation and sale of expensive works of art and design. Auction house fees, called buyer's and seller's commissions or premia, can reach as high as 25 percent (each) to both buyer and seller.
3. *Small buyer pool and slow sale process.* The two issues here are related. As the pool of buyers may be small, placing items into a specialized gallery or auction house may take some time to arrange, negotiate, and begin marketing. This means that there are only a few events per year in which large items or collections can be bought or sold in the context of a major, globally attended auction.
4. *Adverse price dynamics and unclear correlation.* Although great fanfare is attached to spiraling prices of certain selected art pieces, the truth is that 90 percent of works of art achieve their highest price at the time of initial sale. Afterward, at least for many, many years, the price is unlikely to be recovered unless the buyer is extraordinarily perceptive—or extraordinarily lucky.

A Broader Search for Alpha and Creative Alternatives

As with so many other asset classes, alternatives are redefining their role in family portfolios. The long history of value creation through arbitraging inefficiencies between private and public markets is not so easy in a flat financial world. Equally, providing equity funds is also no longer a unique proposition in a well-funded world, where available capital exceeds attractive opportunities in many geographic markets and industrial sectors.

Although the role of alternative assets remains to provide portfolio alpha, the route to success in the future will require more creativity, a broader global search for opportunities, and an ability to spot and capture opportunities ahead of the broader market.

Given the amount of capital and high-quality brainpower dedicated to the sector, there will no doubt be new waves of innovation and opportunity coming through in the future, but the benefits created may require greater creativity and harder work for less return—for families and alternatives managers alike.

CHAPTER 18

Selecting Individual Investments and Investment Managers

A thorough investment analysis goes beyond understanding history, estimating economic cycles, and forecasting the future investment environment to spot trends, risks, and opportunities. Successful investing also involves an assiduous review of each potential investment manager and mandate, including past results, the chosen business model, competitive performance, industry regulatory environment, asset backing, team dynamics, environmental liabilities, forecast results, and other measures relevant for the kind of investment proposed.

After the long-term strategic asset mix has been determined, the investment policy has been documented, and the asset-class universe has been identified, the investor will begin the process of reviewing and selecting investment managers who will manage individual mandates. The actual investment management function can be performed internally within a family office or can be outsourced to any number of external investment managers. The latter is the much more common route families choose due to the complexity of the task and the experience required for successful execution. They choose investment management specialists who will be responsible for managing the funds within specific guidelines and parameters.

It is critical for the investor to probe deeply into the quality of the thinking underpinning the investment thesis and the underlying assets under consideration, rather than simply allocating the capital at hand.

Issues to Consider

There are a number of issues investing families will want to consider as part of the investment decision process and before they select the managers who will look after a portion of their capital. Some of those considerations are discussed in this section.

Active versus Passive Management

One of the most important philosophical decisions a family investor will need to make is how they choose between active and passive investment management. Active investment funds are those that are directed by an individual manager, or a team of managers, who invests to outperform the relevant market benchmarks. For this service, active managers charge a fee to the portfolio. Passive investments (often referred to as *index funds*) manage defined portfolios that are targeted to mirror (not outperform) the components of a market index. Index funds or exchange-traded funds (ETFs) tend to charge much lower fees than active managers and often aim to create beta at low prices rather than seeking to outperform the market. To add further choice, there are now also active management ETFs that are designed to mirror the performance of active managers.

The arguments for passive investing are as follows: The stock market is efficient so, on average, investment managers cannot outperform over the long term. In fact, advocates of passive investing argue that the average manager underperforms the relevant index by the amount of his or her annual fees and trading costs.

It is true that many asset classes (e.g., U.S. large-cap) are considered very "efficient" in the sense that information is widely available and there are many funds chasing the same opportunities. This can make it difficult for managers to actually add value in excess of the benchmark.

Investors can track the upside/downside capture of managers, and they can also track the risk-return record of the manager to help them decide what best fits their family's investment objectives. Selected factors such as outperformance of a benchmark and risk reduction can be worth the additional fees if actually achieved.

Sometimes investors can end up with the worst of both worlds. Many active managers are afraid of straying too far from the index because they fear that frustrated investors will remove their assets from the fund. Some of these managers become what are called *closet indexers*, with portfolios that look very much like the index but still charge the higher active management fees.

Hedge funds managers are the ultimate active managers. They believe that they have significant skill to generate alpha, outperform the market, or produce substantial risk-adjusted returns. Their 2 percent and 20 percent fee structure reflects that confidence and, hopefully, their active management skills.

Dispersion and Persistence

A related issue is dispersion of returns. In more efficient markets (like government bonds or large-cap U.S. stocks), investment manager returns are typically clustered around the average return. In other words, the range between the best managers and the worst managers is not very wide.

In less efficient markets (like small-cap equity or even private equity), the dispersion of returns can be much wider. Figure 18.1 shows the return dispersions between top and bottom quartiles for various asset classes for the 10 years ending June 30, 2010. The larger the dispersion, the more opportunity there is for a very good manager to produce meaningful outperformance over this index and his or her peers, and the greater the rationale for paying active manager fees.

Being able to find managers that can outperform is one significant challenge in the search for superior investment return. The next challenge is finding a manager that can keep outperforming

Bonds	0.6%
U.S. Large-Capitalization Equity	4.5%
Absolute Return	4.9%
U.S. Small-Capitalization Equity	6.5%
Venture Capital	12.4%
Leveraged Buyouts	16.0%
Real Estate	24.8%

Figure 18.1 Dispersion of Returns, 10 Years Ending June 2010
Source: "The Yale Endowment," Yale University, 2011.

year after year, described as "investment persistence" by analysts. In other words, can a good manager stay a good manager?

Sadly, the answer is that it is very difficult. Studies show that most investment managers that outperform for a period of time will almost always lag in a following period, in such a manner and with sufficient magnitude that over time they move toward the average. There are some exceptions, and they are as valuable as they are rare.

Given the low rates of return in the current environment, finding managers who can add 1 to 2 percent above their benchmark or peers can be a very welcome addition to portfolio returns. There is good evidence to suggest that persistence is more often present in some of the less liquid asset classes such as private equity.

Investment Style

Investors will also want to consider the investment style of the managers they choose. The most common equity styles are growth, value, growth at a reasonable price (GARP), momentum, and concentrated, although there is a wide range of other unique styles and approaches across equities, bonds, and all other asset classes.

Investors should consider how the manager style fits with their own understanding and philosophy of investing. For instance, in equity management, value managers tend to be more effective protecting downside, and growth managers will often do better when markets are strong.

Investors will also want to consider the opportunities for diversification that using multiple styles can bring. There are periods of time when value managers outperform and times when growth managers outperform. Some families intentionally choose a mixture of value and growth managers to diversify their portfolios. Concentrated and high-conviction managers are less likely to be "benchmark huggers" because of the small number of positions they own or the large tilt toward a particular security or sector.

Geography

Many investing families will also choose to diversify their holdings regionally and will select managers with expertise and focus in different parts of the world. There are several factors to consider. One of the reasons to hold a global portfolio is that it may offer a broader range of markets and industry groups than a single home country can offer and thus, if assets are well chosen, can produce higher growth rates and returns for the portfolio.

In the past, there have also been significant benefits available from diversifying a portfolio beyond an investor's own borders. In recent years, with the more interconnected world, global markets have begun to move more in tandem, reducing those benefits to some extent. Investors are starting to look for that global diversification by shifting to emerging markets (e.g., Brazil, India, China) and frontier markets (e.g., Vietnam, Ukraine, Indonesia), which are somewhat less correlated with developed markets and in many cases have more rapid growth.

The downside of emerging-market investing is risk and, surprisingly, an excess of enthusiasm for these markets by international portfolio investors. Less developed markets, in particular, typically are more volatile and have lower standards of transparency and regulation, thus increasing the contextual risk to investors.

International markets, especially in the emerging world, are often very sensitive to the flows of international "hot money." Markets are driven by these flows in and out, leaving domestic and long-term investors to see the value of their investment whipsawed by sentiment and the constant search to reduce risk and boost return. The result can be high prices, as seen at the end of the 2012–2013 rebound in markets such as Indonesia and Thailand, or extremely low prices as seen in the 1998 crisis period.

Investment managers who specialize in these regions will typically be aware of the unique factors in these newer markets. Some investors will choose to access emerging markets via exchange-traded funds (ETFs), some via global companies with significant sales in emerging-market countries, and some via direct purchase of companies on emerging-market exchanges or private companies. Given the risk of emerging markets, most inexperienced or broad-based investors will be well served to own exposure to a basket of countries rather than just one or two.

Another decision investors and their advisors will have to make is whether to access global markets by way of one or more global managers (who have the freedom to allocate the funds across many regions) or through a series of regional funds that are focused solely on one particular region. The former approach puts the regional allocation decision in the hands of the investment manager. The latter approach leaves the regional allocation to the family and its chief investment officer (CIO) or advisors.

Another point worth noting is that the definition of what is a nondomestic company is blurring as companies become more global. For instance, Coca-Cola, nominally a U.S. company, earns 80 percent of its revenue outside the United States. The distinction between domestic, international, and emerging markets is becoming increasingly outdated and artificial.

Public versus Private

As a rule, public securities are more liquid, transparent, and less expensive to own than private investments. Private investments, as we have seen, can offer higher return and higher risk, and there is more potential for a manager to outperform his peers and continue to do so.

Investors will need to determine the trade-offs in their own portfolios, such as how much liquidity they are willing to sacrifice for the potential extra return available from private investments. Families with very long investment horizons, who have large liquid investment portfolios and limited debt and personal spending commitments, may easily be able to sustain larger exposures to illiquid private investments and so benefit from the potential higher returns. As mentioned, fees are generally higher on private investments and need to be factored in to the total investment return calculation.

Direct versus Funds

Investors also need to decide on the structure of their investments. They can go direct and buy individual investments—from stocks and bonds to individual private companies to stand-alone pieces of real estate. Alternatively, they can buy a fund that invests in multiple opportunities. Pools or funds are generally more expensive because the investor pays a manager to manage the investments. However, it may be a cheaper way for investors to manage a group of assets than having to set up the infrastructure themselves. Pools also offer the benefit of diversification and a more convenient method of purchase for the investor. This is very much a personal choice on the part of investors and will depend on the costs, the structure they have in their own family office, the time they commit to managing their assets, and the complexity of the assets, and the skill required to manage them.

One consideration taxable investors should bear in mind is that pools or funds can come with an unwelcome surprise. If the fund has had strong performance, it will have embedded capital gains. A new investor buying that fund may be liable to pay the tax on those gains even though he or she did not actually receive the benefit of those gains.

Access

Some investments are easy to access, such as public stocks and bonds. There are others, often run by top-performing hedge fund and private equity managers, that can be far more difficult to access by individual investors.

Managers may limit access to keep a fund smaller and thus more nimble, or simply to create the impression of scarcity, preparing the ground for much larger funds in the future. Other investments can be difficult to access because of the sheer size of the dollar commitment required, like infrastructure investments (e.g., bridges, tolls roads, and hospitals), which are often available only to the largest institutional pension plans or sovereign wealth plans.

Market Exposure (Long versus Short)

Investors will also want to decide whether they want to take a long-only approach to investing (only buying securities) or if they want to incorporate the ability to "go short" into their portfolio. Some asset managers, most notably hedge fund managers, regularly short securities as a diversifying strategy.

Tax Factors

Taxable investors will want to consider if or how their investment managers take taxes into account for their investors. They should be more sensitive to the amount of capital gains tax that will be triggered by active trading of the portfolio and will want to be aware of the character of the returns that are being generated (e.g., interest, dividends, capital gains), depending on how each is taxed in their jurisdiction. Taxable investors may need a manager to be sensitive to the location of their assets in various taxable and nontaxable structures.

"The Five Ps" of Investment Manager Evaluation

Once the preceding factors have been considered, the process for selecting a manager should be carried out in a disciplined manner that takes into account a range of qualitative and quantitative factors. Outlined in this section are five factors that deserve evaluation in the selection of a qualified investment manager.

Performance

Reviewing an investment manager's long-term return is often the starting point in manager evaluation. There are a number of important ways to evaluate performance, including relative performance to peers, relative performance to benchmark, results relative to risk taken, and pure absolute return.

Extensive experience in manager selection over the years suggests that the qualitative factors can also have a significant impact on the ultimate effectiveness and longevity of the manager and his or her investment results. Examples of valuable questions to ask here include:

- Are the manager's investment management activities consistent with the stated philosophy (e.g., a value manager should be expected to protect capital when markets fall)?
- What is the process for risk management and has it been effective?
- Which activities have had the greatest impact on performance in a particular period (asset allocation, regional allocation, or stock selection, an issue usually described as performance attribution)?
- Have there been years with particularly large gains or losses? Can they be explained?
- How do returns compare on an after-fee and after-tax basis and on an absolute and relative return basis? Are the performance numbers comparable and compliant?

People

Far too often, investors spend all their time and due diligence resources reviewing the investment manager's business and quantitative performance numbers. Allocating sufficient effort to understand and assess the people involved can be a valuable part of the approach to any investment analysis.

In a business that is all about the investment decisions made by individuals, it is important to know that the people who have been responsible for the past performance are still at the firm and that these results can potentially be reproduced in the future. An investor may also want to be assured that an investor can have access to the key decision makers.

Similarly, it is important to know if there have been any organizational changes that may affect the key decision makers. An investor might also consider looking at the employee turnover rate, the employment records of the principals, and the firm's compensation structure.

Investors should also want to be confident that the people who are running the firm and managing the portfolio have the appropriate integrity and experience to execute their mandate well, as proven by performance in a wide range of situations and across various market cycles. Due diligence on the people involved in the management or ownership of a business may merit a special review of each key person's background. This may involve taking references, checking backgrounds, and even using a security firm to verify character and curriculum vitae. This is not the time to be polite or deferential.

> *Investors have to ask impertinent questions if [they] are to separate the superior from the inferior managers.*
>
> *Claude Rosenberg Jr.,* Investing with the Best

Research suggests that qualitative factors such as these have a significant impact on the ultimate effectiveness and longevity of the manager and therefore a great impact on investment results.

Philosophy

The fundamental philosophy of investment is what makes a manager unique and what ultimately drives investment decisions. Good managers will have a clear philosophy and be able to articulate it well. It is also helpful to know if the manager has maintained that philosophy or style over the long term, particularly through difficult years, and the degree of future conviction with that investment philosophy.

There is substantial pressure on managers to produce above-average investment returns every quarter. Managers with a sustainable philosophy will resist the temptation to chase short-term performance and adhere to core disciplines through economic cycles.

Process

The investment process is how investment managers operate on a day-to-day basis and how they implement their investment philosophy. Families will want to know if the investment process is proven, if it is clear and understandable, and if it is stable and repeatable. This helps eliminate "one-shot wonders" who may have benefited from a lucky break or one-off event.

Families will also want to know how the manager makes investment decisions and how they manage portfolio risk. Additionally, it is important to know whether the manager has experienced significant changes in the approach or perhaps the size of the portfolio, which could alter the investment process.

It is worth reviewing all key administrative issues in the firm, such as the firm's registration with the appropriate regulatory authorities and its financial and compliance processes, as well as making efforts to understand the impact of the various commercial relationships an investment firm has, including auditors, partners, related-party entities, industry associations, and outsourced suppliers.

It may also be important to assess a manager's experience with private wealth and the ability to deal effectively with taxable accounts, franking credits, and other jurisdictionally specific reporting demands.

Price

Price is always an important factor when hiring an investment manager, but it is particularly relevant in today's low-return environment. Investment management fees can easily eat up a large portion of investment management alpha and even market beta in an extremely low-yield market.

It is important also to be alert to all the ways a firm can generate revenue and be sure they are all disclosed and not contrary to an investor's interests. Placement fees, fee-sharing arrangements with product vendors, "retrocessions" (fee kickbacks from bankers or brokers), and other such arrangements are clear conflicts of interest and should be fully disclosed whenever offered or accepted.

Sample Questions to Ask Investment Managers

- Outline any significant developments that have occurred within your firm in the past year (ownership, company direction, personnel, etc.).
- What percentage of the firm is currently owned by employees? If less than 100 percent, who owns the remainder?
- Have any additional steps been put in place to ensure the firm's continuity (succession planning)?
- Indicate what your future plans may be, involving both investment management and other business activities (business plan projections, asset/regional growth plans, organic growth vs. merger, etc.).
- Indicate the details of any new investment services, products, or mandates an investor has or plans to introduce.
- Do you have any plans to cap the firm's growth in terms of total assets, total number of clients, or total assets in a particular mandate? If yes, please explain.
- What areas of your business do you see growing over the next five years (institutional, private client, funds, etc.)?
- Has your firm or any employee been involved in any legal actions and/or sanctioned by any regulatory body in the past year? If yes, please provide details.
- Has your firm been audited by regulators over the past year? If yes, please provide a copy of the audit.
- Indicate the number of professionals, with additions/deletions over the past five years (please provide an organizational flowchart).
- List names, positions held, and dates of all personnel departures in the past year.
- Have there been significant changes to your compensation structure?
- What is the approximate market value of the total assets managed by your firm?
- Please provide the breakdown of the number of accounts gained and lost during the past year.
- Have there been any significant changes to your investment philosophy/process in the past year? Are there any pending changes?

(*continued*)

- Provide the names and titles for all members of the investment policy or strategy committee.
- Please provide a copy of your most current version of the following documents:
  - Firm's regulatory-related policies
  - Certification of compliance letter
- Are your performance numbers CFA Institute compliant and audited for last year? If yes, please provide a copy of the audited results.

Documentation and Discipline

Although it may be countercultural to document investment proposals and investment decisions, the discipline of capturing them in written form can provide useful information for review and response to inevitable changes in the investing environment or the family's situation.

The use of standardized templates for investment proposals can help to streamline the decision-making process and provide an easy summary for the CIO, family office or investment committee, or other family decision makers to compare investment opportunities and proceed efficiently.

It is also important to recognize that this discipline must leave room for qualitative decision-making elements and entrepreneurial investment style, which may not be fully quantifiable. A check-the-box, mechanistic investment process will not produce the best results.

How a Large Outsourced CIO Thinks about Manager Evaluation

The sourcing and assessment process of investment managers is global in nature. Over the past few years, our investment committee has reviewed several thousand potential investment funds and opportunities, making an effort to select only the best managers that fit our strategic frameworks. The due diligence and analysis process is a highly detailed process that addresses the potential investment's past performance, market and related risks, the firm's range of investment strategies and unique characteristics, and management team.

The overall process is driven by an asset allocation model and by the parameters of the relevant investment policy statement, which is reviewed periodically by the investment committee members. Each potential investment is overseen from start to finish by a project manager, working under the supervision of the CIO and, ultimately, the family's investment committee.

Though each investment is different, investment review mandates generally describe and address the following:

- The specific investment manager recommendation.
- Key decision criteria.
- Expected performance, along with potential exit strategy/ parameters.
- Fees, costs, and tax issues.
- Background/due diligence process.
- Investment strategy and process.
- Portfolio composition.
- Risk assessment and management.
- Investment characteristics, performance, and statistics.
- Management team quality.

Obviously, the more high-quality opportunities we have to assess, the more likely it is that the quality of the final investments will be exceptional in their performance over time. At our firm, for example, the team reviewed over 2,700 funds in order to find the 45 that best fit their demanding investment criteria.

Initial Allocation and Tactical Decisions

Once the eligible managers are chosen, the available capital must be allocated among the managers selected. There may be a wide range of views on the number of managers that should be employed in each asset class and the trade-off between benefits and costs. On the one hand, the investor will want enough managers to ensure sufficient diversification and exposure to various investment styles and strategies. On the other hand, a larger number of smaller exposures to investment managers can cause unnecessary overdiversification, excess complexity, and increased costs due to smaller commitments to each manager.

Another factor investors need to consider is the potential overlap and duplication created by having multiple managers. Investment managers, acting independently, may double up on the same security, creating a significant overweight not readily apparent when the initial mandate was granted. One manager may also sell a security because he no longer wants it in his portfolio, whereas another manager might purchase the same security at the same time because he or she finds it attractive. This creates an unnecessary disposition, potential capital gains tax, and possible compliance issues for the family.

It can be helpful for the CIO or family office to try to coordinate among managers to reduce the incidence of unintended consequences such as these in the portfolio.

CHAPTER 19

Investment Policy Statement (Example)

Investment Policy Statement—the Reynolds Family

Purpose

The investment policy statement (IPS) is a strategic guide to the planning and implementation of the family's investment program. It provides a framework for managing your investment assets and will prescribe the structure, content, and administration of your portfolio.

Specifically, the IPS is intended to:

- Establish a clear understanding of the investment goals and objectives of the family.
- Determine the relevant time horizons in which the funds will be managed an evaluated.
- Set out the structure and process for managing the investment assets, including asset allocations, asset classes, and the composition of the portfolios.
- Describe the criteria by which investments and managers will be selected and any restrictions that must be followed.
- Outline the process by which the investment program will be implemented and administered.
- Define the decision-making process and the responsibilities of all parties involved in the management of the assets.

- Ensure effective communication between the investor and the various parties involved in the investment management process.
- Ensure that the governance and the management funds comply with all applicable fiduciary standards and regulatory requirements.
- Establish a clear basis for reporting on and evaluating the investment results.

Scope

This investment policy is designed for the Reynolds family and its related entities. James (71) and Susan Reynolds (64) are the owners, beneficial owners, and/or trustees of the entities listed below. These investable assets comprise the bulk of the family's net worth, with the exception of their remaining 22 percent share of Reynolds Aviation and their homes and personal use assets. The total investable asset across all entities is $100 million.

- James and Susan Reynolds
- Reynolds family trust
- Artorius Capital
- HEW trust

The Reynolds Family Foundation is viewed as a separate entity with a separate investment objectives and policy and an independent board of directors (even though controlled by James and Susan).

Objectives

The portfolio is to be constructed to:

- Preserve capital.
- Provide income to fund spending and donation requirement.
- Provide reasonable prospects for growth within a moderate-risk context.
- Provide some limited liquidity.

Specifically:

- The portfolio will be expected fund annual family lifestyle income requirements of $1 million.

- The family intends to continue its tradition of funding all education costs of its descendants for as long as possible and discretionary investments in family member's entrepreneurial ventures. In recent years this has averaged $1 million per year. This funding is expected to come from the HEW trust.
- The family would like to be able to provide additional funds to the Reynolds Family Foundation of $20 million on the death of James and Susan.
- The family would like to retain the purchasing power of the capital and grow the funds modestly after distributions.

Investment Principles

The portfolio will be managed based on the following investment principles:

- Diversification among uncorrelated asset classes can help to reduce risk.
- Sound investment in illiquid assets can add to return. The family is able to withstand some illiquidity due to the size of its assets and the long-term nature of its objectives.
- Investment fees should be minimized where possible due to the large negative effect they have on investment returns.
- Since the family and its entities are taxable for the most part, sensible tax savings strategies and tactics should figure into the investment policy where possible.
- Investments should be purchased with a margin of safety where possible. Chasing return, following the crowd, and speculative securities are not appropriate strategies for this portfolio.
- Reinvestment of dividends and investment returns (net of income requirements) is an important way to grow capital.

Expected Return

Within these overall objectives, the portfolio should seek to earn total returns in the range of 6 to 8 percent over the long term before fees and investment expenses. Given historical experience and the ability of the family to invest for the long term with minimal liquidity requirements, this rate of return should be achievable, on average. Of course, the rate of return will vary each year based on developments in the capital markets.

Income Needs

Income will be required from the portfolio to fund the income-oriented objectives and will need to rise with the rate of inflation.

Liquidity

Over the short term, the portfolio should be sufficiently flexible and liquid to accommodate reasonable capital withdrawals that may be required, although none are currently foreseen. However, the specific allocation to short-term investments in the asset mix will be relatively small. Liquidity is likely to be achieved through the income normally generated within the portfolio given the asset mix and the marketability of securities. In addition to planned liquidity amounts, the external investment managers may hold cash positions temporarily, pending their intended eventual reinvestment in the portfolio.

Risk Tolerance

The family recognizes that the long-term objectives of the portfolio cannot be achieved without incurring a certain level of risk, and that there are uncertainties within capital markets. The family's investment profile reflects an acceptance of the degree of volatility associated with a portfolio of equities, fixed income, and alternative or illiquid asset classes, including hedge funds, private equity, real estate, and others. Portfolios with an emphasis on long-term growth will tend to experience wider price fluctuations in the short-term than over a full investment cycle. In those years when returns are above this range, the excess return can either be considered a reserve for those years when the return falls below this range, or an addition to capital on which to earn future income. We believe that the approach of focusing on a long-term target for returns will provide more stability for future planning.

Planning Horizon

Investment recommendations are to be made using a clear long-term horizon, and will be evaluated over a three- to five-year time frame within the context of the planned investment objectives. Results will be measured annually and reported quarterly.

Asset Class Universe

The relatively wide range of objectives the family has (preservation, income, modest capital growth, inflation protection, and modest liquidity) will require a range of asset classes to meet those objectives. The appropriate asset mix will be a key factor in the achievement of the family goals.

Fixed-income and related investments can provide stability of capital, liquidity, and some modest level of income (especially in the current low-interest-rate environment). But they are not generally able to deliver consistently high returns or significant protection from the effects of inflation.

Equities and related growth-oriented assets are designed to provide capital growth, inflation protection, and, in some cases, growth in income/dividends. However, equities can have substantial year-to-year variability, which can impact investor confidence and liquidity.

Other investments have a range of positive and negative factors. Many alternative investments (real estate, private equity, infrastructure, some hedge funds) target higher long-term returns or less variability in returns (absolute return funds) but can sacrifice liquidity.

The goal of a sound investment policy is to balance the risks and rewards of the various asset classes in service of the objectives of the portfolio and the family.

The allowable asset class universe in this investment policy is as follows:

- Cash and money market
- Bonds and fixed income
- Equities—domestic, global, emerging market
- Hedge funds
- Private equity
- Real estate
- Infrastructure
- Insurance
- Gold
- Exchange-traded funds (ETFs)

Asset classes and categories specifically excluded from the investable universe include:

- Structured products
- Commodities
- Speculative securities
- Currencies

- Aviation securities (due to the family's continuing large exposure to the industry via Reynolds Aviation)
- Mutual funds

Proposed Asset Allocation (and Target Ranges)

The recommended allocation takes into account the family's investment needs, time horizon, and ability to tolerate fluctuations in the value of the portfolio. Based on the investment profile and objective of achieving a return in the range of 6 to 8 percent per annum before fees, the overall recommendation is that your portfolio be allocated as follows:

	Target Asset Allocation	Asset Allocation Guideline Ranges	
	Asset Mix	**Minimum**	**Maximum**
Cash	5%	0%	5%
Fixed income	25%	15%	30%
Equities	30%	20%	40%
Hedge funds	10%	0%	10%
Real estate	10%	0%	20%
Private equity	10%	0%	10%
Infrastructure	5%	0%	5%
Gold	5%	0%	5%
Total	**100%**		

Rebalancing

The asset allocation recommended for the portfolio represents what we believe is meant to be an appropriate balance among asset classes given the family's risk tolerance. A rebalancing of the portfolio may be recommended based on a substantial change in the mix of the portfolio caused by relative price movements. At a minimum, this will be reviewed annually. The family office has the authority to make tactical allocations within the asset mix ranges.

Quality Guidelines and Portfolio Constraints

Quality guidelines are designed as a framework for helping to ensure that securities chosen within the portfolio meet certain criteria. The portfolio will be invested prudently, taking into consideration securities ratings, portfolio and industry concentration limits, issuer size, and ensuring that securities are traded either on a recognized public exchange or as qualified public issues.

Issuers of securities that need to be excluded from the investment portfolio are designated in the appendix. There are currently none. In addition, any preexisting assets to be managed on a special-situation basis will be listed in the appendix along with a description of the treatment of and strategies for these securities. There are currently none.

Tax Implications

All of the family entities are taxable, so tax-aware investing is a key component of this investment policy and should be factored into the investment decisions wherever possible.

Investment Manager Selection

Investment managers will be selected by the Mayfair Family Office based on the investment policy. The roster and selection guidelines will be reviewed on a regular basis by the investment committee. The manager selection process will be based on the following Five Ps guidelines.

Performance The manager should have a proven minimum track record (three years) of performance and an ability to meet the objectives of the mandate it is being given. The family will target managers with evidence of a higher-than-average risk-adjusted return over relevant measurement periods relative to their peers, key benchmarks, and/or a minimum absolute rate of return for the mandate.

People The people managing the funds should be of the highest integrity and experience level, and the organization should be stable and profitable. There should be good bench strength, effective incentives and human resource management, and a visible succession plan.

Philosophy The philosophy under which the funds are managed should be reasonable, and the manager should be able to articulate it well. It is also helpful to know if the manager has maintained that philosophy or style over the long term (particularly through difficult years), and his or her degree of conviction in the particular investment philosophy. The investment committee has a preference for the value-oriented manager and his or her focus on downside protection and margin of safety.

Process The manager should have a proven process to implement his or her investment mandate that is sensible, disciplined, and repeatable, as well as sound operational, administrative, and regulatory policies and practices.

Price The fees should be reasonable based on the products offered. The investment committee is sensitive to the level of fees and prefers not to use mutual funds or funds-of-funds where possible.

Investment Decision Making and Responsibilities

The following outlines the responsibilities of the various parties involved in the investment process.

Family Investment Committee The family investment committee is the representative of the family in all investment decisions and is responsible for:

- Participating in developing the investment policy, including the determination of the objectives, risk tolerance, asset mix, and control procedures.
- Approving the initial investment policy statement and reviewing it at least annually.
- Selecting the investment consultant/family office that will provide overall management of the investment process.
- Reporting to the other relevant members of the family on the investment portfolio and any relevant decisions and developments.

The current investment committee is composed of James Reynolds, Jeremy Reynolds, Morgan Reynolds, Gavin Dunston (solicitor and trustee), and Maria Van Holland (friend and university endowment investment manager).

Mayfair Family Office (Investment Advisor/Outsourced CIO)

The family has retained an objective, third-party advisor (Mayfair Family Office) to manage their financial affairs, including their investment portfolio. Mayfair has been delegated the responsibility to lead the investment process by the family investment committee and will:

- Manage the family's investments in the context of the overall wealth plan and family balance sheet.
- Prepare, execute, and maintain the investment policy statement in conjunction with the family investment committee.
- Recommend an appropriate asset mix that is likely to meet the family's objectives.
- Select the investment managers (based on full due diligence) and products to fulfill the asset allocation.
- Negotiate investment fees on behalf of the family.
- Rebalance the investments as needed.
- Monitor and oversee the investments and managers.
- Provide consolidated reporting on all investments to the family investment committee.

Investment Managers

The investment managers selected will have the following responsibilities related to managing a component of the investment portfolio:

- Discretionary investment management, including decisions to buy, hold, or sell individual securities in the mandates assigned to them.
- Ensure "best execution" on all transactions within the mandate, where relevant.
- Diligently follow all regulatory policies and corporate action requirements.
- Communicate to Mayfair all relevant information and changes within the firm or the fund.
- Provide required reporting to Mayfair.

Custodian

The custodian(s) will be responsible for execution, administration, and reporting on the assets. They will:

- Maintain possession of the securities owned by the family in separate accounts based on individual or entity.

- Settle all transactions and collect dividends, income, and distributions.
- Provide monthly valuation and reporting on all holdings and transactions in the account.

Monitoring and Review

Regularly Mayfair will communicate with the investment committee (via James Reynolds, chair) whenever there are relevant issues to discuss.

Monthly The investment committee will receive reports from the custodian(s) each month detailing the holdings and all transactions with the accounts.

Quarterly Mayfair will meet with the investment committee each quarter and will produce formal portfolio statements and transactions for each account together with a written investment outlook. A performance report showing the return of the portfolio and appropriate benchmarks for return will also be provided.

Annually Mayfair will provide a comprehensive portfolio review including performance evaluation, evaluation of financial market conditions, and a review of the specific circumstances of each entity on an annual basis. The investment committee will be asked to review and reapprove the investment policy annually as well.

IMPERATIVE 5

MONITOR PERFORMANCE AND RESPOND TO THE NEED FOR CHANGE

CHAPTER 20

Monitoring Performance against Internal Goals and External Benchmarks

One of the most important elements of a high-quality approach to wealth management is a clear, accurate, and usable set of performance reports. These tools, which measure progress against the plan, can help to keep the family and its advisors on top of developments in the market and understand how they will affect the portfolio and the family's long-term goals.

Typically once a month, and in greater detail each quarter, the family should receive a summary report of its net worth and investment performance by asset class, manager, and individual investment, although many investments such as private equity funds may not provide any meaningful information on less than a quarterly or even an annual basis.

Accurate information can perform many valuable functions: it can guide the review and adjustments of asset allocation, inform specific investment decisions, and highlight the accumulation of risks and costs on a total portfolio basis. Most important, high-quality reporting and control can make a substantial contribution to the achievement of overall investment objectives. With accurate and timely information, wealth managers will be far more able to make the right decisions to keep a portfolio of investments on track to long-term goal achievement.

Family investors, the family office (FO) or the chief investment officer (CIO), and other decision makers will require detailed reporting to facilitate decision making. These reports should be prepared on a regular basis in a consistent, standardized format. The content of the reporting is dependent on what metrics are desired and information availability, but it should cover:

- Current and historic performance summary.
- Variance analysis against target and historic performance.
- Current allocation against target ranges.
- Absolute return for the current and recent past periods (for total portfolio, asset class, and each individual investment).
- Return against benchmark (with performance net of fees).
- Any proposed additions to or exits from the portfolio.
- Upcoming investments, disposals, or potential investments.

Without this kind of strategic monitoring and control, decision makers will have inadequate information for portfolio management, and remedial actions will be difficult to put into effect. Further information of a more detailed nature can be requested for strategic allocation adjustments or tactical decisions as necessary.

Investment Manager Monitoring

In addition to general investment performance monitoring, the pool of managers selected to manage the family's assets should be evaluated on a regular basis by the FO or CIO and his or her staff. Typically, evaluation processes are broken into routine cycles that are conducted on daily, monthly, quarterly, and annual time frames.

The CIO and investment staff should prepare a formal review of the manager annually and sign off on the continued use of the manager for the family. Following are examples of the tasks performed in each time frame:

- *Daily.* Some strategies, particularly those in the public equity markets, can be monitored on a daily basis. For example, manager trades can be monitored on a real-time basis to ensure they are in line with the manager's defined strategy.
- *Monthly.* Performance data are often reviewed monthly against benchmarks, along with a summary of the trading activities of a manager. The review would typically be

completed at a high level, allowing portfolio issues to be investigated in more detail.

- *Quarterly*. Good due diligence would suggest that a conversation is conducted with managers on a quarterly basis to hear their views and review what has transpired in the portfolio over the course of the quarter.

  A detailed quantitative review is typically prepared each quarter and discussed with the manager. In addition, updates from the manager regarding the qualitative aspects of the organization should be required, and any significant changes that may affect the portfolio process or philosophy should be reviewed in detail.
- *Annually*. The annual review process for managers should be the most in-depth review process and should typically include an in-person meeting with the manager. A general update of the original due diligence should be completed. This is typically done through a questionnaire format distributed to the manager in advance of the meeting.

  All aspects of qualitative and quantitative measures should be formally documented. General trends in the manager's qualitative and quantitative factors from previous annual reviews should be evaluated in more detail. For example, growth in the manager's assets under management can create significant challenges to some management styles.

Benchmarks

A constant dilemma for investors and their advisors is which measures they should use to evaluate the performance of the portfolio. There is a wide range of measurement options that can seem helpful, but can also add confusion if not clear and the implications of each measure fully understood.

Multiple benchmarks can also allow investment managers to hide poor performance by switching benchmarks or time frames to suit their circumstances if not correctly and consistently presented with appropriate commentary.

Absolute Benchmarks

Some families will want to develop absolute return targets based on the required return they have developed in the investment planning stage. For instance, if a 5 percent long-term rate of return on the portfolio is sufficient to fund all of the family's goals and commitments, then this will be an important number to review.

The reporting should identify whether the portfolio is on track to deliver the targeted rate return and how likely it is to be achieved in the future. The investor may actually prefer to track a cash number versus a percentage (e.g., $100,000 a month) in cases where there is a specific income requirement from the funds.

Relative Benchmarks

Because capital markets go through significant up-and-down phases, it can be more difficult to achieve a specific absolute return goal in some environments compared to others. Many investors also choose to track relative returns, such as how a particular investment or fund performed relative to market indices (e.g., S&P 500 or HFRI hedge fund index). Figure 20.1 shows the benchmarks used by an actual family investment fund.

Investors may also want to compare the performance to all the other managers who were managing funds in a similar manner. It can also be helpful to track rates of return relative to historical averages (e.g., performance of real estate this year over the past 10 years) and relative to other asset classes (e.g., performance of stocks vs. bonds).

Risk-Adjusted Measurement

Investors looking at portfolio performance should also be aware of the amount of risk the investment manager has taken to achieve the returns. There are a number of measures that will provide these data, such as the information ratio, Sharpe ratio, and Sortino ratio.

Other Factors

Taxable investors will probably want to calculate their returns on an after-tax basis. Investors who expected the portfolio to provide significant distribution over many generations will want to be aware of the real results (i.e., after inflation), after tax and after all costs have been taken into account.

Investors can track all of the preceding data and benchmarks, but it will be helpful if they can identify the key objectives of the portfolio and a few key benchmarks against which they will measure their progress. This kind of alignment is helpful both for the wealth holders and for the managers who are working for them.

The trust will use benchmarks on a quarterly, annual, and three-year basis, to evaluate the success of the strategic model and the investment manager. As a long-term investor, the trust places a higher emphasis on longer-term information than on shorter-term information (see Figure 20.1).

Cash	**No benchmark**
Core Fixed Income	Barclay's Capital 3-5 Year UST Index −20bps
Credit & Distressed Strategies	**Barclay's Capital U.S. High Yield Index**
Global Public Equities • U.S. • Europe & Developec Markets • Emerging Markets–Non-Asia • Asia	 Russell 3000 • MSCI EAFE • MSCI Emerging Markets • MSCI Emerging Markets
Private Equity **• Corporate Buyout & Growth** **• Venture Capital** **• Asia**	 **• Cambridge Associates Private Equity Index** **• Cambridge Associates Venture Capital Index** **• Cambridge Associates PE/VC Indices**
Direct Strategies	Cambridge Associates PE/VC Indices
Absolute Return	**90 day UST+600bps**
Real Assets • Real Estate & Infrastructure • Energy & Commodities	 • Marketable: DJ REIT ETF; CPI + 900bps • Nonmarketable: Cambridge Associates RE Index; CPI+900bps • Marketable: DJ Energy ETF; GSCI-50bps • Nonmarketable: Cambridge Natural Resources—Oil/Gas Index; CPI+600bps
Hard Tradables	**No benchmark**
Foreign Exchange Strategies	No benchmark

Figure 20.1 Sample Portfolio Benchmarks for a Large Family Trust

Analytical Tools

Raw performance data may not be enough for sophisticated investors. There are many analytical tools investors can use to evaluate the performance of an investment portfolio. Analytical and comparative measures may focus on the return relative to the risk (normally defined as *volatility*) taken to achieve that return.

A return of 12 percent with a very high level of volatility might be viewed by a conservative investor as worse than an 8 percent return with relatively lower volatility. Measures such as the Sharpe ratio or information ratio make it easy to compare the returns of various investments after adjusting for risk.

Other tools identify price movements relative to an index or when compared to peers such as upside/downside capture (i.e., how much an investment drops when the overall market drops and how much it rises when the overall market rises) or tracking error, which tracks how closely, or not closely, a portfolio follows its reference benchmark.

Concerns with Standard Statistics

There are several key factors to watch that will help investors see through the numbers to understand the real and useful trends and issues in a portfolio:

- *End-date bias.* Because investment managers will always want to be seen in the best light when presenting investment returns to clients, they will tend to focus reports on the time periods with the best returns. A specific handpicked period may not necessarily be representative of overall historical performance. Investors should ensure that their investment reporting is presented in a standard format with consistent time frames and benchmark calculations for each quarter.
- *Survivorship bias.* Statistics overestimate the impact of funds or investments that have prospered and underestimate the impact of those that have not survived, and are therefore no longer in the index or on the product list. This can skew investors' perspectives of performance by reducing the perceived probability of investment failures.

- *One-hit wonders.* Funds with very strong performance should be carefully investigated to determine whether the results are from a single strong quarter in the past that has influenced the overall average of long-term results. Preferably, the strong results are more evenly distributed across the entire investing period.

  Similarly, in quarterly or annual reporting, it is worthwhile for investors to know the origins of the strong (or weak) performance and whether they came from any one particular security. Performance attribution provides information on how the results are being achieved and, ultimately, whether the performance is likely to be replicated in the future.
- *Window dressing.* Investment managers will often make changes to the portfolio at the very end of a quarter when they have to report the contents of the portfolio to stakeholders to make it look as if they had some of the winning stocks in the portfolio, even if they didn't own them throughout the entire quarter. Investors may thus want to ask their managers about end-of-quarter changes to the portfolio.

Reporting to Multiple Stakeholders

Some families will also choose to report to a broader group of the family, or perhaps to beneficiaries of a trust. Beneficiaries are, in fact, typically entitled to regular reporting from the trustees on the investments within the trust. They require enough information to allow them to assess whether the trustees are acting properly both as fiduciaries and according to the terms of the trust. Timing of reporting to beneficiaries varies among families, with the most popular being on an annual or quarterly basis.

Ultimately, the extent of reporting depends on the resources employed, systems used, and the requirements of the governance process. Good reporting provides all stakeholders with the information that they require to carry out their functions and to evaluate how well policies are being followed.

Sample management reporting metrics for each family group are outlined in Figure 20.2.

Report Type	Wealth Owners (Family Council/ Trustees)	Investment Committee	Beneficiaries
Performance			
Portfolio returns	Yes	Yes	Yes
Returns by manager—quarterly, annual and annualized	Yes	Yes	Yes
Benchmark review and comparison	Yes	Yes	Yes
Peer review and comparison		Yes	
Risk metrics (Sharpe ratio, upside/downside capture, etc.)		Yes	
Other performance metrics as chosen by the investment committee or CIO		Yes	
Asset			
Asset mix	Yes	Yes	Yes
Assets by manager	Yes	Yes	
Summary of all assets by entity	Yes	Yes	
Listing of security or investments held with cost base information		Yes	
Accounting			
Liquidity review	Yes	Yes	
Income streams produced by holdings and the sources of the income streams		Yes	
Reconciliation of the portfolio values		Yes	

Figure 20.2 Sample Reporting Available to Various Stakeholders
Source: Northwood Family Office, 2011.

Other Reports

- *Cash flow management.* The FO or CIO will need to pay close attention to the cash flow position of the family's funds and understand clearly the expected future inflows/outflows.

Integration of the family's needs for cash flow with investment policy, strategy, and processes is crucial for an efficient family office.

- *Investment accounting.* The bookkeeping, reconciliation, and reporting process for the family can take many forms and may be undertaken at different levels of detail. Coordination and management of the process will typically require monthly attention, including a review of all accounts and transactions processed through the accounts.
- *Custodial/banking relationships.* Management of the family's relationship with administrative suppliers such as custodians and banks is generally the responsibility of the FO or CIO and should be built into the regularly scheduled reporting process.
- *Tax reporting.* Depending on the structures selected to hold the family's assets, there may be significant reporting requirements for the preparation of tax returns. Requirements will typically include income calculations; gain/loss calculations, including the maintenance of costs bases; and other required schedules for accountants to prepare annual returns.

Investment Policy Statement Review

The investment policy should also be reviewed on a regular basis to ensure that it is still suitable and appropriate to the purposes of the wealth holder and/or beneficiaries. The IPS may be adjusted based on changes in the family's circumstances or resources, or based on strategic changes expected in capital markets. Asset class allocations, normally set up as ranges around a target, will need to be adjusted on a regular basis to ensure they stay within the target range or are adjusted, if required.

Rebalancing makes sense because it helps keep the portfolio focused on the long-term asset mix that was identified to meet the investment goals. But there are issues to consider. First, it is very difficult to carry out because it requires the investor to sell its winners (the asset class or securities that have gone up in price) and buy its losers (the investments that have declined in price). Second, if a family has decided to earmark a specific amount of capital to fund a specific set of commitments (e.g., funding family lifestyle expenditures with relatively safe assets), rebalancing may reduce that capital amount to a point below the target level. Like many components of investment management, judgment and balance are required to find the best middle way that will meet the ultimate needs of the family.

The Family Wealth Strategic Dashboard

There is a great deal of data that investors and their advisors need to monitor to help protect them from risks, ensure that the portfolio is being well managed, and make changes where and when necessary. Each family should develop its own wealth dashboard that highlights the key factors and indicators that signal a need for further analysis or corrective action.

One of the more valuable tools used in creating and using a strategic dashboard is the application of a "stoplight" scoring system against performance. Those activities in line with plan or ahead of benchmark earn a green dot. Those slightly off course for a short term or in some other kind of mild difficulty are highlighted in a warning shade of yellow. Those items that are substantially off course or measurably off course for a substantial period of time are designated by a red dot in the report.

This simple color coding of performance will make it far faster and easier to see where the issues are in the context of overall progress, and where scarce time and resources can be concentrated to protect against downsides and double up on upside opportunities.

What Gets Measured

The old management adage "what gets measured gets done" would be well applied to family wealth management. Measurement and follow-up are key parts of a successful wealth management plan.

Unfortunately, many existing approaches to reporting lack essential items such as consolidated mark-to-market valuation, see through-costs, net after-fees-and-carry performance on a comparable basis, performance versus benchmarks, risk versus risk parameters, and other measures that are well-suited to guide both strategic and tactical action.

By setting out a clear set of objectives and performance measures, and tracking the most important variables accurately and on a timely basis, a simple strategic dashboard can play an important role in the process beyond mere reporting; it can contribute substantially to the achievement of the larger family vision and supporting objectives.

CHAPTER 21

"White Water Investing" and the Management of Wealth in Turbulent Times

As the history of the past 100 years confirms, it is not always smooth sailing for family investors. There are many periods of volatility, risk, turbulence, and negative market dynamics that can last for decades and severely damage or even destroy a family fortune. Navigating successfully through these particularly difficult years and carefully avoiding the heightened potential for loss during the worst of times can have an extraordinary impact on a family's preservation of wealth.

Adapting to Change

It may be worth remembering again that Charles Darwin did not say "only the strong survive." Instead, his true words were, "It is neither the strongest of the species that survives, nor the most intelligent that survives. It is the one that is the most adaptable to change."

How families adapt their approach to the investment challenges may well make the difference between sustaining family wealth and stature, and falling prey to the all-too-frequent decline from riches to rags in three generations.

In periods of consistently adverse markets, it may be appropriate to adopt a different approach to investment in assets exposed to negative movements in the public or private capital markets.

White Water and Whitecaps

When setting out on an investment voyage in stormy seas, wealthy families might benefit from an approach that adopts the relevant wisdom captured in the experience of sea captains whose vessels successfully completed their voyages despite the danger signs of white water (in a fast running river) and whitecaps (on the swells and waves in a turbulent ocean). These inevitable stormy periods must be managed well, as family fortunes are lost more easily in volatile times.

The nautical analogy, drawing on wisdom from thousands of years and millions of sea voyages, may provide investing families with some helpful and amusing practical reminders of how to cope successfully with a particularly turbulent investing period.

Sailing with the Right Crew

Well-prepared and highly organized families will ensure that they have set up the appropriate strategies required and created the right ecosystem and environment to take advantage of them. Together with their expert crew of advisors, successful family investors adapt their approaches and lay out a course and approach to the journey that is well-suited to the difficulties and dangers of the voyage.

Throttle Back

Curtailing preturbulence expectations and resetting goals more adapted to a changed environment can manage a rising risk profile and forestall inappropriate investment decisions. One wonders whether the *Titanic*'s hopes to set a trans-Atlantic speed record may have influenced the captain's behavior, even at the margin, at a most critical time of limited navigational information, rapidly changing situations, and rising risk from both known and unknown factors.

Proceed with Caution—and Increase Sensitivity to Risks

While some risks are visible and predictable (the "known unknowns"), others are not (the "unknown unknowns"). Hidden dangers and unexpected linkages can have a damaging impact on portfolio values and performance. Moving forward with appropriate caution can have a very positive long-term effect, if even just one major risk is avoided just one time.

Cross-Check

Proceeding carefully also requires high-quality information and insights on the investment environment. On a ship, this requires information on weather, wind, currents, rocks, and shoals as well as the detail of the vessel's operating systems and performance.

In the financial world, this means getting as many insights and views as possible on macroeconomics, capital markets, currencies, companies, risks, and opportunities, and using that information to steer away from risks and toward the opportunities that present themselves over time.

Hold More Frequent Reviews with More Detailed Reporting

During a particularly vicious crisis, monthly meetings may need to become daily or weekly sessions, reporting periods shortened, and fundamental economic reviews undertaken more frequently. Checking progress more regularly and watching the full set of vital signs (financial, fiscal, and family) for early warning signals is an essential part of successful financial navigation through stormy seas.

Remain Flexible

Adhering to an outdated plan or holding on to an underperforming asset can contribute to poor results when not necessary. Remaining flexible and adapting to important changes in the environment can contribute to the survival and continuing prosperity of a family's fortune.

At a very practical level, this may mean focusing more on conservative investments backed by strong strategic positions and cash flows. It may also mean widening the tactical ranges for each asset class within the overall asset allocation model and holding cash for deployment as and when the right opportunities present themselves.

Batten Down the Hatches

Preparation in advance of a crisis can be a valuable contribution to the preservation of family wealth. It is important to ensure that costs are low, information flows and resulting responses are swift and effective, and expectations for progress are reset appropriately.

Family expectations of services, distributions, and acquisition of residences and lifestyle assets may also need to be addressed because prolonged crisis, unmatched by cutbacks in distribution and costs, can have a significantly negative long-term impact on family wealth.

Ensure That the Hull Is Sound

The risk of flaws and faulty seams needs to be avoided. These can include weak counterparties, failing banks, or other sources of unmanaged risk in the system. Regular checks on the solvency of key financial service and other providers can be crucial to the future of a family's wealth plans, as can structuring arrangements to ring fence assets or acquiring reliable policies to ensure against loss.

Jettison Unwanted Cargo

There may be assets, advisory relationships, and encumbrances that no longer fit the current or future needs of the family, and the family would be better off without them. A crisis or difficult trading environment may provide a good opportunity to remove those elements in the family wealth management mix that no longer belong.

Make Needed Change

As one pundit concluded: "It would be a great shame to waste a good crisis." Family leaders can use the crisis environment to make changes that would not be possible under normal operating circumstances.

Changing managers, making adjustments to the ecosystem, redefining roles or replacing staff in the family office, reviewing processes and approval filters, and similar changes can contribute to current tactics and longer-term strategies for the family.

Stay Ahead of or Sail around the Worst Storms

There is no need to engage with every issue, pursue every opportunity, and review every proposed opportunity. By avoiding icebergs and concentrated risks, investment portfolios will be better positioned to survive intact when the worst storms eventually pass.

Seek Safe Harbors

There are times when the economic seas become extraordinarily roiled and the markets are sending warning signals. If investors are savvy enough to foresee these risks, they would be better advised to seek safe harbors for a while, moving into a "risk-off" mode and waiting for the clouds to clear and the storms to pass before venturing forth once again.

Safe harbors can be of many varieties: solid jurisdictions, reliable financial institutions, strong currencies, diversified portfolios, a higher allocation to safe investments, and tight control of costs and fees. In more dramatic times, seeking a new country in which to live, escaping from impending wars or revolutions, and moving away from particularly troubled areas at particularly troubled times can make the entire difference between preserving and losing a family's wealth.

Pick Up Valuable Flotsam

As ever, there are opportunities in crisis. Distressed investing can provide attractive returns if done at the right time with the right team. One large family office, looking deeply at how great fortunes are made in times of economic distress, described some of the most positive results arising from acquisition strategies which "grabbed as many quality operating assets at the lowest possible price and held on as long as possible before selling in a more positive economic time."

Keep Your Crew Focused and Content

Keeping the crew busy, informed, engaged, and motivated through the entire duration of a crisis is a difficult challenge. Retention and motivation remain essential, as the experience gained will be invaluable in the next crisis.

Resume Full Speed When the Crisis Is Over

Once a storm passes and calmer seas are again the order of the day, family wealth plans can gradually regain speed, take on a bit more risk, and deploy some of the cash carefully husbanded during the crisis for sunnier days. There is no preset trigger on when it is safe to begin to reinvest, but it would not be wise to wait until assets are fully priced again, for much of the benefit available toward the end of a crisis is to be had in buying good assets at low prices.

IMPERATIVE 6

SELECT AND MANAGE AN ECOSYSTEM OF TRUSTED FINANCIAL ADVISORS

CHAPTER 22

Designing the Ecosystem and Selecting Advisors

The complex and fast-moving world of wealth management needs a highly capable team and a leadership that is capable, experienced, and trustworthy. All but the most expert private investors should retain capable advisors to help them navigate through the dangerous peaks and troughs of global financial markets, and advise on how best to work through the many issues associated with family wealth. That network of expert advisors has been described as an integrated financial "ecosystem" of the family.*

Finding the right combination of skills in one advisor or a single advisory team is not an easy task. The advisors should be trustworthy, dependable, knowledgeable, qualified, veterans of multiple cycles, good communicators, empathetic, independent, objective, and sensitive to the needs of the family. Any good advisor must clearly be multitalented as well as dedicated to the best interests of the family.

There is also a constant debate about whether key advisors should be in-house, outsourced, or a combination of both. In some cases, responses to the questions arising are easily decided by asset size and affordability (i.e., if a family is not wealthy enough to justify a dedicated in-house resource). In other cases, especially if

---

* *Strategy for the Wealthy Family, Seven Principles to Ensure Riches to Riches Across Generations* (John Wiley & Sons, 2008), from which the material for this chapter has been extended.

the scale of wealth is particularly substantial, there will need to be a careful trade-off between the exclusive focus and dedication of internal staff and the expertise, connections, and broader experience an outside resource can contribute.

Managing the Ecosystem

By its very nature, a family's ecosystem, like any other dynamic system, is constantly evolving, changing, and being redirected and redefined. Thus, it is incumbent on family leaders to review and adjust their responses to these changes on a regular basis. By assessing regularly the current state of the family's ecosystem, and then acting with a long-term forward view in mind, family leaders may well be capable of preempting problems or strengthening the family to face future challenges, which might otherwise pose a substantial threat to family wealth and well-being.

A System Centered on the Family

An ecosystem is a community of interconnected and interdependent people and institutions that live, work, and interact within a single system. The individual components are linked together and have an effect on each other. In the current technology-driven era, this has been described by more than one observer as an interconnected network of networks.

Just like any ecosystem in the natural world, a family ecosystem is made up of a collection of individuals, institutions, influencers, practices, and principles that nourish and shape it—and that it shapes—through various interactions. It has the potential to provide benefit or harm, clarity or confusion, comfort or distress. An example of a family's financial ecosystem, made up of five concentric levels of participants, is set out in Figure 22.1.

The family and its members lie at the heart of the system, supported most immediately and intimately by an inner circle of trusted advisors, some of whom may have been advisors, friends, or employees of the family for more than a generation.

Beyond these two levels of the ecosystem are selected advisors: relationship-based advisors who understand and work toward the family's long-term goals, and transactional advisors selected and managed to provide specific expertise and support on stand-alone projects and initiatives. At the most remote are the institutions, individuals, and influencers who exert gravitational influence on

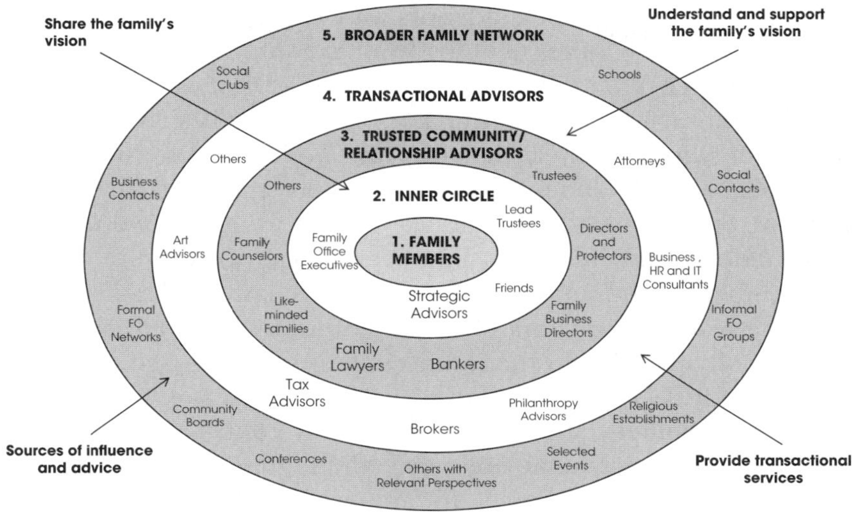

Figure 22.1 Sample Family Wealth Ecosystem
Source: © Rattles Family Wealth Trust

the system as a whole for short or long periods of time but are not involved in specific decisions and their implementation.

The Family Center

While it is obvious that the family sits at the center of its own ecosystem, the role of family leaders and members as conscious managers of that ecosystem may require renewed consideration. Knowingly or not, the family acts as a kind of powerful gravitational center around which revolve dozens of subsidiary and supporting entities, locked into defined orbits and held in place by the gravitational presence of the family.

Unlike solar systems, where all motion is subject to the laws of physics, a family's ecosystem is subject to the conscious and unconscious human decisions and personalities of the family, creating a dynamic system that is created by will, effort, intervention, values, personal choices, and collective aspirations.

The Inner Circle of Trusted Advisors

Just as every president has a "kitchen cabinet" of trusted friends and advisors outside the formal structures of power, and every CEO has a set of close business advisors and trusted friends, the head of a wealthy family often benefits from the integrated insights and practical advice of an inner circle of trusted advisors.

This informal set of powerful advisors operates best as a group of peers with whom family leaders can discuss the most sensitive issues regarding the family and issues of central importance to its wealth management. Such conversations can take place only in an atmosphere of full confidence and without any inhibition or fear of disclosure.

Members of the inner circle may include lawyers, bankers, family office leaders, directors of a family business, tax advisors, and trustees. Membership in the inner circle is usually based on a relationship of trust, capability, and shared experience.

While members of an inner circle can contribute from their own area of professional expertise, their greatest value may be found in offering informed and impartial advice regarding all aspects of the diverse challenges facing the wealthy family, particularly when addressing long-term issues or facing an important transition in the family's affairs. The latter may include the potential sale of a family business or other substantial asset, the transition of leadership or ownership of assets from one generation to another, or in a defining business/family crisis.

Network of Selected Professionals

In the next level of the ecosystem is found a world of professionals with whom the family may have a close working relationship that is based on an understanding of a family. They typically include bankers, private bankers, brokers, lawyers, fund managers, trust and administrative service companies, insurance purveyors, risk management service providers, accountants, and tax experts.

Although it is relatively easy to list the advisors, colleagues, individuals, and institutions that have an impact on a wealthy family, it is far more difficult to determine how to go about influencing the interrelated and dynamic ecosystem that they become. Although the network is usually managed on an informal basis, its importance in determining the family's future prosperity may justify the investment of time and thought in a more structured approach.

What Is Wrong with the Current System?

Although each family's network of advisors is different, a great number of family leaders have expressed their unhappiness with a similar set of issues. They include disappointment with results generated by investment managers, dissatisfaction with fee levels, concerns over a product-push mentality by brokers and bankers, little meaningful risk management systems or systemic insights, and a lack of creativity or understanding to find solutions to family investment issues.

This dissatisfaction has led many to reconsider their span of advisory relationships, become more aggressive on fee control, and ensure that their advisors receive direct feedback on performance and performance shortfalls.

Chief Investment Officer

The chief investment officer (CIO) is the main investment executive in the family ecosystem and is responsible for managing the family's overall investment portfolio in the context of the total family wealth. The CIO role may be an internal staff position or it can be outsourced. If outsourced, it may be independent or part of a multifamily office that serves the integrated needs of the family. Whereas in the institutional world the CIO can focus solely on an investment portfolio and meeting or exceeding the target benchmark rate of return, the CIO of a wealthy family must take a much more integrated approach to investment management. The effective family CIO will need to take into account the other significant assets and liabilities of the family, including businesses, private assets, and multistakeholder, multigenerational funding. In addition, the family CIO will need to understand and work with the full family balance sheet—including soft as well as hard assets and liabilities.

In general, the CIO's role is to work with all of the members of the family and its supporting financial ecosystem to:

- Ascertain and document family investment goals.
- Determine appropriate beneficiary distribution strategies.
- Select eligible asset classes and investment vehicles.
- Craft an investment policy statement.
- Decide on a strategic asset mix designed to meet objectives.
- Review a wide range of investment managers in each eligible asset class.
- Select managers that are suitable for the portfolio.
- Negotiate mandates and fees with each manager.
- Implement the investment process and invest the funds.
- Manage the cash flow, reinvestment, and rebalancing activities of the portfolio.

- Liaise with the financial staff in the family office regarding tax-related investment issues.
- Review and assess investment managers on a regular basis.
- Make changes to the investment policy, asset allocation, and investment managers as needed.
- Provide consolidated investment reporting to the family office and investment committee.
- Provide tax reporting.
- Meet with the family office and other stakeholders to review investment policy, strategy, and results.
- Provide investment education and training to beneficiaries and other stakeholders, as required.

It is essential to preserve the CIO's independence from the pressures of advisors' in-house product sale.

Many private banks offer a finder's fee to trustees, advisors, CIOs, or other influencers. If such an arrangement exists, it should be made known to the investor. A principled investment advisor should not receive any placement fee or reward from any asset or fund manager. Only in this way can the family be sure it receives truly unbiased advice.

Investment Committee

Some particularly wealthy families will choose to set up an investment committee to help guide the family in making sound investment decisions. The investment committee is normally created by the wealth owner and is sometimes a subcommittee of another governance entity, such as a board or trustee group.

The committee is normally responsible for working with the family and/or its family office to engage a CIO and/or investment managers (internal or external), develop and approve changes to the investment policy (normally under the direction of the CIO), monitor the investments (normally on a quarterly basis), advise and guide the CIO, and report to the wealth owner.

Since the role of an investment committee is to oversee a pool of assets, it is imperative that the committee members share an understanding of the goals for that money and that they articulate the goals through the development of a detailed investment policy.

Even in families of more modest means, a formal group that assembles to review and revise investment plans can provide a major contribution to a disciplined and thoughtful investment process.

The investment committee can be composed entirely of family members, or it can be a mix of insiders and selected outside members with investment expertise and a commitment to the family. An external group of committee members can bring experience, perspective, and a good sense of balance that can benefit the family and their investment program.

Selecting and Managing Advisors

- *Start with family visions and goals.* Before setting out to define and select a team to serve family purposes, it is always worthwhile to review what the family is trying to achieve. By setting out in advance the overall goals, the most appropriate supporting resources can be identified to support the family, or to supplement their capabilities to achieve that goal on their own.
- *Set priorities.* Trying to do all things at all times in all places is a recipe for disaster. A few key changes in the ecosystem can be far more effective than blanket coverage of all issues in helping a family to avert disasters and reach a particular destination, perhaps many generations forward. Starting with the highest-priority issues, family leaders can identify the few changes, additions, enhancements, and eliminations from the family's ecosystem that can lead to the greatest and longest-lasting change.

  With a plethora of vendors and suppliers wanting to make their services available to the wealthy family, it is essential to have an organized approach to the management of the internal and external advisor network to avoid wasting time on uninteresting or poor-quality advice.
- *Define the "'ideally constituted'" advisory network team structure.* Once the family's needs and aspirations are defined, the structure of the team of advisors can be determined. In some cases, the team will be purely investment focused; in other cases (perhaps most cases), they will need to be multidisciplinary, with requisite skills in related areas such as tax, trust, and governance. Again, this can be internal staff, external staff, or a combination of the two.
- *The cardinal sin.* One of the most basic mistakes made by many investors is to use the same investment advisor (the

person who selects the funds for an investment portfolio) as a fund manager (the person managing the money). This obvious conflict of interest is most visible in the banking, asset management, private banking, and brokerage worlds. Time and again, "relationship managers" or "personal advisors" push in-house products onto customers, regardless of client needs, fee levels, or likely return.

Since most bankers and brokers are now rewarded on the profitability of the products they sell to clients, and are indifferent to the client's portfolio performance insofar as their own compensation goes, wealthy families need to be aware of the real motivations of their advisors and managers.

- *Decide roles and outline the appropriate selection criteria.* Once the needs for advisory services have been decided, the specific structure of the team can be decided. Will there be a multidisciplinary lead advisor, such as a family office? Will there be a CIO? How many firms and of which type will need to be included? What risk management principles—avoiding concentration risk, security risk, or overdependence on one individual—should be observed?

  Exposure to more than one source of ideas, perspectives, and opportunities has great benefit, but coordination and integration are also crucial. This is the balance the family will need to find when constructing a team of advisors. For example, in the cases where there is no family office, the family may have an established relationship with a "house private bank" with which they have a solid and satisfactory relationship. A second tier of preferred suppliers (e.g., in different geographies) can also be established as appropriate. Other private banks can provide specific transaction opportunities and expert advice as and when needed.
- *List the candidates in each category by area of expertise.* After defining the needs, structure, and approach to its advisory network, the family can then list the candidates in each area of need. From this long list of qualified and appropriate advisory firms and individuals, the family can draw up a short list of the most appropriate candidates to be measured against more rigorous selection criteria. These criteria should reflect both the objective needs of the family and any subjective criteria relating to specific family cultural attributes, values, or operating principles.

In defining a family's specific needs, it can be valuable to solicit input from families in similar situations that may generate general ideas and particular recommendations. This can often serve as a shortcut in an otherwise time-consuming process. If the family already has advisors in a particular area, the factors that make them successful, or not, can also be factored into the selection criteria.

- *Interview and evaluate candidates.* In the interview process, each member of the selection team should have a score sheet of criteria against which each candidate will be assessed, but assessment should not be based solely on that predefined list, as other important but unexpected elements of the decision may arise during the process.

  Many families have found it beneficial to see all candidates for a particular area of support in a compressed time frame, often seeing as many firms or individuals as possible over the course of a few days. This allows comparisons to be made more easily, before memory fades and subtle details and differences are forgotten. Having creative criteria and different participants in the process can also be useful. Family advisors who have had experience of the sell side can be very valuable in understanding what to avoid and what may add value.
- *Test and evaluate the new members of the group.* The successful candidates may be given small pieces of work to confirm their abilities and discretion before being integrated into the broader network. Working together, even briefly, can provide a valuable platform of shared experience for both sides to assess the fit and potential mutual benefits from a longer-term relationship.
- *Manage and refresh the system.* As with the hiring and integration of an employee into a family business, the hiring of internal investment and financial managers or the selection and introduction of a professional firm into the network is just the beginning of a much longer journey. Not all employee hires will rise to the top, nor will they all stay for an extended time period. The same is true for advisors in the broader network.

  Many advisors to wealthy families can become complacent as the relationship continues across the years, delivering work that becomes accepted despite its low or declining standard. Seeking out and addressing such underperformance is a key test of effectiveness for family leadership.

By changing or adding advisors from time to time, the remaining players in the system will stay fresh and eager to provide the required level of service. In most cases, regular and objective reporting on performance against benchmarks, on an after-fees-and-costs basis, is an important part of the management of financial advisors and investment professionals in the network.

Individual Elements and Holistic Team

As with investment strategy, the determination of the right team of advisors needs to be developed at an individual or firm level, but then also seen as an integrated team of advisors working toward the same goal. It is important that team members work well together, do not retreat to their silos of expertise on broad issues, and work in a collegial and focused manner. There is no room for big egos, counterproductive competition between firms, or the pursuit of political agendas and individual ambitions at the cost of overall progress.

In the end, both the team and its individual members should be measured annually against a short list of preset criteria, and team results and dynamics reviewed in a team setting with prior individual feedback from the lead member of the family involved.

The structure, participants, and approaches set out in this chapter need to be put in place and managed well over time in order to ensure that the overall objectives are met, and that the results targeted are achieved.

Advisor Selection: Issues Checklist

Investors should think carefully about the kind of professional help they want and need. Although the criteria for selecting an advisor will be unique to each investor, the following general qualities are worth weighing in assessing the suitability of potential advisors:

Credentials

- What is their wealth management history and experience?
- How important is the wealth management business for them?

- What is the quality and tenure of professionals?
- What is their financial condition?

Strategy and Advice

- Do they have understandable and credible philosophies and processes?
- Do they have proven, relevant track records?
- Do they have a tax-conscious approach?
- Do they take accountability for their decisions?
- Do they coordinate well with other advisors?
- Do they take a full balance sheet view?

Relationship Quality

- Do they ask the right questions?
- Do they answer all of our questions?
- Do they understand and care about each client?
- Is there clear accountability for client success?
- What is the quality of their communications? Are they clear, honest, and relevant?
- Do they have proactive communication and advice?
- Is there a clear client focus (e.g., no sales, revenue, investment research, or other responsibilities)?

Oversight and Control

- What is the transparency of decisions, holdings, and actions?
- What is the level of due diligence: quality and consistency?
- Do they have sufficient asset protection and insurance coverage?
- Do they have internal and external oversight and measures?
- What are their reporting capabilities and standards?

Resources

- Do they have sufficient resources for current and future needs?
- Do they make sufficient investments in technology and training?

Values

- Do they have proven client satisfaction and retention success?
- Is their compensation aligned with clients' interests?

Source: "2020 Vision: The Most Critical Decade." BNY Mellon, 2011 (authors' edits).

CHAPTER 23

The Role of the Family Office

The needs of any family are complex, and the needs of the wealthy multigenerational family are greater in number and more substantial than those of an average family. A family office is a unique multidisciplinary entity that is designed to serve the multifaceted and integrated needs of wealthy families. It provides advice, oversight, and consolidated management of all of the family's financial assets and liabilities, and typically looks after a range of administrative, human capital, property, personal service, and other family-related issues on behalf of the larger family and its members.

Family offices first emerged in the mid-nineteenth century to look after the needs of the extraordinarily and newly wealthy families that emerged from the Industrial Revolution, including the Rockefellers, Pitcairns, Fords, Rothschilds, and Vanderbilts. Typically beginning as offshoots of the family business, over time the family office developed into a professional organization designed to manage the financial and personal affairs of the family.

A few have evolved into private trust companies and multifamily offices (MFOs) established to serve multiple client families, with others fading in significance with the passage of time and the decline of the fortunes they were established to oversee.

Typical Family Office Activities

While every family is different, there are a number of consistent activities shared across most family offices, with the most important being:

- Comprehensive wealth and tax management
- Administration, reporting, and family support services
- Objective advice and counsel

While the needs of wealthy families vary widely, there are many common concerns shared by most. On the financial side, families need integrated, objective advice on a wide range of topics including complex asset structures, tax and estate planning, succession and family transitions, cash flow management, and investment management. On the family side, many families require residence and property management, physical asset and security oversight, education and leadership development, preparation of heirs, management of human capital, governance, and family communication.

Family offices are also usually responsible for reporting, risk management, and bank and other advisor relationship coordination. A family office, at its best, provides a stable team of well-qualified staff who get to know the family needs and become both coordinators of the family's financial activities and trusted advisors. The family office can bring the appropriate expertise to bear as needed in many individual areas, and on the overall integrated approach, working closely with the family's other advisors to develop a coordinated plan and ensure that it will be implemented effectively.

A well-run family office can take a significant load off the shoulders of the family members to whom the financial and family leadership responsibility normally falls, and allow them to invest their time in their business, family, or leisure activities as they wish. In addition to being technical specialists, family office staff members often also act as sounding boards, problem solvers, and objective sources of reliable, dispassionate advice. Given the long-term nature of the relationship, the family office often becomes the "institutional memory" for the family, safeguarding a wide range of important family records, decisions, values, and wishes, often across multiple generations.

This stable, discreet, and dedicated resource can be contrasted with the frustration many private wealth holders face in the current "a la carte" style of management and administration of their financial affairs.

The high level of staff turnover at their private bank or advisory firm often means they have to reexplain their situation to a new person every few years. In addition, the lack of integrated technical expertise in these institutions often requires the client themselves to coordinate the sharing of financial administration and details among their multiple advisors.

Rationale for Having a Family Office

The reasons for starting or engaging a family office also vary but typically include some of the following:

- Aggregation of assets can offer economies of scale, access to superior investment managers, and a way to protect family assets by consolidated professional management.
- Family focus and continuity, especially after the operating business has been sold.
- Integrated strategy, pulling together all of the diverse components of a wealthy family's financial and human capital into one single view.
- Peace of mind that nothing will fall through the cracks.
- Privacy and confidentiality.
- Tailored services to meet the unique and diverse needs of a wide range of family members.
- Time savings, simplification, and coordination of advisors.
- Education and leadership development.
- Governance to establish a framework and process for decision making, particularly in future generations.
- Institutional memory to help retain key financial and family information and plan for the future.
- Mitigation of conflicts by having the family office represent with expertise and objectivity the interests of the family when reviewing conflicting information or views provided by investment advisors, bankers, and brokers.
- Administration and consolidated reporting.

The function, structure, and operations of a family office vary enormously, depending on the family's specific and unique needs. There are, however, some broad areas of commonality between such offices within the same region. In the United States, for example, family offices may be more focused on domestic trusts and investment and philanthropic needs, while in Europe they may be more focused on offshore trusts, tax planning, and family services, along with wealth management and business needs.

In Asia, where family money, family businesses, and family members are still quite closely aligned, the family office may also serve as the de facto headquarters of the family business enterprise or, conversely, the actual business headquarters may perform many of the functions of a traditional Western family office.

In either case, the family office is the single point of contact for planning and implementation, the point of contact with the broader world, sometimes the public face and spokesman for the family, and typically plays the role of coordinator and manager, bringing the appropriate expertise to bear as needed and working closely with the family's other advisors to ensure seamless execution of multifaceted plans and initiatives.

Comprehensive Wealth Management

One of the main functions of most family offices is to support the family's wealth preservation and investment management activities.

This role typically includes investment management functions such as investment policy development, asset allocation, investment strategy, due diligence, selection of asset managers, performance measurement and analysis, portfolio rebalancing, and negotiation of fees. A family office might also develop its own internal investment capabilities, but more often than not those functions are outsourced to professional investment managers. The family office often plays the complementary roles of the family's CIO and financial controller.

This role is becoming increasingly important with the proliferation and increasing complexity of capital markets and financial products. Families often need a trusted financial advisor who can offer objective advice on investment products and asset allocation, without any of the bias that naturally comes from the product provider.

The family office is also responsible for the related planning activities including tax, asset structuring, estate planning, insurance, trust and trustee management, risk management, and cash flow planning. In most cases, the family office will work closely with other advisors who specialize in tax, legal issues, accounting, and investments.

A family office can improve significantly the effectiveness of the collaboration among professionals. For instance, the work of integrated tax planning, estate planning, and will preparation can be streamlined and enhanced with expert coordination and shepherding. The tax savings that can be uncovered from a diligent review of the family wealth and its structures can be substantial.

Risk management is one of the most important, yet most undervalued, roles of a typical family office. Many wealthy families have highly concentrated assets—in their business holdings, their human capital, and/or their financial portfolios. The risk of this degree of concentration may not be fully evident until a major external event occurs, such as the global financial crisis (GFC) of 2008 and 2009, which showed the full downside cost of many embedded family risks, including concentration risk.

Other risks that require attention and mitigation by the family office might include dying without an updated will or being incapacitated without an appropriate power of attorney; unwitting exposure to estate taxes and reporting requirements; improperly structured or managed trusts; marriage without proper protection of family wealth; or poor succession planning and insufficient documentation on the death of the key decision maker.

Administration, Reporting, and Family Services

Family offices also play a key role in the administration of the family's affairs. This can include consolidated financial reporting, advisor coordination, tax compliance, family record keeping, tax preparation, bill payment, bookkeeping, trust administration, family meetings, and many other activities for family members such as housing, insurance, travel, payments and account management, educational services, security, and health care.

The family office will typically keep minutes, records, and relevant documents in an organized fashion for ease of regular access and for succession planning. The structured and professional review process also helps keep the focus on getting things done.

In this case, the family office operates as a chief financial officer (CFO) or chief administrative officer (CAO) for the family. One of the benefits of a family office is that the services can be tailored to each family member, depending on his or her needs.

With so much going on in so many areas, providing accurate and timely reports on priority investment and family activities on a regular basis is an essential part of the value provided by a well-run family office, as is the selection and operation of an enabling technology platform and an appropriate compliance regimen.

Objective Advice and Counsel

In addition to the specific tasks that the family office undertakes for the family and its members, it often becomes a key center of advice and counsel. Due to its family-centric mission and objective status, senior family office staff often become trusted confidantes or *hommes de confiance* helping to guide and support the family leadership as they make and implement important decisions.

A family office must be independent and objective to offer unbiased advice to the family. Normally, this means that the family office does not create or sell any product and is paid only by the client family.

This advisory element commonly includes advice on integrated strategy, family business, investment, distribution policy, accounting and legal matters (often working with existing professional advisors), counseling on charitable activities, and help dealing with family relationships and issues related to individual family members.

Younger family members may also benefit from the mentoring, education, and guidance offered by the family office. Family office value added in the softer areas can also include facilitating family communication and meetings, preparing for succession, educating heirs, and developing philanthropic plans. The family office can also contribute to the memory, culture, continuity, and dedication that can help preserve the important family history and values, develop leadership, and help the family adapt over multiple generations.

Family Office as Repository of Values

One experienced American billionaire, heir to one of the country's great multigenerational fortunes and an articulate spokesman on the role of the family office, has argued very strongly in favor of an approach to family infrastructure in which "a family office should act primarily as a repository and protector of family values across generations." From his perspective, building the correct foundation of values in the younger generations is the best antidote to the risks of financial ruin, family discord, erosion of the family business, or actions likely to bring the family's good name into controversy or disrepute. While not abdicating the responsibility of family leadership, he sees the enlistment of support from his family office in this cross-generational role as an essential part of his approach to long-term family wealth management.

Family Office Services

The following list summarizes the three roles of a family office and the services provided, with a checklist of activities captured within each area:

Comprehensive Wealth Management

- Goal development
- Family balance sheet management
- Long-term strategy
- Investment policy
- Risk management
- Investment manager selection and oversight
- Performance measurement and analysis
- Fee negotiation
- Custody of assets
- Tax and estate planning
- Insurance
- Trust management
- Cash flow and distribution management

Administration, Reporting, and Family Services

- Consolidated financial reporting
- Advisor coordination
- Tax compliance
- Family record keeping
- Regulatory compliance
- Bill payment

- Bookkeeping
- Trust administration
- Family meeting management
- Services for family members such as housing, insurance, travel, payments and account management, educational services, security, and health care

Objective Advice and Counsel

- Integrated strategic advice
- Family business advice
- Accounting and legal advice (often working with existing professional advisors)
- Counseling on charitable activities
- Family relationships and individual members
- Mentoring, education, and guidance
- Facilitating family communication
- Succession planning
- Educating heirs
- Developing philanthropic plans
- Repository of family values

Internal or External?

The family office can be constituted as an in-house staffed organization, typically called a dedicated or single-family office (SFO), or it can be outsourced to a multifamily office (MFO). For families of $1 billion or more, the need for great discretion and confidentiality, the long list of items to be addressed, and the scale of those activities may justify the establishment of a separate office dedicated to serving the needs of the family.

Other families will choose to use an MFO, which provides many of the advantages of a dedicated family office but typically has a lower and more variable cost model because it serves the needs of more than one family and combines resources for efficiency. Also, some families do not want the in-house operating, compliance, and reporting burdens of a complex business entity like a family office, with all of the related cost, human resources, tax, and regulatory issues.

Because an MFO works with a number of families, there can be valuable learning and experience to bring to bear, as well as a wider range of contacts and access to more investment opportunities.

The multifamily approach can also provide a broader range of choices and allow negotiation of lower investment management fees. Because the MFO deals with multiple high-net-worth families, it brings substantial experience and expertise to bear on many of the complex issues that are common to these and other wealthy families.

Organizing and Outsourcing the CIO Function

From an investment perspective, some families will choose to hire a CIO to oversee the banking, direct investment, and portfolio management of family wealth. The CIO role can be an internally staffed position (for very large pools of capital) or an outsourced one—typically through the engagement of an independent advisor, a multifamily office, or investment consultant. However the family decides to approach the choice, there needs to be someone who will be identified as being responsible for the overall investment activities of the family on an integrated basis. Unclear roles and responsibilities are a recipe for disaster.

How a family decides to structure its investment management process will vary by the scale of the family wealth, the vision, investment profile, financial objectives of the family, and its investment sophistication, as well as the resources it has within the family or family office. In all cases, it is critical for the CIO to separate the roles of the central investment manager, who selects fund managers, and the actual management of funds. By maintaining a clear and effective separation of the two roles, conflict of interest can be more easily avoided and the financial interests of the family best represented through an unbiased CIO function.

One of the challenges for single-family offices lies in sourcing and retaining high-quality professionals with the appropriate skills to manage the various aspects of the family's holdings. Many single-family offices are changing their models to focus on the specific strengths that the family office and then outsourcing other functions, such as asset structuring or portfolio management.

Building an investment team in-house requires a minimum level of wealth (but a substantial number indeed) in order to afford to hire in, retain, motivate, and develop individuals with the experience and skills and infrastructure to manage a diverse range of investment classes and individual investments.

In Figures 23.1 and 23.2, an illustration of a sample organizational structure is set out for both an internally managed investment operation and for an outsourced version.

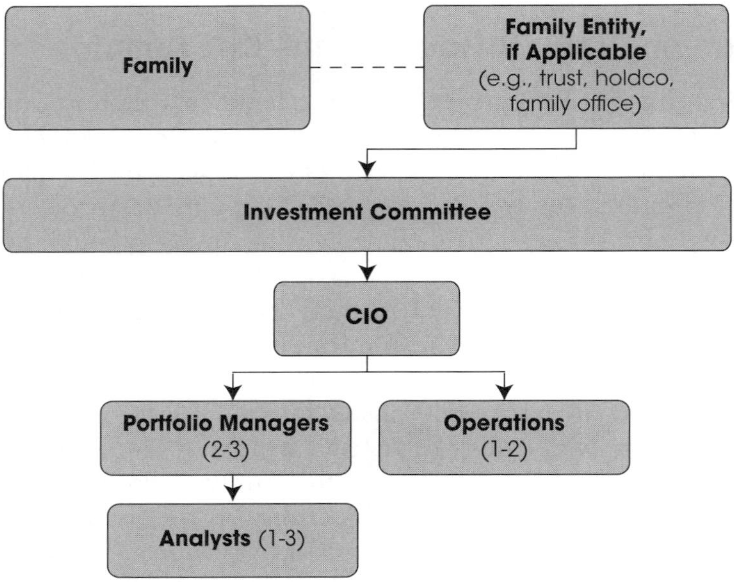

Figure 23.1 Sample Organizational Structure for Internally Managed Investment Operation

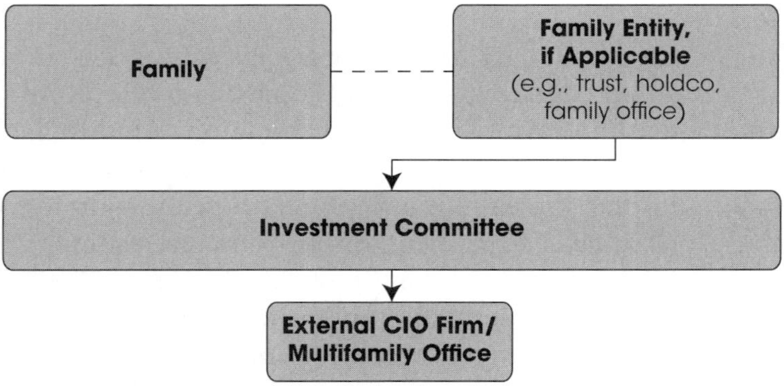

Figure 23.2 Sample Organizational Structure for Externally Managed Investment Operation

Trend toward Outsourcing

According to a 2009 survey by the Family Wealth Alliance:

- Approximately 4 in 10 wealthy families have outsourced discretionary investment management and now use an outsourced CIO model.
- Among smaller family offices (those with $500 million or less in assets), two-thirds use an external advisory on a discretionary basis.
- One-third of all single-family offices think they lack sufficient expertise to analyze investments themselves. This rises to 50 percent for SFOs with $100 million to $500 million in assets.

The staff required to build an investment management operation depends on the approach each family decides to take and how much they want to do internally and how much they want to outsource to external resources.

Source: Inaugural 2009 Single-Family Office Study, Family Wealth Alliance.

Choosing the Right Multifamily Office

If a family has decided to engage a multifamily office instead of establishing its own internal operation, there are some important steps to follow to ensure that the right options and questions are presented and choices are well made in the process of selection and management of the MFO.

Choosing an MFO or outsourced CIO is an exceptionally important decision due to the level of influence over future family wealth management decisions, along with the accompanying trust and disclosure of sensitive information that will be required in the relationship.

Families looking to select among the lengthening list of available MFOs could include the following questions in their analysis of options:

- What is the range of services offered? Which services are provided in-house and which are accessed externally?
- Who are the key staff members and what are their background and experience levels? Describe the roles of key personnel. Who would be the primary contact?

- Who are typical clients—asset size, family size, complexity, geographic location? How many clients do they have? What relevant experience has the MFO had with clients with similar issues?
- Describe the investment process and how the firm develops investment policy for clients. What investment resources does the firm have at its disposal?
- Which investment managers have been selected in the past? Does the firm cover both traditional and alternative managers? What is a typical mix of managers?
- What is the firm's fee structure? Is it based on investable assets, net worth, hourly rate, or annual retainer? Are there any lockups?
- What is the ownership of the firm? What is the business strategy, growth expectation (or ceiling imposed on growth), and succession plan?
- Please provide an example of a consolidated reporting package.
- What regulatory structure governs operations? Have there been any regulatory issues or concerns? What are conflict and compliance procedures? What professional liability insurance is in place (if capable of being disclosed, as some policies may have nondisclosure clauses)?
- What potential conflicts of interest are there? Does the firm receive compensation from any source other than clients?
- What are the policies and procedures to protect client privacy and confidentiality?

These questions may provide some structure to individual conversations, and also, if answered well, provide sufficient data to begin to evaluate options on a relative basis.

Separate from the Family Business

While many family offices begin as an outgrowth of the family business, with the corporate CFO and company administrative staff providing advice, administrative services, and personal financial management, this approach does not often work well for the long term. As the family and its wealth grow in size, scope, and complexity, it is important to separate the management of the family and the family wealth from the management of the family business.

An independent wealth management entity has the ability to provide services such as family education, investment planning, and personal financial planning, which are not within the scope of most operating companies and are difficult to justify as business expenses. It can also serve all family members equally, not just those working in the business, and allows them to receive advice based on an in-depth understanding of their comprehensive asset holdings and family circumstances.

The long-term benefits of this integrated advice—professional tax planning, well-developed investment strategies, and additional lifestyle support services for family members—can easily outweigh the added cost of a separate organization.

A separate family office or wealth management entity can serve as a conduit for bringing the family together to determine their shared vision for the future beyond the business, and can help clarify the strategic plans for reaching future goals. In fact, one of the key reasons for keeping the family office and family business is that the staff of the former may even be reviewing and providing input to the family on the potential sale or restructuring of the latter.

Range of Costs

Given the variations available, it is difficult to set a target cost benchmark for a family office. In one sample of 10 SFOs in the United States, with family assets ranging from US$120 million to US$1.2 billion, the total cost as a percentage of assets managed ranged from 12.5 basis points to 125 basis points—with the highest 1.25 percent being found in the office of the wealthiest ($1+ billion) family surveyed.

Other studies have shown a mean cost level of around 50 to 70 basis points for administrative and accounting services, although even those numbers are hard to use as benchmarks as trust, accounting, administration, investment, and service levels, and therefore team size, vary substantially between offices of families with similar wealth and family complexity.

Cautions

While family offices can bring substantial benefits to wealthy families, as in any endeavor, there are risks of which families should be aware. Because family offices look after so many details for families and their members, the individuals can develop an unhealthy dependence on a family office. This can lead to a diminution of basic financial skills such as budgeting and check writing, a reduction in financial responsibility, and the development of a family culture where too many decisions and family roles are outsourced to third-party employees.

These issues can be compounded, and new concerns can develop, if there is a lack of proper oversight and governance of the family office and its staff. A proper family office structure will develop the individual capabilities and financial education of family members, encourage independence and self-reliance, and ensure a robust governance and oversight process.

A Focus on the Family's Objectives

Whether the primary objective of a family office is fiscal, financial, philanthropic, values-oriented, or aligned behind some other greater purpose, it is essential to have in mind a clear vision for the family and for the family office (with the latter subsidiary to and supporting the former), a supporting set of values, and a set of defined priorities (with a definition of success for each priority element) to keep the family office focused on the correct set of activities and objectives.

Whichever route a family chooses, it is critical to invest time and effort to select the right combination of trusted staff and advisors who will provide the expert, objective advice and counsel the family requires. This may be one of the most important "investments" the family ever makes.

Risk and the Role of a Family Office

Entrepreneurs and very senior business leaders face a unique set of circumstances that can put their families and their personal wealth at more risk than they might have imagined. In most cases, these individuals are highly exposed to one company. The company they own is also the company they work for. Unwittingly, perhaps, the entrepreneur has all of his wealth invested in the company, and only the company. Such a concentration of wealth has never bothered the entrepreneur (indeed, it is how he made his fortune). But with succession planning and retirement not far off, he suddenly realizes that his financial well-being may be at risk because all of his wealth is tied up in his one and only investment—the company. Enter the family office, a team of professionals that can help mitigate the risks and prepare the entrepreneur to manage the shift from creating wealth to sustaining it.

Four Key Risks

Apart from the risks inherent in their businesses, entrepreneurs and business leaders face four broad categories of risk:

1. Concentration risk
2. Management risk
3. Balance sheet risk
4. Succession risk

Concentration Risk

Concentration of investment can be a good way to grow wealth, but diversification is the more prudent path to preserving wealth. The trick is in knowing how and when to convert that single, concentrated asset into a more diversified pool of assets, to mitigate the risk of something bad happening to that one asset. Most entrepreneurs and CEOs discount the riskiness of their own business because they know it so well. But regardless of the type of business, having "all of your eggs on one basket" leaves an investor exposed to a substantial loss if something were to go wrong.

It is important for business owners and executives to have a diversification plan in place, especially since it is not easy to move quickly when difficulties arise. Transitions can be dangerous inflection points. Private businesses are generally illiquid, and significant public shareholders usually have regulatory constraints on their ability to buy and sell shares of their company. So the combination of bad timing and a large concentrated asset can be devastating. And, of course, the "mother of all transitions" comes when the business is sold or the deferred compensation vests (usually on retirement). These events need to be well planned for, from both timing and tax perspectives, to mitigate the potential impact of unforeseen negative events and to help ensure the highest possible value of the asset.

Management Risk

When a business owner sells a business or a CEO retires, and their wealth shifts from a concentrated, relatively illiquid operating company to a more diversified set of financial assets, they are often

(*continued*)

unprepared for the different skills and resources required to manage this new form of wealth. Think about it this way: It would be unimaginable for a CEO or business owner to run an effective operating business totally on his or her own. Most CEOs have a team of executives with diverse skill sets—sales, marketing, manufacturing, accounting—with whom they regularly sit around the boardroom table to strategize and to manage the company.

But somehow that logic does not seem to play a role in the management of substantial financial wealth. Most wealth holders have no specific strategy for their financial assets, and the new set of required senior "executives"—tax, legal, investment, planning, philanthropic—rarely sit around the table together to manage the financial wealth in an integrated, strategic manner. In addition, there is often no active CEO or COO of the financial wealth. The fact is that most business owners and CEOs will admit that management of their personal wealth is not their core strength.

Three factors can exacerbate this management risk. First, behavioral psychology tells us that entrepreneurs and corporate CEOs (particularly men) have an independent streak that helped create their success. At the same time, however, they are subject to feeling overly confident that they can manage anything. But financial wealth is a different animal than an operating business, requiring a different set of skills and at least the same level of attention that the business did. It can be learned, but it takes diligence, effort, and time to do well and to stay current with new developments.

Second, the financial press tells investors that managing financial wealth is easy and an investor should, in fact, expect to be able to regularly outperform indices or be able to select the best investment managers on a consistent basis. Unfortunately, the reality is quite different, as any investor who has been through a few cycles will know.

The third, and perhaps most important, issue is the way the financial services industry is structured. Most firms are organized and offer services around their own areas of expertise or interest, whether it is investments, insurance, or tax planning. However, the needs of the wealth holder are usually integrated and interconnected. In fact, most financial issues cannot be neatly folded into one particular discipline or another. It leaves the wealth holder responsible for connecting all the dots to ensure that an objective, unbiased assessment is made and that all the potential consequences are taken into account.

Balance Sheet Risk

Most entrepreneurs and corporate executives are very comfortable around a corporate balance sheet. They know that there must be enough current assets to meet current liabilities; they recognize the need to balance liquidity, cash distributions, and reinvestment of capital into the business; and they understand how an excess of liabilities can weigh on the health of an enterprise and limit its future options.

The same risks and constraints apply to a family balance sheet as to a corporate balance sheet. Short-term assets with minimal variability (such as cash) must be available to fund current liabilities (such as this month's private school bill). Longer-term assets (such as equity or real estate) will be required to meet long-term liabilities (such as bequests).

Too great a focus on investment returns (versus the entire family balance sheet) can put financial wealth at significant risk. The quest for the highest possible return without appropriate regard for specific objectives, risk of loss, or the appropriate matching of assets and liabilities can push the wealth holder further out on the risk curve than they realize or than they need to be. It can also lead (aided and abetted by the investment industry) to a loose collection of investments that serve no specific purpose on the balance sheet. In fact, most of the investments in wealth holders' portfolios have been sold to them by one of the purveyors rather than bought by them to meet a specific need or to play a particular role on their family balance sheet.

Succession Risk

It is no surprise that the word *success* features prominently in the word *succession*. It is vitally important that the business is prepared to continue its success once the current leader moves on, particularly when the wealth of a family is underpinned by just one asset. A well-planned succession has a significant impact on the continuing cash flow of the founder, if he or she plans to retain a stake in the business, or on the price the buyer is willing to pay for the business. Well-thought-out succession is also relevant to senior corporate leaders, who often continue to own shares in the company, which often form a meaningful component of their wealth.

(*continued*)

The Family Office as a Risk Mitigator

The family office was initially conceived to mitigate the previously mentioned risks and help build sustainability into family wealth. There are three main roles the family office plays in this risk mitigation: diversification, integration, and discipline.

Diversification of the core concentrated asset is often a prudent way to protect the risk of loss should the unthinkable happen. The family office, with its deep knowledge of the family and its goals, as well as its staff's experience in a wide variety of professions of origin, plays an important role in providing the family with objective comparison, perspective, and integrated advice and recommendations. The family office can bring an important level of discipline to bear on managing wealth. This can include independence and objectivity, a less emotional perspective, and a fair and fact-based decision-making process that can significantly improve the workings of a family and the management of its wealth.

IMPERATIVE 7

ENGAGE AND EDUCATE THE FAMILY

CHAPTER 24

Determining the Right Wealth Distribution Strategy

The family's wealth distribution policy, which sets out the principles of who gets what when and for what purpose, can have a significant impact on the growth and preservation of family wealth and the long-term health of the family. It is also essential to manage both the financial and family aspects of distribution if wealth management objectives and imperatives are to be respected.

There are two reasons for this. The first is quantitative and deals with the numbers on family wealth and distribution policy; the second is qualitative and addresses issues related to family values and individual behavior.

In both cases, transfer of wealth, similar to transfer of authority through succession in a family business, is best managed through a three-step process:

1. Preparation and communication.
2. Transfer in an appropriate context.
3. Follow-up to ensure that the distribution or transfer of substantial wealth is having, on balance, the desired effects.

A well-designed approach that follows these three steps can address the series of interrelated issues around distribution decisions: how much (both a quantitative and qualitative issue), when, how, in what context, with what messages and limitations, and with what preparation and obligation on the part of the beneficiary.

The Financial Perspective

The hard fact is that aggregate distributions in excess of real aggregated after-fees-and-costs-and-inflation returns on the portfolio will steadily eat away at the portfolio over time in real (i.e., inflation-adjusted) terms.

Distributions in a year of portfolio losses do the same, only faster. Even if per-member distributions are decreasing, if the number of family members tapping in to the shared pot is increasing faster than the wealth accumulates, the net effect may be diminution of the family wealth over time.

However, a more disciplined approach to distribution policy will confine individual payouts to some share of after-tax-and-inflation portfolio return only, ensuring that family wealth is preserved in real terms before any distributions are made. This approach, adopted by some families new and old, ensures that beneficiaries do not become passive "trust babies" or "trustifarians" who are incapable of finding a job or taking care of themselves, and live only from one unearned distribution check to another, with the option of bridging the time in between distributions with as little effort expended as possible.

The Family and Individual Perspective

Distribution policy can also play a major role in shaping the family's culture, values, and work ethic. By giving too much too soon with too little preparation, family value systems can become warped, and individual family members can fall prey to a narcissistic attitude where "the kids know the price of everything and the value of nothing."

Many sensible family leaders, aware of the risks, are concerned about the pernicious effects that substantial wealth can have on inheritors. They want to find the right balance of helping their children and heirs in a significant way but not enabling them to lose touch with reality. Most families like to think about distributions as a combination of a generous gift, more like sharing than transferring, and one that should not be allowed to compromise each family member's ambition, independence, and motivation.

The long-term effects of a life without financial responsibility or autonomy can be heavy indeed. Families who are unwilling to focus on values, to limit distributions, to enforce a policy of individual autonomy, or to invest in the "soft side" of the family wealth equation face a far greater risk of catastrophic loss of wealth.

A Poisoned Chalice

One member of a multibillion-dollar family described his own painful experience with the transfer of substantial wealth without preparation. "The worst day of my life," he said, "was the day I turned 21 and was told I was going to inherit $200 million." In a very eloquent and painful exposition of the "dark side of wealth," he went on to explain that the problems he had experienced were a product of a total lack of preparation by the family, a lack of knowledge on his part, and a poor grasp on the implications of inheriting, managing, and transferring significant family wealth.

He did, in the end, suffer enormously and experience great disorientation as a result of his overnight transformation from college student to multimillionaire, with little engagement on the essential issues in between. In the end, by overinvesting his wealth in a highly concentrated position in a failing retail business, and by transgressing family principles and governance policies in his personal life, his wealth was either lost soon after receipt or cut off completely by his family trustee from the funds that were meant to be his. His nuclear family fell apart and he was forced into a strange meta-life where he, as the protagonist, lived off only off the memory of money and the allure of a once famous name.

This was a hollow substitute for what could have been a substantial and positive family life, based on better knowledge and discipline, benefiting from more thorough preparation and driven by a more compassionate (and more demanding on both sides) family approach to its individual members.

Philosophy, Practicalities, and Policy

Once the family has decided that they want to fund multiple generations, a detailed set of questions emerges. Those questions include:

- What will be the total capital allocated to future generations?
- How many generations does the family want to fund?
- How many can it fund?
- How much money should each generation receive?

- What is the appropriate structure to protect the assets from tax, where possible?
- Should the assets be kept in one pool or should they be divided (e.g., by subfamily group)?
- What is the appropriate investment policy to ensure that the assets last the desired amount of time and defend as much as possible against the ravages of inflation, beneficiary growth, and spending?
- Will there be criteria or guidelines on the amount and manner of the distributions?

There are rarely easy answers to these questions, and many of the answers to one question are interconnected with others. For instance, how much each generation will receive is highly dependent on how many generations the capital is intended to fund and how the capital will be invested.

There is no right or wrong answer when trying to determine the best amount to distribute, but in all cases the decision should be made with reference to the family's values and long-term vision.

Hard Issues in Distribution Policy

The first step in determining distribution plans is to get a picture of the size of the assets and how long they could last. The estate structure and distribution options the family decides on will have an impact on the long-term ability of the family capital to grow and support future generations.

In the following example, a number of simplifying assumptions were made to measure and illustrate the impact of two variables—distribution amounts and number of generations a family could fund:

Current capital	\$100 million
Return on capital	0%
Current number of beneficiaries	4
Children per beneficiary	1.8
Childbearing age	30 (all children born in the first year of the generation)
Life expectancy	90

Assuming no return on the portfolio and that the capital will be fully depleted, Table 24.1 shows that the family can divide all the funds among the members of the current four-person second generation

Table 24.1 Sample Number of Descendants and Distribution per Beneficiary

Generations	Birth Year of Children of the Generation	Number of Beneficiaries Born into the Generation	Number of Living Beneficiaries from Previous Generations (over 18)	Number of Cumulative Beneficiaries	Lifetime Financial Distribution per Beneficiary
1	0	0	0	0	$100,000,000
2	1971	4	4	4	$25,000,000
3	2001	8	8	12	$8,333,333
4	2031	16	12	28	$3,579,429
5	2061	32	24	60	$1,666,667
10	2211	1,024	768	2,044	$48,924
15	2361	32,768	24,576	65,532	$1,526
20	2511	1,048,576	786,432	2,097,148	$48

at the rate of $25 million each (over their lifetime). Alternatively, they can fund 10 generations (2,044 beneficiaries) at the rate of $48,924 each, or use many other combinations and permutations in between. This simple analysis begins to give the family some context in which to make distribution plans and decisions.

A Sustainable Rate of Withdrawal

One of the current dilemmas for many families is the low rate of return in many asset classes over the past decade. Many families have previously counted on a certain level of income from their fixed income and equity investments and those have been under pressure. In the past, a rule of thumb for a sustainable distribution rate over many years would have been in the range of 2 to 4 percent of family investable assets.

Research has shown that portfolios with average risk should have generated 6 to 8 percent per annum over a decade, considering economic cycles both positive and negative. Taking a 7 percent average investment return, and then subtracting three costs will leave far less available for distribution than one might think:

- Investment fees of 1 to 2 percent of assets per year.
- Tax and transfer costs of another 1 percent (when averaged over a generation).
- Inflation of 3 percent.

Families are thus are left with 2 percent for distribution to retain the purchasing power of the wealth. There is no absolute requirement to retain family capital in real terms. Many families simply, and perhaps voluntarily, liquidate their family wealth over time as more and more beneficiaries make greater and greater demands on a diminishing pool of assets, eventually killing off the goose that laid their golden eggs.

The preceding calculation of returns reflects the economics of the last half-century, rather than the most recent decade. In the past, a relatively safe income could be had from fixed income, and solid gains were generated by core equity and real estate investments, providing solid returns above inflation, with excess income also generated for spending and to preserve and enhance capital value.

In the past decade, investment yields and returns have dropped, making sustainable distribution in a time of sharply declining value a fading fancy and a lively topic of discussion for many wealthy families, their advisors, and their trustees.

Reculer pour Mieux Sauter

Wealthy families often have many options regarding the current and future state of their balance sheet and family and investment goals. For instance, the French phrase *reculer pour mieux sauter*, which roughly translates as "step back in order to jump higher" or "retreat to advance better," can provide useful guidance to families at risk of placing excessive demands on a limited resource pool.

By holding back or reducing distributions for a period in order to restore the capital base to a sustainable level, family leaders can provide for the greater family's needs for far longer.

What Is the Right Amount to Leave to an Heir?

This is one of the most important questions wealthy families face, and one with the widest range of answers, literally ranging from everything to nothing.

Some families leave everything to their children on an unencumbered basis, others leave virtually everything to the eldest son only in an age-old system of primogeniture which keeps family wealth intact but excludes the vast majority of bloodline descendants and, historically, also excluded women entirely, and still others leave nothing at all to their children, preferring to fund charitable activities or leave their financial wealth to better earthly and divine causes.

Each family will have very different views on how much of the family wealth will be dedicated to funding activities of the current generations and how much will be left as a legacy for future family members. In some cases, the decision will be determined by the current generation deciding what it will need and what balance, if any, will be left to future progeny.

In other cases, a family leader will have a specific vision for what money could do for the family or the community for many years to come and will make a broader and more inclusive strategy for wealth distribution both within and outside the family.

How Much Is Too Much?

The words "I want leave my children enough so that they can do anything, but not so much that they can do nothing" capture a spirit of balance that makes an interesting point of departure for any conversation about inherited wealth.

There are pros and cons of wealth, particularly when it is inherited and not earned. On the positive side, beneficiaries will benefit from a more comfortable life and may be freed up to pursue passions and interests that they might not have been able to do without the support and benefit of inherited family wealth. On the negative side, inheriting too much money too soon can get in the way of a sense of accomplishment and can reduce self-esteem.

At What Age?

Many families of wealth have some set of age-related, and in some cases capability-related, tests. The most common age at which next-generation members begin to inherit starts at 25, with the possibility of some kind of phased approach up to age 35, or even beyond. Obviously, for testamentary and other inheritance events that are not determined in advance, death or disinheritance can intrude into the picture and tip over any carefully set plans.

The reason most families choose 25 as a minimum age is that by then most children will have finished their education, have taken a few steps toward their career goals, been forced to live within a small budget based on their own after-tax earnings, and learn to plan accordingly before beginning to take on the benefits and related responsibilities of greater wealth.

Practical Distribution Options

There are a number of ways to set up an individual's income and capital distributions to provide the desired motivation and independence. They will typically require a relevant and meaningful reference point to create the calculation. The following are examples of methods that can be used:

- *Income-linking approach.* Link the beneficiary payout to a publicly published average national or more specific salary level.
- *Income-matching approach.* The individual's employment income is matched by the trust. This approach needs to be developed carefully, as one of the possibly unintended consequences of this approach is that an heir who is already a highly paid investment banker would double up on a large salary, while a schoolteacher or charity worker would receive far less; full-time mothers would, possibly, receive nothing for fulfilling a very valuable role for the family and larger society.
- *Milestone approach.* Link distributions to normal lifetime milestones that most people reach.

While there is nothing wrong with any of the preceding alternatives, some families with a strong desire to see the future generations develop "as normally as possible" have favored the milestone approach, as it most closely resembles the experience of other members within the same society.

Not giving large sums of capital or income, but rather helping with capital and income amounts over the course of the beneficiary's lifetime allows them to continue to relate to their peers and the issues that they encounter as they age.

By linking access to family wealth to a defined set of behaviors or accomplishments, for example, finishing college, demonstrating a "work ethic" lifestyle, or maintaining certain family traditions or assets, forward-thinking family leaders can channel some, or even all, of their wealth to preserving valuable assets of all kinds and do their best to help to protect future generations from the dark side of wealth that can be so destructive.

Similarly, providing funds for the continuing ownership and upkeep of a family home, or funds to cover travel to and from an annual family meeting, can ensure that a family's sense of place, harmony, and unity can be carried forward over time as well.

Milestone Methodology

Linking the beneficiary's income and capital payments to key life-cycle milestones may help provide motivation and goals for the individual and, if desired, can help motivate beneficiaries toward the energetic pursuit of selected achievements.

For example, specific capital distributions could be provided for major life events during the crucial financial development years of 18 to 30, such as education funding, graduation capital, wedding capital, and home down payment.

Figure 24.1 shows a sample milestone methodology for one particular family's income and capital distributions.

Life Milestone	Age	Milestone Policy	Income	Capital
Education funding	18–25	Funding of undergraduate and one graduate degree	$25,000	—
Capital at graduation	**25**	**—**	**—**	**$100,000**
Wedding	—	—	—	$50,000
Home down payment	**—**	**Average detached home price in major metropolitan area**	**—**	**$500,000**
Annual income supplements per year	25–65	125% of average national family income (beyond what they might choose to earn themselves)	$100,000	—
Retirement	**55**	**Lump sum payment payable at the age of 55**	**—**	**$1,500,000**
Total of all payments			**$4,175,000**	**$2,150,000**
Combined total of income and lump sums				**$6,325,000**

Figure 24.1 Sample Milestone Methodology

Source: Northwood Family Office, 2012.

Making Their Own Way

There are many benefits to allowing beneficiaries to "make their own way," not the least of which is the satisfaction and self-esteem that they develop over their lifetimes from their own successes. Inheriting too much too early can get in the way of this sense of accomplishment. Phasing as well as conditionality can provide useful input to balanced wealth-life management.

One particular family was trying to find this balance between providing generous financial assistance for beneficiaries and also stimulating a desire for independence and self-motivation. They settled on a combination of step-by-step income and capital distributions that place the onus on the beneficiary to seek employment and handle normal expenses and life decisions before any distributions were available.

The amount they decided to distribute was significant and would make any family's life far more comfortable, but was not so much that it would dramatically alter existing and more "normal" lifestyles. While some beneficiaries could choose to live only on the distributions, most beneficiaries from successful families would not, and would seek employment and the pursuit of a life characterized by greater engagement and accomplishment.

Criteria and Values

Some families also establish minimum requirements or policies that beneficiaries must fulfill to entitle them to receive distributions. While some families may see these policies and practices as too formal or structured, it is worth keeping in mind that they are intended to apply not just to the current generations, but to the generations, even as yet unborn, that will follow them. Examples of minimum requirements include:

Family Employment Policy

- Development of a family employment policy, which includes minimum requirements for employment in the family business/family office.
- Typically, this includes a requirement to work outside the family business/family office for a certain period of time (often 3 to 5 years, but even extending to 10 in some cases) before receiving income from the family's assets.

Family Code of Conduct

- Frequently, well-organized family leaders will require adherence to a defined family code of conduct. Examples include an absence of addictive, abusive, destructive, or criminal behavior; avoiding behavior "unbecoming of the family"; or not making public statements about the family, its members, and its affairs.

Beneficiary Financial Management Skills

- A required family financial management course, coupled with a series of required planning and investment exercises, can help ensure that the beneficiaries start to build the required knowledge and skills to receive and manage distributions and greater family capital over time.

Developing Responsibility and Self-Esteem in Beneficiaries

Experience with wealthy families provides a few general guidelines when it comes to considering distribution policies:

- *Allow people to develop normally.* People are better off when they have some purpose in life and some control over their own destiny. Too much money can eliminate these opportunities.
- *Less is more.* Giving beneficiaries "too little money" won't have the desired effect of providing them with a noticeably more comfortable lifestyle. "Too much money" can create entitlement and dependence. Each family has to find the right balance, but in many cases "less is more."
- *Later is better.* Giving significant amounts of money later in life allows time for people to build their own lives. Giving money too soon can stunt or warp their individual development and life experience.
- *Responsibilities as well as rights.* There should be some requirements or responsibilities expected from the people receiving money. A simple handout can feel like charity and devalue the recipient's experience as an active and valued participant in the family.
- *Magic moments.* There are certain key times in life when extra money will be greatly appreciated (e.g., education, house

(*continued*)

purchase, raising children, etc.). Matching the funds with those critical financial moments can be a good way to help at critical times, yet still allow independence and self-reliance at most times.

- *Careful communication.* Thoughtful preparation and execution of a plan that sets out the timing, context, and messages being sent is critical. Long before informing intended heirs and heiresses of "the number" of total family wealth and their share in that wealth, a phased program of communication that involves both talking and listening on both sides, and a discussion of the general benefits and burdens of wealth and the family's specific values and policies may be among the most important factors in a successful wealth transfer.

While each family is different and unique in its culture, financial resources, and philosophy, the related goals of beneficiary independence and lifelong personal motivation are usually among the most important for all families.

A Contrarian View: All in the Family? Maybe

Ed Lazar

Family management guru Jay Hughes, in his classic and influential book, *Family Wealth: Keeping It in the Family* (Princeton, NJ: Bloomberg Press, 2004), provides a road map for families who wish to work together as a group to preserve their human, intellectual, and financial assets. When done well, managing wealth cohesively as a family has enormous advantages, both financially and emotionally. However, family leaders and their advisory teams too often presume that newly liquid wealth ought to be managed—and controlled—as one unit. Despite the advantages of doing so, make no mistake about the hardships such a journey will almost certainly bring.

Don't get me wrong—being a unified "financial family" is not an all-or-nothing proposition. Invariably, most families have one or more assets that must be managed as a single unit. The key question is how best to create a balance between singular, unified management of wealth and the human autonomy often desired by individual family members. More than one family situation has gone awry because this balance of unity and autonomy was never discussed, debated, and decided.

If a family is already emotionally strained or lacks capacity to create compromise without regret, its members may not be ready to sit down to a dinner of financial stew. Serious heartburn can result. Further, dad and/or mom, in the name of protecting the hard-earned financial wealth from taxing authorities and creditors, may become willing pawns in the creation of byzantine legal structures. Worse yet, they may attempt to use money as a tool to control offspring and their behavior. These situations can only increase the toxicity of the family environment.

Assuming up-front motivations are pure, families must enter into a long-term financial arrangement with the same level of diligence one might use when undertaking any investment with third parties. It is typically best to first examine the plan's intent and structure as if doing so through the eyes of an unrelated third-party private investor.

- Why would we want to do this together as a group, versus either going it alone or with some other group?
- What do we seek to gain by working together, both for ourselves and for those who will or might come after?
- How will we make decisions?
- What are our respective roles and responsibilities?
- How will we communicate and act with each other? How often and to what extent will information be shared? What about communication outside the family, understanding that those on the outside world have certain assumptions of their own—not always well intentioned?
- How often should our up-front assumptions and agreements be revisited?
- If I or others are no longer willing or able to be a part of the family financial cabal, what is the process for unwinding our affairs in an orderly and civil way?

Once the preceding questions are discussed and alignment is achieved, families should test their plan against the grizzled veterans who have paved the path before them. Wealth-owning families are surprisingly candid and constructive in one-on-one peer discussion about their experiences. Family leaders are wise to choose not only advisors who know families with experiences to share, but those who are willing and able to connect peer families with one another. As family-to-family facilitators, advisors must have the knowledge,

(*continued*)

courage, and network of resources to help these peer connections succeed.

The aphorism "shirtsleeves to shirtsleeves in three generations" has become a universal and truthful proverb. Driven in part by human behavior, the inertia of generational family wealth often follows a pattern: The first generation creates the wealth, the second preserves it, and the third spends it. Mr. Hughes posits that families can break this generational cycle and preserve or build wealth for generations if they employ strategies already proven by a handful of legendary financial families. I have no quarrel with this wisdom. However, I do caution that those eager to accept this approach must consider thoughtfully whether and how much of this family journey should be done as a group. If family relationships are not on solid emotional footing, real groundwork will be necessary before joint pursuit of wealth preservation will solidify the family's footing and ultimately achieve financial success.

Ed Lazar is a certified public accountant and has helped guide families of wealth for more than 25 years. He currently serves as president of the Threshold Group, a family office organization founded by the Russell family (Russell Investments), located in Gig Harbor, Washington.

CHAPTER 25

Preparing the Family for Successful Management and Transfer of Wealth

One of the key features of private wealth, and also one of the most important factors family leaders must take into account, is the need to prepare for and support the transfer of wealth across generational and other family divides.

This involves addressing the formal educational needs with regard to family governance and all of the disciplines necessary to support high-quality wealth management programs. While necessary, this may not be sufficient on its own to ensure a successful transfer of wealth from one generation to the next. Formal education on finance and investment needs to be augmented by a more complex psychological and individual effort to ensure that there is sufficient engagement and motivation on the part of the individuals concerned to do a good job when effort, attention, and expertise are most needed.

This dual role of ensuring both engagement and education is a vital task, as much can go wrong in the complex and delicate process of wealth handover from one generation to the next.

A Tidal Wave of Wealth

There is a massive tidal wave of wealth about to transfer across generational lines in the next 40 years. By some estimates, the total wealth faced with the challenge of successful transition exceeds $40 trillion over this time period. Many of these wealth transfers will ultimately be unsuccessful. The main reason for this unhappy record, according to most experts, is the lack of preparation of heirs and heiresses for the inheritance. Traditionally, there is a great deal of attention paid to the management of money, with only a very small amount of time allocated to individual preparation and the organization of the family. All too often, the enormously important task of preparing heirs and heiresses for what is to come is left to schools, dinner table conversations, and occasional discussions.

Given the importance of this task and the high rate of failure in successful maintenance and transfer of wealth across generations, one could argue that this standard approach is a massive underinvestment in one of the most critical areas for the enhancement of family wealth: the engagement and education of the entire family, with particular attention paid to the needs and challenges of the next generation—and beyond. Figure 25.1 looks at the challenges to an enduring legacy.

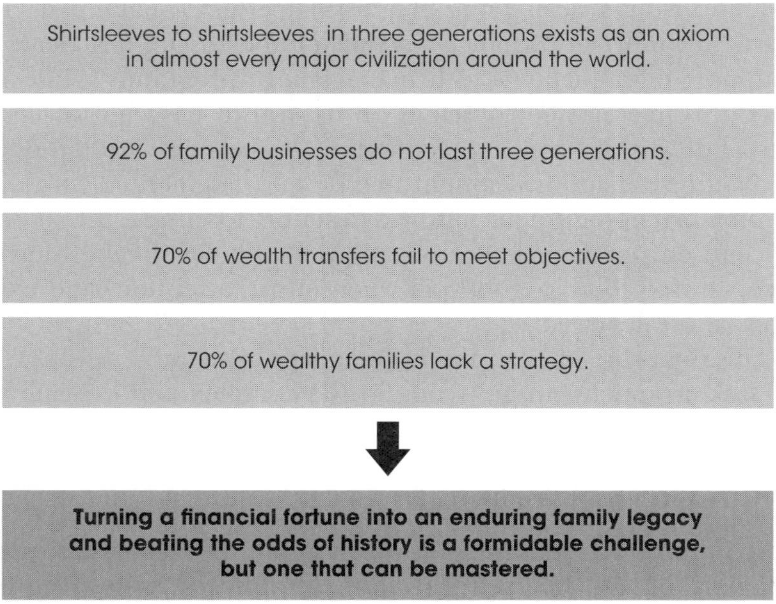

Figure 25.1 The Challenge of Enduring Legacy

Engagement and Education

The two concepts captured in the heading of this section are, in fact, very different, but both are highly relevant to the successful management transfer of wealth.

Engagement has to do with a state of mind, attitudes based on beliefs, which will manifest itself in the degree to which individuals choose to spend time, invest effort, and feel a sense of ownership in the management of family wealth. Some experts call this *emotional ownership*, which is far easier to find in "business families" with a substantial and continuing operating business than in an "investing family" with a portfolio of changing financial investments with which younger family members may have little connection or interest and even less understanding.

Finding a way to engage family members, especially the young, can be a major challenge, and one in which the family leaders may need to invest in a broad set of family activities in which the financial element is embedded but not the sole content.

Emotional Ownership

It is hard for many to imagine that managing substantial family wealth, with all of the benefits and advantages it brings, can be seen to be a burden rather than as an opportunity. Yet for some, the complexities of fund analysis, tax planning, investment selection and risk management are areas of little expertise and daunting complexity.

While creating shared emotional ownership and a substantive connection with an operating business may have its own challenges, forging a motivational or even inspirational engagement with a portfolio of funds and trading accounts is even more difficult. Although not easy, the task of engaging the attentions of the relevant family members of different generations at least can be made to be of greater interest if knowledge and support are preconditions for distributions and the role is intertwined with a broader and fully disclosed family responsibility. Alternatively, investment activities can often be made to be more visibly a part of a shared family activity (e.g., sitting on an investment committee) or made more fun (e.g., dividing the portfolio into two, with two teams competing for best results) if family leaders are well tuned into the attitudes and interests of the members involved.

For the more expert and motivated, pursuing related work experience, or even working in an asset management firm in another country, can all help to create a sense of commitment, enthusiasm, and interest in the task.

The answer to the challenge may be a blend of expectation management, tailored experience, obligation (in order to receive benefits), and personalized approaches, which adapt the response to a given individual's personal capabilities and preferences.

What Do We Need to Learn?

Consistently throughout this narrative we have argued that the taxonomy of family wealth management—the structure and essence of its content—is a mix of family and financial elements that come together, sometimes under pressure or forged in the heat of a crisis, into a single whole that is entirely unique and specific to one single family. The educational needs are thus equally allocated between the two, requiring mastery of family structures and governance, as well as asset structures and financial management.

Depending on the interest and expected role of the inheritor, skills and condensed experience should be provided in key areas from economic history to capital markets to financial planning. In families where the capital base has the ability to last for multiple generations, it will be important to be intentional about passing on the skills and structures to allow for the continued stewardship of those assets, both financial and nonfinancial.

It is easy to focus simply on the needs, skills, and personalities of the current investment tasks and the needs of the current generation, but current generations will disappear over time and be replaced by new family members whose preparation needs to start long before they take over.

In addition to the skills to manage and disperse the capital, there are a number of other aspects of the family that should be passed on to future generations to help ensure preservation of both the family identity and financial assets:

- *Family history.* This can be accomplished by telling stories of past generations to make sure family history is known by all beneficiaries and provides a way of linking family members together.

- *Family values.* This is important to ensure common reference points and principles on which decisions can be made for the common good of the family.
- *Culture of stewardship.* The continued ability to maintain and grow assets over time will be dependent on beneficiaries understanding that they are managing assets for future generations, just as past generations did for them.

There are also many specific financial education tools that can be deployed, depending on the age range of the children involved.

Checklist for Financial Education

Learning about the financial world and its multiplicity of elements is a lifelong journey. There is no end to what can and should be known, and no limit to available ideas and information. The purpose of a tailored program of financial education for a family is to inform and prepare family members with the information they need to fulfill their wealth management responsibilities well. This can range from a high-level understanding of issues and options to a detailed understanding of the macroeconomy and every asset class, manager, and product in the family portfolio.

While there are many courses, teachers, and books available on the various elements of wealth management, the table of contents of this work, and its contents as well, may serve to provide a good view of all aspects of family wealth management. Further course work, seminars, readings, and engagement with expert advisors and investors can give members of the family valuable insights, knowledge, and wisdom that can contribute to an overall effort to fill the needs of their continuing education and relevant experience base.

Educational needs will vary over time, and an annual check on evolving needs and progress in responding to those needs should be part of the family's planning activities. Inclusion into the long-term strategy (LTS) and investment policy statement (IPS) of a nonfinancial metric on progress in family education, for example, can be an important step forward in ensuring that the family is well-prepared to both manage and transfer wealth as and when needed.

Engagement, Education, and Experience

While an educational program on the individual components of family wealth is important, it may not be sufficient to preserve and enhance wealth in both the financial and broader senses of the word if provided as a merely passive learning experience to younger family members whose interests and attention may lie elsewhere. A tough-minded assessment of each family member's needs (rather than wants) should be the foundation of a program of focused engagement in the issues, a complementary educational program, and a set of appropriate jobs, internships, educational institutions, and other sources of real-life wisdom and knowledge.

There is no substitute for difficult experiences. Positive experience merely reinforces what we already know. It is the more difficult experiences that help us to learn, to grow as individuals, and to develop the skills and instincts necessary for survival and prosperity. Far too often, great wealth deprives individuals of the experiences they need to grow into mature and independent adults; wealth all too often severs individuals from the real and the meaningful.

Maturity can come late, if ever, to individuals and generations never facing a tough performance review, never failing to obtain a desired job, never testing their skills in a real meritocracy, and not exposed to situations in which they need to manage without the outcome-controlling presence of financial wealth.

As one wealthy individual said, "I don't want my kids to know that there is a big, comfortable safety net below them at all times. That can make them reckless and lack seriousness about what they need to learn and how they need to be. I don't want to give away my wealth, but I also don't want it to ruin my kids' lives either."

Family Structures

Figure 25.2 reflects a standard set of family organizational entities on which family members of all ages can sit as members, leaders, or spectators. A well-crafted, creative, and engaging family structure may motivate involvement by younger family members on a wider range of family issues than a pure investment committee or wealth management review board might offer.

Readers interested in more information on this topic may refer to the more extended content of *Family Legacy and Leadership: Preserving True Family Wealth in Challenging Times.*

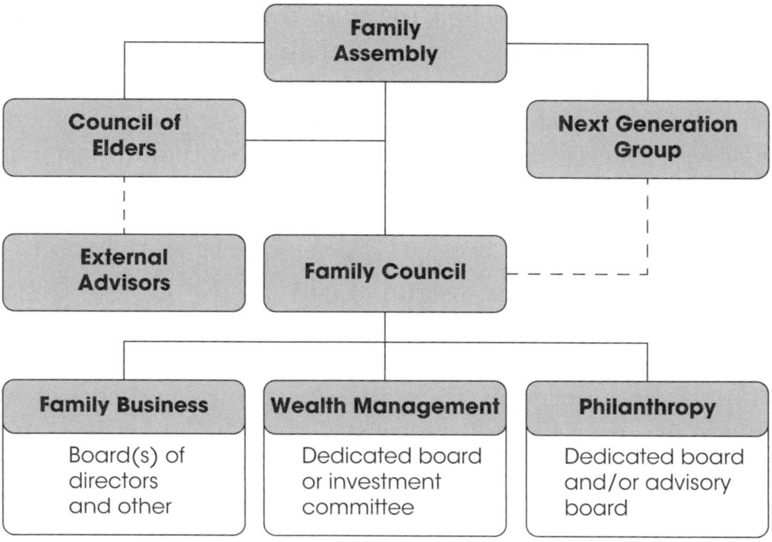

Figure 25.2 Sample Family Organization Structure

Costs of Disengagement

While sometimes inevitable, rancorous disengagement by one or more family members from the family system can create problems of great concern and magnitude. Investing time and money to solve problems before they arise always makes sense. Beginning at an early age, the benefits of engagement with family should be made clear, and the values necessary to create the right attitude reinforced in age-appropriate ways.

Education, however, is about obtaining both the knowledge and wisdom necessary to become an effective private investor and contributor to the stewardship of the family wealth. The skills and experiences here are more granular than they are for the attitude-driven challenges of engagement.

Knowledge about accounting, capital markets, investment classes, asset allocation, risk management, and similar issues is more easily taught to the willing.

History and Values

A family's history and sense of place are important foundations for a shared future, providing a common platform of ancestry and a shared set of current values to guide the family forward. This is the rock on which families can build their own successful and prosperous futures. According to the *New England Journal of Psychology*, this is a source of proven motivation in younger people. Called the *ancestor effect*, the contemplation of family history and past accomplishment of family members gives a measurable boost to confidence, motivation, and results.

The eloquent words of Robinson Jeffers (1887–1962) that capture the full spirit of this insight: "Lend me the stone strength of the past and I will give you the wings of the future."

Presuming that the values and attitudes have been properly prepared and the individuals are ready to begin the process of fuller engagement and tailored education, the challenge has already been partially mastered.

As discussed elsewhere, this dual nature of the challenge can be captured in two balanced sets of activities:

1. Preparing the heirs for the money.
2. Preparing the money for the heirs.

Although very different in scope of activity, both of these points are equally important in ensuring that the wealth of any one family remains intact as it makes the delicate transition from one generation to the next.

Preparing the Money for the Heirs

Preparing an inheritance from the structuring side is an essential part of the process. Ensuring that the philosophy and purposes of wealth in the future generation are well understood and reflected in the overall portfolio is just as important. The same is true of tax structuring, clear trustee and advisor roles, implications for family governance and reporting (which may need to be adjusted to conform with the capabilities and interests of the inheriting generation), planning and reporting cycles, asset allocation, and portfolio management of assets, risk and costs.

In this area, the LTS and IPS will be invaluable aids in transferring ownership and responsibility of substantial assets from one individual to another, or from one generation to another.

Preparing the Heirs for the Money

The set of activities necessary to prepare an individual, or even an entire generation, for inheritance has been colloquially dubbed *heir conditioning*. The full range of activities stretches across a lifetime, and can include exposure to ideas, institutions, activities, and experiences that can prepare heirs and heiresses for their future inheritance and roles as persons of wealth.

This is an enormously complex task and requires an understanding of the person, the family, and the environment. Preparation will include moral orientation as well as the economics of investment. It will need to highlight the full taxonomy and sets of knowledge necessary to achieve an appropriate set of objectives as a person and as an owner of wealth.

Treating the heir or heiress as a whole person, and addressing all elements of true family wealth and their own holistic nature as individuals, can be enormously motivating, and a great start to full and lasting engagement.

Understanding and Engaging with the Full Definition of Wealth

Wealth has always meant more than just money. In fact, the word *wealth* is derived from the Old and Middle English words *wela* and *weal*—more akin to the concept of welfare and well-being than to pure finance.

The elements of true family wealth, as defined across cultures, languages, and time, include those in the following sidebar. It is

Definition of True Family Wealth

- Financial wealth
- Integrity
- Accomplishment
- Physical security, health, and fitness
- Knowledge, wisdom, and spiritual growth
- Family harmony
- Individual happiness

Source: Mark Haynes Daniell, *Strategy for the Wealthy Family: Seven Principles to Assure Riches to Riches Across Generations* (Singapore: John Wiley & Sons, 2010).

Individual Responsibilities of Next Gen Members

Along with the considerable rights and advantages that accompany substantial family wealth are the related and substantial responsibilities. Shouldering these responsibilities is one of the signs that an individual is starting to understand just how difficult it is to preserve a family fortune.

A brief list of wise counsel for next-gen members includes:

- Understand and accept that, without substantial effort and a little luck, your family will probably lose its money.
- "Know thyself" and accept assessment and feedback as a sign of strength and a key part of a personal development program.
- Be humble and treat others with exceptional respect, no matter what their position or interest.
- Learn as much as possible from as many sources as possible.
- Listen before speaking, and listen "actively" to understand the intent in addition to the words spoken.
- Be prepared for every meeting; read the papers, ask any questions needed to understand (even before the meeting, if necessary), and have a point of view on the issues presented.
- Take responsibility for the design and pursuit of your own progress and program of development.

Far too many people—usually the lazy or disengaged—think their education is someone else's responsibility. By overcoming the obvious limitations of this dangerous attitude, a fortunate few are far more likely to make a contribution to, rather than escalate the risks associated with, the preservation and enhancement of family wealth.

important that heirs understand this broader picture of family wealth to be well prepared as family leaders and influencers.

How Can We Best Learn What We Need to Know?

There is no single approach that will tick all of the boxes for both education and engagement. Engagement requires a more psychological approach and more personal engagement, while the educational side, which benefits from a personal touch as well, can more easily be accomplished through courses, schooling, on-the-job training, internships, and other structured experiences designed to enhance and accelerate the necessary knowledge and wisdom required for the tasks at hand.

Especially at a time within a family when a significant generational transition is looming or there is a change in leadership roles and responsibilities, extra thought should be given to ensure that both engagement and educational preparation are adequate for the challenge.

How Much Should Be Invested in Family Education and Engagement?

It is easier to determine how and where financial assets should be allocated. It is harder to assess how much investment is needed in the so-called soft areas of family strategy. Perhaps a relatively simple formulaic approach might be useful.

Let's assume that the likelihood of a family's retaining its wealth across three generations, if everything is done right, is fixed at a very generous 30 percent. The average experience is probably closer to 10 percent.

With focused investment in high-priority areas in both the family and finance areas, those odds can be improved. Although not mathematically precise, a formula might look something like the following:

Percentage of full potential achieved in financial approach	×	Percentage of full potential achieved in family preparation	×	Rate of success in retaining family wealth if everything is done right	=	Chance of long-term success in family wealth management

Thus, an above-average family, following an excellent program of extended investment, might produce the following results:

90 percent of full potential achieved in financial approach	×	**80 percent** of full potential achieved in family preparation	×	**30 percent** rate of success in retaining family wealth if everything is done right	=	**22 percent chance** of long-term success in family wealth management

However, a more negligent or simply unprepared family might fail to make these investments, thereby dramatically reducing their potential for wealth return. Their calculus might look as follows:

50 percent of full potential achieved in financial approach	×	**20 percent** of full potential achieved in family preparation	×	**30 percent** rate of success in retaining family wealth if everything is done right	=	**3 percent chance** of long-term success in family wealth management

Quantum of Investment When we add in the actual costs of preparing the heirs to this calculus, the most striking thing is how minimal the costs are, particularly those of organized education, on the important aspects of the family. A family with $10 million may be able to boost the probability of success dramatically with one half of 1 percent of their wealth—$50,000—of incremental investment per year. At higher numbers of wealth, even smaller percentages can have a far greater return.

Return on Investment The return on this small investment can be extraordinary. The probabilistic outcome is highly levered and can be easily justified in the value of improved risk management for a family. Investment in the individual members and collective family can reduce aggregate risk as improvements in family and intellectual capital are spread across an entire invested portfolio.

Two Key Questions

Would-be testators and stewards of family wealth might ask themselves two simple questions:

- Over the past year, how many hours have we spent structuring and managing family financial wealth?
- Over the same period, how many hours have we spent preparing the recipients to be good owners of wealth?

As in so many aspects of family wealth management, the successful transfer of wealth across generations is a balance of family and financial principles and approaches. Addressing both in an integrated fashion is obviously the best way forward.

A Shared Responsibility

Education and engagement are a shared responsibility. Younger-generation members who come in with an attitude of "you can teach me if you can motivate me" have already lost the battle.

Values, most notably humility and a willingness to work hard, a sense of responsibility instead of entitlement, and a desire to give as well as to receive in a team context should all be in place by the time a family member reaches his or her age of majority, and certainly long before any substantive wealth passes to him or her.

A Divergence of Outcomes

In the world of the wealthy, there are many different outcomes than can proceed from different family approaches to wealth, despite a shared starting point of equal financial fortunes.

How Not to Do It

One European G1 entrepreneur, having spoiled his only child for years, stepped back from running his enormous fortune after 20 years of entrepreneurial success. After protracted and heated discussions, he managed to convince his only daughter, who was more interested in her friends and her local tennis club, to invest two days a week in the family office.

Recently divorced and without children, her father thought this an ideal time to inject her into the affairs over which she would, at some point, exercise control. This she did with reluctance and ill will, despite spending more than $10 million per year on her own residences and personal expenses, including domestic staff, vehicles, travel, clothing, and so on.

The time she spent in the office was ineffective and actually damaging for both the daughter and the family wealth, as she was neither prepared for meetings she was intended to run, nor yet capable of making the decisions her father assigned to her.

The situation went from bad to worse. The family office staff resented her lack of interest and clear disinterest in their work. Lacking both the

(*continued*)

requisite capabilities and commitment, the daughter adopted a dismissive style as a defensive mechanism, which only exacerbated the problems. Worried about the poor decision making and deteriorating situation, the entrepreneur overruled his daughter's worst decisions, which confused matters further.

Not surprisingly, the better members of the family office team started to drift away. Obviously, there would have been a higher probability of success if values had been instilled earlier, if succession had been planned for or implemented earlier, and a process of family office and ecosystem design had been undertaken to provide the best possible support in an admittedly suboptimal situation.

It is also easy to see that this lack of investment in family preparation will have a substantially negative impact on the likelihood of this family's retaining its wealth and prestige across one, let alone two or three, generations.

Doing It Right

In sharp contrast, a long-established European family has taken an entirely different approach, which begins virtually at birth and is focused on values and a shared sense of responsibility for the family's wealth and well-being. This approach has supported many successful generational transitions and transfers of both family wealth and leadership.

The current leader of their large family operating business explained that the most important aspect of their individual development and family culture was in their common dedication as a family to retain their humility. In addition, despite enormous wealth and stature as a family and as individuals, they worked together with a tough-minded focus on family unity and values, had very clear role definitions within the family and the business, undertook regular objective assessments of capabilities and performance, included independent advisors and team members in their business decisions, demanded attention to respectful manners and behaviors, and made sure they had exposure to the most capable people they could find across a broad set of disciplines.

By meeting and understanding the most competent advisors with the most interesting ideas—related to art and athletics as well as business and family matters—this family ensured that its members were fully equipped in all generations to rise to the challenges they faced.

On the financial front, the family was conservative in their investment objectives, highly informed of their international investment opportunities, and "not overly generous" in their wealth distribution policies. The net effect of the overall approach to family and finance was notable success in investment return, family unity, and individual opportunity to both support the family and pursue independent roles as appropriate.

Two Sides of the Coin

It is critical to both prepare the heirs for the money and prepare the money for the heirs. One without the other is likely to result in frustration and will certainly not accomplish the goals of the family. Families wishing to ensure that both family and funds survive and prosper over many generations will do well to pay close attention to both sides of this important coin.

They will want to invest the time to create a long-term plan, a governance structure, financial skills, and a culture of responsibility and stewardship that will increase the odds of success in an essential but challenging pursuit.

An Entrepreneurial Family Culture and the Preservation of Wealth

Professor Heinrich Liechtenstein

The importance of family culture is becoming increasingly clear over time as playing a key role in preserving family wealth across generations. In particular, the value of an entrepreneurial culture in a family of wealth is one of the defining characteristics of those families, with and without a principal operating business, that keep and grow their wealth across economic cycles and through periods of adversity from within or surrounding the family.

In a number of academic studies completed over the past few years, family culture, values, and other "soft" factors were rated by families as equally important as—and in some cases even more

(*continued*)

important than—the hard variables such as asset allocation and investment advisor selection in preserving family financial prosperity.

Two Key Insights

Research completed on two separate occasions has reinforced two basic insights. First, as demonstrated by analysis completed for a private roundtable in the United Kingdom for a group of substantially wealthy international families, family culture was an area of exceptionally high importance. When asked to rank-order the critical elements of family legacy, the relative importance of formal governance documents and structures, leadership, and culture were selected consistently as the top three issues. Of these, culture came out as a surprising first choice among the families present. Second, in an earlier and more comprehensive analytical study, it was the entrepreneurial nature of family culture that was most highly appreciated—and determined to be the most important factor in preserving family wealth over time.

In the business world, it is becoming increasingly well known that "culture overcomes strategy"; identifying the nature and need for change within a corporate culture must be an essential part of any business strategy or organizational study. The same has now been found to be true in the area of family business, family continuity, and family wealth management.

What is most interesting about these insights is that they are, as yet, not fully supported by any detailed understanding of what makes up a family culture and how those elements can best be managed to create change in the culture which can lead to the desired outcome of a strong, cohering, positive, and entrepreneurial family culture.

Practical Advice on Individual Experience and Family Culture

As the research develops and understanding deepens over time of what culture is, there are already a number of proven practices that can be put in place today to shape the experience and attitudes of a new generation. These experiences may, if shared broadly across a whole family or targeted generational group, affect the broader family culture as well.

These ideas include:

- Internships within the businesses and family offices of other, like-minded families.

- External work experience for a significant period of time, say three to five years, with real performance feedback.
- Running a small company.
- Participating in an MBO (actually an MBI—management buy-in) of one of the family companies.
- Taking up a role in social entrepreneurship in another country, creating three types of experience: foreign environment, social focus, and entrepreneurship.
- Spending some time as an executive assistant to a successful start-up entrepreneur (described by one family member as "working with one of the beasts").
- Working in an emerging country.

In all cases, those experiences should be accompanied with real feedback, pay linked to performance, a reporting relationship to someone other than a family member and, if possible, the establishment of a relationship with a family or family business mentor who can help carry forward the lessons learned during the experience.

By creating these kinds of opportunities, and shaping the experience of the future leaders of the family, current leadership teams can influence both individual capability and family culture for the better, and improve the odds of keeping both family and family wealth intact and thriving into the next generation.

Professor Heinrich Liechtenstein is an associate professor of finance at the IESE Business School in Barcelona, Spain, and a director of his family's nonprofit Liechtenstein Academy. His work addresses many relevant areas for legacy families and their governance, business, and investing activities.

CONCLUSION

CHAPTER 26

Pulling It All Together: The Successful Management and Transfer of Wealth Across Generations

At the end of the day, a long-term family wealth strategy and current investment policy will need to be looked at on a top-down as well as bottom-up basis, observing the holistic nature of the strategies as well as the content of each individual piece of the strategy.

Any gaps need to be filled, contradictions need to be removed, and any remaining wrinkles ironed out. The entire fabric of the approach needs to be whole, seamless, and fit for the family purposes it is designed to achieve. Stress testing will be a final step in the "manufacturing" process.

While each element is important on its own, and the linkages between the pieces are equally critical, it is most essential that the whole of the effort should be far greater than the sum of the parts: the alignment with family purposes and financial goals, the focus and quality of selected investments, the active engagement of the family, and the overall impact of the family wealth management ideas and activities fully aligned with the family's long-term vision.

The ultimate goal of family wealth management, as stated in the early pages of this work, is to help families and their advisors to compound their wealth successfully over time, and to do so in a manner that creates the greatest possible benefit—family and financial—for all involved.

Serving Multiple Family Purposes

Family wealth management is not just about developing and applying an amended version of Modern Portfolio Theory, incorporating a more engaged model of principled investing, or developing a more global asset allocation model that better preserves and enhances family wealth at an aggregate level. It is about defining very specific purposes of family wealth over the long term, both capital and income, and ensuring that all best efforts are made to fulfill the purposes described across many years and through many generations of the family.

Family wealth management is about fulfilling a defined set of specific purposes on a long-term basis, not just achieving short-term portfolio results.

Before applying any of the possible approaches to investment set out in this book, the purpose of the exercise needs to be defined, and the exact set of family goals and financial objectives needs to be specified in order to generate the strategies and tactics that will best fulfill the demands of each defined purpose and support the achievement of the overarching family vision.

Adopting a New Approach

To achieve consistently superior results, we have argued for consideration of a long list of potential changes and additions to more traditional forms of investing.

The following list, subject to the comments about the value and need for an integrated approach, may serve as a checklist and reference guide for family wealth management programs once they have been prepared in an initial form. The new approach is marked by a number of substantial changes from many past models and would include building an approach to family wealth management that is:

- *Guided by family vision and values.* Successful family wealth management is always characterized by a family-centric approach guided by a family's long-term vision and generational aspirations. Adapted to the nature of family investing, a specific program will need to reflect both family-specific values and investment goals.

- *Incorporating family purposes and state-of-the-art integrated financial management.* A correctly defined family wealth plan will reflect the full array of options for asset management and structuring to support the achievement of multiple family purposes and take advantage of legitimate tax and planning opportunities. Both investment performance (supply) and distribution objectives (demand) for individuals, family philanthropy, and other defined stakeholders need to be harmonized, and both lifetime and legacy plans put in place.
- *Capable of avoiding the most dangerous recurring risks in private investment.* At the same time that the approach is firmly family led and family-centric, it also takes into account the omnipresent risks inherent in private and family investing. Learning the lessons of private investment history and applying them with discipline is an essential part of family wealth management. Strategy is often as much about what is not done as it is about affirmative action. Putting in place an informed and disciplined approach may be the best vaccination (or possibly antidote if the portfolio is already in trouble) against the ever-present risks of human frailty and ego in private investment.
- *Creative and evolutionary in adopting a more active and engaged "postmodern" theory of portfolio investment.* This step forward avoids purely passive asset allocation and manager selection. It includes active engagement in a full range of investment classes. It also embraces activities related to goals-based wealth management, shifting asset allocation as the environment changes, applying sound risk management to the portfolio, adapting to change in the markets, and pursuing beta and alpha in ways both efficient and effective.
- *Based on a practical investment model that incorporates both past experience and the requirements of a new world order.* That program needs to be very specific and capable of being implemented, monitored, and adapted as necessary in the face of inevitable changes in the environment.
- *Well-adapted to maintaining performance in a colder and more volatile context.* The new world order in which we are now operating, and will likely operate in for some time to come, is characterized by enormous sums of money searching for positive outcomes in a world of more information, lower capital

returns and yield, more complex opportunities, larger risk, higher taxes for both individuals and companies, and greater competition for scarce alpha opportunities. The most sophisticated approaches will need to be adapted to current and future external environments and therefore need to be scenario-based and forward looking.

- *Addressing both strategic and tactical risk in a thoughtful program of risk management.* This will need to incorporate sensitivity to a fuller range of risk—from tail to advisory—and for families to set priorities and implement appropriate programs of risk mitigation as a matter of both urgency and importance.
- *Encompassing the entire new world of investment opportunities.* In order to identify and access the few opportunities for positive return, family investors will need to contemplate the full global set of asset classes, products, geographies, and currencies on offer. Given the enormous size of the "buffet" available taking an informed approach from the outset, narrowing down the areas of interest and exploration, and working with high-quality advisors is a must.
- *Supported by a more efficient, effective, and aligned ecosystem.* The network of advisors and the process by which they work, separately and together, needs to be driven by a high-quality set of advisors with aligned interests, increasingly open to sharing with like-minded families in a similar situation, considering coinvestment and cooperation where appropriate, and providing advice on a cost-effective and transparent basis.
- *Carries long-term value through engaging and educating the family across generations.* Family wealth management begins and ends with the family. Future transfers of wealth across generations are not easy and require preparation of both heirs and heritage. It is a process that needs to begin years before the actual transfers are effected and should be subject to a constant educational experience across the entire lifetime of family members involved with the management and transition of family wealth.

Integrated Approach

No one element, on its own, can assure that a family will invest well and thus both preserve its wealth and enhance its stature over time. Yet the combination of elements addressed in these pages, well understood, adapted, and pursued in the context of a single and unique family, can go a long way toward improving investment return and reinforcing the achievement of a given family's wealth purposes.

The same need for an integrated and holistic view is necessary for best-practice portfolio management within and between asset classes. It is important to understand each individual asset-class selection and the investments within it. It is equally important to understand how a family's overall investment portfolio will behave in different economic environments. This will require stress testing and risk management assessments to provide an understanding of how a particular portfolio will behave if interest rates, energy prices, consumer demand, or a particular currency or stock market rises or falls within the investment horizon.

Achieving Consistently Superior Returns

Ultimately, all of these observations and areas for potential change are but a means to the end goal of improving the results an investing family obtains from the intelligent deployment of its financial capital. They are also about how that family uses its intellectual and family capital in that process to pursue an overarching family vision, reinforce family values, and ensure that the financial strength is there to support the full set of other goals of the family.

Achieving sustainable, reliable, and superior results is the objective of the exercise; progress against this high-level goal should be an essential element of any structured program of family wealth management.

Successful Transfer of Wealth Across Generations

Annual success, while important, is only part of the picture for long-term preservation and enhancement of a family fortune. One of the greatest noninvestment challenges in a family wealth management plan is the ability to transfer wealth, and the responsibility for wealth, across generational borders successfully.

Research shows that up to 70 percent of wealth transfers fail to meet all objectives of the generation or individual making the transfer, which is due primarily to poor preparation of the heirs and heiresses on the other side of the divide.

As a program of family wealth management needs to address all elements in the mix that could have a material impact—positive or negative—on the preservation or enhancement of family financial capital, this transfer issue and the "heir conditioning" challenge it implies, need to be fully considered in a family's program of development, education, and preparation for the future.

That program of preparation and practice will need to include at least three high-level sources of content. Those three areas would embrace interrelated aspects of family and finance:

- *Individual, relationship and family issues,* which include a personal profile, strengths and weaknesses, time management, performance reviews, family governance, leadership skills, meeting disciplines, team motivation, dispute resolution, succession planning, communication, positive psychology, and an understanding of relationship dynamics and family culture
- *Investment expertise,* based on an integrated approach to family wealth management, scenario planning, asset allocation, investment selection, monitoring, advisor and manager selection, tax and trust planning, team alignment, ecosystem design and oversight, advisor selection, family office design and operation, external resources and third-party advisors, and benchmarking
- *Family business and management expertise,* which needs to include strategy, organization, management skills, leadership, team motivation, priority setting, competitive analysis finance, accounting, growth strategies, mergers and acquisitions, ecosystem, and personal effectiveness

By putting in place a special program for family leaders, those charged with the responsibilities of wealth management and preservation across generations, legacy families will be far more likely to achieve their objectives once stuck into the hard graft of managing and transferring wealth across generations.

Hope Is Never a Strategy

There is no substitute for hard work, insight, planning, and action in pursuit of specific goals with defined responsibilities and objectives. Successful pursuit of family objectives will rely on individual roles and responsibilities operating within an integrated and well-managed plan of action.

Family wealth management is all about beating the odds, providing insight, and pursuing actions that can help a given family thrive and prosper in good and bad times. By engaging with all that has been learned and all that can be done, families and their leaders will be far better placed to emerge as one of the few winners in a challenge of great importance to them, their families and the communities in which they live, and the many generations yet to be born who could benefit enormously from their efforts.

At the beginning of this book, we talked about the preservation of family wealth and its parallel in the metaphor of a fire and the illumination and warmth it provides in our lives. This fire needs to be built and tended, as well as enjoyed, if it is to last. In the same way, by carefully preparing the way and managing critical processes well, wealth owners and their families will be far better placed to beat the odds and create a rare story of wealth preservation and family harmony across many generations of an enduring and successful family.

Bibliography

Bailey, Jeffery, Jesse Phillips, and Thomas Richards. *A Primer for Investment Trustees.* Research Foundation of CFA Institute, October 2010.

Barberis, Nicholas, and Richard Thaler. "A Survey of Behavioral Finance." In *Handbook of the Economics of Finance,* Volume 1B, Chapter 18, edited by G. M. Constantinides, M. Harris, and R. M. Stulz. St. Louis, MO: Elsevier Science and Technology Books, 2003.

Bernstein, Peter. *Against the Gods: The Remarkable Story of Risk.* New York: John Wiley & Sons, 1996.

Bernstein, Richard. "An Alternative to Alternatives." Richard Bernstein Advisors, May 2012.

Bodie, Zvi, and Paula Hogan. "The Emerging New Model for Wealth Management." CFA Institute, *Private Wealth Management* 1, no. 1 (March 2008).

Bogle, John. "The Lessons of History: Endowment and Foundation Investing Today." Conference remarks, The NMS Investment Management Forum, Washington, DC, September 2011.

Bogle, John C., "Three Challenges of Investing: Active Management, Market Efficiency, and Selecting Managers." Conference remarks, Boston, MA, October 21, 2001.

Boone, Norman, and Linda Lubitz. *Investors, Policy and Change.* Greenwood Village, CO: College of Financial Planning, 2010.

Burns, Terence. "Investment Counseling for Private Clients." *AIMR Conference Proceedings,* August 1999: 1–5.

Brunel, Jean. *Integrated Wealth Management: The New Direction for Portfolio Managers.* London: Euromoney Institutional Investor, 2006.

Brunel, Jean. "Revisiting the Asset Allocation through a Behavioral Lens." *Journal of Wealth Management,* Fall 2003.

Carter, Marty. "The Psychology of Wealth." *AIMR Conference Proceedings,* Investment Counseling for Private Clients V. July 2003: 52–57.

Chhabra, Ashvin. "Beyond Markowitz: A Comprehensive Wealth Allocation Framework." *Journal of Wealth Management* 7, no. 4 (2005): 8–34.

Chirelstein, Marvin. "Learned Hand's Contribution to the Law of Tax Avoidance." *Yale Law Journal* 77, no. 3 (January 1968): 440–74.

Curtis, Greg. "White Paper No. 32: Identifying Managers Who Will Outperform." Greycourt & Co., 2004.

Daniell, Mark Haynes. *Strategy for the Wealthy Family: Seven Principles to Assure Riches to Riches Across Generations.* Singapore: John Wiley & Sons, 2010.

Daniell, Mark Haynes, and Sara Hamilton. *Family Legacy and Leadership: Preserving True Family Wealth in Challenging Times.* Singapore: John Wiley & Sons, 2010.

Das, Sanjiv, Harry Markowitz, Jonathan Scheid, and Meir Statman, "Portfolio Optimization with Mental Accounts." *Journal of Financial and Quantitative Analysis* 45, no. 2 (April 2010): 311–34.

Dembo, Ron, and Andrew Freeman. *Seeing Tomorrow: Rewriting the Rules of Risk.* New York: John Wiley & Sons, 2001.

"Elements of an Investment Policy Statement for Individual Investors." CFA Institute, *Codes, Standards and Position Papers* (May 2010): 1–9.

Ellis, Charles. *Investment Policy: How to Win the Loser's Game.* New York: McGraw-Hill Professional, 1992.

"The Essentials of Portfolio Construction." Morgan Stanley, April 2010.

Evensky, Harold, and Deena Katz. *Investment Think Tank: Theory, Strategy, and Practice for Advisers.* Hoboken, NJ: John Wiley & Sons, 2004.

Fitzgerald, F. Scott. *Babylon Revisited: Taps at Reveille.* 1935.

"The Future of Long-Term Investing." World Economic Forum, 2011.

Garland, James. "To Thine Own Self Be True." Jeffrey Company, 1995.

"Global Yearbook." Credit Suisse, 2012.

Grantier, Bruce. "Benjamin Graham and Risk." Brandes Institute, 2009.

Grubman, James, Dennis Jaffe, and Keith Whitaker. "Immigration to the Land of Wealth." *Private Wealth* (March/April 2009).

Gunther, Marc. "Yale's $8 Billion Man." *Yale Alumni* 68, no. 6 (July/August 2005).

Hamilton, Sara, and Joline Godfrey. "Preparing the Next Generation for the Responsibilities of Ownership." *Journal of Wealth Management* 10, no. 3 (Winter 2007): 8–16.

Hauser, Barbara. "Family Governance." *Journal of Wealth Management* 5, no. 2 (Fall 2002): 10–16.

Horan, Stephen. "CFA Institute: Asset Liability Management for Private Clients." Presentation, 2012.

Ilmanen, Antti. *Expected Returns on Major Asset Classes.* Hoboken, NJ: Wiley, 2012.

"Investing Like the Harvard and Yale Endowment Funds." *Frontier Investment Management,* March 2012.

"The Investment Policy Statement." Commonfund Whitepaper, 2011.

Jeffrey, Robert (Tad). *The Long Search for a Better Way: The Evolution of a Tailor-Made Strategy.* Jeffrey Company, 2009.

Jennings, William, Stephen Horan, and William Reichenstein. "Private Wealth Management: A Review." CFA Institute, 2010.

Kiefer, Leslie. "Investment Policy Best Practices: Communication, Creation and Commitment." *CFA Institute Conference Proceedings Quarterly* 24, no. 1 (March 2007).

Klement, Joachim. "Investment Management Is Risk Management," *Journal of Wealth Management* 14, no. 3 (Winter 2011): 10–16.

Kyrychenko, Vladyslav. "Optimal Asset Allocation in the Presence of Nonfinancial Assets," *Financial Services Review* 17 (Spring 2008): 69–86.

Levin, Ross. *The Wealth Management Index: The Financial Advisor's System for Assessing and Managing your Client's Goals and Plans.* New York: McGraw-Hill, 1997.

"The Longest Pictures." Bank of America Merrill Lynch, June 2012.

Lowenhaupt, Charles. "Freedom from Wealth," *Journal of Wealth Management* 11, no. 3 (Spring 2008): 1–4.

Lucas, Stuart. *Wealth: Grow It, Protect It, Spend It, and Share It.* Upper Saddle River, NJ: Pearson Prentice Hall, 2006.

Marston, Richard. *Portfolio Design: A Modern Approach to Asset Allocation.* Hoboken, NJ: John Wiley & Sons, 2011.

Masters, Seth. "The Case for the 20,000 Dow." AllianceBernstein, 2009.

Maynard, Robert. "Conventional Investing in a Complex World." *Journal of Investing* 22, no. 1 (Spring 2013): 57–73.

Nevins, Daniel. "Goals-Based Investing: Integrating Traditional and Behavioral Finance." *Journal of Wealth Management* 6, no. 4 (Spring 2004): 8–23.

Padgett, Miles, and Louisa Wright Sellers. "The 'Integration' in Integrated Wealth Management: How Does It Work in Practice?" *Journal of Wealth Management* 8, no. 3 (Winter 2005): 19–25.

Piketty, Thomas. "Inequality in America: The 1% in International and Historical Perspective." Presentation, Paris School of Economics, Columbia University, September 2012.

Pittman, Sam, and Russ Greenshields. "Adaptive Investing." Russell Investments, March 2012.

Pompian, Michael. *Behavioral Finance and Wealth Management: How to Build Optimal Portfolios that Account for Investor Biases.* Hoboken, NJ: John Wiley & Sons, 2006.

Pompian, Michael. *Advising Ultra-Affluent Clients and Family Offices.* Hoboken, NJ: John Wiley & Sons, 2009.

"A Primer for Investment Trustees." Research Foundation of CFA Institute, October 2010.

"Retirement: Plan Early and Often." AllianceBernstein, February 2007.

Rosenberg, Claude Jr. *Investing with the Best: What to Look for, What to Look Out for in Your Search for a Superior Investment Manager.* John Wiley & Sons, 1993.

Schulmerich, Marcus. "Behavioral Finance in Asset Management: A Primer." *SSgA Capital Insights,* 2011.

Sebold, Sean. "Succession Planning for Business Owners." *CFA Institute Conference Proceedings Quarterly* (October 2005): 48–54.

Senge, Peter. *The Fifth Discipline: The Art & Practice of the Learning Organization.* New York: Currency Doubleday, 1994.

Singer, Gregory, and Brian Wodar. "Moving from P&L to Portfolio: Advice for Business Owners." CFA Institute, *Private Wealth Management Feature Articles,* 2011.

Sordoni, Nicholas. "Decision-Making Processes in Equity Investing: The Case for Investment Frameworks." Lazard Freres, 2010.

Swedroe, Larry. "Risk: What Exactly Is It?" Buckingham Asset Management, August 2003.

Taleb, Nassim Nicholas. *The Black Swan: The Impact of the Highly Improbable.* New York: Random House, 2010.

Trachtenberg, Andrea. "Value of Advice: Breaking Cycle of Emotion." *Journal of Wealth Management* (Winter 2001).

"2020 Vision: The Most Critical Decade." BNY Mellon, 2010.

Wilcox, Jarrod. "Risk Management for Private Wealth." CFA Institute, *Conference Proceedings Quarterly,* 2005.

Williams, Roy, and Vic Preisser. *Preparing Heirs: Five Steps to a Successful Transition of Family Wealth and Values.* San Francisco: Robert D. Reed Publishers, 2003.

"Working with Taxable Clients." Association for Investment Management and Research, August 1999.

"The Yale Endowment." Yale University, 2011.

Zeeb, Rodney, and Ryan Zeeb. "Guidelines for Effective Family Governance." Heritage Institute, 2008.

List of Essay Writers

"Profile and Trends of the World's Wealthy," Mykolas Rambus, Chapter 2

"The Future Global Investment Context," Thierry Malleret, Chapter 2

"Investment Discipline: An Undervalued Asset," H. F. "Rick" Pitcairn, Chapter 4

"The Importance of Clarifying Values in a Family Wealth Plan," Dr. James Grubman and Dr. Dennis Jaffe, Chapter 5

"The Implications of Differing Investment Philosophies: 'Egg Farmers' versus 'Chicken Farmers,'" James Garland, Chapter 6

"Three Pathways to Evolutionary Survival," Dr. Dennis Jaffe and Jane Flanagan, Chapter 8

"The Family Business and the Family Portfolio: Another Relationship to Consider," Dr. Stephen Horan, Chapter 8

"Integrated Goals-Based Wealth Management," Jean Brunel, Chapter 9

"Welcome to Risk Management 2.0," Dr. Erwann Michel-Kerjan, Chapter 11

"Delivering the Promise of Alternative Investing through Principled Strategies," Stephen J. George, Chapter 13

"The Role of Property in a Family Portfolio," Basil Demeroutis, Chapter 17

"A Contrarian View: All in the Family? Maybe," Ed Lazar, Chapter 24

"An Entrepreneurial Family Culture and the Preservation of Wealth," Professor Heinrich Liechtenstein, Chapter 25

List of Figures and Tables

List of Figures

Figure 1.1	Integrated Family Framework	10
Figure 1.2	Structure of Business and Financial Families	18
Figure 2.1	Forbes Top 20 U.S. Rich List 1918	26
Figure 2.2	Historical Highest U.S. Marginal Income Tax Rates	28
Figure 2.3	A Dead Decade: Dow Jones Industrial Average, 2000–2010	35
Figure 2.4	U.S. Household Net Worth, Percentage Change from Five Years Earlier	36
Figure 2.5	A History of U.S. Home Values, 1890–2011	36
Figure 4.1	Eisenhower Matrix	58
Figure 5.1	Philosophy of Wealth	77
Figure 6.1	Investment Risk Pyramid	92
Figure 6.2	Lifetime and Legacy Requirements	93
Figure 6.3	Sample Lifetime and Legacy Portfolios	97
Figure 6.4	Family Balance Sheet	98
Figure 6.5	Calderon Family Balance Sheet	101
Figure 7.1	Health, Education, and Welfare (HEW) Trust	109
Figure 7.2	Traditional Trust Structure	110
Figure 7.3	Diversified Structure	113
Figure 7.4	U.S., UK, and German Inheritance Tax Rates, 1900–2010	114
Figure 8.1	Magnitude of Human Capital	129
Figure 9.1	Classification of Assets and Liabilities Using the Wealth Allocation Framework	144
Figure 10.1	Evolution of Asset Allocation	150
Figure 10.2	The Investment S-Curve	152
Figure 10.3	Average Endowment Asset Allocation	155
Figure 10.4	Large ($1+ billion) Endowment Asset Allocation	156
Figure 10.5	Yale Endowment Asset Allocation, 1986–2011	157
Figure 10.6	Sample Global Scenarios	160

Figure 11.1	Key Risks Faced by Wealthy Families	172
Figure 11.2	U.S. Gross Federal Debt as a Percent of GDP	173
Figure 11.3	U.S. Income Distribution, 1774, 1860, and 2010	174
Figure 13.1	Share of Global GDP	202
Figure 13.2	GDP by Country, 2010	204
Figure 13.3	GDP by Country, 2050	204
Figure 16.1	10-Year Treasury Entry Yield and Subsequent 10-Year Return	253
Figure 16.2	Correlation among Key Asset Classes During the Crisis	257
Figure 16.3	S&P Dividend Yield and 10-year Treasury Yield	258
Figure 16.4	S&P 500 Rolling 10-Year Average Annual Total Return	259
Figure 16.5	Eleven Decades of Returns on U.S. Stocks	260
Figure 16.6	Mean Reversion Following Poor Equity Performance	262
Figure 18.1	Dispersion of Returns, 10 Years Ending June 2010	287
Figure 20.1	Sample Portfolio Benchmarks for a Large Family Trust	315
Figure 20.2	Sample Reporting Available to Various Stakeholders	318
Figure 22.1	Sample Family Wealth Ecosystem	331
Figure 23.1	Sample Organizational Structure for Internally Managed Investment Operation	350
Figure 23.2	Sample Organizational Structure for Externally Managed Investment Operation	350
Figure 24.1	Sample Milestone Methodology	369
Figure 25.1	The Challenge of Enduring Legacy	376
Figure 25.2	Sample Family Organization Structure	381

List of Tables

Table 2.1	Dow Jones Industrial Average—Returns by Decade	34
Table 12.1	The Macdonald Family	195
Table 12.2	The Bardali Family	195
Table 15.1	Old and New Purposes of Asset Classes in a Portfolio	238
Table 24.1	Sample Number of Descendants and Distribution per Beneficiary	365

About the Authors

Mark Haynes Daniell

Chairman, Raffles Family Wealth Trust Pte Ltd., Singapore

Mark Haynes Daniell is the founder and chairman of the Raffles Family Wealth Trust, a Singapore-based strategic advisory boutique focused on strategies for wealthy families and their investments, transactions, and businesses. Raffles also provides services to wealthy families and their family offices in establishing and operating selected activities in Singapore, Europe, and other parts of the world. He is also the founder and chairman of his own family office in Singapore.

Mr. Daniell is a former senior partner at Bain & Company, director of Wasserstein Perella, and president of k1 Ventures, a strategic investment company publicly listed in Singapore. He created and chaired the Private Wealth Management Initiative as part of the Singapore government's Economic Review Committee in 2002. He is a director of various listed and private companies, including Olam International, Tiryaki Agro, Aquarius Investment Advisors Pte Ltd. (vice chairman), Sacoven PLC (chairman), and a cofounder of Capital Partners of Georgia.

He is the author of several books, including *Strategy for the Wealthy Family: Seven Principles to Ensure Riches to Riches Across Generations* (John Wiley & Sons, 2008), *Family Legacy and Leadership: Preserving True Family Wealth in Challenging Times* (coauthored with Sara Hamilton; John Wiley & Sons, 2010), *Wealth Wisdom for Everyone: An Easy to Use Guide for Personal Financial Planning and Wealth Creation* (World Scientific, 2006), *Strategy: A Step-by-Step Guide to the Creation and Presentation of World Class Business Strategy* (Palgrave Macmillan 2008), *The Elements of Strategy: A Pocket Guide to the Essence of Successful Business Strategy* (Palgrave, Macmillan, 2009), *World of Risk: Next Generation Strategies for a Volatile Era* (John Wiley & Sons, 1999), and *World of Risk: An Alternate Model of Global Strategy and Leadership* (World Scientific, 2004; reprinted 2006). He also contributed chapters to *China's Century: The Awakening of the Next Economic Powerhouse* (John Wiley & Sons, 2001) and the *Handbook of Business Strategy* (Emerald Press, 2006). His first book, *World of Risk*, was a *Sunday Times of London* Business Book of the Week and appeared in numerous foreign language editions.

Mr. Daniell is a graduate of Harvard Law School (JD), Oxford University (University College, BA and MA), Amherst College (BA), and the Phillips Exeter Academy. Mr. Daniell also has earned diplomas from the Institut d'Etudes Politiques de Paris and the l'Université Paris-Sorbonne (Paris IV). He has lectured at INSEAD, Harvard Business School, IMD, IESE, NUS, and other institutions, and is a frequent guest on the BBC, CNBC, CNN, Bloomberg, Channel NewsAsia, and other media channels.

Tom McCullough

Chairman, CEO, and CIO, Northwood Family Office, Toronto

Mr. McCullough is the cofounder, chairman, CEO, and CIO of Northwood Family Office, a leading global multifamily office based in Toronto. Northwood looks after the integrated family and financial needs of an exclusive group of wealthy families and has consistently been ranked the number one family office in Canada in the Euromoney Private Banking Survey.

He is one of the founders of the Wigmore Association, an association of independent family offices from around the world, of which Northwood Family Office is an active member.

Mr. McCullough is also an adjunct professor of finance at the Rotman School of Management at the University of Toronto, one of the leading research universities in the world. He teaches Management of Private Wealth in the Rotman MBA program.

Prior to founding Northwood Family Office, he was a senior executive and member of the executive committee at RBC Wealth Management.

He is a member of the editorial board of the *Journal of Wealth Management*, the founding chair of the Canadian Private Family Office Summit, and an entrepreneur-in-residence at the Ivey School of Business at Western University.

Mr. McCullough is a graduate of the University of Toronto (BCom) and the Schulich School of Business at York University (MBA). He holds other designations including Chartered Investment

Manager, Chartered Strategic Wealth Professional, and holds a certificate in Family Business Advising.

He is married with two adult children, lives in Toronto, and is active in charitable pursuits, most notably microfinance and poverty alleviation in the developing world.

About the Raffles Family Wealth Trust

RAFFLES
FAMILY WEALTH TRUST

Based in Singapore, but with an ability to work worldwide, the Raffles Family Wealth Trust is a boutique advisory business focused on serving the needs of legacy families to preserve their financial fortunes and enhance their true family wealth across generations.

Services include integrated multigenerational family strategy, strategic family wealth management, merger and acquisition transaction support, family business strategy (including listing and sale), family office reviews, offshore presence and service provision, education and training, and access to a global set of like-minded families interested in pursuing coinvestment opportunities.

Our overall vision is:

> To create a unique enterprise to support leaders of legacy families to protect and grow their true family wealth across generations.

In pursuit of this vision, we focus on strategies and initiatives that create or are aligned with the protection and enhancement of family wealth in both financial and nonfinancial matters, and on both a strategic and transactional level. The elements of our business model and service offering to our clients that differentiate us from other firms include:

- *A deep knowledge of integrated family strategy and multigenerational legacy planning*, addressing all elements of true family wealth, including the financial and nonfinancial aspects of strategy for both newly wealthy and long-established families.
- *Support and services from a Singapore base, offering an established offshore presence and operation* with "purpose, substance and form" in a global financial center and an operating presence in a sound primary (or alternative) jurisdiction.
- *Pure (conflict-free) family advisory service*—no in-house funds or products of any kind and hence full client alignment in providing services and advice to legacy families; and with an ability to identify the best service providers and negotiate fees on behalf of the family with private banks, trust companies, banks, custodians, technology providers, and other intermediaries.
- *A platform to provide co-investment opportunities with a network of like-minded families* and family offices in an international family office/ultra-high-net-worth individual (FO/UHNWI) network.
- *Access to Asian and related growth capital opportunities* to support families in their search for alpha in a challenging investment climate.
- *An experienced and highly capable team,* familiar with all aspects of family offices, family business, and private wealth, characterized by the highest levels of trust and discretion.
- *Complementary services, often with expert and focused partners,* to support family educational programs and the other needs of family leaders, family offices, multifamily offices, trustees, private banks, and other existing advisory relationships.

In particular, the Singapore location can provide access to selected Asian and emerging market investment opportunities and be a critical part of creative solutions to fiscal, financial, and family challenges, drawing on:

- State-of-the-art knowledge of global tax planning and asset structuring.

- Family office design, establishment, assessment, and relocation or provision of a back-up jurisdiction for an offshore "satellite" family office in Asia.
- Singapore's sound government, world-class legal and financial infrastructure, pro-business culture, low taxes, new trust laws, and a credible reputation as a global financial and regional investment center.
- Creative asset structuring and risk management capabilities through the use of trusts, corporations, and alternative structures (Singapore family-owned investment holding companies [FIHCs], SCC/PCCs, private trust companies [PTCs], limited liability companies [LLCs], limited partnerships [LPs], family partnerships [FPs], etc.).
- An offshore set of expert investment professionals.
- High-value trustee services with a deep understanding of family investment and distribution objectives.
- A real interest in the long-term success of the family, providing integrated family wealth management strategies, specific investment advice, and asset structuring opportunities, along with family education and individual development programs to support the real long-term needs of the family and its members.

For more information, please visit www.rafflestrust.com.

About Northwood Family Office

NORTHWOOD
FAMILY OFFICE

Northwood Family Office is a global multifamily office based in Toronto that looks after the integrated family and financial needs of an exclusive group of wealthy families. Northwood acts as the personal chief financial officer (CFO) for clients, coordinating and managing the complexities of investments, financial affairs, and family issues.

Founded in 2003, Northwood has quickly become one of the leaders in its field and has been consistently ranked as "the #1 family office in Canada" in *Euromoney*'s Global Private Banking survey.

Northwood is a member of the Wigmore Association, an exclusive international association of independent family offices from around the world, including the United Kingdom, United States, Germany, Brazil, Australia, and Canada. It brings an important set of global connections and resources to Northwood clients.

Northwood clients have complex family structures and own a diversity of investments and business and real estate interests. They value the independence, objectivity, and organization that a family office can provide. Northwood serves as the single point of contact for clients on all issues related to their family and financial affairs. Northwood clients have family net worth in the $10–$500 million range.

Northwood's mission is to bring direction, perspective, and confidence to the management of its clients' net worth. The firm helps families define a clear sense of the direction they want to take and develop an integrated perspective. It works closely with clients' professional advisors to ensure that everything is coordinated and integrated so families will have a high level of confidence that they and their wealth are being well looked after.

Northwood also carefully selects external specialists from all relevant financial disciplines to round out the interdisciplinary service team it manages for each family. The firm has a strong emphasis on building lasting relationships of trust with each of its client families and maintains absolute confidentiality of their personal and financial information.

Northwood offers nine core services for client families, examples of which are outlined as follows:

1. **Integrated net worth plan.** Overall family wealth diagnosis and plan, goal setting, balance sheet analysis, integrated tax planning and implementation, income splitting strategy, asset protection structures, retirement planning, cash flow planning and management, citizenship, immigration and offshore planning, holdco setups, windups and consolidations, currency management, personal residences planning.
2. **Investment strategy and implementation.** Defining investment objectives of the family, investment policy development, global asset allocation and investment strategy, investment manager selection and monitoring, custodial oversight, concentrated asset oversight, tax analysis of investments, art and collectibles management.
3. **Wealth transfer planning.** Development of objectives, estate planning, legal and tax strategies, will and power of attorney preparation, beneficiary distribution planning and implementation, explanation of plans to owners, financial modeling, succession planning, marriage and prenuptial contracts.
4. **Trustee-related services.** Trust setup and management, organization and management of trustee meetings, management of family shareholdings, selection and training of trustees and protectors, trustee fee negotiation, beneficiary education and mentoring, and family policies (e.g., medical, property usage)
5. **Liability/risk management.** Risk management plan, property and casualty insurance assessment, life and disability

insurance analysis, personal security, collectibles inventory, appraisal, and protection.

6. **Administration, management, and projects.** Tax compliance coordination, bank financing analysis and negotiations, advisor coordination, expense tracking and management, financial reporting, bookkeeping, document management, bill paying and banking, efficient cash flow management among entities, cross-border reporting and structure integration, vehicle management, management of aging parents' affairs, education cost management, new business setup, access to a network of peer families.
7. **Client information management.** Consolidated net worth reports, investment performance reports, benchmark and peer performance comparison, entity accounting and reporting, cash flow analysis, meetings minutes, task lists and timely reminders, family records inventory, data and document management.
8. **Family continuity/client education.** Family governance, family education, family values and vision, family constitution, family communication, family meeting coordination and support, mentoring and coaching for family members, leadership training, career management.
9. **Family philanthropy.** Philanthropic planning, formulating giving strategy, setup and administration of charitable foundations, foundation trustee training, governance and board development, foundation and grant administration, technical advice on charities.

For more information, please visit www.northwoodfamilyoffice.com.

Index

Absolute benchmarks, 314–315
Absolute return:
  bonds and, 251
  evolution of asset allocation and, 150
  funds as alternative asset, 277–278
  importance of, 141
Access to investments, professional advisors and, 291
Accounting reports, performance monitoring and, 319
Active versus passive management issues, professional advisors and, 286–287
Advisors. *See* Investment management; Professional advisors
Africa, 203, 205
Age issues:
  in distribution strategies, 367
  longevity and risk of wealth depletion, 171, 180
Aging, health care and mega-theme investing opportunities and, 206–207
Agricultural land, as alternative asset, 205–206, 271
Alpha:
  alternative investments and, 213–214, 282–283
  asset allocation strategies and, 150
  expert's approach to asset allocation and, 161–162
Alternative assets and strategies, 267–283
  alpha and, 213–214, 282–283
  alternative opinions about, 269–270
  asset-backed income sources, 271–272
  changing role of asset classes and, 238–240
  collectibles, 281
  commodities, 279
  credit strategies, 277
  direct investments, 280–281
  exotica and passion investing, 281–282
  family interests in, 267–269
  foreign exchange, 279–280
  hedge funds and absolute return funds, 277–278
  infrastructure, 276–277
  Islamic products, 281
  mega-trend investing and, 200–209
  performance shortfalls of, 270–271
  private equity, 275–276
  real estate, 272–274
  real estate, Demeroutis on role of, 273–274
  sustainable and principled investing, 209–213
  swaps, derivatives, and structured notes, 278–279
Ancestor effect, 382

Annual review of investments, 313
Anstalts, 110
Antinori wine family, 120
Arrow, Kenneth, 138
Asia:
  family wealth in, 31
  mega-theme investing and, 201–202
Aspirational risk bucket, goals-based wealth management and, 143–144
Asset allocation, 149–164
  cash flow and, 192
  "chicken- and egg-farmer investors," 102–104
  core and satellite strategy, 150–151
  endowment model of, 155–158, 163–164, 268–271, 275
  evolution of, 149–150
  expert family office's approach to, 159–162
  expert family office's example allocation, 162–163
  historic background, 135–136
  holistic and active portfolio management, 159
  investment policy statement and, 241
  in investment policy statement example, 302–304
  in long-term strategy, 193–196
  in long-term strategy document example, 227–230
  risk management and, 181
  scenario planning's role in, 158
  S-curve strategy, 151–154
  simple structure's advantages, 163–164
  variety of opportunities and choices, 154–155
Asset classes and investment strategies:
  changing role of, 237–240
  investment policy statement and, 245
  in long-term strategy document example, 230–232
  old and new purposes of, 238–240
Asset structuring, 105–117
  balance sheets and, 100–101
  citizenship and residency issues, 115–116
  with corporations and companies, 111
  distinct pools of wealth and, 106–107
  with LLCs and LLPs, 111
  marriage issues, 117
  multijuridisctional approaches to, 112–113
  with other vehicles, 111–112
  with partnerships and dedicated fund structures, 111
  steps for dividing assets, 106–107
  tax issues, 113–114
  with trusts, 108–109
  values across generations and, 107–108
Asset-backed income sources, as alternative asset, 271–272
Assets, rethinking role of traditional, 249–265
  cash and bonds, 249–256
  equities, 256–261
  index performance and, 261–263
  reversion to the mean and, 261, 262
  value investing and, 263–265
Australia, 113, 205

Balance sheet, for family, 96, 98–99, 102
distribution and growth requirements and, 83
in long-term strategy document example, 223–224
Balance sheet risk, family office and, 356
Banking reports, performance monitoring and, 319
Bardali family, example of long-term strategy asset allocation, 195–196
Behavioral biases, private and institutional investing differences, 51–53
Behavioral finance:
goals-based wealth management and, 142–145
Modern Portfolio Theory and, 139
risk management and, 181
Bemberg family, 125
Benchmarks:
evaluating performance against, 313–315
in long-term strategy document example, 234
monitoring performance and costs against, 15–16
Bequests. *See* Heirs
Berkshire Hathaway, 264
Bernstein, Peter, 138, 179
"Best" and "next" practice," 4, 11, 40, 65–66, 137, 399
Beta:
asset allocation strategies and, 150
index funds and, 268
Black swan events, 167, 178, 180, 244
Black Swan: The Impact of the Highly Improbable, The (Taleb), 167
Blair, Tony, 183
Blind trusts, 110
Bogle, John, 258
"Bolthole" risk management strategy, 175–176, 230
Bonds:
capital preservation and, 249–250
income and, 251
laddered portfolios, as element of long-term strategy, 190, 250–251
liquidity and, 250–251
past and future returns, 252–254
risk management and, 177–178, 179
value of, in volatile markets, 254–256
Bonhoeffer, Dietrich, 41
Brandes Institute paper, 138
Brazil, 205, 289
Brunel, Jean, 145–147
"Bucketing approach," to asset allocation, 143–145
Buffett, Warren, 9, 15, 263–265
Business. *See* Family business
Business risk, 169
Business Week, 126

CAARB countries and continents, 205
Calderon, Jose and Maria, asset structuring example, 100–101
Camus, Albert, 184
Canada:
GAAR legislation in, 113
immigration incentives and, 112
natural resources in, 205
trusts in, 112

Capabilities, of family members, 84–85
Capital gains taxes, "chicken- and egg-farmer investors," 103–104
Capital preservation:
bonds and, 249–250
excess assets and, 147
in long-term strategy document example, 220–221
real estate and, 273
Captive insurance companies, 111
Cash:
as asset class, and changes in investment policies, 238–240
management of, in long-term strategy document example, 230–231
risk management and, 175
Cash flow:
forecast of, as element of long-term strategy, 191–192
management reports, 318–319
private and institutional investing differences, 47–48
real estate and, 273
role in long-term strategy, 192, 196–197
Change:
managing in disciplined investment process, 68
within new wealth management approach, 3–4
Charitable donations. *See* Philanthropy
Chhabra, Ashvin, 143–145
"Chicken-farmer investors," 102–104
Chief investment officer (CIO), 159, 296–297
in family ecosystem, 333–334, 349
outsourcing of, 306–307, 351
reports and, 318–319
China, 207, 289
Citizenship:
asset structuring and, 115–116
family law and divorce issues, 116
mobility issues, 115
risk management and, 175–176
tax issues, 116
Climate change and environment:
global investment outlook and, 42
mega-theme investing, 204–205
"Closet indexers," 287
Coca-Cola, 290
Code of conduct, distribution to heirs and, 371
Coinvestment transactions, 208
as alternative asset, 280–281
changing role of asset classes and, 238–240
Collateralized debt obligations (CDOs), 33, 272, 274
Collateralized loan obligations (CLOs), 33, 272, 274
Collectibles, as alternative asset, 281
Commodities, as alternative asset, 279
Communication:
importance to distribution strategies, 372
investment policy statement and procedures for, 241
risk management and speed of, 184
Competence risk, private and institutional investing differences, 54–55
Complexity risk, 170
Concentrated investing, 256, 288

Concentration risk, 169, 355
Conservative investment assumptions, risk management and, 181
Consistency:
disciplined investment process and, 68
new wealth management approach and, 18–19
Continuity, within new wealth management approach, 3–4
Contributions. *See* Philanthropy
Control risk, 171
Core and satellite asset allocation strategy, 150–151
Correlation to market, family businesses and, 130
Costs, of investment management:
family office and, 353
hedge funds and absolute return funds, 277–278
impact on cash flow, 192
in long-term strategy document example, 222–223, 233–234
professional advisor evaluation and, 294, 306
rethinking of, 14–15
risk management and, 180–181
Counterparty risk, 169
Credit strategies, as alternative asset, 271, 277
Crises. *See* "White water investing"
Culture of family. *See also* Values, of family; Vision, of family
defined, 76
distribution strategy issues, 362–363, 370–371
emotional ownership of family wealth and, 378–379, 381–383
financial goals and, 91
in long-term strategy document example, 218
private and institutional investing differences, 53–54
Currency:
as alternative asset, 279–280
currency risk, 169
in long-term strategy document example, 230
Custodial relationship reports, 319
Custodial risk, 169
Custodian, in investment policy statement example, 307–308

Daily review of investments, 312
Darwin, Charles, 321
Das, Sanjiv, 146
De Voe, Raymond, 177
Debt, personal. *See also* Sovereign debt
changing role of asset classes and, 238–240
family balance sheet and, 98–99
in long-term strategy document example, 221, 222
risk management and, 181
Decision making and responsibilities, in investment policy statement example, 306–308
Deed of settlement, 109
Demeroutis, Basil, 273–274
Demographics, global investment outlook and, 42
Derivatives, as alternative asset, 278–279
Direct investments:
as alternative asset, 280–281
versus fund issues, 290–291

Direct investments (*continued*)
in long-term strategy document example, 232
mega-theme investing, 208
professional advisors and, 289, 290–291
Disasters, risk management and, 180, 182–184
Disciplined investment process, 57–69
Eisenhower urgent and important matrix, 58–59
goals and definitions of success, 58, 65–67
imperatives of, 59–65
professional advisors and, 296
as undervalued asset, 67–69
Dispersion and persistence issues, professional advisors and, 287–288
Distribution and growth requirements, investor profile and, 83
Distribution strategies, 361–374
amount and age issues for heirs, 366–367
estimating returns and sustainable rates of withdrawal, 365–366
family culture and, 362–363
family values and, 370–371
financial perspective on, 362
Lazar on balancing unity and autonomy, 372–374
question of number of generations to fund, 363–365
responsibility development in heirs, 371–372
risks of poor preparation for, 363
strategy options, 368–369
as three-step process, 261
Diversification:
asset allocation theory and, 136
family businesses and, 130
in Modern Portfolio Theory, 137
rethinking role of traditional asset classes, 256–257
risk management and, 177, 181
Divorce:
asset structuring and, 117
citizenship and residency issues, 116
wealth destruction and, 28
Documentation, professional advisors and, 296
Donations. *See* Philanthropy
Dow Jones Industrial Average:
in early 21st century, 35
in late 20th century, 33, 34
"Dreams and nightmares," family goals and, 146–147
Dynasty trusts, in Canada, 112

Economic and market perspectives, in long-term strategy document example, 226–227
Economic growth, risk management and, 180
Economic perspectives, in long-term strategy document example, 226–227
Ecosystem, of family, 329–339
centering on family, 330–331
checklist for advisor selection, 338–339
chief investment officer in, 333–334
example of, 331
investment committee in, 334–335

in long-term strategy document example, 226
new wealth management approach and, 14–15
private and institutional investing differences, 55–56
risk and, 170–171
selected professionals in, 332
selecting and managing advisors for, 335–338
trusted advisors in, 331–332
wealth destruction and, 29
Education and engagement, of next generation, 16, 375–391
asset structuring and, 107–108
challenges of, 375–376
costs of disengagement, 381
divergent outcome possibilities, 387–389
as element of long-term strategy, 16, 189
emotional ownership and, 377–378
family and financial elements of, 378–380
family balance sheet and, 99
family business survival pathways, 120–124
family organizational structure and, 380–381
history, values, and full definition of wealth, 381–383
investment in, and odds of success, 385–386
Liechtenstein on preserving family wealth, 389–391
as shared responsibility, 384, 387
Education sector, investing in, 206
Efficient frontier, 135–136, 140
"Egg-farmer investors," 103–104
Eisenhower matrix, 58–59
Emerging markets:
economic crisis and, 34
list of, 289
mega-theme investing, 203, 204
professional advisors and, 289
Emotional ownership:
of family business, 124–125
of family wealth, 377–378
Employee Retirement Income Security act (ERISA), 149–150
Employment, of heirs. *See* Work experience
End-date bias, 316
Endowment effect, private and institutional investing differences, 53
Endowment model, of asset allocation, 155–158, 163–164, 268–271, 275
Energy-producing assets, as alternative asset, 271
Engagement, of heirs. *See* Education and engagement, of next generation
Entrepreneurial business, defined, 120
Environment and climate change, mega-theme investing, 204–205
Environmental audits, before investments, 210–211
Equities:
expected return and, 258–261
in long-term strategy document example, 231
rethinking role of traditional asset classes, 256–257
Estate planning, as element of long-term strategy, 189

Event risk, 140
Exchange-traded funds (ETFs):
  in asset allocation strategies, 150–151
  professional advisors and, 286–287, 289
Exotica and passion investing, as alternative asset, 281–282
Expenses. *See* Costs, of investment management

Family banks, Rothschilds and, 20
Family business, integrating into wealth management strategy, 13–14, 119–131
  buying new business, 125
  emotional ownership and, 124–125
  family firm defined, 120
  generational issues and business survival, 120–124
  human capital and asset allocation, 128–131
  in long-term strategy document example, 222
  Marlot family asset mix example, 126–127
  performance consequences to portfolio, 126
  risk profiles and, 124
  selling business to create liquidity, 127–128
  separating family office from, 352–353
Family Business Network, 121
Family context and elements, in long-term strategy document example, 217–220, 225–226
Family Firm Institute, 121
Family law, citizenship and residency issues, 116
Family Legacy and Leadership: Preserving True Family Wealth in Challenging Times (Daniell, Haynes, and Hamilton), 380
Family office, 341–358
  administration, reporting, and family services tasks, 345–348
  advice and counsel from, 346, 348
  cautions about, 353–354
  choice of internal or external, 348–349
  comprehensive wealth management and, 344–345, 347
  costs of, 353
  expert's approach to asset allocation, 159–162
  importance of separating tasks in, 349
  in investment policy statement example, 306–307
  multifamily office choice, 341, 348–349, 351–352
  objectives and, 354
  organization of, in long-term strategy document example, 226
  outsourcing trend, 351
  rationale for having, 343–344
  as repository of values across generations, 346–347
  risk and role of, 354–358
  separating family business from, 352–353
  services of, 347–348
  typical activities of, 342–343
Family Office Exchange, 121

Family risks, 170–171
Family roles and relationships:
investment policy statement and, 247
private and institutional investing differences, 50–51, 54
wealth destruction and, 28
Family size, family businesses and, 130–131
Family wealth, definition of "true," 383
Family Wealth: Keeping It in the Family (Hughes), 372–374
Family wealth management, inflection point in history of, 23–43
accumulation of wealth, 29
"best" and "next" practices, 4, 11, 40, 65–66, 137, 399
current fears about lack of future returns, 32
cycles of change, 38–39
Dow Jones Average in early 21st century, 35
Dow Jones Average in late 20th century, 33
financial events and wealth destruction, 31–32
global megatrends, 41–42
lack of confidence in past investment approaches, 37–38
old investment truths and, 39–40
patterns and sources of wealth destruction, 27–29
potential outcomes, 40–41
20th century changes in fortunes, 24–26
21st century net worth drops, 35–37
Family wealth management, new approach to, 3–21
changing economic climate and, 4–6
consistent governance and leadership and, 17
consistent purposes and, 18–19
continuity and change in investing and, 3–4
engagement and education of family, 16
family business and, 13–14
family-centric aspects of, 7–8
financial ecosystem and, 14–15
global opportunities and, 12–13
goal and benchmarks monitoring, 15–16
goal-based approach, 9–10
imperatives of, 7
integrated, holistic approach to, 10–11, 17, 395–401
integrated management aspects, 17–18
management for horizons, not headlines, 11–12
multiple purposes of, 8
need for, 9
risk definition and management, 14
sustainable and principled aspects, 13
"Fat tail" incidents, 140
Fees. *See* Costs, of investment management
Financial education, importance for next generation, 379
Financial ethics, 212
Financial experience, investor profile and, 85

Financial management skills, distribution to heirs and, 371
Financial planning, as element of long-term strategy, 189
Financial risks, management of, 169–170
Five Ps of manager evaluation, professional advisors and, 292–294
Fixed income:
  changing role of asset classes and, 238–240
  in long-term strategy document example, 231
  rethinking role of traditional asset classes, 249–256
Flanagan, Jane, 120–124
Forbes magazine, "rich list" in 1918, 25–26
Foreign direct investing, 201
Foreign exchange (forex), as alternative asset, 279–280
Fragmentation risk, 170
France, 174
Freezer trusts, 110
"Friend following," private and institutional investing differences, 52
Frontier markets, professional advisors and, 289
Funds and pools, professional advisors and, 290–291
Future commitments, family balance sheet and, 98–99

GAAR (general anti-avoidance rules) legislation, 113, 174
Galbraith, John Kenneth, 19
Garland, James, 103–104
GARP (growth at a reasonable price) investing, 256, 288
General anti-avoidance rules (GAAR) legislation, 113, 174
General partners (GPs), 111
Generation-skipping tax, 110
Geocultural contexts, shift in family wealth and, 30–31
Geographic investment issues, professional advisors and, 288–290
Geography, diversification issues and, 288–290
Geopolitical conflicts, global investment outlook and, 27, 38, 42, 171–172
George, Stephen J., 213–216
Germany, 114
Global Financial Crisis (GFC), 2008–2009
  bonds and, 243–255
  equities and, 257
  goals-based wealth management and, 145–147
  Modern Portfolio Theory and, 139–142
  risk and, 5, 166
Global investing, 288–290
  expert's approach to asset allocation, 161, 162
  megatrends and, 41–42
  new wealth management approach and, 12–13
Global Reporting initiative, 212
Globalization, risk management and, 183
Goals, setting of high-level financial, 89–104
  balance sheet for family, 96, 98–99

"chicken- and egg-farmer investors," 102–104
hierarchy of, 92
lifetime legacy framework, 93–97
questions to be asked about, 90, 91
sample goals, 90–92
Goals and objectives, of family:
disciplined investment process and, 68
as elements of long-term strategy, 189–190
family office and, 354
investment policy statement and, 241, 243–244
in investment policy statement example, 300–301
in long-term strategy document example, 220–223, 230
monitoring performance and costs against, 15–16
Goals-based wealth management (GBWM), 9–10, 135–147
asset allocation theoretical background, 135–136
basics of, 142–143
Brunel on, 145–147
"bucket approach" and, 143–145
Modern Portfolio Theory and, 137–141
optimality and, 145
Post-Modern Portfolio Theory and, 139–140
Gold, risk management and, 175
Governance, of family:
as element of long-term strategy, 189
investment policy statement and, 247
Government debt. *See* Sovereign debt
Graham, Benjamin, 263
"Granny trusts," in Canada, 112
Green investing, 211
Growth at a reasonable price (GARP) investing, 256, 288
Growth economies. *See* Emerging markets
Growth investing, 256
Growth requirements, investor profile and, 83
Grubman, Dr. James, 78–79, 86–89
Guidelines and constraints, in investment policy statement example, 304–305

Hand, Learned, 114
Harvard University, 49, 155–157, 268–269, 275
Health, education, and welfare (HEW) trusts, 108, 109, 221, 223
Health and wellness issues, mega-theme investing, 206–207
Hedge funds:
as alternative asset, 277–278
aspirational risk bucket and, 144–145
in asset allocation strategies, 150–151
changing role of asset classes and, 238–240
in long-term strategy document example, 231
professional advisors and, 287
risk management and, 165
survivor bias and, 270

Heirs. *See also* Education and engagement, of next generation
bequest and gifts to, 99
preparing for money, 383
preparing money for, 382
values of family and, 87–88
Herding, private and institutional investing differences, 52
Hierarchy of needs framework, for goals, 92
History, wealth destruction and, 27
Horan, Dr. Stephen, 128–131
Household net worth, drop in early 21st century, 35–37
Hughes, Jay, 372–374
Human capital, as asset, 98
family businesses and, 122–123, 124
family businesses and asset allocation, 128–131
in long-term strategy document example, 222
Humility, as family value, 388

"Immigrants and natives," to wealth issues, 78–79
Immigration tax incentives, 112
"Immigration to the Land of Wealth" (Grubman and Jaffe), 78–79
Impairment of capital, risk management and, 167
Imperative 1: Establish family vision, values, and goals, 7, 60
determining purpose of wealth, setting financial goals, 89–104
documenting philosophy, vision, and values, 75–88
integrating family business into wealth management strategy, 119–131
structuring assets and aligning investments for multiple purposes, 105–117
Imperative 2: Set a practical framework for family investment, 7, 60–61
asset allocation approaches, 149–164
goals-based wealth management, 135–147
risk management, 165–184
Imperative 3: Set long-term strategy and define the asset allocation model, 7, 61–62
long-term investing, mega-themes and principled investing, 199–216
long-term strategy document example, 217–234
long-term strategy elements, 187–197
Imperative 4: Draft the investment policy statement and refine investment tactics, 7, 62–63
assessing alternative assets and searching for recurring alpha, 267–283
investment policy statement example, 299–308
refining investment tactics and drafting annual statement, 237–248
rethinking role of traditional asset classes, 249–265
selecting individual investments and investment managers, 285–298

Imperative 5: Monitor performance and respond to the need for change, 7, 63
monitoring performance against goals and benchmarks, 311–320
"white water investing" in turbulent times, 321–325
Imperative 6: Select and manage an ecosystem of trusted advisors, 7, 63–64
designing ecosystem of selecting advisors, 329–339
role of family office, 341–358
Imperative 7: Engage and educate the family heirs, 7, 64–65
determining right distribution strategy, 361–374
preparing family for successful management and transfer of wealth, 375–391
InBev Group, 125
Income, from investments:
bonds and, 251
impact on cash flow, 192
income-linking distribution strategy, 368
income-matching distribution strategy, 368
investment policy statement and, 244, 302
Index funds:
in asset allocation strategies, 150
beta and, 268
professional advisors and, 286–287
rethinking role of traditional asset classes, 261–263
India, 207, 289
Indonesia, 34, 205, 208, 289
Inflation:
distribution strategy issues, 362
risk management and, 180
Information ratio, 314, 316
Infrastructure projects:
as alternative asset, 276–277
principled investing and, 211
Inheritance tax rates, 114
Institutional investing. *See* Private and institutional investing differences
Integrated family framework, 10–11
Integrated management, 17–18, 188–189
Interconnection risk, 170
Interdependencies, risk management and, 183
Interest rates, bond yields and, 252
Intergenerational and interbranch conflict, private and institutional investing differences, 54
International asset structure, 112–113
International Finance Corporation (IFC), 210
Internet bubble, 34
Investment committee (IC):
in family ecosystem, 334–335
in long-term strategy document example, 226
Investment management:
bad decisions and wealth destruction, 29
as element of long-term strategy, 189
as engineering issue, 191
family office and, 355–356
procedures and investment policy statement, 241

Investment persistence, professional advisors and, 287–288
Investment policy statement (IPS), 11, 53, 62–63, 194
as bridge between insight and action, 248
drafting of, 240–243
main issues needing to be covered, 243–248
purpose of, 241
simplicity and, 248
success and, 242
Investment policy statement (IPS) example, 299–308
asset allocation, 304
asset-class universe, 302–304
decision making and responsibilities, 306–308
expected return, 301
financial education and engagement of heirs, 379, 382
guidelines and constraints, 304–305
income needs, 302
investment manager selection, 305–306, 307
investment principles, 301
liquidity, 302
monitoring and review, 308
objectives, 300–301
planning horizon, 302
purpose, 299–300
rebalancing, 304
risk tolerance, 302
scope, 300
tax issues, 305
Investment principles, in investment policy statement example, 301
Investment process. *See* Disciplined investment process
Investment S-curve strategy:
elements of, 151–153
in long-term strategy document example, 228
purpose of, 153
timing and, 153–154
Investment selection, investment policy statement and, 246
Investor profile, 82–84
Irrevocable trusts, 110
Islamic bonds, 281
Islamic investors, infrastructure assets and, 276–277

Jaffe, Dr. Dennis, 78–79, 86–89, 120–124
Japan, 207
Jeffers, Robinson, 382
Just-in-time society, risk management and, 184

Key person risk, 171
Keynes, John Maynard, 258

Laddering of bonds, 190, 250–251
Large purchases, family balance sheet and, 99
Latin America, family wealth in, 31
Lazar, Ed, 372–374
Legacy assets, as element of long-term strategy, 191
Legacy goals, 94–95
as element of long-term strategy, 190
with lifetime assets, in single portfolio, 96, 97
in long-term strategy document example, 228
matching to lifetime assets, 95

Letter of wishes, 85–86, 109
Leverage, risk and, 169, 181, 222
Levin, Ross, 93
Liechtenstein, Heinrich, 76, 389–391
Lifestyle maintenance, in long-term strategy document example, 220, 222
Lifetime asset requirements, 93–94
  as element of long-term strategy, 189–190
  family balance sheet and, 98, 99, 102
  with legacy assets, in single portfolio, 96, 97
  matching to legacy assets, 95
Lifetime legacy framework, for financial goals, 93–97
  legacy goals, 94–95
  lifetime requirements, 93–94
  portfolios and, 96, 97
Limited liability companies (LLCs), 111
Limited liability partnerships (LLPs), 111
Limited partners (LPs), 111
Liquidity:
  bonds and, 250–251
  creating by selling family business, 127–128
  investment policy statement and need for, 244
  in investment policy statement example, 302
  investor profile and preference, 83
Liquidity risk, 169
  alternative assets and, 269, 273
  cash and, 238
  as element of long-term strategy, 190
  in long-term strategy document example, 229
Longevity, risk and, 171, 180
Long-term megatrends, expert's approach to asset allocation, 160
Long-term strategy, elements of, 187–197
  asset allocation and, 193
  cash flow forecast in, 191–192
  cash flow's core role in, 192, 196–197
  change and obsolescence of strategies, 196
  constraints on planning, 196–197
  family objectives and, 189–190
  financial education and engagement of heirs, 379, 382
  indicative allocation, 194–196
  integrated framework's importance, 188–189
  legacy assets in, 191
  mega-trend investing, 200–209
  noninvestment factors, 193–194
  plan components, 187–188
  sustainable and principled investing, 209–213
Long-term Strategy (LTS) document, 11, 61, 194
Long-term Strategy (LTS) document example, 217–234
  asset allocation and investment strategies, 227–230
  asset classes and investment strategies, 230–232
  balance sheet, 223–224
  economic and market perspectives, 226–227

Long-term Strategy (LTS) document example (*continued*)
 family context, 217–220
 family elements, 225–226
 financial ecosystem and, 226
 goals and objectives, 220–223
 long-term strategy, 224–225
 operational considerations, 233
 performance reporting and risk and cost management, 233–234

Macdonald family, example of long-term strategy asset allocation, 194, 195
Macroeconomic context, expert's approach to asset allocation, 159–160, 161
Macroeconomic risk, 169
Malleret, Thierry, 41–43
Marital issues, wealth preservation and, 28, 114, 117
Market exposure issues, professional advisors and, 291
Market perspectives, in long-term strategy document example, 226–227
Market risk bucket, goals-based wealth management and, 143–144
Market values, "chicken- and egg-farmer investors," 103
Markowitz, Harry, 135, 136, 138, 146
Marmot family, 126–127
Mega-theme investing, 200–209
 Africa, 203, 205
 agricultural land, 205–206
 Asia, 201–202
 climate change and environment, 204–205
 direct and co-investing, 208
 education and related activities, 206
 emerging markets, 203, 204
 health and wellness issues, 206–207
 priorities and, 208–209
 resources and energy, 205
Mental accounting, goals-based wealth management and, 142–145
Mexico, 208
Michel-Kerjan, Erwann O., 182–184
Middle East, family wealth in, 31
Milestone methodology, in distribution strategy, 368–369
Milton, John, 23
MIST countries, 208
Modern Portfolio Theory (MPT), 135, 149
 assumptions and observations of, 51, 137–139
 definition of risk as volatility, 5
 diversification and, 37
 new wealth management approach and, 9
 risk management and, 166
 60-40 stock and bond allocation and, 140–141
Momentum investing, 256, 288
Monitoring of investments:
 analytical tools for, 316
 against benchmarks, 313–315
 importance of, 311–312
 importance of measurements, 320

against internal goals and external benchmarks, 311–320
intervals of, 312–313
investment policy statement and roles of, 247–248
in investment policy statement example, 308
investment policy statement review and, 319–320
multiple stakeholders and, 317–318
specific reports, 318–319
standard statistics and, 316–317
Monte Carlo simulations, 158, 179
Monthly review of investments, 312–313
Montier, James, 180
Mortality risk, 171
Mortgages, in long-term strategy document example, 222
Multifamily office (MFO), 341, 348–349, 351–352
Multijurisdictional assets allocation, 112–113
Multiple investment purposes. *See* Asset structuring
Multiple investor profiles, 82–83

Nahal, Sarbjit, 207
Negative investment screens, 81–82, 210–211
Nevada, 112
New England Journal of Psychology, 382
New Hampshire, 112
New Zealand, 112
"Next practice." *See* "Best" and "next" practice"
Normal distribution, in Modern Portfolio Theory, 137, 139, 166, 244
Nuclear energy, investment opportunities and, 210

Obesity, mega-theme investing, 206–207
Office. *See* Family office
One-hit wonders, 317
Operational considerations, in long-term strategy document example, 233
Optimism, private and institutional investing differences, 52
Organisation for Economic Cooperation and Development (OECD), 206, 240
Organizational structure, of family, 380, 381
Overconfidence, private and institutional investing differences, 52
Ownership approach, to wealth, 77–78, 79

Partnerships, asset structuring and, 111
Passion investing, risks of, 282
Passive management, professional advisors and, 286–287
Passports, 115
Past performance, limits of predictive usefulness, 138
Penaflor, 125
People, professional advisor evaluation and, 292–293, 305
Performance of investments. *See also* Monitoring of investments
professional advisor evaluation and, 292, 305
reporting of, 233–234

Persistence, professional advisors and, 287–288
Personal risk bucket, goals-based wealth management and, 143–144
Philanthropy:
  family balance sheet and, 99
  goals and strategies for, 221, 222
Philosophy, of family:
  consensus and coexistence issues, 79
  family balance sheet and, 99
  "immigrants or natives" to wealth issues, 78–79
  investment implications, 80
  professional advisor evaluation and, 293–294, 305–306
  stewardship or ownership approach, 77–78, 79
Philosophy, vision, and values documentation, 75–88
  capabilities and constraints, 84–85
  culture of family and, 76
  history of family and, 75
  importance of value clarification, 86–89
  in long-term strategy document example, 219–220
  philosophy of wealth, 77–80
  scale, sophistication, and experience of family, 85
  trust deeds and letters of wishes, 85–86
  values of family, 81–84
  vision of family, 80–81
Physical security risk, 170
Pitcairn, H. F. "Rick," 67–69
Plague, The (Camus), 184
Planning horizon, in investment policy statement example, 302
Pools of wealth, 106–107
Portfolio constraints, investment policy statement and, 246
"Portfolio Optimization with Mental Accounts" (Das, Markowitz, Scheid, and Statman), 146
Post-Modern Portfolio Theory (PMPT), 139–140
Primogeniture, wealth preservation and, 27, 366
Principled investing, 13, 209–213
  broadening definition of success and, 212–213
  financial ethics, 212
  George on strategies for, 213–216
  green investing, 211
  negative screens and, 210–211
  redefining return, 209
Private and institutional investing differences, 45–56
  behavioral biases, 51–53
  cash flow patterns, 47–48
  challenges and opportunity, 56
  personal relationships and family complexity, 50–51
  risk and opportunity, 47
  risk identification and management, 53–56
  summary of, 46
  taxation, 47–48
Private equities:
  as alternative asset, 275–276
  changing role of asset classes and, 238–240
  characteristics of, 275–276
  in long-term strategy document example, 231–232

Private investment in public utility (PIPE), 208
Private investments, professional advisors and, 290
Probability-adjusted scenario analysis, 158
Process of investing:
- private and institutional investing differences, 55
- professional advisor evaluation and, 294, 306

Professional advisors, 285–298. *See also* Investment management
- access to investments issues, 291
- active versus passive management issues, 286–287
- alpha and beta and, 150–151
- direct investment versus fund issues, 290–291
- dispersion and persistence issues, 287–288
- documentation and discipline issues, 296
- in family ecosystem, 331–332
- Five Ps of manager evaluation, 292–294
- geographic investment issues, 288–290
- initial allocation and tactical decision issues, 297–298
- investment policy statement and role of, 247
- in investment policy statement example, 305–306
- investment style and, 288
- market exposure issues, 291
- private and institutional investing differences, 53
- public versus private investment issues, 290
- rethinking role of, 14–15
- sample questions to ask, 295–296
- selecting and managing of, 335–338
- tax issues, 291

Property. *See* Real estate investments
Public securities, professional advisors and, 290

Quality guidelines, investment policy statement and, 246
Quantitative inputs, expert's approach to asset allocation and, 160
Quarterly review of investments, 313
Quilmes, 125

Rabbi trusts, 110
Rambus, Mykolas, 30–31
Real estate investments:
- as alternative asset, 272–274
- changing role of asset classes and, 238–240
- drop in value in early 21st century, 35, 37
- in long-term strategy document example, 221, 232
- risk management and, 177–178

Rebalancing, in investment policy statement, 245, 304, 319
Reculer pour mieux sauter, 366
Relative benchmarks, 314
Reporting risk, 171
Representativeness, private and institutional investing differences, 52

Residency status:
- asset structuring and, 115–116
- family law and divorce issues, 116
- mobility issues, 115
- tax issues, 116

Resource risk, private and institutional investing differences, 55
Resource scarcity, global investment outlook and, 42
Resources and energy, mega-theme investing, 205
Responsibility, developing in next generation, 371–372, 384
Return on investments:
- distribution strategy issues, 365–366
- expected, in investment policy statement example, 301
- expected return from equities, 258–259
- investment policy statement and, 244
- in long-term strategy document example, 229
- redefining for principled investments, 209
- required rate of return, 192, 194
- risk management and, 179

Reversion to the mean, of investment returns, 261, 262
Revocable trusts, 109–110
Risk and risk management, 165–184
- basic principles of, 176–179
- black swan events, 167, 178, 180, 244
- "bolthole" strategy for, 175–176, 230
- "chicken- and egg-farmer investors," 103–104
- citizenship issues, 115–116, 175–176
- controllable factors, 180–182
- defining and managing, in new approach, 14
- evolution of risk, 168–169
- family businesses and, 124, 130
- family office benefits and, 345
- family risks, 170–171
- financial risks, 169–170
- geopolitical risks, 170–171
- in goals-based wealth management, 143
- investment policy statement and, 244
- investment pyramid and, 92
- investor profile and, 84
- legacy assets and, 94
- lifetime assets and, 94
- in long-term strategy document example, 229–230, 233–234
- Michel-Kerjan on, 182–184
- in Modern Portfolio Theory, 137
- new challenges of, 166–167
- political risks and, 172–173
- private and institutional investing differences, 47, 53–56
- risk defined, 167–168
- risk tolerance, in investment policy statement example, 302
- role of, 5
- role of family office and, 354–358
- tax risks, 173–174
- uncontrollable factors, 179–180
- in "white water" times, 322

Risk-adjusted measurement, of investment performance, 314
Rosenberg, Claude J., 293

Rothschild, Nathan Mayer, 20–21
Rothschild family, 265
Russia, 205, 207

Safe harbors, 324–325
Scale of family wealth, investor profile and, 85
Scenario analysis, in asset allocation, 158, 179, 194
Scheid, Jonathan, 146
Scientific asset allocation, 135–136
S-curve strategy:
  elements of, 151–153
  in long-term strategy document example, 228
  purpose of, 153
  timing and, 153–154
Self-esteem, heirs and distribution strategies and, 371–372, 384
Settlement risk, 169
Sharpe, William, 136
Sharpe ratio, 136, 314, 316
Singapore, 112
Single-family office (SFO), 348, 350
60-40 stock and bond allocation, Modern Portfolio Theory and, 140–141
Societal trends, mega-theme investing, 199–200
Sortino ratio, 314
South Africa, 208
Sovereign debt:
  changing role of asset classes and, 240
  global investment outlook and, 42
  risk and, 172–173
Speculative return, 258–259
Stakeholders, reporting to multiple, 317–318
Statman, Meir, 146
Stewardship approach, to wealth, 77–78, 79, 80
Stiftungs, 110
"Stoplight" scoring system, 320
"Strategic dashboard," 16, 320
Strategic risk, expert's approach to asset allocation, 161
Strategy, disciplined investment process and, 68
Structured investment vehicles (SIVs), 274
Structured notes, as alternative asset, 278–279
Success, defining of, 65–67, 212–213
Succession. *See also* Education and engagement, of next generation
  family office and, 357
  private and institutional investing differences and, 55
Survival stockpile strategy, 175
Survivorship bias, 316
Sustainability reporting, 212
Sustainable investing, 13, 39, 232. *See also* Principled investing
Swaps, derivatives, and structured notes, as alternative asset, 278–279
Swenson, David, 262
SWOT analysis, in long-term strategy document example, 224
Systematic risk, 136
Systemic risk, 169

Tactical risk:
  expert's approach to asset allocation and, 161

Tactical risk (*continued*)
investment policy statement and, 245–246
management of, 181
Taleb, Nassim Nicholas, 167
Taxation issues:
asset structuring and, 113–114
"chicken- and egg-farmer investors," 104
citizenship and residency issues, 116
distribution strategy issues, 362
family office benefits, 345
goals-based wealth management and, 147
immigration incentives and, 112
investment performance and, 314
investment policy statement and, 246, 305
new wealth management approach and, 8
paying no more than law demands, 114
planning for, as element of long-term strategy, 189
private and institutional investing differences, 47–48
professional advisors and, 291
reporting requirements, 319
risk management and, 170, 173–174, 180
trusts and exemptions from, 110
types of taxes, 114
wealth destruction and, 27–28
Technology and service area, principled investing and, 211
Templeton, John, 177
Thai baht, 34
Thailand, 289
Three generation issues, wealth preservation and, 27, 126, 374
Timeframe for investing:
impact on cash flow, 192
investment policy statement and, 245
in investment policy statement example, 302
investor profile and, 83
in long-term strategy document example, 229
Tolstoy, Leo, 76
Tracking error, 316
Transaction costs, risk management and, 180–181
Treasury bonds, 252, 253–254
Treasury inflation-protected securities (TIPs), 238–240
Trends, private and institutional investing differences, 52
Triple-bottom-line reporting, 212
Trust deeds, 85–86
Trusts:
forms of, 109–110
HEW trusts, 108–109, 221, 223
traditional structure, 110
Turkey, 208

Ukraine, 289
Uncertainty. *See also* "White water investing," risk management and, 184
Uncorrelated investments, alternative assets and, 269. *See also* "White water investing"
United Kingdom:
family wealth in, 31
GAAR legislation in, 113
inheritance taxes in, 114

United States:
family wealth in, 31
tax income versus government spending in, 173
trusts and taxes in, 110
Unmanaged risk, 84
Unsystematic risk, 136
Upside/downside capture, 316
Urgent versus important tasks, 58–59

Value investing, 256, 263–265
Values, of family, 81–84
disciplined investment process and, 68
distribution strategy issues, 370–371
importance of clarifying, 86–89
investor profile and, 82–84
relevance to investing, 81–82
wealth destruction and, 28–29
Vanderbilt, Cornelius, 19–20, 21
Vanderbilt, William, 20
Vietnam, 289
Vision, of family, 80
in long-term strategy document example, 225
vision statement example, 81
Volatility. *See also* "White water investing"
as return relative to risk, 316
risk and behavioral finance, 143
risk management and, 167–168

Wealth Allocation Framework, of Chhabra, 143–145
Wealth management. *See Family wealth management entries*
Wellness issues, mega-theme investing and, 206–207
Werklund, Dave, 209
"White water investing," 321–325
adapting to change, 321–322
investment changes, 324–325
procedural changes, 322–324
risks and, 322
"Why of Wealth Management, The" (Levin), 93
Window dressing, investment managers and, 317
Work experience, heirs and, 370, 378, 380, 390–391

Yale University, 49, 155–157, 268–269, 275